When should  *e?*
Where do I go *tions?*
What's the best and easiest way to plan and book my trip?

frommers.travelocity.com

Frommer's, the travel guide leader, has teamed up with **Travelocity.com,** the leader in online travel, to bring you an in-depth, easy-to-use resource designed to help you plan and book your trip online.

At **frommers.travelocity.com,** you'll find free online updates about your destination from the experts at Frommer's plus the outstanding travel planning and purchasing features of Travelocity.com. Travelocity.com provides reservations capabilities for 95 percent of all airline seats sold, more than 47,000 hotels, and over 50 car rental companies. In addition, Travelocity.com offers more than 2,000 exciting vacation and cruise packages. Travelocity.com puts you in complete control of your travel planning with these and other great features:

Expert travel guidance from Frommer's – over 150 writers reporting from around the world!

Best Fare Finder – an interactive calendar tells you when to travel to get the best airfare

Fare Watcher – we'll track airfare changes to your favorite destinations

Dream Maps – a mapping feature that suggests travel opportunities based on your budget

Shop Safe Guarantee – 24 hours a day / 7 days a week live customer service, and more!

Whether traveling on a tight budget, looking for a quick weekend getaway, or planning the trip of a lifetime, Frommer's guides and Travelocity.com will make your travel dreams a reality. You've bought the book, now book the trip!

Travelocity.com
A Sabre Company

Frommer's®
™

A New Star-Rating System & Other Exciting News from Frommer's!

In our continuing effort to publish the savviest, most up-to-date, and most appealing travel guides available, we've added some great new features.

Frommer's guides now include a new **star-rating system.** Every hotel, restaurant, and attraction is rated from 0 to 3 stars to help you set priorities and organize your time.

We've also added **seven brand-new features** that point you to the great deals, in-the-know advice, and unique experiences that separate travelers from tourists. Throughout the guide look for:

Finds	Special finds—those places only insiders know about
Fun Fact	Fun facts—details that make travelers more informed and their trips more fun
Kids	Best bets for kids—advice for the whole family
Moments	Special moments—those experiences that memories are made of
Overrated	Places or experiences not worth your time or money
Tips	Insider tips—some great ways to save time and money
Value	Great values—where to get the best deals

We've also added a **"What's New"** section in every guide—a timely crash course in what's hot and what's not in every destination we cover.

Other Great Guides for Your Trip:

Frommer's Canada

Frommer's Nova Scotia, New Brunswick & Prince Edward Island

Frommer's Montréal & Québec City

Frommer's British Columbia & the Canadian Rockies

Ottawa

1st Edition

by Louise Dearden

Here's what the critics say about Frommer's:

"Amazingly easy to use. Very portable, very complete."

—Booklist

"The only mainstream guide to list specific prices. The Walter Cronkite of guidebooks—with all that implies."

—Travel & Leisure

"Complete, concise, and filled with useful information."

—New York Daily News

"Detailed, accurate and easy-to-read information for all price ranges."

—Glamour Magazine

Independent Thinkers

Toronto ON

About the Author

Canadian writer **Louise Dearden** fell in love with travel during her first visit to Europe as a child. Six years later, after impatiently completing high school in Ontario, she flew to England in search of adventure and managed to turn a 12-month visit into an extended stay of 15 years. During that time, she traveled extensively in the U.K. and visited mainland Europe, particularly France, as often as possible. For the past 11 years she has resided in Ontario with her husband and two children. She happily spends many hours at her keyboard, interspersed with excursions in pursuit of her travel interests, which include food & wine, getaways, and family vacations. Louise is also the author of *Frommer's Ottawa with Kids.*

Published by:
John Wiley & Sons Canada, Ltd.
22 Worcester Road
Etobicoke, ON M9W 1L1

National Library of Canada Cataloguing in Publication Data

Dearden, Louise
    Frommer's Ottawa/Louise Dearden.—1st ed.

Includes index.

ISBN 1–894413–42–3

1. Ottawa (Ont.)—Guidebooks. I. Title. II. Title: Ottawa.

FC3096.18.D419 2002   917.13'84044   C2002–901899–4
F1059.5.08D419 2002

Editorial Director: Joan Whitman
Associate Editor: Melanie Rutledge
Publishing Services Director: Karen Bryan
Cartographer: Mapping Specialists, Ltd.
Illustrations: Frommer's US and Bart Vallecoccia Illustration
Text layout: IBEX Graphic Communications
Cover design: Kyle Gell
Front cover photo: Bill Brooks/Masterfile
Back cover photo: Larry Fisher/Masterfile

Special Sales

For reseller information, including discounts and premium sales, please call our sales department: Tel.: 416-646-4584. For press review copies, author interviews, or other publicity information, please contact our marketing department: Tel.: 416-646-4584; Fax.: 416-646-4448.

1 2 3 4 5 <tk> 06 05 04 03 02

Manufactured in Canada

Contents

6 What to See & Do in Ottawa   93

7 Active Ottawa   134

8 Ottawa After Dark   157

9 Shopping   171

10 Exploring the Region   188

Appendix: Ottawa in Depth   208

Index   215

List of Maps

Acknowledgments

Thanks to Joan Whitman, who helped me to navigate the challenges of this project. Special thanks to my husband and children for their continuing patience and tolerance over the years in dealing with a spouse and parent who works in a home office.

—Louise Dearden

An Invitation to the Reader

In researching this book, we discovered many wonderful places—hotels, restaurants, shops. And more. We're sure you'll find others. Please tell us about them, so we can share the information with your fellow travelers in upcoming editions. If you were disappointed with a recommendation, we'd love to know that too. Please write to:

Frommer's Ottawa, 1st Edition
John Wiley & Sons Canada, Ltd. • 22 Worcester Road • Etobicoke, ON M9W 1L1

An Additional Note

Please be advised that travel information is subject to change at any time—and this is especially true of prices. We therefore suggest that you write or call ahead for confirmation when making your travel plans. The authors, editors, and publishers cannot be held responsible for the experiences of readers while traveling. Your safety is important to us, however, so we encourage you to stay alert and be aware of your surroundings. Keep a close eye on cameras, purses and wallets, all favorite targets of thieves and pickpockets.

New! Frommer's Star Ratings & Icons

Every hotel, restaurant and attraction listing in this guide has been ranked for quality, value, service, amenities, and special features using a star-rating scale. In country, state, and regional guides, we also rate towns and regions to help you narrow down your choices and budget your time accordingly. Hotels and restaurants in the Very Expensive and Expensive categories are rated on a scale of one (highly recommended) to three stars (exceptional). Those in the Moderate and Inexpensive categories rate from zero (recommended) to two stars (very highly recommended). Attractions, towns, and regions are rated according to the following scale: zero stars (recommended), one star (highly recommended), two stars (very highly recommended), and three stars (must-see).

In addition to the rating system, we also use seven icons to highlight insider information, useful tips, special bargains, hidden gems, memorable experiences, kid-friendly venues, places to avoid, and other useful information:

(*Finds* (*Fun Fact* (*Kids* (*Moments* (*Overrated* (*Tips* (*Value*

The following abbreviations are used for credit cards:

AE	American Express	DISC	Discover	V	Visa
DC	Diners Club	MC	MasterCard		

FROMMERS.COM

Now that you have the guidebook to a great trip, visit our website at **www.frommers.com** for travel information on nearly 2,000 destinations. With features updated regularly, we give you instant access to the most current trip-planning information available. At Frommers.com, you'll also find the best prices on air fares, accommodations, and car rentals—you can even book travel online though our travel booking partners. At Frommers.com you'll find the following:

- Daily Newsletter highlighting the best travel deals
- Hot Spot of the Month/Vacation Sweepstakes & Travel Photo Contest
- More than 200 Travel Message Boards
- Outspoken Newsletters and Feature Articles on travel bargains, vacation ideas, tips & resources, and more!

The Best of Ottawa

Canadians are proud of their capital city, with good reason. Ottawa lies in a magnificent natural setting on the south shore of the Ottawa River, with the picturesque rolling hills of the Outaouais region as a backdrop. The Parliament Buildings perch graciously on the escarpment, their architectural grandeur on display for all to admire. Ottawa's symbolic location on the border of English and French Canada serves to strengthen the relationship between the two cultures.

Ottawa's appeal lies in its charming blend of sophistication and informality. Businessmen in somber wool overcoats clutch briefcases as they skate to work on the Rideau Canal. Sleek black limousines ferry foreign dignitaries to their engagements, in-line skaters and cyclists darting around them. Rows of tulips stand like sentries wearing multi-colored tunics, while students and tourists lounge on the grass, soaking up the spring sun. National museums feature world-class exhibits with entrance fees that the man in the street can afford to pay. Throughout the year, the region fizzes and sizzles with festivals and events to entertain the whole family.

In 2001, Ottawa was suddenly catapulted to a new position as the fourth-largest city in Canada, when 11 municipalities and the region of Ottawa–Carleton amalgamated to become the "new" city of Ottawa. With a population of 800,000, which is projected to grow by 50% over the next 20 years, Ottawa has become a mega-city. Citizens and politicians alike hope this will translate into a brighter future for Canada's capital city.

My personal introduction to Ottawa was as a guest at the biggest birthday party I'd ever attended. There were thousands of party-goers decked out in red and white, but the atmosphere in the huge crowd was benevolent and relaxed. As we threaded our way along the downtown streets, we exchanged smiles and greetings with strangers, bound simply by our nationality. I remember the day as a blur of pageantry, ceremony, music, and dancing, punctuated by a grand finale of fireworks exploding in the sky. Celebrating Canada Day in the nation's capital sparked an affection for Ottawa that has blossomed over the past seven years. Each time I catch my most cherished image of the city, which is the vivid red and white Canadian flag silhouetted against the intense blue of the sky atop the Peace Tower on Parliament Hill, raw emotion never fails to surface.

For a time, I was fortunate enough to live close to the city. Suddenly, I felt more like a resident than a tourist. I began to shop, explore, and dine in Ottawa on a regular basis and grew to appreciate the city more and more as I discovered its many treasures.

I have marveled at the national museums, slept comfortably in hotels and B&Bs, been intrigued by heritage attractions, been entertained by world-class performers, tasted superb cuisine, shopped beyond my budget, walked the network of pathways, cruised the Ottawa River, and hiked through the autumn leaves. Having experienced Ottawa as both a researcher and a tourist, I can enthusiastically recommend the city and the surrounding region as a great vacation destination. I'm not a native, so I may be accused of looking at the city through tourist-tinted glasses, but I find Ottawa to be bursting with attractions and activities. I hope that you do too.

1 The Best of Ottawa Experiences

- **Celebrate Canada's Birthday:** Spend Canada Day in the nation's capital—there's no experience quite like it. Head downtown and prepare for a full day of uniquely Canadian celebrations. Start the day with the ceremony of the Changing of the Guard. Watch the Canadian flag rise above the Peace Tower on Parliament Hill, chat with the friendly Mounties mingling with the crowds (don't forget to ask if they'll pose for a photo), and take in a free concert. Have your face painted or tattooed (temporarily) in red and white, wave a paper flag, and buy a hat or T-shirt with a Canadian symbol to blend in with the throngs of people wandering the streets. Watch the Snowbirds air show overhead at midday, and in the evening, cast your eyes skyward again for the best fireworks display of the year. See chapter 2, page 20.

- **Skate on the Rideau Canal:** Even if you live in a part of the country where ice-skating is a winter activity, it most likely takes place at an indoor community rink, where you end up skating around . . . and around . . . and around. An hour or two of that is enough to make anyone hang up their blades for good. But in Ottawa, you can experience the world's ultimate skating rink—the Rideau Canal— which offers almost 8km (5 miles) of wide-open space and ever-changing scenery. Warm-up huts are stationed along the way where you can sip a hot chocolate or munch a Beaver Tail pastry. Skate and sled rentals are available. See chapter 7, page 154.

- **Enjoy the Waterways:** Ottawa's history is deeply tied to the waterways in the region, and today the scenic Ottawa River, Rideau River, and Rideau Canal make a major contribution to the beauty of the city. You can watch the locks in operation, take a cruise on the Ottawa River or the Rideau Canal, rent a paddleboat, canoe, or kayak on Dow's Lake, picnic on the city's riverbanks, sizzle on a sandy beach, or ride the white water of the Ottawa River northwest of the city. See chapter 6, page 107.

- **Spend a Day at the Canadian Museum of Civilization:** This stunning, award-winning building is home to world-class museum exhibits. Life-size renderings of the social, cultural, and material history of Canada since the landing of the first Europeans in A.D. 1000 will captivate even the most reluctant museum-goer. The majestic Grand Hall displays more than 40 gigantic totem poles from the Pacific Northwest. A hands-on Children's Museum, which invites children to take a trip and experience the fascinating cultural mosaic of the world we live in, is housed within the complex. The Canadian Postal Museum, an IMAX theater, two restaurants, two boutiques, and an extensive outdoor children's playground round off the attractions. Spend a day here?

You might want to spend two. See chapter 6, page 102.

- **Play in the Snow at Winterlude:** This annual winter festival, held during the first three weekends of February, is filled with snow, ice, and loads of fun. Downtown Ottawa and Hull are transformed into winter wonderlands filled with gigantic snow sculptures, glittering ice sculptures, and a Snowflake Kingdom especially for kids. There's entertainment, dog sled rides, horse-drawn sleigh rides, snowboarding demonstrations, and more. Winterlude activities are based at Parliament Hill, New Ottawa City Hall and Festival Plaza, Confederation Park, the Rideau Canal Skateway at Fifth Avenue, Dow's Lake, and Jacques-Cartier Park in Hull. See chapter 2, page 17.

- **Sink Your Teeth into a Beaver Tail:** Visit the original stand in the ByWard Market of this now-famous fast-food treat, which was first served in 1978 and now enjoys a huge following. But don't worry—there are no real furry creatures involved. Beaver Tails are flat, deep-fried pastries shaped like a beaver tail. Choose drizzled chocolate, cinnamon and sugar, garlic, cheese, or other toppings. Don't count the calories; you can easily burn up a Beaver Tail or two by skating on the canal or biking on the scenic pathways. See chapter 5, page 82.

- **View the Parliament Buildings and the Ottawa Skyline:** From the Alexandra Bridge, Jacques-Cartier Park in Hull, and the pathways along the north shore of the Ottawa River, you'll get a breathtaking view of the Parliament Buildings and the Ottawa skyline. The view from the Capital Infocentre on Wellington Street facing toward the front of Parliament Hill is one of the most photographed views in Ottawa. See chapter 3, page 42.

- **Ride to the Top of the Peace Tower:** When you've taken in the grace and majesty of the exterior of the Parliament Buildings, hop in the elevator and ride up to the observation deck at the top of the Peace Tower. Built between 1919 and 1927, the 92-m (302-ft.) tower is a memorial to the more than 60,000 Canadian soldiers who lost their lives during World War I. The glass-enclosed observation deck offers magnificent views in all directions. See chapter 6, page 97.

- **Stroll the ByWard Market:** The ByWard Market district has something for everyone, from funky shops to swank restaurants, outdoor cafes, and an authentic farmer's market with excellent quality fresh produce and flowers. The place bustles with activity and bubbles with personality. See chapter 6, page 121.

- **Shop in the Glebe:** This fashionable shopping district stretches along Bank St. between the Queensway and the Rideau Canal. Most retailers are independent and the merchandise is good quality. It's well worth spending a morning or afternoon strolling up one side of the street and down the other. See chapter 9, page 172.

- **Tiptoe through the Tulips:** Visit Ottawa in mid-May and you'll be dazzled by literally millions of tulips blooming throughout the capital region. Commissioner's Park, alongside Dow's Lake, features an orchestrated display of tulip beds with over 300,000 blooms. Many of the events of the 10-day Canadian Tulip Festival take place in Major's Hill Park, northeast of the Parliament Buildings and behind the Fairmont

Château Laurier Hotel. Ottawa's festival of tulips began with a gift of several thousand bulbs from the Dutch royal family after World War II. Since then, the tulips of Ottawa have grown to represent international friendship and the arrival of spring in Canada. See chapter 2, page 18.

• **Be Dazzled by the Autumn Leaves:** Gatineau Park, a wilderness area covering 361 km² (141 mile²) in Quebec's Gatineau Hills, is a short drive from downtown Ottawa. It's beautiful in all seasons, but the abundance of deciduous trees makes it especially colorful in the fall. There are many hiking trails to suit a variety of ages and fitness levels. Maps are available. See chapter 10, page 194.

2 Best Hotel Bets

• **Best Historic Hotel:** The elegant Edwardian **Fairmont Château Laurier** (1 Rideau St. ✆ **800/ 441-1414** or 613/241-1414) has preserved and maintained the exterior and interior of the building most admirably. If you're looking for tradition, luxury, and attentive service, this is the place to stay. The extensive health club and pool area, added in 1929, superbly demonstrate Art Deco design.

• **Best for Business Travelers: ARC the.hotel** (140 Slater St. ✆ **800/ 699-2516** or 613/238-2888) scoops the award in this category. A sophisticated blend of luxury and efficiency is the hallmark of this upscale boutique hotel. Striving to anticipate and meet the needs of frequent travelers, ARCthe.hotel provides a relaxing retreat from the demanding world of the business traveler while providing essential services for those who wish to work while a guest at the hotel.

• **Best for Families:** With so many Ottawa hotels offering family packages and facilities for children, it's not easy to choose a single property as the best of the bunch. For many years, the **Delta Ottawa Hotel and Suites** has unofficially earned the local title of tops for children. The two-story indoor waterslide is a big hit. In addition, there's a children's playroom, game room, and seasonal children's programming. Suites have kitchenettes.

• **Best Moderately Priced Hotel:** The **Hampton Inn** has oversize guest rooms, spacious bathrooms, mini-kitchenettes, a sparkling clean indoor pool, and complimentary continental breakfast for a rack rate of C$125 (US$78). Now *that's* value for money.

• **Best Luxury Hotel:** The breathtaking splendor of the new (2001) **Hilton Lac Leamy,** adjacent to Casino du Lac-Leamy (3 boulevard du Casino, Hull ✆ **866/488-7888** or 819/790-6444) has set a new standard of luxury in Canada's capital region. The main lobby features a spectacular blown-glass sculpture. Public areas are adorned with ceramic and marble. Views of Lac Leamy, Lac de la Carrière with its trademark fountain, and the Ottawa skyline are stunning. Guest facilities include spa, indoor/outdoor pool, tennis courts, fitness center, adjacent performance hall, and adjacent award-winning fine dining restaurant.

• **Most Unusual Accommodation:** The **Ottawa International Hostel** (75 Nicholas St. ✆ **613/235-2595**) is housed in the former Carleton

County Gaol (1862–1972). Your bed for the night is a jail cell bunk. If you'd rather not sleep behind bars, you can overnight in one of the dorms. Guided tours of the former prison are available.

- **Best Suite Hotel:** There's an abundance of good suite hotels in the city, as you'll see if you browse through chapter 4, "Accommodations." Sharing the top spot by a whisker are the **Marriott Residence Inn** (161 Laurier Ave. W. ℭ **800/331-3131** or 613/231-2020) and **Minto Place Suite Hotel** (433 Laurier Ave. W. ℭ **800/267-3377** or 613/782-2350). Both have beautifully appointed, spacious suites with well-equipped kitchens. Their convenient downtown locations, clean indoor pools, and courteous, friendly staff earn them top marks.

- **Best Location:** The **Westin Ottawa** (11 Colonel By Dr. ℭ **888/625-5144** or 613/560-7000) is just steps from Parliament Hill and the ByWard Market. The third floor of the hotel provides direct access to the stores and services of the Rideau Shopping Centre. The National Arts Centre and the Rideau Canal are also on the doorstep.

- **Best Facilities for Kids:** There are a number of Ottawa hotels with excellent facilities for kids. Earning top spot is **Cartier Place and Towers Suite Hotel** (180 Cooper St. ℭ **800/236-8399** or 613/236-5000). This hotel boasts a clean indoor pool, well-equipped indoor playroom, pre-school-size play structure adjoining the pool area, and an outdoor courtyard with a climbing gym, children's play equipment, and skating rink.

- **Best Resort:** Leisure and recreational activities are outstanding at **Chateau Cartier Resort** (1170 chemin Aylmer, Aylmer ℭ **800/807-1088** or 819/777-1088), just a short drive from Ottawa or Hull. There's an 18-hole golf course on the 62 hectare (152 acre) property. Tennis courts, racquetball and squash courts, fitness center, indoor pool, spa, and sports equipment rental ensure there are activities to suit every guest. In winter, enjoy the skating rink or a horse-drawn sleigh ride, or go tobogganing, tubing, cross-country skiing, or snowshoeing. Most rooms are junior suites and they're above average in amenities and decor.

3 Best B&Bs and Inns

- **Best Retreat:** The **Carmichael Inn & Spa** (46 Cartier St. ℭ **613/236-4667** or 613/563-7529) is a quiet oasis in the heart of the busy city. Enjoy the calm, restful atmosphere. Relax on the sheltered veranda in spring and summer or curl up in an armchair by the fireplace in colder weather. A luxurious spa is located on the lower level. Packages available for the day or overnight and special getaways for couples are popular features.

- **Most Friendly:** You'll feel completely at ease at **A Rose on Colonel By** (9 Rosedale Ave. ℭ **613/291-7831**). Owner Ann Sharp cheerfully welcomes guests and her friendly nature ensures a relaxing stay in this charming home.

- **Most Romantic: Brighton House** (308 First Ave. ℭ **613/233-7777**) has six units available between two neighboring Edwardian homes in the Glebe. All are tastefully furnished, but for the most romantic atmosphere, ask for one of the suites. One suite has an adjoining sunroom with a pretty view of the garden, but the most popular suite for couples is the one with an antique brass bed draped in lace and an adjoining sitting room with a fireplace.

- **Best Period Decor:** You'll find many period details throughout the distinguished Victorian **Auberge "The King Edward" B&B** (525 King Edward Ave. © 800/841-8786 or 613/565-6700). The front parlor is a peaceful oasis of tropical plants, accented by a trickling fountain. Antiques are featured throughout the principal rooms. Original fireplaces, plaster moldings, pillars, and stained-glass windows complete the picture. At Christmastime, a 3.6-m (12-ft.) high tree trimmed with Victorian decorations is a sight to behold.

- **Best Contemporary Decor:** In the historic residential district of Sandy Hill east of the Rideau Canal, **Benner's Bed & Breakfast** (539–541 Besserer St. © 877/891-5485 or 613/789-8320) encompasses two elegant Edwardian brownstone houses. The stunning interior is a seamless blend of original architectural features and sleek contemporary decor. Features include exposed brick, artful lighting, thoughtfully placed sculptures, and a polished maple staircase.

- **Best All-Rounder:** There's lots to like about **Alanbury House** (119 Strathcona Ave. © 613/234-8378). The owners are pleasant and welcoming. The interior has been meticulously decorated with chic Montreal style and taste. Fabrics and furnishings, including several antique pieces, have been carefully selected to complement this beautiful three-story Victorian home. The location is close to downtown, the Canal, the shops of the Glebe, and pretty little Central Park.

4 Best Dining Bets

- **Best Bagels:** You could also call **Kettleman's Bagels,** 912 Bank St. (© 613/567-7100), the best show and probably the best breakfast (if you're a bagel person). Watch the bagel bakers at work as they deftly cut strips from huge mounds of dough, shape them into circles, line them up on long wooden planks, and slide them into the open wood-burning oven. The result is delicious. There are two other locations at 2177 Carling Ave. (© 613/722-4357) in the west end and 1222 Place D'Orléans Dr. (© 613/841-4409) in the east end.

- **Best Afternoon Tea:** There is nothing more civilized than after-noon tea, and **Zoe's** at the **Fairmont Château Laurier** (1 Rideau St. © 613/241-1414) does it very well. Guests will appreciate the white linen, silver tea service, Victorian scones with Devonshire cream and strawberry jam, and attentive service from gracious waiters in waistcoats and bow ties.

- **Best Vegetarian: The Green Door** (198 Main St. © 613/234-9597) is a casual eatery with buffet-style service. Many dishes are certified organic. Choose from vegetable stir-fries, tofu, pasta, salads, breads, fresh fruit, cakes, and pies.

- **Best Desserts: Oh So Good Desserts Café** (108 Murray St. © 613/241-8028), has its delectable desserts lined up in a shiny glass showcase. There's only one serving size (huge) and the selection of cakes and pies is dazzling.

- **Best Crepes:** Maybe this category should be amended to "Most Generous Portions," because the crepes at **Crepe de France** (76 Murray St. ℭ **613/241-1220**) are big enough to share with a friend. There's a large selection of savory and sweet crepes in addition to French brasserie staples such as steak *frites* (steak with fries) and mussels.
- **Best Cafe:** At the north end of the ByWard Market building you'll find **Le Moulin de Provence,** 55 Byward Market (ℭ **613/241-9152**), a lively mix of bakery, cafe, pâtisserie, and light fare. The French pastries are irresistible. Huge picture windows are perfect for people-watching, an essential ingredient of any good cafe. Cup your hands around a bowl of café au lait and sip as you watch the world go by.
- **Best Gourmet Takeout:** For an ever-changing selection of take-home food, visit **Thyme & Again** (1255 Wellington St. W. ℭ **613/722-6277**). The list of soups, salads, side dishes, main dishes, dips, vinaigrettes, and desserts reads like a fine dining menu. You may never cook again!
- **Best Canadian:** The freshest available regional, seasonal, and often organic products are employed to create uniquely Canadian dishes on the constantly changing menu at **Domus** (87 Murray St. ℭ **613/241-6007**).
- **Best French:** A distinctly French atmosphere prevails at **Le Pied de Cochon** (248 rue Montcalm, Hull ℭ **819/777-5808**). The food is excellent and the service attentive.

- **Best Casual Italian:** Housed in a heritage stone building, **Mamma Grazzi's Kitchen,** 25 George St. (ℭ **613/241-8656**), is especially pleasant in the summer, when you can dine alfresco in the cobblestone courtyard at the rear. The quaint courtyard is flanked by the terraces of several other eateries, lending a European atmosphere.
- **Best Traditional Italian:** In the heart of Little Italy, **La Roma** (430 Preston St. ℭ **613/234-8244**) has a solid reputation for good quality cuisine. Service is impeccable. Italian specialties include veal, chicken, and pasta dishes. The recently expanded all-Italian wine list is impressive in both length and variety.
- **Best Fusion:** Intense Caribbean colors surround diners at **Savana Café** (431 Gilmour St. ℭ **613/233-9159**). West African–style vegetable stir-fry, sweet basil shrimp, coconut rice, and pad thai are just a few of the divine dishes.
- **Best American:** Ottawa's **Hard Rock Café** (73 York St. ℭ **613/241-2442**) caters to rock music fans and lovers of burgers, steaks, fajitas, ribs, barbecued chicken, milk shakes, and ice cream sundaes. The collection of memorabilia from rock's most legendary performers is jaw-dropping.
- **Best Croissants:** Reputed to have the flakiest, richest, most buttery croissants in the city, the **French Baker/Le Boulanger Français,** 119 Murray St. (ℭ **613/789-7941**) also has authentic baguettes and other breads and pastries.
- **Best Cheese:** The gourmet food shop **L'Amuse Gueule,** 915 Bank St. (ℭ **613/234-9400**), is a little slice of France. Taste local and imported cheeses and pick up a baguette or two. There are a few tables and chairs inside, but this

is primarily a takeout and catering operation.

- **Best Newcomer:** Intent on turning the spotlight on individual flavors and aromas, **Infusion** (825 Bank St. (℃ **613/234-2412**) takes its culinary creations seriously. The imaginative dishes will take your breath away.
- **Best Ice Cream:** I always say you can never have too much ice cream, and it's impossible for me to walk or drive past **Pure Gelato,** 350 Elgin St. (℃ **613/237-3799**), without stopping in for a dish of their delicious gelato.
- **Best Pasta: Luciano's,** a take-home-only pasta shop at 106 Preston St. (℃ **613/236-7545**), is the place to go to stock your freezer with ravioli, agnolotti, and tortellini stuffed with yummy fillings like sun-dried tomato, spinach and ricotta, and butternut squash. Choose spaghetti, fettucine, linguine, or rigatoni and top it with one of their homemade sauces.
- **Best Pizza:** Pizzas almost fly from the oven onto tables and out the door at **Café Colonnade,** 280 Metcalfe St. (℃ **613/237-3179**). Their famous pizza has a thick crust with a sprinkling of cheese around the edge, a generous smear of tangy tomato sauce, and gooey mozzarella to hold the toppings in place. On warm summer days

and evenings you can hang out on the outdoor terrace that stretches along one side of the building. Takeout is also available.

- **Best Seafood:** You know how fresh the fish is at the **Pelican Fishery & Grill** (1500 Bank St. (℃ **613/526-0995**) because you walk right past the eye-catching display of fresh fish and seafood on the way to your table. The menu changes daily, depending on what's available.
- **Best Bistro:** One of the best places to eat in the ByWard Market area, the **Black Tomato,** 11 George St. (℃ **613/789-8123**), gets top marks for the food and the surroundings. The kitchen has heaps of culinary talent, so prepare yourself for a hedonistic culinary experience.
- **Best View:** Having the distinct advantage of a converted boathouse setting, the **Canal Ritz,** 375 Queen Elizabeth Dr. (℃ **613/ 238-8998**), boasts an outstanding view of the Rideau Canal and a constantly changing panorama. In summer, boats glide right past the terrace. In the winter, when the canal freezes and transforms itself into the world's longest skating rink, you can watch the myriad of skaters slipping and sliding along the ice.

5 The Best of Ottawa for Families

There are as many different kinds of children as there are parents. Some families like to be active outdoors, others like to explore museums, and many like to join in local festivals and special events. Whatever your family's favorite kind of vacation, Ottawa and the surrounding region delivers. There's so much to see and do, you'll find yourself planning a return visit even before the first is over.

- **Best Attractions:** Ottawa has so many top attractions appealing to all age groups that it's difficult and perhaps a little unfair to single

out a few. Browse the animal barns, demonstrations, and special events at the **Canada Agriculture Museum,** and take in the dinosaurs, rocks and minerals, and creepy critters at the **Museum of Nature.** At the **RCMP Musical Ride Centre,** tour the stables and watch the Mounties rehearse their routines free of charge. Visit the **Canada Aviation Museum,** with its large collection of authentic aircraft, and the exceptional **Canadian Museum of Civilization,** with its world-class exhibits, IMAX films, and **Children's Museum.** See chapter 6.

- **Best Accommodation:** Although a one- or two-bedroom hotel suite may be out of the reach of some budgets, it's a luxury worth paying for when you're traveling with children. The flexibility of having at least one separate bedroom and the convenience of a kitchen in which to prepare snacks and meals makes the entire vacation less stressful for everyone. Ottawa has an unusually high proportion of suite hotels, and many offer family packages during peak vacation periods. See chapter 4.
- **Best Outdoors:** Head for **Gatineau Park** across the river in Quebec in any season and enjoy the trails. Drop into the visitor center before you hike, bike, or ski and buy a trail map showing the topography in detail so you can select trails to suit your fitness level and ability. See chapter 10, page 194
- **Best Events:** Join the fun at **Winterlude,** celebrating Canada's chilliest season. The first three weekends of February are filled with snow, ice, and loads of family fun. In mid-May, the **Canadian Tulip Festival** will dazzle young and old with the blooming of over three million tulips in a rainbow of colors. Between May and October, the **RCMP Musical Ride** performs a musical show with

their majestic horses. They tour throughout Canada, with some Ottawa dates. Not to be missed is the **Changing of the Guard,** a half-hour ceremony performed daily (weather permitting) on Parliament Hill between late June and late August. Finally, it's worth the effort to experience **Canada Day** in the nation's capital.

- **Most Fun Dining:** Experience the unique atmosphere of **Marchélino** (Rideau Shopping Centre, 50 Rideau St. ✆ 613/569-4934). Wander among the colorful displays of fruits, salads, breads, and pastries and watch the staff at work rolling out dough, baking bread, roasting chickens, sliding pizzas in and out of the stone hearth oven, assembling sushi, and flipping crepes.
- **Best Casual Dining:** The **Elgin Street Diner,** 374 Elgin St. (✆ 613/237-9700), is a comfy, neighborhood kind of place where you can saunter in, flop into a chair, and hang out with a coffee while the kids slurp milk shakes and chomp peanut butter and jam sandwiches. There are plenty of old-fashioned dinners on the menu, including meat loaf, shepherd's pie, and liver and onions. See chapter 5, page 78.
- **Best Shopping:** All the major malls seem to attract families like magnets, but there are two that have particularly good facilities for parents and kids. **Place d'Orléans Shopping Centre** (110 Place d'Orléans Dr. ✆ 613/824-9050) has an area for parents of young children called Place Bébé. Facilities include changing rooms and breastfeeding rooms. There's also an indoor playground, a play-care center run by the YMCA/YWCA, and a good selection of clothing

stores for kids and teens. **St. Laurent Shopping Centre** (1200 St. Laurent Blvd. © **613/745-6858**) has an entertainment wing with a climbing wall and high-tech arcade zone. Nursing rooms, family washrooms, designated parking for expectant mothers and new parents, and highchairs in the food court are some of the family amenities. Lots of kids and teen clothing stores. Anchors are Toys "Я" Us, The Bay, and Sears.

2

Planning a Trip to Ottawa

Whether you're usually a careful think-ahead type of person or a spur-of-the-moment decision maker, to make the most of your trip you'd be well advised to take some time planning. You've already made the right decision in choosing Ottawa as your vacation destination—the city is bursting with attractions and activities for everyone to enjoy.

1 Visitor Information & Entry Requirements

VISITOR INFORMATION

FROM NORTH AMERICA Your starting point is the **Capital Infocentre,** 90 Wellington St., Ottawa, ON K1P 1C7 (© **800/465-1867** or 613/239-5000; www.canadascapital.gc.ca), which provides information on Ottawa and the surrounding region and is administered by the National Capital Commission. The call center provides visitor information Monday to Friday 8:30am to 8pm and on weekends 8:30am to 5pm from mid-May to Labour Day. The rest of the year it's open from Monday to Friday 8:30am to 5pm and Saturday and Sunday 9am to 5pm. To receive written material on the National Capital Region, write to the Capital Infocentre at 40 Elgin St., Room 202, Ottawa, ON K1P 1C7.

The **Ottawa Tourism and Convention Authority Inc. (OTCA),** 130 Albert St., Suite 1800, Ottawa, ON K1P 5G4, publishes a comprehensive annual visitor guide, which includes maps and listings of cultural sites, things to see and do, accommodations, places to dine and shop, and services. You can obtain a free copy of the guide by phoning © **800/465-1867.** Allow up to 2 weeks for delivery. You can also pick up a copy at the Capital Infocentre when you arrive in the city. Websites with visitor information

include **www.canada.com, www.ottawakiosk.com** and **www.festival seeker.com**.

The **Ontario East Tourism Association,** © **800/567-3278,** can provide details of Eastern Ontario attractions, including the Thousand Islands and St. Lawrence Valley Corridor, the Rideau Heritage Corridor, and the Ottawa Valley.

For information about the entire province of Ontario, contact **Ontario Tourism Marketing Partnership** (an agency of the Ontario Ministry of Tourism, Culture, and Recreation), at © **800/ONTARIO** or www.ontario travel.net. You can write for tourist information to the Ontario Ministry of Tourism, Culture, and Recreation, Hearst Block, 900 Bay St., 10th Floor, Toronto, ON M7A 2E1.

The official website of the **Canadian Tourism Commission, www. travelcanada.ca,** offers customized information for visitors depending on their country of origin.

There are around a dozen Canadian Consul General's offices in the U.S. that can direct U.S. citizens to resources to help you plan your trip to Ottawa. Visit the website of the U.S. Embassy in Ottawa for travel tips and tourist information at **www.usembassy canada.gov** or contact the Embassy at 490 Sussex Dr., Ottawa ON K1N 1G8 (© 613/238-5335).

FROM ABROAD The following consulates can provide information or refer you to the appropriate offices.

U.K. and Ireland: The **Canadian High Commission,** 1 Grosvenor Sq., London W1K 4AB (© **0207/258-6600**).

Australia: The **Canadian High Commission,** Commonwealth Avenue, Canberra, ACT 2600 (© **02/6270-4000**), or the Consul General of Canada, Level 5, Quay West Building, 111 Harrington St., Sydney, NSW 2000 (© **02/9364-3000**). The consul general also has offices in Perth.

New Zealand: The **Canadian High Commission,** 3rd Floor, 61 Molesworth St., Thorndon, Wellington (© **644/473-9577**).

South Africa: The **Canadian High Commission,** 1103 Arcadia St., Hatfield 0083, Pretoria (© **012/422-3000**).

ENTRY REQUIREMENTS

It is key to know and follow these guidelines carefully.

DOCUMENTS

Entry requirements for Canada have tightened in recent years and security has been heightened at border crossings and other points of entry since the tragedy in the U.S. on Sept. 11, 2001. All visitors to Canada must show proof of citizenship. U.S. citizens and permanent U.S. residents do not need a passport to enter Canada, though it is the easiest and most convenient method of proving citizenship. If you don't have a passport, you should carry a certificate of naturalization, a citizenship certificate, or a birth certificate with photo ID. Permanent U.S. residents who are not U.S. citizens must carry their Alien Registration Cards (green cards). If you plan to drive into Canada, be sure to bring

your car's registration papers. If you are traveling with children under the age of 19, make sure they carry identification papers. If you are not their parents or legal guardians, you must also carry a written statement from their parents or guardians granting permission for the children to travel to Canada under your supervision.

Citizens of most European countries and former British colonies, as well as certain other countries (such as Israel, Korea, and Japan), do not need visas but must carry passports. Entry visas are required for citizens of more than 130 countries. You must apply for and receive your entry visa from the Canadian embassy in your home country. For detailed information, call your local Canadian consulate or embassy.

CUSTOMS
WHAT YOU CAN BRING IN

Generally, you are allowed to bring in goods for personal use during your trip into Canada, although there are restrictions on plants, meats, and pets. Fishing tackle poses no problem, but the bearer must possess a nonresident license for the province where he or she plans to use it. There are severe restrictions on firearms and weapons. All guns must be declared—otherwise, they may be seized by customs officers. Handguns require a special permit and may be imported only under specific conditions. Long guns can be brought into Canada only under special circumstances, such as for use in competitions or for hunting in season. Provided you are 19 or older, you can bring with you up to 200 cigarettes, 50 cigars or cigarillos, 200 tobacco sticks, and 200 grams (7 oz.) of manufactured tobacco without having to pay duty. In Ontario, if you are 19 years or older you can bring in no more than 1.14 liters (40 fl. oz.) of liquor, or 1.5 liters (52 fl. oz.) of wine or wine coolers, or 24 containers of beer (355ml, or 12 fl. oz., each) duty-free. Dogs, cats, and most other pets can enter Canada with their owners, but you should bring a valid rabies vaccination certificate with you.

For more details concerning customs regulations, call the **Canada Customs and Revenue Agency**'s 24-hour Automated Customs Information Service at © **800/461-9999** (within Canada) or © **204/983-3500** (in the U.S.). Detailed information for Canadian residents and visitors to Canada, including border wait times, can be found at the CCRA website at www.ccra-adrc.gc.ca. In some major U.S. airports, you'll find Customs Service kiosks—self-service computers with touch-screen displays that can assist you with customs regulations for the country you're planning to visit.

WHAT YOU CAN BRING HOME

- **U.S. citizens** should contact the **U.S. Customs Service,** 1300 Pennsylvania Ave. NW, Washington, D.C. 20229. Information is also available at www.customs.ustreas. gov. *Be warned:* Cuban tobacco products purchased in Canada cannot be brought back to the United States.
- **U.K. citizens** can contact **HM Customs and Excise** online at www.hmce.gov.uk or use the National Advice Service by calling © **0845/010-9000** Monday to Friday 8am to 8 pm.
- **Australian citizens** should contact the **Australian Customs Service** at www.customs.gov.au or phone the Customs Information Centre at © **1300/363-263.**
- **New Zealand citizens** may contact **New Zealand Customs Service** by writing to The Custom House, 17–21 Whitmore St., Box 2218, Wellington, by calling © **0800/428-786,** or by visiting their website at www.customs. govt.nz.

2 Money

CURRENCY

The currency of Canada is the Canadian dollar, made up of 100 cents. U.S. visitors enjoy a distinct advantage—the Canadian dollar has been fluctuating at around 62 cents in U.S. money, give or take a couple of points' variation. What this means is that your American money gets you about 60% more the moment you exchange it for local currency. Since the cost of many goods is roughly on par with U.S. prices, the difference is real, not imaginary. The British pound has been hovering at around C$2.30, which translates into excellent value for visitors from the U.K. Be aware that although sales taxes are high in Canada, you may be able to claim a tax refund for some purchases (see "Taxes" under "Fast Facts" in chapter 3, "Getting to Know Ottawa").

Paper currency comes in $5, $10, $20, $50, and $100 denominations. Coins come in 1¢, 5¢, 10¢, and 25¢ (penny, nickel, dime, and quarter) and $1- and $2 denominations. The common name for the brass $1 coin is a "loonie" because of the loon on its "tails" side. The more recently released $2 coin has been dubbed the "toonie."

Most tourist establishments in Canada will accept U.S. cash, but to get the best rate, change your funds into Canadian currency upon arrival. The most widely accepted credit cards are MasterCard and Visa, with American Express gaining ground.

If you do spend American money at Canadian establishments, you should understand how the conversion is calculated. Often there is a sign at the cash register stating "U.S. Currency 50%." This 50% is the "premium," which means that for every U.S. greenback you hand over, the cashier will consider it $1.50 Canadian. For example, to pay a $15 tab you'll need only $10 in U.S. currency. Be aware that the exchange rate may not be as favorable as you would get at a financial institution or currency exchange booth.

The Canadian Dollar, the U.S. Dollar & the British Pound

The prices in this guide are given first in Canadian dollars, then in U.S. dollars. Amounts over $5 have been rounded to the nearest dollar. Note that the Canadian dollar is worth about 40% less than the American dollar but buys nearly as much. At the time of writing, C$1 was worth about US$0.62 and that was the equivalency used to figure the prices in this guide. The U.K. pound is included here for your reference with C$1 worth about £0.43. Note that exchange rates are subject to fluctuation, and you should always check the most recent currency rates when preparing for your trip. Here's a quick table of equivalents:

C $	U.S. $	U.K. £	U.S. $	C $	U.K. £
1	0.62	0.43	1	1.60	0.69
5	3.10	2.15	5	8.00	3.45
10	6.20	4.30	10	16.00	6.90
20	12.40	8.60	20	32.00	13.80
50	31.00	21.50	50	80.00	34.50
80	49.60	34.40	80	128.00	55.20
100	62.00	43.00	100	160.00	69.00

You'll usually get the best rate of exchange through an **ATM,** and it's handy not to have to carry large amounts of cash or traveler's checks around. Always bring sufficient Canadian funds to take you through your first day or so, when you'll likely need cash for cab or bus fare and a snack. Try to limit your ATM transactions because you will pay a fee for each withdrawal. You can find ATMs at most banks. You can also get cash advances against your MasterCard or Visa, but you'll need a personal identification number (PIN) to access this service. Note that the credit card company will begin charging interest on the cash advance immediately and may charge a fee for this service.

If you prefer the extra security of **traveler's checks,** almost all hotels, restaurants, shops, and attractions accept U.S.-dollar traveler's checks, and you can exchange them for cash at banks if you show ID. There may be a charge for this service. Be sure to keep a record of the serial numbers of your traveler's checks (separately from the checks, of course), so you're ensured a refund if they're lost or stolen.

American Express (© 800/869-3016 in Canada or the U.S.) is the most widely recognized traveler's check; depending on where you purchase them, expect to pay a 1% to 4% commission.

Credit cards are invaluable when traveling—they provide a safe way to carry money and a convenient record of all your expenses. Almost every credit card company has an emergency toll-free number to call if your credit card is lost or stolen. They may be able to wire you a cash advance from your credit card immediately, and in many places they can deliver an emergency card in a day or two. In Canada, **MasterCard** holders should call ✆ **800/307-7309, Visa** customers should call ✆ **800/847-2911,** and **American Express** cardholders should call ✆ **800/869-3016.** Information is also available online at www.master card.com, www.visa.com, and www. americanexpress.com. You can also call a toll-free information directory at ✆ **800/555-1212** to get Canadian toll-free numbers. The best and fastest way to get assistance when you are in your home country is to call your card issuer.

What Things Cost in Ottawa	C$	U.S.$	U.K.£
Shuttle from airport to downtown hotel	11.00	6.82	4.73
Newspaper	.70	.43	.30
Local telephone call	.25	.16	.11
Movie ticket	10.00	6.20	4.30
Ticket for the NAC	50.00	31.00	21.50
Taxi fare, typical 5-km (3-mile) ride	9.00	5.58	3.87
Bus ticket (adult single)	2.25	1.40	.97
Bus day pass (unlimited travel)	5.00	3.10	2.15
Two-course lunch for one (moderate)*	25.00	15.50	10.75
Three-course dinner for one (moderate)*	40.00	24.80	17.20
Parking meter, downtown per hour	1.50	.93	.65
All-day parking lot, downtown	9.00	5.58	3.87
Museum entrance fee	7.00	4.34	21.07
Roll of Kodak film, 24-exposure print	6.00	3.72	2.58
Cup of coffee	1.50	.93	.65
Bottle of juice	2.00	1.24	.86
Hot dog from corner umbrella cart	2.00	1.24	.86
Large takeout pizza	20.00	12.40	8.60
*Includes tax, tip, and nonalcoholic beverage.			

3 When to Go

Many special events and festivals are scheduled for the peak periods of June, July, and August. Special packages are often available from hotels—always ask for a deal when making a reservation. During the summer months and the Christmas and March breaks, many of Ottawa's museums and attractions offer special workshops and programs for children and families. The city is most crowded with visitors at these times, though, and there are other wonderful times of the year to enjoy the region. The spring weather in May, when the tulips are in bloom, is often bright and refreshing; the sunshine is warm but you'll need light jackets for cooler days. If you visit in the fall, you can bike or hike through the beautiful

Gatineau Hills and enjoy nature's art show. In mid-winter, enjoy skating on the Rideau Canal Skateway. The Skateway is usually open from late December until late February or early March. Up-to-the-minute information on ice conditions on the canal is available by calling © **613/239-5234.** The first three weekends in February bring Winterlude, Ottawa's annual winter festival. March is maple syrup season, so head out to a sugarbush to see some tree tapping and sample this classic Canadian treat. For an exuberant birthday celebration, visit the nation's capital over Canada Day, on July 1. Hotel rooms fill up quickly for the Canada Day weekend, so book well ahead.

THE CLIMATE

Spring runs from late March to mid-May (although sometimes there's a late snowfall in April); **summer,** mid-May to mid-September; **fall,** mid-September to mid-November; and **winter,** mid-November to late March. The average annual high is 10°C (50°F) and the average annual low is 0°C (32°F). In winter, fluctuations in temperature sometimes cause freezing rain, a serious hazard for drivers.

Ottawa's Average Temperatures (°C/°F)

	Jan	Feb	Mar	Apr	May	June	July	Aug	Sept	Oct	Nov	Dec
High	–4/25	–6/22	3/37	9/48	17/63	20/69	23/74	22/72	18/64	12/54	5/42	–3/27
Low	–18/0	–18/0	–13/9	–1/31	8/47	14/58	17/62	15/59	11/52	2/36	–6/21	–15/5

HOLIDAYS

On most public holidays, banks, government offices, schools, and post offices are closed. Museums, stores, and restaurants vary widely in their policies for holiday openings and closings, so to avoid disappointment, call before you go.

Please note that between mid October and late April, most museums in Ottawa are closed on Mondays. Ottawa celebrates the following holidays: New Year's Day (January 1), Good Friday and/or Easter Monday (March or April), Victoria Day (Monday following the third weekend in May), Canada Day (July 1), Civic Holiday (first Monday in August), Labour Day (first Monday in September), Thanksgiving (second Monday in October), Remembrance Day (November 11), Christmas Day (December 25), and Boxing Day (December 26).

OTTAWA CALENDAR OF EVENTS

The following list of events will help you to plan your visit to Ottawa. Contact the **Capital Infocentre** (© **800/465-1867**) to confirm details if a particular event is a major reason for your vacation. Even the largest, most successful events sometimes retire, a few events are biennial, and dates may change from those listed here. In addition to the following events, numerous smaller community and cultural events take place throughout the year. **Lansdowne Park** hosts many trade and consumer shows catering to special interests—contact **Lansdowne Park** at © **613/580-2429**. Various websites list upcoming events. Have a look at www.canada.com/ottawa, www.canadascapital.gc.ca, www.ottawakiosk.com, or www. festivalseeker.com.

January

The Governor General's New Year's Day Levee is held at Rideau Hall, the official residence of the governor general. Members of the public are invited to meet the governor general, visit the historic residence's public rooms, and enjoy entertainment and light refreshments. © **866/842-4422.** www.gg.ca

The Ottawa-Hull International Auto Show at the Ottawa Congress Centre (adjoining the Rideau Centre) brings you up-to-date on what's happening in the world of cars, minivans, pickups, and SUVs. ✆ 613/563-1984.

February

Winterlude. Every year, the first three weekends of February are filled with family winter fun in the snow and ice, as the city celebrates its chilliest season. Downtown Ottawa and Hull are transformed into winter wonderlands filled with gigantic snow sculptures, glittering ice sculptures, and a Snowflake Kingdom especially for kids. Children's entertainment, craft workshops, horse-drawn sleigh rides, snowboarding demonstrations, dog sled rides, and more are on offer for little ones. Activities are based at Parliament Hill, New Ottawa City Hall and Festival Plaza, Confederation Park, the Rideau Canal Skateway at Fifth Avenue, Dow's Lake, and Jacques-Cartier Park in Hull. A free shuttle bus operates between sites. ✆ 800/465-1867. www.canadascapital.gc.ca

Canadian Ski Marathon. The world's longest cross-country ski tour is a skier's paradise and offers some of the best wilderness trails anywhere. You can ski as little as 15km (9 miles) or as much as 160km (99 miles)—you set the pace. The marathon attracts 1,500 to 2,000 novice and veteran skiers from ages 3 to 85. ✆ 819/770-6556. www.csm-mcs.com

Keskinada Loppet. Close to 3,000 skiers from more than a dozen countries gather to participate in Canada's biggest cross-country ski event, held annually in Gatineau Park. There's a 5-km (3-mile) and a 10-km (6-mile) family race. Kids under age 13 can ski, snowshoe, or walk the 2-km (1.25-mile) Mini-Keski. ✆ 800/465-1867 or 819/595-0114. www.keskinada.com

Ottawa Boat, Sportsmen's & Cottage Show. Revel in the outdoors at this show for fishers, hunters, and weekend cottagers, held at Lansdowne Park. Dozens of demos feature everything from tying a fly to paddling a canoe. ✆ 613/580-2429.

Ottawa Spring RV and Camping Show. Mobile homes, travel and tent trailers, vans, and sport utility and all-terrain vehicles motor into Lansdowne Park for this trade show. ✆ 613/580-2429.

March

Ottawa Spring Home Show. More than 300 exhibitors gather to showcase furnishings, swimming pools, landscaping, plumbing, kitchens, and baths at Lansdowne Park. Seminars on renovating, gardening, and interior design are also featured. ✆ 613/580-2429.

Ottawa Paddlesport & Outdoor Adventure Show. The show highlights the latest in camping, canoe, and kayak gear, as well as adventure sport activities such as white-water rafting, rock climbing, mountain biking, scuba diving, parachuting, and backpacking. ✆ 613/580-2429.

April

Kiwanis Music Festival. This annual competitive music festival, held in local venues, brings together close to 4,000 competitors of all ages and at all levels of training and ability. Teachers and performers of the highest professional standing come from across North America to act as adjudicators. ✆ 613/226-7572.

The Ottawa Lynx. Ottawa's premier baseball team, the Triple-A affiliate of the Montreal Expos, provides fun and affordable family entertainment at JetForm Park. The Lynx play 72 home games between April and September. The 10,332-seat stadium boasts a full-service restaurant, luxury suites, and a picnic area. ☎ **800/663-0985** or 613/747-LYNX (5969). www.ottawalynx.com

Ottawa Antiques Event. This annual show features 30,000ft² of authentic antiques. Held at the Aberdeen Pavilion, Lansdowne Park. ☎ **613/580-2429.**

May

Canadian Tulip Festival. A visit to this spring festival in mid-May will dazzle you with the blooming of over three million tulips in a rainbow of colors. The 10-day tulip festival includes concerts, an arts and crafts market, fireworks displays, and the colorful Tulip Flotilla, a floating parade on the Rideau Canal. Stroll along the banks of the canal and through the gardens at Dow's Lake to catch the full effect of the carpet of flowers. ☎ **800/66-TULIP** (668-8547) or 613/567-4447. www.tulipfestival.ca

National Capital Race Weekend. Thousands of runners, volunteers, spectators, and visitors gather for this world-class 42-km (26-mile) marathon, run as two laps of 21km (13 miles). Several other events, ranging from 2km (1 mile) to 21km (13 miles) are held. Families, in-line skaters, and beginner runners are welcome. ☎ **613/234-2221.** www.ncm.ca

Wind Odyssey Sound and Light Show on Parliament Hill. This free, dynamic show illuminates Parliament Hill on summer evenings. The accomplishments and experiences of Canadians are featured, revealing the essence of Canada through stirring music and visual projections on the Parliament Buildings. ☎ **800/465-1867.** www.canadascapital.gc.ca

Mother's Day Celebration. The ByWard Market is the place to be on Mother's Day. More than 75 ByWard Market restaurants roll out the red carpet for mom and the family, and many offer special menus. The ceremonial opening of the outdoor market season is staged the same weekend. ☎ **613/562-3325.** www.byward-market.com

Classic Cars. Owners and enthusiasts are invited to Place d'Orléans Wednesday evenings from 6 to 9pm, May to September, to view 350 classic cars during this outdoor, family event. ☎ **613/824-9050.**

Sheep Shearing Festival. The Canada Agriculture Museum presents its annual sheep-shearing extravaganza with shearing demonstrations, displays of sheep-herding by border collies, rare breed exhibits, wool crafts, children's activities, and much more. ☎ **613/991-3044.** www.agriculture.nmstc.ca

Odawa Spring Pow Wow. Held at Nepean Tent and Trailer Park, this energetic and colorful event is designed to bring First Nations culture to Native and non-Native audiences through the sharing of music, dance, art, and food. ☎ **613/722-3811.** www.odawa.on.ca

RCMP Musical Ride. From May to October, the world-famous Royal Canadian Mounted Police and their majestic horses perform a musical show for appreciative audiences throughout Canada, with some dates in Ottawa. Tours of the stables are offered year-round. ☎ **613/998-8199**. www.grc.ca

Strings of the Future. This biennial international string quartet festival is a multifaceted educational and musical experience devoted to the string quartet. Next held in 2003. ℂ **613/851-8668.** www.stringsofthefuture.com

June

Festival 4–15 (Ottawa Festival of the Arts for Young Audiences). Formerly known as the Ottawa Children's Festival de la Jeunesse, this event brings the best of live theatrical arts to children at sites in and around the Canadian Museum of Civilization. Families will enjoy music, theater, crafts, and other kids' entertainment. Other performing arts events for children are staged throughout the year at various local venues. ℂ **613/241-0999.** www.ottawachildrensfestival.ca

Gloucester Fair. This old-fashioned fair offers agricultural displays, gymkhana and western horse shows, a demolition derby, a lumberjack show, midway rides, bubblegum-blowing contests, pony rides, face painting, and more. ℂ **613/744-2671.** www.Gloucester-fair.on.ca

Festival Franco-Ontarian. One of the most important French celebrations in North America is held in the ByWard Market area, with a variety of musical and theatrical performances to entertain all ages. ℂ **613/741-1225.** www.ffo.ca

National Capital Dragon Boat Festival. Held at the Rideau Canoe Club at Mooney's Bay, this festival features dragon boat races, multicultural stage performers, exhibits, and activities for children. Admission is free. ℂ **613/238-7711.** www.dragonboat.net

Changing of the Guard. This half-hour ceremony is one of Ottawa's most outstanding attractions. From late June to late August, the Ceremonial Guard parades from the Cartier Square Drill Hall to Parliament Hill daily between 9:30 and 10am. The ceremony begins at 10am, weather permitting. ℂ **800/465-1867.** www.canadascapital.gc.ca

ByWard Market Auto Classic. On the first Sunday in June, the ByWard Market hosts the Auto Classic, a showcase of automotive history with over 150 vintage, classic, and high-performance cars on display for fun and prizes. The event is free to the public and classic car owners alike. ℂ **613/562-3325.** www.byward-market.com

Italian Week. Corso Italia (Preston Street), the commercial heart of Ottawa's Little Italy, is the place to be in mid-June to celebrate the food, music, pageantry, and art that is Italy. The year 2002 will mark the 28th anniversary of the festival. ℂ **613/726-0920.** www.prestonstreet.com

Carnival of Cultures. The picturesque outdoor Astrolabe Theatre is the setting for a summer kaleidoscope of cultures, with music, food, and dance from around the world. The dynamic entertainment includes international artists and Ottawa's top folk dancers, singers, and musicians. ℂ **800/465-1867.**

UniSong. Over 400 members of youth and children's choirs from across Canada perform 4 days of concerts at the National Arts Centre and other locations. Enjoy a full program of Canadian music and celebrations on Canada Day at the Festival Plaza, on Laurier Avenue near Elgin Street, 4:30pm, free. ℂ **800/267-8526** or 613/234-3360.

Garden Party at Rideau Hall. The governor general hosts the annual garden party at Rideau Hall on the last Saturday afternoon in June. Her Excellency greets visitors on the upper terrace of the gardens. The first Changing of the Guard ceremony of the summer is held before the party. Guests can explore the residence's public rooms, gardens, and greenhouses, and children can enjoy many special activities on the grounds, including entertainment and crafts. Light refreshments are served. ℂ **866/842-4422** or 613/991-4422. www.gg.ca

Canada Dance Festival. This biennial festival, scheduled for early June 2002, showcases the finest in new Canadian contemporary choreography. Performances fill the stages, streets, and parks of Ottawa and feature emerging independent artists as well as established companies. ℂ **613/996-5051.** www.canadadance.ca

Ottawa Fringe Festival. A wide range of exciting and vibrant theatre, dance, music, visual arts, video, and film can be enjoyed on six stages in the heart of Ottawa's arts and theatre district. The arts and theatre district was created in 1997, when the shopping district known as Downtown Rideau expanded to include Arts Court at 2 Daly Ave. and the surrounding area. The boundaries are Sussex Drive/Colonel By Drive to the west, George St. to the north, King Edward Ave. to the east, and MacKenzie King Bridge/Wilbrod St. to the south. Over 70 companies stage more than 300 shows. ℂ **613/232-6162.** www.ottawafringe.com

July

Canada Day. Each July 1, hundreds of thousands of Canadians gather in Ottawa to celebrate Canada's birthday. Activities center around Parliament Hill, Major's Hill Park, and Jacques-Cartier Park in Hull. Shows, street performers, and concerts mark the event. Don't miss the spectacular fireworks display over the Ottawa River.

ℂ **800/465-1867.** www.canadas capital.gc.ca

Helping Other People Everywhere (HOPE). HOPE, a nonprofit charitable organization, holds the largest beach volleyball tournament in the world, with 1,000 teams playing on 79 courts. The tournament attracts over 30,000 participants and spectators, who flock to Mooney's Bay in support of HOPE. ℂ **613/237-1433.** www.hopehelps.com

International Youth Orchestra Festival. The festival offers joint shared concerts, broadcasts, demonstrations, and a gala mass concert. Call the Capital Infocentre ℂ **800/465-1867.**

The Ottawa Chamber Music Festival. North America's largest chamber music festival and one of Canada's most respected cultural events features the finest musicians from across Canada, the United States, and Europe. Some of the most beautiful churches in downtown Ottawa host 78 concerts over 2 weeks. ℂ **613/234-8008.** www.chamberfest.com

Ottawa International Jazz Festival. For 10 days in July, the finest jazz musicians in the world perform in intimate studio spaces and open-air venues for thousands of fans. ℂ **613/241-2633.** www.ottawa jazzfestival.com

Cisco Systems Bluesfest. Canada's biggest blues festival presents an outstanding array of blues musicians. Traditionally held over 4 days at Lebreton Flats, the festival may be seeking a new location for 2002 and beyond. ℂ **613/247-1188.** ottawa-bluesfest.ca

Pride Week Festival. The Ottawa area highlights its gay, lesbian, bisexual, and transgender community with a week of events including the annual Pride Parade. ☎ **613/238-2424.** www.gayottawa.com

Capital Classic Show Jumping Tournament. Canada's top equestrians compete at this annual event. Held at the National Capital Equestrian Park, the tournament draws lots of family spectators. Call the Capital Infocentre ☎ **800/465-1867.**

Children's Hospital of Eastern Ontario Teddy Bear Picnic. Bring your kids and their bears to this annual picnic, held on the beautiful grounds of Rideau Hall on the second Saturday of July. Meet a Mountie, enjoy a pancake breakfast, visit the petting zoo, and watch live entertainment. ☎ **613/737-7600.**

August

Ice Cream Festival. The Canada Agriculture Museum celebrates creamy, dreamy ice cream. From milking cows to mixing the ingredients, discover the process of making ice cream and other frozen treats. ☎ **613/991-3044.** www.agriculture.nmstc.ca

Ottawa Folk Festival. This gathering celebrates Canada's rich folk traditions with music, dance, storytelling, and crafts. Some of Canada's finest acoustic musicians perform evening concerts on the main stage, and afternoon musical stages feature such themes as song writing, Ottawa Valley fiddling and step dancing, Celtic music, and vocal harmonics. A fun-filled area offers crafts, activities, costumes, and children's performers. Held in Britannia Park. ☎ **613/230-8234.** www.ottawafolk.org

Central Canada Exhibition. This is wholesome family entertainment at a great price. "The Ex" combines interactive theme exhibits, agricultural programs, entertainment, and a large midway with more than 60 rides, including a roller coaster. ☎ **613/237-7222.** www.the-ex.com

Ottawa Greek Festival. Ottawa's Greek-Canadian community celebrates all things Greek at this annual festival. Hosted by the Hellenic Community of Ottawa. ☎ **613/225-8016.** www.greekfest.com

The Sparks Street Mall International Busker Festival. The second-largest busker festival in Canada presents jugglers, comedians, storytellers, fire-eaters, mimes, musicians, and magicians to entertain audiences of all ages. ☎ **613/230-0984.**

September

Gatineau Hot Air Balloon Festival. Some 150 balloons take to the skies at Canada's largest balloon festival, held on Labour Day weekend. There are plenty of shows and activities, fairground rides, and a dazzling fireworks display. ☎ **800/668-8383** or 819/243-2330. www.ville.gatineau.qc.ca

Bytown Days. Step into 19th-century Bytown and experience life in Ottawa's early days. The ByWard Market district is the heart of the settlement established by Lieutenant Colonel John By in 1827 to house the workers involved in the construction of the Rideau Canal. Sample the fall harvest, watch demonstrations of 19th-century workmanship and handicrafts, take a horse-drawn hayride, and munch your way through the corn roast. ☎ **613/562-3325.** www.byward-market.com

Ottawa 67's. Watch Ontario Hockey League (OHL) action at the Civic Centre, Lansdowne Park. The regular season runs from September to April. ☎ **613/232-6767.** www.ottawa67s.com

Ottawa Senators. The Sens take on the National Hockey League's best at the Corel Centre. The regular season runs from September to April. ✆ **613/599-0100.** www.ottawasenators.com or www.corelcentre.com

Fall Rhapsody. Workshops, guided tours, nature interpretation programs, and other outdoor activities take place in Gatineau Park against a spectacular backdrop of fall leaves. Kids can watch and participate in games and crafts. The towns and villages surrounding Gatineau Park celebrate autumn with exhibits of arts and crafts and activities for the whole family. ✆ **819/827-2020.** www.capcan.ca

National Capital Air Show. Held at Ottawa International Airport on the second weekend in September, the air show features 2 full days of static and flying demonstrations, including exhibits of military and civilian aircraft and performances by the Canadian Forces Snowbirds and Parachute Team and the Sky Hawks. There are interactive displays and activities for children of all ages. ✆ **613/526-1030.** www.ncas.ottawa.com

Fall Home Show. You'll find everything for the home at this Lansdowne Park event, from wood-burning stoves to windows, roofing, and hot tubs, along with seminars and demonstrations. ✆ **613/580-2429.**

October

Ottawa Wine and Food Show. Thousands flock to this annual event at the Ottawa Congress Centre. Sample fine wines, beers, and spirits from around the world. Taste the delicious food, be entertained by celebrity chefs, or attend a wine seminar. Limited to persons ages 19 and over. ✆ **613/563-1984.** www.playerexpo.com

International Student Animation Festival of Ottawa. This biennial animation event, which alternates with the Ottawa International Animation Festival (see below), is devoted to students and first-time animators. Competitions, workshops, recruiting, and a trade fair are part of the event. ✆ **613/232-8769.**

Great Pumpkin Weigh-Off. At the ByWard Market on the first Saturday in October, growers from Ontario, Quebec, and the northeastern United States bring their entries to compete for the title of the Great Pumpkin. Some of the monsters weigh in at 450kg (1,000 lb.). Expert carvers are on hand to produce jack o' lanterns. ✆ **613/562-3325.** www.byward-market.com

Ski and Snowboard Show. Head to Lansdowne Park to check out the latest, fastest, and most technologically advanced skis and snowboards. ✆ **613/580-2429.**

Ottawa International Animation Festival. Film industry people from around the world gather in Ottawa for this biennial event (alternating with the Student Animation Festival, see above). Programs include competitions, retrospectives, workshops, children's days, and more. ✆ **613/232-8769.**

November

Help Santa Toy Parade. On the third or fourth weekend in November, the annual Santa Claus Parade winds its way through downtown Ottawa. Floats, bands, and clowns entertain the crowds lining the streets. The Fire Fighter's Association collects toys along the parade route and distributes them to less fortunate children in the Ottawa area. © 613/526-2706. www.toy parade.org

Welton Beauchamp Curling Championships. Held at various curling clubs around the city, more than 100 teams from around the world compete for cash prizes. Tickets are available to the public. © 613/235-9946. www.thewelton beauchamp.com

Lebanorama. At Ottawa City Hall's Festival Plaza, a weekend festival of Lebanese visual and performing arts takes place in mid-November. © 613/742-6952.

December

Christmas Lights Across Canada. In the heart of the capital, more than 200,000 colorful lights glow to celebrate the beginning of the Canadian winter and to welcome the New Year. © 800/465-1867. www.canadascapital.gc.ca

Christmas Carollers. Leading up to Christmas, local choirs sing Christmas carols while riding around the historic ByWard Market district in a horse-drawn carriage with sleigh bells. © 613/562-3325. www.byward-market.com

Ottawa Rebel. The National Lacrosse League team plays at the Corel Centre. The regular season runs from December to April. © 613/599-0123.

Canadian Urban Music Festival. The festival features live rhythm and blues, reggae, worldbeat, and tropical dance. © 613/564-1771. www.urbanmusicfestival.com

---

 Hey, I Didn't Know That about Ottawa!

- The name Ottawa is adapted from *Outaouak,* the name of the Algonquin people who settled and traded furs in the area.
- The world's largest gold depository is found in the Bank of Canada gold vaults, which lie under one of Ottawa's main streets, Wellington Street.
- Ottawa's official relationship with tulips began in 1945 when Queen Juliana of the Netherlands presented 100,000 bulbs to the city as a gift. They were given in appreciation of Canada's granting of a safe haven to the Dutch Royal Family during World War II and in recognition of the role that Canadian troops played in liberating the Netherlands. Half a century later, three million tulips bloom in the city's parklands in May.
- The sport of basketball was invented by Dr. James Naismith, who hailed from Almonte, a small town just west of Ottawa.
- Canada's last public hanging took place at Ottawa's first jail. The building is now operated by Hostelling International, and guests can actually sleep behind bars in the cells.
- The Governor General's New Year's Day Levee at Rideau Hall originated from the French governors' practice of shaking hands and wishing a happy New Year to the citizens of Quebec City, a tradition begun in 1646.
- The grounds of Parliament Hill were laid out in 1873 by Calvert Vaux, the same landscape architect who designed New York's Central Park.

- The 7.8-km (4.5-mile) Rideau Canal Skateway, the world's longest skating rink, is used by approximately 750,000 skaters each winter and has an average skating season of 64 days.
- The world's first international telephone call was made from Ottawa in 1927, when Canadian prime minister Mackenzie King called the British prime minister.
- North American entertainment stars Paul Anka and Rich Little were born in Ottawa and have streets named after them in the city's south end.
- Actor Dan Ackroyd was born in the region and attended Carleton University. Singer Alanis Morrisette was also born here, and rock star Bryan Adams went to school in Ottawa.
- The Ottawa Senators was originally the name of a local football club in the 1920s. In 1992, the name was reclaimed for Ottawa's first National Hockey League team.
- The Stanley Cup was born in Ottawa. In 1892, Governor General Lord Stanley Preston commissioned a silversmith in England to make a gold-lined silver bowl on an ebony base, which became the premier trophy of professional hockey in North America.

4 Health & Safety

MEDICAL

Medical care in Ontario is provided to all residents through the Ontario Health Insurance Plan (OHIP), administered by the provincial government. Visitors from abroad are ineligible for OHIP coverage and should arrange for **health insurance** coverage before entering Canada. For more information, contact a private insurance company directly, or call the **Canadian Life and Health Insurance Association** ℂ **800/268-8099;** www.clhia.ca. Canadian travelers are protected by their home province's health insurance plan for a limited time period. Check with your province's health insurance agency before traveling.

There are emergency services available at several hospitals in the Ottawa area. For adult care, there are three hospital campuses with emergency care—the **General,** the **Civic,** and the **Riverside**—all under the umbrella of the Ottawa Hospital. In addition, the **Children's Hospital of Eastern Ontario** is a pediatric teaching hospital with emergency care services. For details on these hospitals, see chapter 3, "Getting to Know Ottawa."

For non–life-threatening emergencies that require a physician consultation, go to a **walk-in clinic.** These clinics operate just as the name implies—you walk in and wait your turn to see a physician. Look in the Yellow Pages or ask your hotel to recommend one. Payment procedures vary between clinics, so call ahead and ask about their billing policy for non-residents of Ontario or Canada. Most clinics will accept health cards from other provinces, although Quebec residents may be required to pay cash and obtain reimbursement from their provincial government. Out-of-country patients may be required to pay cash—checks or credit cards may not be accepted. Some doctors will make house calls to your hotel.

For minor health problems, consult a **pharmacist.** These professionals are trained in health consultation and will recommend whether you should see a doctor about your particular condition. Many pharmacies are open evenings and weekends and advertise their hours in the Yellow Pages. **Shopper's Drug Mart** has one **24-hour** location at 1460 Merivale Rd. (at Baseline Rd.) 𝄐 **613/224-7270.**

TRAVEL INSURANCE

Before you decide to purchase travel insurance, check your existing insurance policies to see whether you're already covered when you travel. Some credit cards offer automatic **flight insurance** when you buy an airline ticket with the card, providing insurance coverage for death or dismemberment due to a plane crash.

If you plan to rent a car, check with your credit card issuer to see if they pick up the **collision damage waiver (CDW)** in Canada. The CDW can run as high as C$16 (US$11) per day, adding up to 50% to the cost of car rental. Check your car insurance policy, too—it might cover the CDW. If you are a homeowner or have contents insurance for a rental property, see if your policy covers off-premises **theft and loss** wherever it occurs. Ask your insurance agent what procedures you need to follow to make a claim. If you're traveling on a tour or package deal, or you hold an airline ticket that is nontransferable or nonrefundable, consider protecting your investment by buying **trip cancellation insurance.**

If, after checking your existing insurance policies, you decide you need additional insurance, ask your travel agent for assistance. Some comprehensive travel policies cover all contingencies—health, emergency assistance, theft and loss, and cancellation.

SAFETY

As large cities go, Ottawa is generally safe, but be alert and use common sense, particularly at night. Sadly, in recent years, the number of homeless people and panhandlers has increased, but they are not generally aggressive in nature. The liveliest and rowdiest areas tend to be around the bars in the ByWard Market and Elgin St. neighborhoods, especially late at night.

6 Tips for Travelers with Special Needs

FOR TRAVELERS WITH DISABILITIES

To find out which attractions, accommodations, and restaurants in Ottawa are accessible to people with disabilities, refer to the Ottawa visitor guide, available from the **Capital Infocentre** (𝄐 **800/465-1867**). The guide includes symbols next to each listing to indicate whether the entry and/or washrooms are accessible. **Full accessibility** is defined as independently accessible to people using wheelchairs or with limited upper-body strength. Services should include automatic front doors, ramps, sufficient turning space for a wheelchair in the rooms or bathrooms, and wider doorways (84cm, or 33 in.). **Basic accessibility** indicates that people using wheelchairs may require assistance to use the services within the establishment. The owners and managers of each establishment determine whether their property is accessible. For more information, call **Disabled Persons Community Resources** (𝄐 **613/724-5886**). If you are purchasing tickets to an entertainment event, indicate that you require special seating when you make your reservation.

OC Transpo, which provides **public transit** in Ottawa, is increasing the number of fully accessible buses, with a target set at 25% of the fleet by the end of 2001. Fully accessible buses have low floors and no stairs to climb, providing easier access for seniors, passengers with limited mobility, people using wheelchairs, and parents with small children or strollers. These buses lower to the curb and have an extendable ramp for wheelchair users. You can spot low-floor buses by the blue and white wheelchair symbol on the upper corner on the front of the bus.

For persons with permanent or short-term disabilities who are unable to walk to or board regular transit, **Para Transpo** is available. Both visitors and residents can use this service, but you must register and book a reservation a day in advance. You must also have the application form signed by an appropriate health professional. Call ✆ **613/244-1289** for information and registration, or ✆ **613/244-7272** for reservations.

FOR SENIORS

Many city attractions grant senior discounts, and some hotels offer special rates. Carry a form of photo ID that includes your birth date. Becoming a member of a senior's organization may earn you a discount on travel arrangements. Consider joining the **Canadian Association of Retired Persons (CARP),** Suite 1304, 27 Queen St. E, Toronto, ON M5C 2M6 (✆ **416/363-8748;** www.50plus.com) or the **American Association of Retired Persons (AARP),** 601 E St. NW, Washington, D.C. 20049 (✆ **800/424-3410**).

FOR STUDENTS

Students seem to always be on a shoestring budget, and obtaining an **International Student Identity Card (ISIC)** will provide both high school and post-secondary students with valuable discounts and benefits for transportation, accommodation, food, entertainment, museums, retail stores, and more. Contact the **International Student Travel Confederation** to obtain a card. In Canada, call ✆ **888/838-2887** or visit one of the Travel CUTS offices in major cities across the country. See www.travelcuts.com

for a full listing. In Ottawa, Travel CUTS is located at 222 Laurier Ave. E., 2nd Floor ✆ **613/238-8222.** In the U.S., a network of student travel specialists stretches across the country. Most U.S. offices are listed at www.counciltravel.com or www.statravel.com. The New York office is Council Travel, 205 East 42nd St., New York NY 10017 ✆ **212/822-2700.**

Students who would like to attend lectures, seminars, concerts, and other events at post-secondary institutions will find plenty of choices. Ottawa has several colleges in addition to **Carleton University,** 1125 Colonel By Dr. ✆ **613/520-7400** www.carleton.ca and the **University of Ottawa,** 550 Cumberland ✆ **613/562-5700** www.uottawa.ca.

FOR GAY & LESBIAN TRAVELERS

To find out what's happening in Ottawa that's of interest to gays and lesbians, pick up a copy of *Capital Xtra!,* a monthly newspaper distributed to over 300 locations throughout the Ottawa area, Eastern Ontario, and Montreal. News, arts, culture, entertainment, and local events are covered. To receive a copy in advance of your visit, write to Capital Xtra!, 177 Nepean St., Suite 506, Ottawa, ON K2P 0B4 ✆ **613/237-7133;** www.capitalxtra.on.ca.

FOR FAMILIES

Luckily for visitors with kids in tow, Ottawa has a good selection of suite hotels, which are equipped with kitchenettes or full kitchens and one or two bedrooms; some have two bathrooms. Suite hotels often have children's programs, play centers, or indoor pools. When booking your accommodation, always ask if family packages are available.

When you're deciding which time of year to visit, try to schedule your trip during the school vacation periods, which in Ontario run for 2 weeks during Christmas/New Year, one week in mid-March, and the months of July and August. Special events and workshops are held for families at various museums and other locations during school holidays.

Many of Ottawa's attractions are clustered downtown within walking distance of one another, so it's possible to plan your vacation without the need for a vehicle.

 ## A History Lesson on Canada's Capital

Here's a brief rundown of the history of the nation's capital. See "Appendix: Ottawa in Depth" for a more detailed look at Ottawa's past.

Early Days   Ottawa's history can be traced to the region's development as a trading site by the **Algonquins,** although other Native peoples had used the mighty Ottawa River as a transportation route for thousands of years.

1613   The French explorer **Samuel de Champlain** is the first European to arrive in the region.

1800   Philemon Wright, a United Empire Loyalist, arrives from Massachusetts with settlers and lumberjacks to establish the first non-Native settlement on the north side of the Ottawa River. Wrightsville, now known as Hull, Quebec, grows and prospers along with the expanding lumber trade in the area.

1826–1832   Under the stewardship of British engineer Lieutenant Colonel John By, the Rideau Canal is constructed, creating a 202-km (125-mile) navigable waterway between Lake Ontario and the Ottawa River.

1827   A settlement was established in the vicinity of the Rideau Canal construction site. It was named Bytown in honor of Lieutenant Colonel John By.

1850–1855   The Chaudière Falls on the Ottawa River are harnessed as a source of mechanical power and the region becomes a major lumber producer, with the largest concentration of milling operations in the world. Stores, banks, newspapers, and schools serve Bytown's population, which has risen to 10,000. The city is renamed Ottawa, to commemorate the 200th anniversary of the first descent of the Outaouak Native people down the river.

1857   Queen Victoria chooses Ottawa as the capital of the British Provinces of Upper and Lower Canada, despite protests from Kingston and Toronto.

1866   The **Parliament Buildings,** modeled on the British Houses of Parliament, are completed.

1867   With **Confederation,** Ottawa becomes the capital of the new Dominion of Canada.

1916   A devastating fire sweeps the Parliament Buildings—only the Parliamentary Library is saved. The Parliament Buildings must be almost completely rebuilt.

Post–World War II　French planner **Jacques Gréber** is commissioned by Prime Minister William Lyon Mackenzie King to lay out a new plan for the growing city. Gréber's design is largely responsible for the protected parkland surrounding much of the city.

2001　A new city of Ottawa is born, as 12 local municipal governments are amalgamated to create one new municipality of Ottawa. The population of the new city is 800,000.

7 Getting There

BY PLANE

When arranging flights, always contact all airlines that service your planned route and ask for the lowest fare available. If your arrival and departure dates can be flexible, you'll have a better chance of landing a deal.

The weekend Travel section of major city newspapers often carries advertisements for ticket brokers and consolidators. These companies buy airline tickets in bulk and sell them at a discount. By purchasing your tickets through these companies, you may be able to fly for less than the standard advance (APEX) fare. You may not be able to get the lowest price quoted in the ad, but you're likely to pay less than the price quoted by the major airlines. Be aware that tickets purchased in this way are often non-refundable. If you change your itinerary after purchase, you will probably be charged a stiff penalty.

Since the tragedy of September 11, 2001, airport security has been enhanced. New procedures may cause increased processing times for passengers, both at the check-in counters and the security checkpoints. Ask your airline for recommended check-in times.

If you're traveling with children, ask your air carrier in advance about child safety restraints, transport of strollers, times of meal service, availability of children's meals, and bulkhead seating (which has extra room to stretch out). Mention any food allergies or other medical concerns.

 Travel-planning Websites

If you're a Net surfer, it's possible to get some great cyber deals on airfare, hotels, and car rentals. Here's a selection of websites to get you started. Keep in mind that websites often evolve, change, or move—this list is a press-time snapshot only.

www.frommers.com　Arthur Frommer's Budget Travel Online is a good place to start. You'll find indispensable travel tips, reviews, monthly vacation giveaways, and online booking services. One of the most popular features of this site is the regular "Ask the Expert" bulletin board, where you can post questions and have them answered online by Frommer's authors. You can also sign up for an electronic newsletter to receive the latest travel bargains and insider travel secrets in your e-mailbox every day. The Destinations Archive lists more than 200 domestic and international destinations, with information on great places to stay, travel tips, and things to do while you're there.

www.travelocity.com; www.previewtravel.com; www.frommers.travel ocity.com **Travelocity** is Frommer's online travel-planning and booking partner. Travelocity uses the SABRE system to offer reservations and tickets for more than 400 airlines, plus reservations and booking services for more than 45,000 hotels and 50 car-rental companies. The site includes a Destination Guide with updated information on more than 250 destinations throughout the world—supplied by Frommer's.

expedia.com **Expedia** is Travelocity's major competitor. It offers several ways to obtain the best possible fares. Features include everyday deals, today's deals, maps, currency converter, driving directions, and lots more. Expedia focuses on the major airlines and hotel chains, so don't expect to find many lower-cost airlines or unique B&B properties here.

www.trip.com **TRIP.com** is a site with innovative features and a highly personalized approach, which appeals to both leisure and business travelers. Manage your travel needs using an Internet-ready mobile device with trip.com's wireless service. Sign up for a weekly newsletter and get the scoop on travel news and deals. You can even check the status of an airborne commerical flight within North America with flightTRACKER.

travel.yahoo.com **Yahoo!** is a popular Internet information portal, and its travel site is a comprehensive mix of online booking, daily travel news, and destination information. The Best Fares area can be customized to suit your needs.

WITHIN CANADA Air Canada, which also operates under regional names such as Air Ontario, offers direct flights from the following Canadian cities: Calgary, Fredericton, Halifax, London, Montreal (Dorval), Quebec City, Toronto (Pearson and City Centre), Vancouver, and Winnipeg. The central reservation number for all Air Canada–operated airlines is © **888/247-2262;** www.aircanada.ca. Bearskin Airlines (© **800/465-5039;** www.bearskinairlines.com) serves Buttonville Airport northeast of Toronto and several cities in Northern Ontario, including North Bay, Sudbury, Thunder Bay, Timmins, and Sault Ste. Marie. Montreal and Northern Canada, including Cambridge Bay, Iqaluit, Kuujjuaq, Nanisivik, Resolute, and Yellowknife, are served by First Air (© **800/267-1247;** www. firstair.ca). Trillium Air (© **877-263-0333;** www.trilliumair.com),

primarily serving the high-tech business sector, flies between Silicon Valley North (aka Ottawa) and Kitchener–Waterloo. For a direct flight from Hamilton, Regina, Saskatoon, or Calgary, contact WestJet (© **877/956-6982** or 800/538-5696; www. westjet.com).

FROM THE U.S. Direct flights from Boston, Chicago, New York (LaGuardia and Newark), Washington (Dulles and Reagan National), San Jose, and Raleigh-Durham are operated by Air Canada (© **888/247-2262;** www.aircanada.ca). American Airlines (© **800/433-7300;** www.amr corp.com) flies direct to Ottawa from Chicago and St. Louis. American Eagle (© **800/345-3400;** www. delta-air.com) operates direct flights from Boston. From Newark, Continental Express (© **800/525-0280;** www.flycontinental.com) flies direct to Ottawa. Travelers in the Detroit area can fly with Northwest Airlink (Mesaba Airlines) (② **800/225-2525;** www.nwa.com). US Airways (US Airways Express) (② **800/4284322;** www.usairways.com) operates direct flights from Philadelphia and Pittsburgh. ASA Delta Connections serves Atlanta with direct flights (② **800/ 221-1212**).

FROM ABROAD   Air Canada flies direct to Ottawa from London (Heathrow). From the rest of the world, there's frequent service (direct or indirect) to Toronto. A 1-hour connector flight from Toronto will land you in Ottawa.

ARRIVING IN OTTAWA

From the Ottawa International Airport, in the south end, you have several options for traveling to the city. The Ottawa Airport Shuttle (② **613/ 260-2359**) runs between the airport and several downtown locations. The cost is C$11 (US$7) per adult one-way, and C$18 (US$11) round-trip. The shuttle operates daily with departures every 30 minutes, starting at 5am. The following hotels have scheduled stops: Novotel, Les Suites Hotel, the Westin, the Fairmont Château Laurier, the Lord Elgin, the Sheraton, the Delta Ottawa, the Crowne Plaza, and Minto Place. The shuttle will drop off and pick up at the following hotels on request: Quality Hotel, Capital Hill Hotel, Cartier Place & Towers, the Aristocrat, the Business Inn, Embassy Hotel and Suites, Marriott Residence Inn, the Ramada Hotel & Suites, Howard Johnson Hotel, Travelodge Hotel, Albert at Bay Suite Hotel, Best Western Victoria Park Suites, and Ramada Inn 417.

If you wish to take public transit, OC Transpo provides high-frequency rapid service along the scenic Transitway, a roadway built specifically for buses. Route 97 will whisk you downtown in less than 25 minutes; adult fare is C$2.25 (US$1.40). You can also hop in a taxi; the fare will be around C$21 (US$13). Several major car rental companies have offices at the airport. A 20-minute drive north along the Airport Parkway will take you to the heart of downtown.

BY TRAIN

VIA Rail trains to Ottawa operate as part of the Windsor–Quebec City corridor. The **Ottawa VIA Rail Station** (② **613/244-8289**) is located at 200 Tremblay Rd., near the Riverside Drive exit from Highway 417, just east of downtown. VIA Rail often has special fares, and booking in advance may also get you a substantial discount. For rail information, contact **VIA Rail Canada** at ② **888/ VIA-RAIL** (888/842-7245); www. viarail.ca. If you're traveling from the United States, call **Amtrak** at ② **800/ USA-RAIL** (800/872-7245) or visit their website www.amtrak.com. Several major car rental companies have offices near the rail station and offer free pick-up and drop-off service at the station for their customers.

BY BUS

The **Ottawa Bus Station** (② **613/ 238-5900**) is located at 265 Catherine St., near the Kent Street exit from Highway 417, on the edge of the downtown core. **Greyhound Canada** (② **800/661-TRIP**, or 800/661-8747) provides coast-to-coast bus service with connections to Ottawa. Book online or obtain schedule and fare information at www.greyhound.ca. **Voyageur** (② **613/238-5900**; www. voyageur.com) links Eastern Ontario and Western Quebec, servicing routes between Kingston, Ottawa, and Montreal. **Greyhound USA** (② **800/231- 2222;** www.greyhound.com) provides bus service between the United States and Canada.

Traveling by bus may be faster and cheaper than the train, and if you want to stop to visit towns along the way, its routes may offer more flexibility. But there's also less space to stretch out, toilet facilities are meager, and meals are taken at roadside rest stops, so consider carefully, particularly if you're planning to bring children with you.

Investigate offers such as unlimited-travel passes and discount fares. It's tough to quote typical fares because bus companies, like airlines, are adopting yield-management strategies, resulting in frequent price changes depending on demand.

BY CAR

With the completion in 2001 of Highway 416 as the link between Highway 401 and Ottawa, the approach from south and west of Canada's capital is a smooth and easy drive. *Warning:* Be alert to the possibility of deer suddenly appearing in the roadway in rural forested areas, particularly on Highway 416 and most often at night. Unless you're headed for the west end of the city, take exit 57 from Highway 416—look for the sign that reads BANKFIELD ROAD (COUNTY ROAD 8)/AIRPORT/ SCENIC ROUTE. Follow County Road 8 east to Highway 73 north through the countryside until you reach Hunt Club Road on the southern edge of the city. From here, you can take one of several routes downtown—Prince of Wales Drive and Riverside Drive are the most pleasant. The Airport Parkway/Bronson Avenue is the most direct, and Bank Street will take you past the most shops. From Montreal and Eastern Canada, travel west along Highway 417 and enter the city via Montreal Road.

If you're arriving from south of the border, there are several convenient crossing points. From Vermont, enter Canada via Interstate 89 or 91, travel toward Montreal, and pick up the westerly route (Hwy. 417). In New York State, Interstate 81 crosses at Hill Island to Highway 401; you can also take Route 37 and enter at Ogdensburg–Johnstown or Rooseveltown–Cornwall. On Interstate 87 in New York State, cross into Quebec, travel toward Montreal, and keep to the west of the city, taking Highway 417. If you're driving from Michigan, you'll enter Ontario at Detroit–Windsor (via I–75 and the Ambassador Bridge) or Port Huron–Sarnia (via I–94 and the Bluewater Bridge).

Here are approximate driving distances in miles to Ottawa: from Boston, 465; Buffalo, 335; Chicago, 800; Detroit, 525; New York, 465; Washington, D.C., 580.

Be sure to carry your driver's license and car registration if you plan to drive your own vehicle into Canada. You should carry proof of automobile liability insurance as well.

If you are a member of the American Automobile Association (AAA), the **Canadian Automobile Association (CAA)** North and East Ontario branch provides emergency roadside assistance (*(C)* **800/222-4357**). The member services call center is open Monday to Friday from 9am to 5pm, Saturday from 10am to 1pm; *(C)* **800/267-8713.**

Survival Tips for Traveling with Kids

- Don't try to see and do as much as you would if you were traveling without your children.
- Make a list of everything you want to do on vacation, then cut it in half.
- Choose accommodations close to a park or playground.
- Alternate sightseeing or travel days with unstructured play days.
- Bring medication, paper towels, and plastic bags in case of travel sickness.
- Plan meal times in advance and *always* carry snacks to appease hungry tummies.
- If you're traveling to a different time zone, schedule meals and bedtime for the new time a few days before leaving—to help children adjust more quickly.
- Bring a few favorite bedtime stories.
- Bring toys, but avoid ones with lots of small parts that can get scattered or lost.
- Bring an umbrella stroller—it's lightweight, it folds easily, and it can be used as a feeding chair or napping place when necessary.
- Let kids pack their own entertainment backpacks.
- Buy each child a portable cassette player with earphones. You can get stories on tape as well as children's music. The trip will be *so* quiet!
- If you have a long trip, splurge at the dollar store on a few simple toys and treats. Pack them in a bag, and each time you have a rest stop, let the kids take a "lucky dip."
- Give older children their own budget to spend on souvenirs.
- Call your hotel to find out what items they have on hand for infants and small children. You may be able to leave at least half the kitchen sink at home.
- Finally, if you can swing it, try to schedule some vacation time away from your children.

3

Getting to Know Ottawa

Ottawa is not what it used to be. Having successfully shaken off its staid image as the solemn seat of federal government (an old joke refers to the city rolling up its streets and turning into a ghost town outside of office hours), the city has taken on a more colorful and vibrant hue in recent years.

Ottawa's personality is both refreshing and eclectic. The nation's top historical landmark, Parliament Hill, stands in Canada's most wired city, where 8 out of 10 households have a computer. The pomp and ceremony of the parade of the Ceremonial Guard contrasts with the relaxed attitude of the young and affluent high-tech community. And through it all run ribbons of green and blue—the region's green space, parks, and waterways.

At the level of local government, Ottawa has recently undergone a major transformation. On January 1, 2001, a new capital city was created for Canada as 12 local municipal governments were amalgamated to create one new municipality of Ottawa. The region was more than ready for municipal reform. Social and economic development had been hindered by the existence of 12 municipalities, each representing local interests and each with its own bureaucratic administration. In fact, three decades of political indecision preceded the launch of the new city.

The new Ottawa, now the fourth-largest city in Canada, spans 2,760 km² (1711 mile²) and includes more than 150 communities. The population at the time of amalgamation was 800,000, and the number of residents is expected to top one million by 2003.

With its proximity to Quebec and its high concentration of federal government employees, Ottawa is a bilingual city, offering a stimulating blend of English and French culture. As you stroll around the city, you are just as likely to hear French spoken as English. But don't worry if you don't speak French. The people you will meet as a visitor—hotel staff, restaurant servers, museum and attractions employees—are usually fluent in both official languages.

Added to the blend of English- and French-speaking citizens is an increasing ethnic population. One in five Ottawa residents is an immigrant, contributing to the city's rich ethnic diversity of German, Lebanese, Italian, Polish, Dutch, Portuguese, Asian, and Greek populations, among others.

Ottawa is a wonderful city to explore. Its people are friendly, the streets and parks are clean, and there's plenty to keep visitors entertained all year around. Experience one of the lively festivals, visit a couple of national museums, and leave plenty of time to play and relax along the waterways and amid the greenspaces. Enjoy!

1 Orientation

VISITOR INFORMATION

Across the street from the Parliament Buildings and within easy walking distance of many major tourist attractions is the **Capital Infocentre**, at 90 Wellington Street. The building has a windowed gallery facing Parliament Hill, offering a dramatic photo opportunity. The Terry Fox Memorial is situated in the square out front.

The Capital Infocentre is packed with brochures and dynamic exhibits. As you enter the building, you'll see a great orientation tool—a huge three-dimensional map of the central region. For a dazzling overview of Canada's capital and what's on offer for visitors, attend a presentation at the multimedia theater. Also check out the souvenir shop, which offers maps, guide books, clothing, and a few items for children.

To customize your itinerary in the capital, visit one of the "passport kiosks" in the Infocentre. Using the touch-sensitive screens, you can ask the computer for information on sites and attractions that suit your tastes and interests. The system then prints out a personalized passport with your chosen itinerary. If you prefer more personal interaction, orientation counselors are available to answer questions on Ottawa and the surrounding region and to help you plan your visit. For phone inquiries, contact the **Capital Call Centre** at ✆ **800/465-1867** or 613/239-5000, open Monday to Friday 8:30am to 8pm and weekends 8:30am to 5pm from mid-May to Labour Day. The rest of the year it's open Monday to Friday 8:30am to 5pm and Saturday to Sunday 9am to 5pm. The call center is closed Christmas Day, Boxing Day, and New Year's Day. If you're online, visit the Capital Infocentre website at **www.canadascapital.gc.ca**. Other websites with visitor information include **www.canada.com, www.ottawakiosk.com,** and **www.festivalseeker.com.**

The **Ottawa Tourism and Convention Authority (OTCA)** publishes an annual visitor guide, with maps and descriptions of cultural sites, things to see and do, accommodations, places to dine and shop, and services. The guide is available at the Capital Infocentre and at other locations around the city. The OTCA can be reached via the toll-free number for the Capital Call Centre listed above, or at ✆ **613/237-5150.**

For listings of upcoming events, pick up a copy of *Where,* a free monthly guide to entertainment, shopping, and dining, available at hotels and stores throughout the city. The daily newspapers are the *Ottawa Citizen,* the *Ottawa Sun,* and *Le Droit,* Ottawa's French-language newspaper. The *Ottawa Citizen* includes a comprehensive Arts section on Fridays, with film listings and reviews, and a special Going Out section on Saturdays, with listings of upcoming live entertainment events. *Capital Parent,* a free monthly newspaper, and *Ottawa Families,* a free bimonthly newspaper, contain articles of interest to parents and often advertise family-friendly events. For news and information about regional arts events and activities, drop in to **Arts Court,** 2 Daly Ave. (✆ **613/564-7240**), or call the **Council for the Arts in Ottawa (CAO)** (✆ **613/569-1387**). The area is well served by weekly Arts and Entertainment newspapers. *Xpress* serves the English-speaking community and *Voir* highlights francophone events and news. Ottawa's gay and lesbian community has several publications including *Capital Xtra!,* a monthly newspaper.

Tips **Smoke-Free City**

All public places and workplaces, including restaurants, bars, bingo halls, billiard halls, and all places of employment, were declared smoke-free as of August 1, 2001. The City of Ottawa Smoke-Free By-laws are designed to protect citizens of Ottawa from the dangers of secondhand smoke.

CITY LAYOUT

The Ottawa River—Canada's second longest, at over 1,100km (700 miles)— sweeps around the northern edge of the city. Most of the major attractions are clustered in the downtown area on the south bank of the Ottawa River. The **Rideau Canal** takes center stage, curving through the city and dividing the downtown area in two—**west of the canal** (often called Centretown) and **east of the canal** (often called Lower Town). In the downtown area west of the canal you'll find **Parliament Hill,** the **Supreme Court,** and the **Canadian Museum of Nature** (a few blocks south). Situated on the east side of the Ottawa Locks where the Rideau Canal meets the Ottawa River is the majestic **Château Laurier,** Ottawa's most elegant hotel. Continuing east, the **ByWard Market** district hosts dozens of restaurants, boutiques, bars, and clubs. Along Sussex Drive (which follows the south bank of the Ottawa River), you'll find the **National Gallery,** the **Canadian War Museum,** the **Royal Canadian Mint,** and the prime minister's residence. Crossing the **Rideau River,** you can pass by the gates of many embassies and their official residences. **Rideau Hall, Rockcliffe Park,** the **Canada Aviation Museum,** and the **RCMP Musical Ride Centre, Rockcliffe Stables** are all east of the Rideau River. The area south of the Queensway (Hwy 417), west to Bronson Avenue and east to the canal, is known as the **Glebe** and offers wonderful shopping and trendy cafes along Bank Street. North across the river, in Quebec, lie the communities of **Hull, Gatineau,** and **Aylmer,** connected to the east end of Ottawa by the Macdonald-Cartier and Alexandra bridges and to the west by the Portage and Chaudière bridges. At the north end of the Alexandra Bridge stands the architecturally stunning **Museum of Civilization.** The **Casino de Hull,** with its theater, convention center, and luxury hotel, is situated on Lake Leamy in Hull. North and west of Hull stretches breathtaking **Gatineau Park,** 361 km² (141 mile²) of wilderness managed by the National Capital Commission.

Finding your way around town can be a challenge, since some streets halt abruptly and then reappear a few blocks farther on, one-way streets are common in the downtown core, and some streets change names several times. Ottawa's main east–west street, for example, starts as Scott Street, changes to Wellington Street as it passes through downtown in front of the Parliament Buildings, switches to Rideau Street in downtown east, and finally becomes Montreal Road on the eastern fringes of town. Take my advice: Carry a map.

Tips **The Main Street**

The main streets running east–west through downtown are **Wellington, Laurier,** and **Somerset;** the **Rideau Canal** separates east from west (Lower Town and Centretown); and the main north–south streets are **Bronson, Bank,** and **Elgin.**

Ottawa-Hull

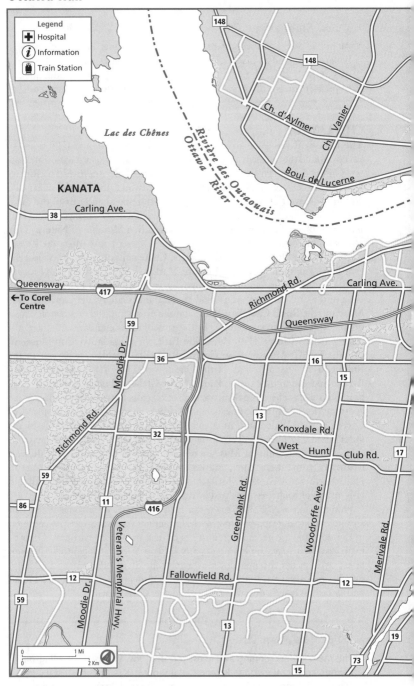

Legend
- Hospital
- Information
- Train Station

148

148

Ch. d'Aylmer

Ch. Vanier

Boul. de Lucerne

Lac des Chênes

Rivière des Outaouais

Ottawa River

KANATA

38

Carling Ave.

Queensway

417

←To Corel Centre

Richmond Rd.

Carling Ave.

Queensway

59

Moodie Dr.

36

16

15

Richmond Rd.

13

32

Knoxdale Rd.

West Hunt

Club Rd.

17

59

Greenbank Rd.

Woodroffe Ave.

Merivale Rd.

86

11

416

12

Veteran's Memorial Hwy.

Fallowfield Rd.

12

59

Moodie Dr.

13

19

0   1 Mi
0   2 Km

15

73

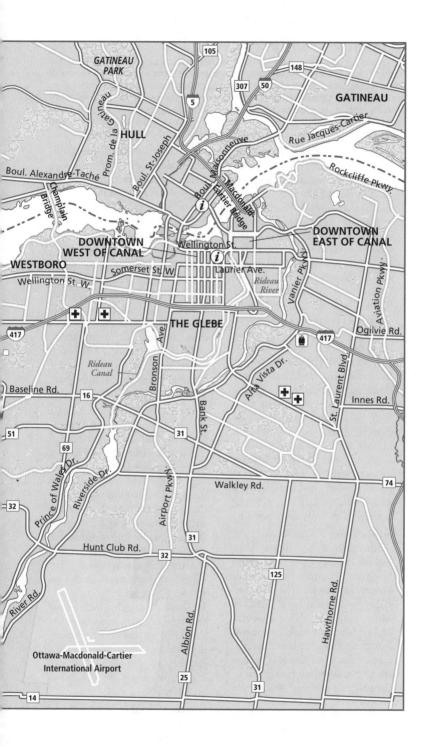

NEIGHBORHOODS IN BRIEF

The architecture and layout of the city of Ottawa has been said to reflect Canada's bilingual heritage. Many residents speak or understand both French and English, and a number of ethnic groups have also brought their cultures to the city. Nowhere is this diversity more apparent than in Ottawa's distinct neighborhoods. The various business and residential areas each has its own mix of shops, cuisine, architecture, and sights and sounds, representing different cultures and traditions from around the globe. Strolling through the various neighborhoods will give you an appreciation of the city's heart and soul—its people.

ByWard Market and Downtown, East of the Canal   Situated northeast of the Parliament Buildings, on the east side of the Rideau Canal and bordered by the Rideau River to the east, this historic neighborhood is the oldest section of Ottawa. Originally, **downtown, east of the canal** (also known as **Lowertown**) was an uninhabitable cedar swamp. During the construction of the Rideau Canal, the land was drained and a mix of settlers soon moved in, including canal workers, shantymen, rivermen, and their families. The area was populated by poor Irish immigrants and French Canadians, and a reputation for general rowdiness and unlawfulness soon took hold. The building of the farmers' market in the mid-19th century helped to boost the local economy. The **ByWard Market** district, with its eclectic mix of boutiques, cafes, and bars, is now a prosperous, attractive city neighborhood with a vibrant personality.

Sussex Drive   Winding along the south shore of the Ottawa River, historic Sussex Drive is a grand boulevard featuring many well-known landmarks. The National Gallery of Canada, Royal Canadian Mint, Canadian War Museum, Notre Dame Basilica, U.S. embassy, French embassy, residence of the prime minister of Canada (24 Sussex Dr.), and Rideau Hall (home of the governor general) are all found on this route. Also on Sussex Drive are the scenic Rideau Falls and the imposing Lester B. Pearson Building, home of the Federal Department of Foreign Affairs. Earnscliffe, the residence of the British high commissioner, was originally the home of Canada's first prime minister, Sir John A. Macdonald. It sits high on a cliff overlooking the Ottawa River.

Downtown, West of the Canal   Ottawa's downtown business district (also referred to as Centretown) is a maze of office towers in an area stretching several blocks to the south of Parliament Hill. There are many excellent hotels, restaurants, and shops in the area. The Sparks Street Mall, Canada's first pedestrian shopping street, is located here.

Somerset Village   This downtown neighborhood, centered on a stretch of Somerset Street between Bank and O'Connor streets, is characterized by a cluster of historic redbrick dwellings. It was revitalized in the mid-1980s after the owners of commercial buildings in the area commissioned a heritage-style streetscape design. Five-globe streetlamps, redbrick sidewalks, trees and shrubs, and benches now line the 19th-century streets. The village encompasses 15 buildings, 13 of which were built around 1900 or earlier, with a lively mix of shops, offices, bars, restaurants, and residential structures. In addition, the Embassy of the Ukraine, the Embassy of Zimbabwe, and the High Commission for Bangladesh are located here.

Somerset Heights   Step into the Far East as you travel further west along Somerset Street to the neighborhood stretching from Bay to Rochester streets. Intriguing markets sell a variety of Asian produce, crafts, traditional Chinese medicinal ingredients, hand-painted silk garments, and many more fascinating treasures. Thai, Vietnamese, and Chinese restaurants appear on every corner, tempting visitors with their distinctive cuisine.

Little Italy   The heart of Ottawa's Italian immigrant population is Preston Street, also fondly known as Corso Italia (both names appear on the official street signs). The area serves as the commercial and cultural center of Little Italy. An abundance of cafes, trattorie, and pizzerias celebrate the essence of Italy—its wonderful cuisine. Irish, French, and Asian Canadians also call the neighborhood home. Every June, the street comes alive with the festivities of Italian Week, culminating in a street party stretching over three evenings.

Westboro Village   Originally a small village on the outskirts of the city, Westboro has retained its friendly small-town atmosphere. This traditional city neighborhood west of downtown has enjoyed a revitalization, which began in the late 1990s. The addition of Richmond Road Mountain Equipment Co-op spurred retail growth in the west end of Westboro's commercial ribbon, and there is hope that the area will eventually link with Wellington Street West to form a shopping district much like the ByWard Market and the Glebe.

The Glebe   Just south of downtown, between the Queensway and Lansdowne Park, lies Ottawa's first suburb. In the 1870s, residential development began to encroach on farmland south of the city. The construction of exhibition grounds at Lansdowne Park and of a streetcar link between the Glebe and the city fueled the growth of this neighborhood. The middle classes settled here in large numbers. Today, the Glebe is an upscale middle-class neighborhood served by a stretch of trendy, high-end stores, services, and eateries on Bank Street. It's well worth spending a morning or afternoon strolling up one side of the street and down the other. If you begin at the north end, take a break near the canal before making your return journey. Brown's Inlet and Park are tucked a block or two west of Bank Street, north of Queen Elizabeth Drive. If you start at the canal end, rest in Central Park, which straddles Bank Street in the vicinity of Powell and Clemow avenues. For winter strolling, take refuge in the atrium at Fifth Avenue Court, about midway down this section of Bank Street.

2 Getting Around

BY PUBLIC TRANSPORTATION

CITY BUSES   **Public Transit** in Ottawa is provided by **OC Transpo.** This is an economical and efficient way to get around since buses can bypass rush-hour traffic through Transitway, a rapid-transit system of roadways exclusively for buses. Routes 95 and 97 are the two main Transitway routes, operating 22 hours a day. All OC Transpo bus routes travel along parts of the Transitway or connect at one of the stations. OC Transpo stations, many of which are located next to major shopping or employment centers, offer convenient transfer points with heated waiting areas, information displays, and phones. Many have bike racks and vendor kiosks. For transit information call *©* **613/741-4390;**

www.octranspo.com. There are five sales and information centers in the city—one in the Rideau Centre shopping mall, one in Place de Ville (on Kent Street between Albert and Queen streets), and three more at various transit stations.

The regular exact-cash fare is C$2.25 (US$1.40) adult single or C$1.25 (US80¢) child. It's cheaper to use tickets, at C85¢ (US55¢) each, since the adult fare is two tickets and the child fare is one ticket. The exception is during weekday rush hours, when some express routes charge a three-ticket fare. Day passes are a good buy at C$5 (US$3) for unlimited rides. You can buy bus passes and tickets at more than 300 vendor locations across the city.

The number of buses that are fully accessible to **people with disabilities** is on the rise, with a target set at 25% of the fleet by the end of 2001. Sixteen bus routes currently support low-floor buses. Fully accessible buses, marked by a blue and white wheelchair symbol on the front of the bus, have low floors to provide access for seniors, people with limited mobility, people using wheelchairs, and parents with small children or strollers. The buses lower to the curb so there are no stairs to climb, and drivers can extend a ramp to accommodate wheelchairs. In addition, these buses are equipped with air-conditioning, cloth seats, yellow grab rails and pull cords, and easy-to-reach stop-request buttons.

For persons with permanent or short-term disabilities who are unable to walk to or board regular transit, **Para Transpo** is available. Both visitors and residents can use this service, but you must have the application form signed by an appropriate health professional, and register and reserve a day in advance. Call ℭ **613/244-1289** for information and registration, or ℭ **613/244-7272** for reservations (reservations office open daily 9am to 5pm).

Public transit throughout **Hull, Gatineau,** and the **Outaouais** region on the Quebec side of the Ottawa River is provided by **Société de transport de l'Outaouais (STO)** (ℭ **819/770-3242** for information; open Monday to Friday 8:30am to 12noon and 1 to 4:30pm; www.sto.ca).

LIGHT RAIL TRAIN (O-Train)   The **Light Rail** pilot project was launched in October 2001. Designed to go where the Transitway doesn't, the O-Train uses an 8-km (5-mile) stretch of existing Canadian Pacific rail line running between Greenboro Transitway Station in the south end and Bayview Station in the north end of the city. **Greenboro Station** has parking available for more than 600 vehicles and connects to Ottawa International Airport via bus route 97. **Confederation Station** is close to Vincent Massey Park. **Carleton Station** serves students and staff of Carleton University. **Carling Station** is conveniently close to Dow's Lake and Little Italy. **Bayview Station** is minutes from downtown, with a high-frequency bus service. Each state-of-the-art train, built by the Canadian company Bombardier, consists of three air-conditioned cars, accommodating 135 seated and 150 standing passengers. The front and rear diesel-powered units allow the train to travel in either direction on the track without having to turn around. A low-floor design ensures easy access for passengers and a quiet, comfortable ride.

Operating hours are Monday to Friday 6:30am to 11:30pm, Saturday 7am to 11:30pm, and Sunday and holidays 7:30am to 11pm. The fare is C$2 (US$1.25). You may transfer to an OC Transpo bus at no extra charge, except for rush-hour routes, which require a top-up of a single bus ticket or C$1.25 (US80¢).

The current rail line is the first step toward citywide light rail transit. Several extensions are being considered, including links to Ottawa's downtown core, Hull, and Ottawa International Airport.

BY TAXI

You can hail a taxi on the street, but you'll find one more readily at taxi stands in front of most hotels, many government buildings, and some museums. You can also summon a taxi by phone. In the Ottawa area, 24-hour cab companies include **Blue Line** (*C* **613/238-1111**), with a fleet of more than 600 cabs, and **Capital Taxi** (*C* **613/744-3333**). **West-Way Taxi** (*C* **613/727-0101**) has drivers who have been trained to transport people with disabilities.

BY TOUR BUS

There are so many interesting buildings, monuments, attractions, and views in Ottawa that hopping on a tour bus is a great idea, especially if it's your first visit to Canada's capital. Tours are fully narrated so you don't miss anything while you're cruising around town. On-and-off privileges allow you to take a break to stretch your legs, or, if you see somewhere you'd like to visit, you can just hop off the bus and join it again later. Tickets are valid for three days. The best bet is to take the full tour on the first day without leaving the bus, making a note of the places you'd like to stop and explore. On the second day, execute your grand plan.

Gray Line Sightseeing Tours   Choose an open-top double-decker bus or a vintage trolley bus for a 90-minute tour. Step on or off the bus any time you wish at the following stops: Parliament Hill, Museum of Civilization, Notre Dame Basilica, Rideau Hall, Musical Ride Centre, RCMP Rockcliffe Stables, Canada Aviation Museum, National War Museum, Royal Canadian Mint, National Gallery, ByWard Market, Rideau Canal, Dow's Lake, the Central Experimental Farm, and the Canadian Museum of Nature. If you call ahead, the bus will pick you up at your downtown hotel. Tours operate from May to October. Tickets are valid for three days and prices are reasonable—a family of four can get a three-day, on–off privilege ticket for C$52 (US$32); adult single C$17 (US$11). For departure times and other information, call Gray Line at *C* **800/297-6422** or *C* **613/565-5463;** www.grayline.ca.

Capital Double Decker & Trolley Tours   This locally owned and operated tour company also offers open-top double-decker buses and historic trolley bus tours between April and October. Tours are fully narrated and take 2 hours to complete. Hotel pick-up and return are free, and you can hop on and off all day. Cost for a family of four is C$56 (US$35) and an adult single ticket is C$20 (US$12). For more information, call *C* **800/823-6147** or *C* **613/749-3666.**

BY CAR

So many of Ottawa's attractions are downtown and within walking distance of each other that you can have a wonderful vacation without ever getting behind the wheel of a car. If you traveled to Ottawa by car, leave it in the hotel parking garage unless you're planning to venture out on a day trip. If you reached the city by plane, train, or bus, you could rent a car for a day or two to explore Ottawa's surrounding regions, and spend the rest of the time traveling by city bus, tour bus, and bicycle or on foot.

If you do decide to drive, be prepared for one-way streets that don't follow any predictable pattern. Keep an eye out, as well, for traffic blocks, designed to prevent vehicles from using residential streets as thoroughfares. Some streets change name several times along their length and others stop abruptly, only to continue a few blocks over. Needless to say, a map is essential if you're driving in city areas. You'll have the added convenience of being able to locate major tourist attractions, parking lots, and other useful destinations.

The View from Here

- For views of **Parliament Hill** and the **Ottawa River,** visit Major's Hill Park or Nepean Point.
- To take in the **Ottawa skyline facing south,** as well as **Parliament Hill,** look across from Victoria Island or the Canadian Museum of Civilization.
- For a photo of the stunning architecture of the **Museum of Civilization,** look across the Ottawa River from Parliament Hill.
- To capture **tulips** on film, visit the numerous public parks and gardens throughout the city during the month of May. Visit the Dutch tulip gardens at the northern tip of Dow's Lake in Commissioner's Park, where 300,000 bulbs create a breathtaking display of color.
- To see beautiful **waterfalls,** visit Rideau Falls and Hog's Back Falls.
- View the **Ottawa skyline facing north** from the Arboretum and the Central Experimental Farm.
- Enjoy a vista of the **Ottawa Valley** from Champlain Lookout in Gatineau Park.
- To see the wide sweep of the **Ottawa River** and the **Quebec shoreline,** pay a visit to Rockcliffe Lookout.

RENTAL CARS   If you decide to rent a car during the high season, try to make arrangements in advance to ensure the vehicle you want will be available. If you are traveling from outside Canada, you may obtain a reasonable discount by booking before you leave home. The rental fee depends on the type of car, but the starting point is around C$45 (US$30) a day, plus taxes. This price does not include insurance, but some credit cards offer automatic coverage if you charge the full amount of the car rental to the card (check with your credit card issuer before you travel). Be sure to read the fine print of the agreement and to do a complete visual check for damage before accepting the vehicle. Some companies add conditions that will boost your bill if you don't fulfill certain obligations, such as filling the gas tank before returning the car. Major rental companies with offices at Ottawa International Airport and downtown locations include **Thrifty** (𝒞 800/847-4389), **Avis** (𝒞 800/879-2847), **Budget** (𝒞 800/268-8900), **Hertz** (𝒞 800/263-0600), and **National** (𝒞 800/227-7368).

Note: If you're under age 25, check with the rental company—some will rent on a cash-only basis, some will rent only if you have a credit card, and others will not rent to you at all.

PARKING   When parking downtown, you have a choice of meters or lots. Parking meters are color-coded: Meters with a 1-hour time limit have gray domes, those with a 2-hour limit have green domes, and those for tour-bus parking only have yellow domes. Meters accept quarters, loonies, and toonies. Always read the signs posted near parking meters to find out if there are any parking restrictions. One of the most common restrictions is a ban on parking weekdays between 3:30 and 5:30pm on certain streets, to improve traffic flow during the evening rush hour. City-owned and private lots charge up to C$10 (US$7) for all-day parking. Your best bet is to use a municipal parking lot, marked with a large green "P" in a circle. On weekends, parking is free at city lots and meters in the area west of the canal, east of Bronson Avenue, and north of the Queensway. If you must leave your vehicle on a city street overnight, ask hotel staff or your B&B host whether there are parking restrictions.

Tips Overnight Winter Parking Ban

From November 15 to April 1 there is an overnight parking ban from 1am to 7am on city streets. In practice, this only takes effect if an accumulation of 7cm (3 in.) of snow or more is forecast. Call the City of Ottawa Snowline at © 613/580-2460. Motorists should be aware that snow removal crews may be working to remove snow from recent storms at any time; signs informing the public are placed in snow banks several hours before beginning work.

DRIVING RULES   In Ontario, a right turn on a red light is permitted after coming to a complete stop unless posted otherwise, provided you yield to oncoming traffic and pedestrians. Be aware that once you cross the Ottawa River, you enter the province of Quebec, where you *cannot* turn right on a red light. There have been experiments in some communities to introduce right turns on reds, but it strikes fear in the hearts of most Quebec pedestrians, so the jury is still out on whether the law will change. Better to err on the side of caution. Wearing your seat belt is compulsory. Fines for riding without a seat belt are substantial. Speed limits are posted and must be obeyed at all times. Always stop when pedestrians are using the crosswalks, but also be careful of pedestrians crossing against the lights—Ottawans seem to have a mild disregard for pedestrian crossing signals in the downtown core. Beware, as well, of drivers running red lights. Always check that the intersection is clear before advancing when the light turns green, especially if your vehicle is going to be the first one through the intersection. In 2001, Ottawa began an intersection safety program by equipping eight city intersections with red-light cameras, with the aim of reducing the number of drivers who run red lights.

Tips Watch for Cyclists!

With the excellent network of bike pathways in the city, Ottawa has a large population of cyclists. Keep your eyes open for cyclists, especially when opening your car door on the street. Opening your door into a cyclist's path is a traffic violation, and, even worse, could cause serious injury to the cyclist.

BY BICYCLE

A great way to get around in Ottawa is by bicycle. Ottawa and the surrounding regions offer a comprehensive network of pathways and parkways where people can bike and in-line skate through beautiful natural scenery. A number of city streets also have designated bike lanes. For **maps** of the pathways and more information, drop in to the **Capital Infocentre,** opposite Parliament Hill at 90 Wellington Street (© **800/465-1867** or 613/239-5000; www.canadas capital.gc.ca). If you find your planned bike route overly ambitious, hop on the bus: **OC Transpo** has installed bike racks on 170 buses, including most buses on routes 2, 95, and 97. Each rack holds two bikes, and loading and unloading is quick and easy. There's no additional cost to use the rack. The program runs from spring through fall.

If you didn't bring your own equipment, numerous places in Ottawa rent out bicycles and in-line skates. See chapter 7, "Active Ottawa," for a list of rental outfits.

Some specific rules apply to cyclists. All cyclists under age 18 must wear a **bicycle helmet.** Cyclists cannot ride on the sidewalk and must not exceed speeds of 20km per hour (12.5 mph) on multi-use pathways. Be considerate of other road or pathway users, and keep to the right. Pass only when it is safe to do so, and if you're on a bicycle use your bell or voice to let others know you're about to pass.

If you're in the vicinity of the Rideau Centre and the ByWard Market, you can **park** your bike at a supervised facility. Located at Rideau and William streets, the facility operates daily 8:30am to 5:30pm, from Victoria Day until Labour Day weekend (third Saturday in May to first Monday in September). The maximum charge is C$2 (US$1.30).

 FAST FACTS: Ottawa

Airport   For general inquiries, and for information on flights, baggage, air freight, call the appropriate airline company—see "Getting There" in chapter 2. You can also obtain general information from the Airport switchboard (© **613/248-2000**) and on the Web at **www.ottawa-airport.ca.** The airport is located in the south end of the city at 50 Airport Road. For information on transportation from the airport to downtown, see "Getting There" in chapter 2.

Air Travel Complaints   The Canadian Transportation Agency's Air Travel Complaints Commissioner handles unresolved passenger complaints against air carriers. Information and complaint forms are available at **www.cta.gc.ca.** For more information call the Canadian Transportation Agency © **888/222-2592.**

American Express   For card member services, including traveler's checks and lost or stolen cards, call © **800/869-3016.** There is an American Express Travel Agency, which provides travel and financial services, at 220 Laurier Ave. W. © **613/563-0231.**

Area Codes   The telephone area code for Ottawa is **613;** for Hull and surrounding areas it's **819.** When calling from Ottawa to Hull, you don't need to use the area code.

ATMs   Walk-up cash machines that link to the Cirrus or PLUS networks can be found every few blocks at various bank branches. You can also get cash advances against your MasterCard or Visa at an ATM, but you'll need a separate personal identification number (PIN) to access this service. ATMs generally charge a fee for each withdrawal.

Babysitting   Hotel concierge or front desk staff can usually supply names and phone numbers of reliable sitters.

Business Hours   Most **stores** are open Monday to Saturday from 9:30 or 10am to 6pm, and many have extended hours one or more evenings.

Sunday opening hours are generally from noon to 5pm, although some stores are now opening at 11am and others are closed all day. **Banks** generally open at 9:30am and close by 4pm, with extended hours one or more evenings; some are open Saturdays. **Restaurants** open at 11 or 11:30am for lunch and at 5pm for dinner, although many in the ByWard Market district stay open all day. Some **museums** are closed on Mondays from October to April. Many stay open on Thursdays until 8 or 9pm.

Car Rentals   See "Getting Around," earlier in this chapter.

Climate   See "When to Go" in chapter 2.

Currency Exchange   Generally, the best place to exchange your currency is at a bank or by obtaining local currency through an ATM. There are a number of foreign exchange services in Ottawa. **Calforex** in the Rideau Centre, 50 Rideau St. (© **800/769-2025** or 613/569-4075), is open daily and provides no-fee American Express traveler's checks and other foreign currency services. **Custom House Currency Exchange** is located at 153 Sparks St. (© **613/234-6005**).

Dentists   For emergency dental care, ask the front desk staff or concierge at your hotel for the name of the nearest dentist, or call Ottawa Dental Society Emergency Care daily 9am to 9pm © **613/523-4185.**

Directory Assistance   For numbers within the same area code, call © **411.** For other numbers, call © **555-1212,** prefixed by the area code of the number you're searching for. There is a charge for this service.

Disability Services   Most of Ottawa's museums and public buildings, as well as many theaters and restaurants, are accessible to travelers with disabilities. For details, refer to the Ottawa visitor guide, available from the Capital Infocentre, 90 Wellington St. (across from Parliament Hill) (© **800/465-1867** or 613/239-5000). Public transit (OC Transpo) is increasingly accessible for passengers with disabilities. For those who are unable to board regular transit, Para Transpo provides alternative transportation. See "Tips for Travelers with Disabilities" in chapter 2.

Doctors   Ask hotel staff or the concierge to help you locate a doctor. Some physicians will visit hotels. Walk-in clinics are available to out-of-province and foreign visitors, but be prepared to pay for services on the spot with cash. For more information, see "Health & Safety" in chapter 2.

Documents   See "Entry Requirements" in chapter 2.

Driving Rules   See "Getting Around," earlier in this chapter.

Drugstores   **Shopper's Drug Mart** has one **24-hour** location: 1460 Merivale Rd. (at Baseline Rd.) (© **613/224-7270**).

Electricity   It's the same as in the United States—110–115 volts, AC.

Embassies/Consulates   All embassies in Canada (more than 100 in total) are located in Ottawa; consulates are primarily located in Toronto, Montreal, and Vancouver. Embassies include the Australian High Commission, 50 O'Connor St., Suite 710, Ottawa, ON K1P 6L2 (© **613/236-0841**); the British High Commission, 80 Elgin St., Ottawa, ON K1P 5K7 (© **613/237-1530**); the Embassy of Ireland, 130 Albert St., Ottawa, ON K1P 5G4 (© **613/233-6281**); the New Zealand High Commission, 727–99 Bank St., Ottawa, ON K1P 6G3 (© **613/238-5991**); the South African High Commission, 15 Sussex

Dr., Ottawa, ON K1M 1M8 (℗ **613/744-0330**); and the Embassy of the United States of America, 490 Sussex Dr., Ottawa, ON K1N 1G8 (℗ **613/ 238-5335** for general inquiries). For U.S. citizen services, visit in person Monday, Tuesday, Thursday, or Friday between 8:30am and noon or call ℗ **800/529-4410** (open 24 hours).

Emergencies   Call ℗ **911** for fire, police, or ambulance. For Poison Control, call ℗ **613/737-1100.**

Eyeglasses   For same-day service (it may be as quick as 1 hour) on most prescriptions, call **Hakim Optical,** which has five Ottawa locations, including the downtown store at 229 Rideau St. (℗ **613/562-1234**). **Lenscrafters** is conveniently located in major malls, including Bayshore, Place d'Orléans, the Rideau Centre, and St. Laurent Shopping Centre.

Hospitals   The **Children's Hospital of Eastern Ontario (CHEO),** 401 Smyth Rd. (℗ **613/737-7600**), is a pediatric teaching hospital affiliated with the University of Ottawa which services a broad geographical area, including Eastern Ontario and Western Quebec. The hospital has an emergency department. For adult care, the **Ottawa Hospital** is a large academic health sciences center with three campuses, all with emergency departments. The **Civic** campus is located at 1053 Carling Ave. (switchboard ℗ **613/761-4000,** Emergency Services ℗ **613/761-4621**), the **General** campus at 501 Smyth Rd. (switchboard ℗ **613/737-6111,** Emergency services ℗ **613/737-8000**), and **Riverside** campus at 1967 Riverside Dr. (switchboard ℗ **613/738-7100,** Urgent Care Centre ℗ **613/738-8200**).

Internet Access   You can check your e-mail and send messages at the **Internet Café,** 288 Bank St., at Somerset (℗ **613/230-9000**).

Kids Help Phone   Kids or teens in distress can call ℗ **800/668-6868** for help.

Laundry/Dry-Cleaning   Most hotels provide same-day laundry and dry-cleaning services or have coin-operated laundry facilities.

Libraries   The recently amalgamated city of Ottawa now has 33 branches of the Ottawa Public Library. Drop into any branch to pick up a current brochure of special events or visit the website at www.library.ottawa.on.ca. The main branch is located at 120 Metcalfe Street (℗ **613/236-0301**).

Liquor   You must be 19 years of age or older to consume or purchase alcohol in Ontario. Bars and retail stores are strict about enforcing the law and will ask for proof of age if they consider it necessary. The Liquor Control Board of Ontario (LCBO) sells wine, spirits, and beer. Their flagship retail store, at 275 Rideau St. (℗ **613/789-5226**), has two floors of fine products from around the world, as well as a Vintages section with a wide selection of high-quality products. Wine accessories are also available, and seminars and tastings are regularly scheduled. This store is well worth a visit. Ontario wines are available at the Wine Rack and at individual winery outlets. Beer is also available through the Beer Store, with about 20 locations in Ottawa.

Mail   Mailing letters and postcards within Canada costs C48¢ (US30¢). Postage for letters and postcards to the United States costs C65¢ (US40¢), and overseas C$1.25 (US80¢).

Maps   Maps of Ottawa are readily available in convenience stores and bookstores, as well as at the **Capital Infocentre,** 90 Wellington St. (© **800/ 465-1867** or 613/239-5000). For a good selection of maps and travel guides, visit **Place Bell Books,** 175 Metcalfe St. (© **613/233-3821**). Specializing in city and country travel books and maps, this bookstore has a hefty selection of vacation guides. Local guide books and scenic photography books of the Ottawa region are also on hand.

Members of Parliament   Call the **Government of Canada** information line at © **800/O-CANADA** (622-6232) or 613/941-4823. Your call will be personally answered in the official language of your choice.

Newspapers/Magazines   The daily newspapers are the *Ottawa Citizen,* the *Ottawa Sun,* and *Le Droit,* Ottawa's French-language newspaper. Keep an eye out for *Capital Parent* and *Ottawa Families,* two local free publications that advertise family-friendly events. *Where Ottawa* is a free monthly guide to shopping, dining, entertainment, and other tourist information. You can find it at most hotels and at some restaurants and retail stores. *Ottawa City Magazine* and *Ottawa Life* are city monthlies. Arts and Entertainment newspapers include the Anglophone *Xpress* and the Francophone *Voir.* Gays and lesbians should check out *Capital Xtra!* For a great variety of international publications, visit **Mags and Fags,** at 254 Elgin St. (© 613/233-9651), or **Planet News,** at 143 Sparks St. (© 613/232-5500).

Police   In a life-threatening emergency or to report a crime in progress or a traffic accident that involves injuries or a vehicle that cannot be driven, call © **911.** For other emergencies (a serious crime or a break-and-enter) call © **613/230-6211.** For all other inquiries, call © **613/236-1222.**

Post Offices   Canada Post, 59 Sparks St., at Elgin St. (© **613/844-1545**), offers postal products and services and collector's stamps. Most convenience stores and drugstores offer postal services, and many have a separate counter for shipping packages during regular business hours. Look for the sign in the window advertising such services.

Radio   The **Canadian Broadcasting Corporation (CBC)** broadcasts on **91.5FM** and **103.3FM.** For news and talk radio, tune in to **CFRA 580AM.** Ottawa's classic rock station is **CHEZ 106FM.** The local easy-listening music station is **Majic 100FM. The BEAR,** on **106.9FM,** broadcasts a mix of current and classic rock. To keep up with the latest on the sports scene, including broadcasts of the Ottawa Senators and Ottawa 67's, listen to **THE TEAM, SPORTS RADIO 1200. KOOL 93.9FM** broadcasts a mix of hits and fun. Those with a preference for New Rock Alternative can tune in to **101.1 X-FM.** For country music fans, there's **Young Country Y105FM.**

Safety   Ottawa is generally safe, but be alert and use common sense, particularly at night. The ByWard Market area and Elgin Street are busy at night with the bar crowd.

Taxes   The national Goods and Services Tax (GST) is 7%. The provincial retail sales tax (PST) is 8% on most goods; certain purchases, such as groceries and children's clothing, are exempt from provincial sales tax. Prepared food, including purchases in restaurants, is taxed at 8%. Liquor, beer, and wine sold in bars and restaurants are taxed at 10%, and retail purchases are taxed at 12%. For amusement venues, admission charges that are over C$3.95 (US$2.60) are taxed at 10%. The accommodations tax is 5%. In Quebec, there is a 7.5% tax on food, liquor, merchandise, and accommodations.

In general, nonresidents may apply for a tax refund. They can recover the accommodations tax, the sales tax, and the GST for nondisposable merchandise that will be exported for use, provided it is removed from Canada within 60 days of purchase. The following do not qualify for rebate: meals and restaurant charges, alcohol, tobacco, gas, car rentals, and such services as dry-cleaning and shoe repair.

The quickest and easiest way to secure the refund is to stop at a duty-free shop at the border. You must have original receipts with GST registration numbers. You can also apply through the mail, but it will take several weeks to receive your refund. For an application form and information, write or call the **Visitor Rebate Program,** Canada Customs and Revenue Agency, Summerside Tax Centre, 275 Pope Rd., Suite 104, Summerside, PEI C1N 6C6 (✆ **800/668-4748** within Canada or 902/432-5608 from outside Canada). *Note:* As of November 1, 2001, Quebec no longer provides rebates of provincial sales tax to nonresidents.

Taxis   See "Getting Around," earlier in this chapter.

Telephone   A local call from a telephone booth costs C25¢ (Canadian and U.S. coins are accepted at face value). Watch out for hotel surcharges on local and long-distance phone calls; often a local call will cost at least C$1 (US65¢) from a hotel room. The United States and Canada are on the same long-distance system. To make a long-distance call between the United States and Canada, use the area codes as you would at home. Canada's international prefix is **1.** Phone cards can be purchased at convenience stores and drugstores.

Time   Ottawa is on **Eastern Standard Time. Daylight Saving Time** is in effect from the first Sunday in April (clocks are moved ahead 1 hour) to the last Sunday in October (clocks are moved back 1 hour).

Tipping   Basically, it's the same as in major U.S. cities—15% in restaurants, 10% to 15% for taxis, C$1 (US70¢) per bag for porters, C$2 (US$1.30) per day for hotel housekeepers.

Transit Information   The public transit system is a bus service provided by Ottawa-Carleton (OC) Transpo (✆ **613/741-4390**) to the communities of Ottawa, Nepean, Vanier, Rockcliffe, Gloucester, Kanata, and Cumberland. Besides using public roads, OC Transpo has a convenient system of roadways used exclusively by buses—the Transitway. Two main lines operate on the Transitway, with transfers possible at many stations along the routes. Route 95 connects the southwest end of the city with the east via downtown. Route 97 runs between Kanata in the west to the airport in the south via downtown. For more information, see "Getting Around," earlier in this chapter.

Weather   For the weather forecast, check the daily newspaper, catch a radio broadcast, or tune in to the weather channel on TV. Some hotels post this information at the front desk.

4

Accommodations

Visitors looking for a place to stay in the National Capital Region are fortunate. Government and corporate clients have traditionally provided brisk and reliable business for Ottawa hoteliers, and tourists often reap the benefits by scooping up weekend and holiday bargains when hotels are scrambling to fill the void left by their weekday residents.

Ottawa offers accommodations to fit every style and budget. Whether your idea of the perfect place to stay is a grandly proportioned Loire Valley Renaissance château, an ultra-modern self-catering suite, a romantic B&B, or a chic boutique hotel, you'll find something in this chapter to catch your interest. If all you're looking for is a clean place to rest your head, you'll find that too—university digs, airport inns, and even a converted jail.

If you're traveling with children, I strongly recommend staying in a one- or two-bedroom suite if your budget will allow. You'll have invested in a comfortable base for your vacation with space for everyone to spread out, a place to make meals at your convenience (which will also save you money), and a couple of TVs. If you're lucky, there'll be a balcony to sneak onto once the kids are asleep where you can enjoy a glass of wine with your spouse as you watch the city lights twinkle.

Many of the accommodations listed in this chapter are within walking distance of the capital's major attractions. Others are only a short drive away. If you choose to stay a little farther out from the downtown core and you don't want to navigate the maze of one-way streets or the dizzying lane changes of the Queensway, use the complimentary shuttle service provided by Capital Double Decker and Trolley Tours, available at approximately 50 hotels, inns, and B&Bs during the main tourist season (see chapter 3, "Getting to Know Ottawa").

PARKING If you have a vehicle with you, remember to factor in parking charges when estimating the cost of your chosen accommodation. Hotel parking rates vary from C$4 (US$2.50) to C$25 (US$16) per night in the downtown area. Most lots are underground and some do not allow in-and-out privileges, which restricts your flexibility. Overnight street parking is allowed where signs are posted. From November 15 to April 1, a city bylaw prohibits overnight on-street parking from 1 to 7am. When a snowfall of 7cm (3 in.) or more is forecast (including ranges such as 5–10cm, or 2–4 in.), the city will issue an overnight winter parking ban, broadcast through the local media. These bans are actively enforced, and those who fail to comply could end up with a C$50 (US$33) ticket.

AN IMPORTANT NOTE ON PRICES The prices quoted in this chapter are **rack rates,** the highest posted rates. Rooms are rarely sold at the full rack rate, but I've quoted rack rates for every property to allow you to compare prices. In each listing, the prices include accommodations for two adults sharing. Discounts can result in a dramatic drop in the rate, typically anywhere from 10% to 50%.

Almost every hotelier I spoke with mentioned that weekend specials or family packages are available at various times throughout the year. A 5% accommodations tax and 7% GST (Goods and Services Tax) are added to accommodation charges, but the taxes are refundable to nonresidents upon application (see "Taxes" under "Fast Facts: Ottawa" in chapter 3).

A NOTE TO NONSMOKERS Most hotels reserve floors for nonsmokers. However, people who want a smoke-free environment should make that clear when reserving a room. Rooms for smokers are often concentrated on certain floors or clustered together at one end of the hallway, and the rooms and even the hallways adjacent to those areas tend to smell strongly of smoke, even in the cleanest hotels. Never assume that you'll get a smoke-free room if you don't specifically request one. The smoking by-laws in the city of Ottawa and the new city of Gatineau (which includes Hull) differ enormously. You'll find smoking bans in all public areas in Ottawa, whereas in Quebec you can light up in most places. You can't really get away from secondhand smoke in Quebec, which will irritate some people and not bother others. I'm just letting you know in advance what to expect.

A NOTE ABOUT POOLS Please be aware that hotel pools are not supervised by hotel staff. If you have children with you, please make sure they are under your direct supervision in pool areas at all times.

BED-AND-BREAKFASTS Ottawa has an abundance of gracious, older homes, some of which have been transformed into charming B&Bs. For the most part, B&Bs are located in quiet residential neighborhoods with tree-lined streets. If you're traveling solo or as a couple, then a B&B presents an economical and delightful alternative to a hotel room, but families will usually need to rent two rooms in order to secure enough sleeping room and that must be taken into account when estimating costs. Also, be aware that B&Bs and inns are usually geared to adult visitors. Many homes have expensive antiques on display and guests are expecting a quiet, restful stay. If you have children with you and they're young, boisterous, or both, then you're better off in a downtown suite hotel with a pool.

Two organizations in the city can help you choose a B&B. The **Ottawa Tourism and Convention Authority (OTCA),** 130 Albert St., Suite 1800, Ottawa, ON K1P 5G4 (© **800/465-1867** or 613/237-5150; www.canada.com) has more than two dozen B&Bs listed as members. There is also a walk-in accommodation reservation desk operated by the OTCA at the **Capital Infocentre,** 90 Wellington St. (across from Parliament Hill), Ottawa, ON (© **800/465-1867** or 613/239-5000). If you're a surfer by nature, visit **BBCanada.com** and have a look at more than 70 properties in the city and around the region that offer bed-and-breakfast accommodation.

CAMPING Across the Ottawa River in Quebec, Gatineau Park's 36,000 hectares or 88,000 acres of woodlands and lakes has two campgrounds. Phillipe Lake Family Campground has around 300 sites. There is also a limited number of canoe-camping sites at La Pêche Lake. For details on these and other camping facilities, contact the **Gatineau Park Visitor Centre,** 318 Meech Lake Rd., Old Chelsea, PQ J0X 1N0 (© **819/827-2020**), or call the **National Capital Commission** at © **800/465-1867.**

REDUCING YOUR ROOM RATE *Always* ask for a deal. Corporate discounts, club memberships (CAA, AAA, and others), and discounts linked to credit cards are just a few of the ways you can get a lower price.

In Ottawa, hotels are especially eager to boost their occupancy rates with families on weekends, when their corporate and government clients desert them. Weekend rates and family packages are often available. Even though March break, Winterlude, the Canadian Tulip Festival, and the summer months are all peak tourist times, many hotels offer packages, which may include complimentary museum passes, restaurant vouchers, or other money-saving deals.

1 Downtown (West of the Canal)

This area has the highest concentration of high-rises and the most traffic congestion, complicated by one-way streets, occasional traffic blocks, and time-limited meter parking, but it's close to many major attractions. Parliament Hill spreads majestically along the banks of the Ottawa River at the north end of this district. In addition to the Parliament Buildings, where you can catch the Changing of the Guard and the RCMP Musical Ride during the summer, you'll find the National Arts Centre, the Museum of Nature, and many great restaurants and retail stores, especially along Elgin, Bank, and Sparks streets. Many other attractions, including the Rideau Locks, the National Gallery, the Canadian War Museum, the Royal Canadian Mint, ByWard Market, and the Rideau Centre, are just across the canal to the east.

VERY EXPENSIVE

Delta Ottawa Hotel and Suites ★/★ *Kids*   From the moment you step into the spacious lobby with its efficient check-in system, you experience the quality of service you'd expect from an upper-end hotel. Over the past couple of years an extensive refurbishment has brightened up everything from pool tiles and the children's playroom to carpets, wall coverings, and fabrics in the guest rooms. There's a choice of three on-site dining facilities, all of which provide above-average fare. Families flock here on weekends, during March break, and over the summer. The giant two-story indoor waterslide is a major hit with kids. In addition to standard guest rooms, the hotel offers studios with kitchenettes (fridge, four-ring hot plate, and microwave) and one- and two-bedroom suites with balconies and kitchenettes. Cordless keyboards have been recently added to all units, providing convenient access to the Internet via TV.

361 Queen St., Ottawa, ON K1R 7S9. ☎ **800/268-1133** or 613/238-6000. Fax 613/238-2290. www.delta hotels.com. 328 units, 63 with kitchenette. C$300 (US$186) double; C$340 (US$211) studio; C$360 (US$223) 1-bedroom suite; children 18 and under stay free in parents' room. Rollaway/crib free. AE, DC, DISC, MC, V. Parking C$16 (US$10). Small domestic pets accepted. C$50 (US$31) cleaning charge applies for stays of 5 nights or more. **Amenities:** 2 restaurants, 1 lounge; indoor pool with adjacent waterslide; exercise room; Jacuzzi; sauna; children's center; seasonal children's program; game room; concierge; business center; secretarial services; salon; limited room service; massage; babysitting; washers and dryers; same-day dry cleaning/laundry; executive floor. *In room:* A/C, TV w/ pay movies, dataport, kitchenette in some units, minibar, coffeemaker, hair dryer, iron.

 Tips

If you're visiting on Canada Day, request a higher-floor room or suite at the **Delta Ottawa,** overlooking the Ottawa River. A few years back, we watched the Snowbirds airshow over the Parliament Buildings at lunchtime and the fabulous fireworks display in the evening through our upper-floor suite window.

EXPENSIVE

Albert at Bay Suite Hotel ★★ (Kids)   This all-suite hotel welcomes families and even goes so far as to provide a free children's program during July and August. The kids' club offers a wide variety of supervised activities for kids ages 3 to 12 daily from 9am to noon and 1 to 5pm. Although there isn't a pool, a bright and sunny exercise room with a Jacuzzi and an adjacent rooftop patio provide a refuge for parents who want to sneak in and relax while the children are busy at the kids' club. The downtown location is a great base for visitors traveling without children as well. You're within strolling distance of Parliament Hill (3 blocks), the National Arts Centre (7 blocks), and the Rideau Centre (8 blocks). A five-minute walk will take you right down to the pathway along the banks of the Ottawa River. All units have a kitchen with full-size appliances, including a dishwasher; one or two bedrooms; and two TVs. Some suites have two bathrooms.

435 Albert St., Ottawa, ON K1R 7X4. ✆ 800/267-6644 or 613/238-8858. Fax 613/238-1433. www.albert atbay.com. 197 units. C$239 (US$148) 1-bedroom suite; C$299 (US$185) 2-bedroom suite. Children 16 and under stay free in parents' room. Rollaway C$10 (US$6), crib free. AE, DC, DISC, MC, V. Parking C$11 (US$7). **Amenities:** 1 restaurant; Jacuzzi; sauna; seasonal children's program; limited room service; washers and dryers; same-day dry cleaning/laundry; executive suites. *In room:* A/C, TV w/ pay movies, dataport, kitchen, coffeemaker, iron.

Albert House Inn ★   This gracious Victorian structure has operated as an inn for the past 20 years. It was designed and built by Thomas Seaton Scott, a renowned architect whose work includes the Cartier Drill Hall, the Langevin Block (home of the prime minister's offices), and many other federal buildings. The furnishings and decor enhance the historic atmosphere. Its convenient downtown location is only a short walk from the Parliament Buildings and a beautiful pathway along the Ottawa River. The environment is adult-oriented, but older children are welcome.

478 Albert St., Ottawa, ON K1R 5B5. ✆ 800/267-1982 or 613/236-4479. Fax 613/237-9079. www. albertinn.com. 17 units. C$175 (US$109) double. Rates include breakfast. AE, DC, MC, V. Free parking. **Amenities:** Business services, washers and dryers. *In room:* A/C, TV, dataport, hair dryer.

ARC the.hotel ★★★   Aiming to blend efficiency with luxury, ARC the.hotel focuses on meeting the needs of sophisticated travelers. The ARC experience will leave you feeling relaxed, pampered, and refreshed. Down-filled duvets, oversize pillows, Egyptian cotton sheets, Frette bathrobes—the list goes on. Nightly turndown service thoughtfully includes cold spring water and Godiva chocolates. You can indulge in Bvlgari toiletries, put a little background music on the CD player, enjoy a complimentary glass of sparkling wine on arrival, or catch up on your reading in the library. The hallways are scented with carefully selected aromatherapy fragrances. The ARC lounge serves signature martinis and "tapatizers" at the cocktail hour. The tempting dinner menu changes seasonally. Autumn 2001 featured spiced tuna sashimi, roasted sea scallops, duck breast roulade, and other dishes, with a fine selection of cheeses and desserts. If you wish to customize your return visit, make your preferences known to the front desk staff and on your next trip you'll feel even more at home. Guests with allergies can request non-allergenic bedding and toiletries. Children can be accommodated, although there are no specific facilities available for kids.

140 Slater St., Ottawa, ON K1P 5H6. ✆ 800/699-2516 or 613/238-2888. Fax 613/235-8421. www.arc thehotel.com. 112 units. C$220 (US$136) double; C$425 (US$264) 1-bedroom suite. Children 12 and under

stay free in parents' room. Rollaway free. AE, DC, MC, V. Parking C$18 (US$11). **Amenities:** 1 lounge/restaurant; exercise room; bike/in-line skate rental; concierge; business center; limited room service; same-day dry cleaning/laundry. *In room:* A/C, TV w/ pay movies, dataport, minibar, fridge, coffeemaker, hair dryer, safe.

Aristocrat Suite Hotel *☆*   With a full-size kitchen in every unit, the Aristocrat guarantees self-sufficient accommodation. Located within walking distance of many downtown attractions and a short stroll from the banks of the Rideau Canal, it's a good base for tourists. The bedrooms and living room are a decent size, but with a table and chairs taking up floor space, the kitchen is a bit short on elbowroom. Be prepared to roll up your sleeves to wash the pots—there isn't a dishwasher. Suites have only one TV (in the living room), which may be seen as an oversight or a blessing, depending on your point of view. In 2001, a new Italian restaurant opened on the main floor, serving breakfast, lunch, and dinner daily. There is no pool, but the hotel offers a number of specialty services. If you're arriving by air, the Aristocrat will arrange for a limousine, with a driver to greet your flight inside the airport. As another bonus, you can have groceries delivered to your suite to save you the trouble of shopping. Ask about special family rates.

131 Cooper St., Ottawa, ON K2P 0E7. *©* **800/563-5634** or 613/236-7500. Fax 613/563-2836. 200 units. C$129 (US$80) studio or 1-bedroom suite; C$179 (US$111) 2-bedroom suite. Children 17 and under stay free in parents' room. Rollaway C$10 (US$6), crib free. AE, DC, MC, V. Parking C$9 (US$6). **Amenities:** 1 restaurant; exercise room; Jacuzzi; sauna; secretarial services; limited room service; massage; babysitting; washers and dryers; same-day dry cleaning/laundry. *In room:* A/C, TV, kitchen, coffeemaker, hair dryer, iron.

Best Western Victoria Park Suites *☆/☆*   Freshly decorated in 2000 and offering an additional 24 newly constructed units in 2001, this hotel has comfortable and spacious studios and one-bedroom suites, all with kitchenettes. Parliament Hill is 10 blocks north, which is a bit far for some folks, but a bus or taxi will whisk you there in no time if you'd rather leave your car in the underground lot. The magnificent Museum of Nature, with its huge dinosaurs, creepy insects, beautiful birds, and life-size woolly mammoth family, is just a block away. Nearby Bank Street is lined with shops and eateries. Wired guests can enjoy Web TV and Nintendo in every unit. A complimentary continental breakfast is included in the rates, and CAA members can save a few bucks with free parking. In the summer months when the kids' club is running at Victoria Park Suites' sister hotel, the Albert at Bay Suite Hotel, you can take your children there for free supervised fun and games.

377 O'Connor St., Ottawa, ON K2P 2M2. *©* **800/465-7275** or 613/567-7275. Fax 613/567-1161. www.victoriapark.com. 124 units. C$209 (US$130) studio; C$239 (US$148) 1-bedroom suite. Children 16 and under stay free in parents' room. Rollaway/crib free. AE, DC, DISC, MC, V. Parking C$9 (US$6). **Amenities:** 1 breakfast room; exercise room; sauna; secretarial services; babysitting; washers and dryers; same-day dry cleaning/laundry. *In room:* A/C, TV w/ pay movies, kitchenette, fridge, coffeemaker, iron.

Bostonian Executive Suites *☆* *Value*   Renovations to an existing high-rise building in the downtown core have resulted in the addition of another suite hotel to Ottawa's accommodations listings. Opened in March 2001, the Bostonian suites have full kitchens and a choice of studio or one-bedroom models. High-speed Internet access, voice mail, 24-hour business support services, ergonomic seating, and long-stay options make the Bostonian an ideal base for business travelers. Families will enjoy the convenience of laundry facilities, grocery delivery, microwave, and dishwasher.

341 MacLaren St., Ottawa ON K2P 2E2. *©* **866/320-4567** or 613/594-5757. Fax 613/594-3221. www.thebostonian.ca. 117 units. C$149 (US$92) studio; C$179 (US$111) 1-bedroom suite. Children under 16 stay free

in parents' room. Rollaway/cribs free for under 16; C$10 (US$6) 16 and over. AE, MC, V. Parking C$10 (US$6). Pets sometimes accepted. **Amenities:** Game room; concierge; business services; washers and dryers; same-day dry cleaning. *In room:* A/C, TV w/ pay movies, dataport, kitchen, coffeemaker, hair dryer, iron.

Carmichael Inn & Spa ⋆⋆   A quiet oasis in the heart of the busy city awaits guests at the Carmichael Inn & Spa. The inn is a designated heritage site, built in 1901 as the retirement residence of a local businessman. The atmosphere is calm and restful. You may catch the scent of spiced pear as you enter the inn, which is decorated predominantly in soft greens, golds, and browns. Many fine antiques are displayed in public areas and guest rooms. Flowering trees, including a magnolia, shelter the veranda, making it a favorite resting place in spring and summer. When the weather is cold, curl up in an armchair by the lounge fireplace. The inn is best suited to adult guests. The luxurious spa is located on the lower level and offers massages, body wraps, foot treatments, herbal baths, and facials. Locals visit the spa as day guests. Ask for package details. The entire building is nonsmoking.

46 Cartier St., Ottawa ON K2P 1J3. ℂ **613/236-4667.** Fax 613/563-7529. www.carmichaelinn.com. 11 units. C$149–C$179 (US$92–US$111) double. Rates include breakast. AE, DC, MC, V. Free parking. **Amenities:** Business services; massage; washers and dryers; same-day dry cleaning/laundry. *In room:* A/C, TV, dataport, hair dryer, iron.

Cartier Place and Towers Suite Hotels ⋆⋆⋆ *(Kids)*   This higher-end suite hotel has wonderful amenities for children. Besides the indoor pool, bathed in natural light streaming through glass doors (which are thrown open in the summer and lead onto a sundeck), there is a well-equipped children's playroom and even a preschool-size play structure in the pool area. An outdoor courtyard features a climbing gym and children's play equipment in summer and a skating rink in winter. Redecoration and replacement of kitchen appliances has been ongoing for the past few years, a couple of floors at a time, so many of the suites are fresh and bright. All units are suites with full kitchens and private balconies with garden chairs.

180 Cooper St., Ottawa, ON K2P 2L5. ℂ **800/236-8399** or 613/236-5000. Fax 613/238-3842. www.suite dreams.com. 253 units. C$229–C$269 (US$142–US$167) suite. Children 16 and under stay free in parents' room. Rollaway/crib free. AE, DC, DISC, MC, V. Parking C$12 (US$7). Small pets accepted C$8 (US$5). **Amenities:** 1 restaurant/lounge; indoor pool; exercise room; Jacuzzi; sauna; children's playroom; outdoor playground; skating rink; game room; business services; limited room service; babysitting; washers and dryers; same-day dry cleaning/laundry. *In room:* A/C, TV w/ pay movies, dataport, kitchen, coffeemaker, hair dryer, iron.

Crowne Plaza Ottawa ⋆⋆   If you're looking for contemporary luxury in a traditional hotel room, this is a fine place to stay. After more than C$11 million (US$7 million) in extensive renovations, the former Citadel Hotel has been transformed. The public areas reflect a sophisticated Art Deco style, with clean lines, expanses of wood, and a rich, earthy color scheme. The upscale decor continues into the hallways and guest rooms, which have been refurbished with new carpets, draperies, wall coverings, furniture, and redesigned bathrooms. An underground shopping arcade, open primarily during weekday office hours, is accessible from inside the hotel. The extensive health club features a large fitness center, aerobic classes, and squash courts. The indoor pool area, nicely set in a light-filled space, has patio doors leading onto a courtyard. Staff are attentive, courteous, and efficient. International cuisine is served in the sophisticated atmosphere of 101 Café & Bar.

101 Lyon St., Ottawa, ON K1R 5T9. ℂ **800/227-6963** or 613/237-3600. Fax 613/237-2351. www.crowne plazaottawa.com. 411 units. C$239 (US$148) double. Children 17 and under stay free in parents' room.

Rollaway/crib free. AE, DC, DISC, MC, V. Valet parking C$21 (US$13), self-parking C$14 (US$9). **Amenities:** 1 restaurant, 1 lounge; indoor pool; health club; Jacuzzi; sauna; concierge; business center; limited room service; babysitting; same-day dry cleaning/laundry; executive floors. *In room:* A/C, TV w/ pay movies, dataport, fridge in some units, coffeemaker, hair dryer, iron.

Lord Elgin Hotel ✦   This established hotel, with its elegant lobby incorporating a recently added bar, is centrally located near Parliament Hill and the Rideau Centre shopping mall and a stone's throw from the National Arts Centre and the Rideau Canal. Directly across the street you'll find Confederation Park, a small but pretty city park that provides respite from the dense metropolis of skyscrapers crowding the business district west of the hotel. The park is a great place to people-watch, let your kids run around, or take your pooch for a walk. If you venture north along Elgin Street, you'll find plenty of pleasant eateries, lively pubs, and shops. Construction of 60 new units, an expanded health facility, and an indoor pool is due to be completed in 2002. Guests enjoy the convenience of voice mail, complimentary newspapers, and a cash machine on the premises. The rooms are not overly spacious and the bathrooms are utilitarian. Rooms at the back are quieter, but you lose the view of the park. Staff are formal and efficient.

100 Elgin St., Ottawa, ON K1P 5K8. ✆ **800/267-4298** or 613/235-3333. Fax 613/235-3223. www.lord elginhotel.ca. 300 units. C$170 double (US$105). Children 17 and under stay free in parents' room. Rollaway/crib free. AE, DC, DISC, MC, V. Valet parking C$14 (US$9). Pets accepted in some rooms but cannot be left alone. **Amenities:** 1 restaurant, 1 lounge; exercise room; bicycle rental nearby; concierge; salon next door; limited room service; babysitting; same-day dry cleaning/laundry. *In room:* A/C, TV w/ pay movies, dataport, coffeemaker, hair dryer, iron.

Marriott Residence Inn Ottawa ✦✦✦   The units in this all-suites hotel are at least 50% larger than those in standard hotels. If you're staying in town longer than a night or two, it's nice to be able to spread out a little in comfort. If you have kids with you, splurge on a two-bedroom suite, which boasts a well-equipped kitchen, two full bathrooms, and three TVs. It's well worth the money, and if it's going to push you over budget, take advantage of the grocery service and cook meals in the suite. The health club's pool has a uniform 1.1-m (4-ft.) depth. For round-the-clock caffeine cravers and hungry tummies, there's a 24-hour Tim Horton's right on the doorstep, with access from the main lobby. Expect cheerful faces and friendly greetings from staff whenever you cross their path. The hotel has been open just over two years, and the furniture and decor still look brand-new, a credit to the meticulous housekeeping. Two one-bedroom suites are equipped for guests with disabilities.

161 Laurier Ave. W., Ottawa, ON K1P 5J2. ✆ **800/331-3131** or 613/231-2020. Fax 613/231-2090. www. residenceinn.com. 171 units. C$179 (US$111) studio; C$299 (US$185) 2-bedroom suite. Rollaway C$12 (US$7), crib free. AE, DC, DISC, MC, V. Parking $C12 (US$7). Pets C$150 (US$99) flat fee; can be left alone if owners can be reached by phone. **Amenities:** 1 lounge serving complimentary breakfast and snacks; indoor pool; health club; hot tub; sauna; spa next door; concierge; secretarial services; laundry room (some units have washers/dryers); same-day dry cleaning/laundry. *In room:* A/C, TV w/ pay movies, dataport, kitchen (equipment varies with suite size), fridge, coffeemaker, hair dryer, iron.

Minto Place Suite Hotel ✦✦✦ (*Value*)   Beautifully appointed, spacious suites with kitchenettes or full kitchens make Minto Place one of Ottawa's top choices for accommodations. Adding to its appeal is direct access to an indoor shopping concourse with a bank, walk-in clinic, post office, food court, car rental outlet, and retail stores. The 19.5-m (65-ft.) long indoor pool, lit by skylights, is a uniform 1.2m (4 ft.) deep and sparkling clean. A sundeck leads off the pool area. Vacationing families are well-catered to; in the summer, your kids can even sign up for the fun and games at the kids' club. Staff are courteous, pleasant, and experienced in helping visitors to make the most of their stay in Ottawa. Two suites are designed specifically for guests with disabilities.

433 Laurier Ave. W., Ottawa, ON K1R 7Y1. © **800/267-3377** or 613/782-2350. Fax 613/232-6962. www.mintohotel.com. 417 units. C$155 (US$96) studio; C$194 (US$120) 1-bedroom suite; C$262 (US$162) 2-bedroom suite. Children 18 and under stay free in parents' room. Crib free. AE, DC, DISC, MC, V. Parking C$12 (US$7) weekdays, C$4 (US$2) weekends. **Amenities:** 2 restaurants; indoor pool; exercise room; Jacuzzi; sauna; seasonal children's program; secretarial services; shopping arcade; limited room service; babysitting; washers and dryers in some suites; same-day dry cleaning/laundry. *In room:* A/C, TV w/ pay movies, dataport, kitchen or kitchenette, coffeemaker, hair dryer, iron.

Ottawa Marriott ★★

Ottawa's downtown Marriott has the distinction of having the only rooftop revolving restaurant in the region, where diners can gaze at an ever-changing view of the nation's capital while enjoying global cuisine highlighted with Canadian products. With the aim of attracting families on weekends and during school holidays, the hotel has recently expanded its facilities for children. The Kids Zone features an activity and craft center, game room for teens, mini-golf, basketball half-court, and big-screen movies. Family packages are available with discounted room prices. Two guest rooms have been fitted to accommodate guests with disabilities. High-speed Internet with cordless keyboards in all rooms.

100 Kent St., Ottawa, ON K1P 5R7. © **800/853-8463** Canada or 613/238-1122. Fax 613/783-4229. www.marriotthotels.com. 481 units. C$189 (US$117) double; C$285 (US$177) larger corner room. Children under 18 stay free in parents' room. Rollaway/crib free. AE, DC, MC, V. Valet parking C$20 (US$12), parking C$14 (US$9). Pets accepted. **Amenities:** 2 restaurants (1 revolving); indoor pool; exercise room; Jacuzzi; sauna; bike/in-line skate rental; children's center and programs; game room; concierge; business center; shopping arcade; 24-hour room service; massage; babysitting; washers and dryers; same-day dry cleaning/laundry; executive floors. *In room:* A/C, TV w/ pay movies, dataport, fridge on request, coffeemaker, hair dryer, iron.

Sheraton Ottawa Hotel ★★

The Sheraton is a classy hotel, as you'll note from the moment you enter the elegant lobby and are greeted by the impeccably dressed doorman. A spiral staircase leads to the second floor, but you can opt for the more conventional elevator. Even the restaurant is posh, furnished with rich, dark wood, gleaming brass, and sparkling chandeliers. Rooms are spacious, and the complete refurbishment in 1998 included upgraded vanities and ceramic tiles in the bathrooms. The spotless indoor pool complex features a bank of windows at one end to allow natural light to flood the space. If luxurious surroundings are a priority on your vacation, you won't be disappointed here.

150 Albert St., Ottawa, ON K1P 5G2. © **800/489-8333** or 613/238-1500. Fax 613/238-2723. www. sheraton.com. 236 units. C$260 (US$161) double. Children 16 and under stay free in parents' room. Rollaway/ crib free. AE, DC, DISC, MC, V. Valet parking C$18 (US$11). Small pets accepted. **Amenities:** 1 restaurant, 1 lounge; indoor pool; exercise room; sauna; concierge; business center; room service; babysitting; same-day dry cleaning/laundry; executive rooms. *In room:* A/C, TV w/ pay movies, dataport, coffeemaker, hair dryer, iron.

 Tips

Hotel pools do not usually provide lifeguards or other supervisory personnel. It is the parent's responsibility to closely supervise their own children in the pool area. Exercise extra caution when the pool is crowded. Enjoy your swim and always follow pool safety rules.

MODERATE

Capital Hill Hotel & Suites *Value*   This comfortable but far from ritzy hotel offers good value and the advantage of a downtown location. Various hotel room and suite accommodations are available, including standard rooms with one queen- or king-size bed, studios with two queen-size beds and a kitchenette, and one-bedroom suites with two queen-size beds, a kitchenette, and a pullout couch. About half of the 150 units are equipped with a stove or microwave, a small fridge, dishes, and utensils, but none have dishwashers. The top four floors (9 through 12) have been refreshed with a bright, neutral decor; floors four through eight are currently being renovated. The room size is average and bathrooms tend to be small. Guests receive complimentary passes to a health club situated in the Rideau Centre shopping mall, a few minutes' walk away.

88 Albert St., Ottawa, ON K1P 5E9. *℃* **800/463-7705** or 613/235-1413. Fax 613/235-6047. www. capitalhill.com. 150 units. C$129 (US$80) double with kitchenette; C$149 (US$92) 1-bedroom suite. Children 17 and under stay free in parents' room. Rollaway/crib free. AE, DC, DISC, MC, V. Parking C$10 (US$6). Pets accepted. **Amenities:** 1 restaurant, 1 bar; secretarial services; massage; same-day dry cleaning/laundry; executive rooms. *In room:* A/C, TV w/ pay movies, dataport, kitchenette in some units, coffeemaker, hair dryer, iron.

Embassy Hotel and Suites   All units in this hotel have a full kitchen (minus dishwasher). The bathrooms and bedrooms tend to be small, but there is plenty of seating in the living rooms of the one-bedroom suites. Some units have new carpet and linens; others are in need of refurbishing. The on-site restaurant/coffee shop serves breakfast and lunch only.

25 Cartier St., Ottawa, ON K2P 1J2. *℃* **800/661-5495** or 613/237-2111. Fax 613/563-1353. www.embassy hotelottawa.com. 130 units. C$130 (US$81) studio; C$150 (US$93) 1-bedroom suite; C$230 (US$143) 2-bedroom suite. Children 16 and under stay free in parents' room. Rollaway/crib free. AE, DC, DISC, MC, V. Limited parking C$8 (US$5). **Amenities:** 1 restaurant; 1 lounge; exercise room; sauna; limited room service; coin-op washers and dryers; same-day dry cleaning/laundry. *In room:* A/C, TV, kitchen, coffeemaker, hair dryer, iron.

Ramada Hotel & Suites Ottawa *★*   If you're searching for moderately priced accommodation with self-catering, the Ramada fits the bill. The property is situated at the quiet end of Cooper Street, just steps from the banks of the Rideau Canal and a few blocks west of the shops and restaurants of Elgin Street. All rooms with two double beds have a kitchenette with a two-ring hot plate and small fridge. A microwave can be supplied on request. One-bedroom suites are equipped with a full kitchen, and a small number have a connecting door to a single room, effectively creating a two-bedroom suite. Executive-level rooms include a full Canadian breakfast and have added luxuries including upgraded toiletries, bathrobes, and heated floors in the bathrooms.

111 Cooper St., Ottawa, ON K2P 2E3. *℃* **800/267-8378** or 613/238-1331. Fax 613/230-2179. www. ramada.com. 233 units. C$151 (US$94) double with kitchenette; C$201 (US$125) 1-bedroom suite; executive room C$176 (US$109) double. Executive room rate includes breakfast. Children 18 and under stay free in parents' room. Rollaway/crib free. AE, DC, DISC, MC, V. Parking C$10 (US$6). Pets accepted. **Amenities:** 1 restaurant, 1 lounge; exercise room; secretarial services; 24-hour room service; babysitting; washers and dryers; same-day dry cleaning/laundry; executive rooms. *In room:* A/C, TV w/ pay movies, dataport, kitchen or kitchenette, coffeemaker, hair dryer, iron.

INEXPENSIVE

Arosa Suites Hotel   If your budget is tight, consider the Arosa Suites. The living quarters are compact and the decor is dated, but the price is right. A maximum of four occupants plus one baby in a crib is the limit to each

Accommodations

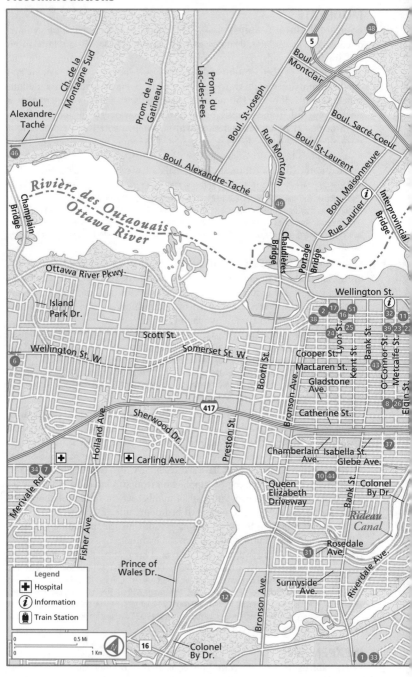

Legend

✚ Hospital

ⓘ Information

🚆 Train Station

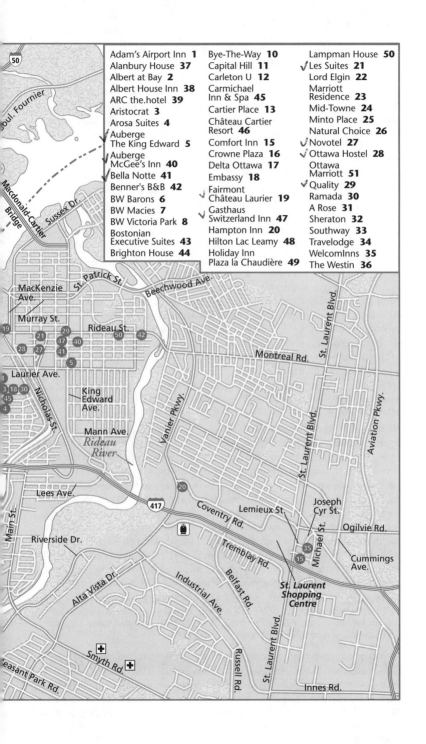

Adam's Airport Inn **1**
Alanbury House **37**
Albert at Bay **2**
Albert House Inn **38**
ARC the.hotel **39**
Aristocrat **3**
Arosa Suites **4**
Auberge
The King Edward **5**
Auberge
McGee's Inn **40**
Bella Notte **41**
Benner's B&B **42**
BW Barons **6**
BW Macies **7**
BW Victoria Park **8**
Bostonian
Executive Suites **43**
Brighton House **44**

Bye-The-Way **10**
Capital Hill **11**
Carleton U **12**
Carmichael
Inn & Spa **45**
Cartier Place **13**
Château Cartier
Resort **46**
Comfort Inn **15**
Crowne Plaza **16**
Delta Ottawa **17**
Embassy **18**
Fairmont
Château Laurier **19**
Gasthaus
Switzerland Inn **47**
Hampton Inn **20**
Hilton Lac Leamy **48**
Holiday Inn
Plaza la Chaudière **49**

Lampman House **50**
Les Suites **21**
Lord Elgin **22**
Marriott
Residence **23**
Mid-Towne **24**
Minto Place **25**
Natural Choice **26**
Novotel **27**
Ottawa Hostel **28**
Ottawa
Marriott **51**
Quality **29**
Ramada **30**
A Rose **31**
Sheraton **32**
Southway **33**
Travelodge **34**
WelcomInns **35**
The Westin **36**

one-bedroom suite. Almost half the residents, many of them corporate or government employees, are long-term occupants, but you'll see more families and other tourists around in the summer. Parking is cheap, but be warned: The parking lot doesn't have room for every vehicle—it's first-come, first-served. Most kitchens have a dishwasher, and all units but three have a private balcony.

163 MacLaren St., Ottawa, ON K2P 2G4. © **613/238-6783**. Fax 613/238-5080. www.arosahotel.com. 62 units. C$91 (US$56) double 1-bedroom suite; C$96 (US$60) four adults sharing 1-bedroom suite. Children 16 and under stay free in parents' room. Crib free. AE, DC, DISC, MC, V. Limited parking C$4 (US$2). **Amenities:** Exercise room; washers and dryers. *In room:* A/C, TV, kitchen, coffeemaker.

Mid-Towne Heritage B&B ★★ (Value)   Built in 1891 as a fashionable Victorian family home, this is one of the most charming bed-and-breakfasts in Ottawa. It has been recently restored, with original fireplaces, stained glass, wood, and plaster. The shade trees and small gardens are set in one of the last remaining private yards in the city core. The owners reckon their home is the closest B&B to Parliament Hill, which is only a 10-minute stroll away, along Wellington Street. Breakfasts are delightful. This is one of the few B&Bs to offer suites. The second floor offers a choice of two—a one-bedroom suite with ensuite bathroom and private sitting room with adult-size day bed, and a two-bedroom suite with a bathroom accessible from both bedrooms and a private sun porch. The rooms are fresh and pretty, with Victorian decor. The entire building is nonsmoking. As with most B&Bs, the owners accept children at their discretion, and suggest that ages 8 and up are best suited to the tranquil charm of this home. For travelers who conduct their lives at a gentle pace, this will be a lovely base for an Ottawa vacation.

220 Lyon St., Ottawa, ON K1R 5V7. © **888/669-8888** or 613/236-1169. www.bbcanada.com/closestbnb. 4 units. C$95 (US$59) and up double; C$129 (US$80) double suite; C$139 (US$86) four adults sharing suite, including breakfast. AE, DC, MC, V. Free parking. *In room:* A/C, TV, hair dryer, no phone.

Natural Choice/4 Nature B&B   If you take a nuts-and-granola kind of approach to life, you'll feel right at home in this vegetarian, nonsmoking B&B facing the Canadian Museum of Nature. The bedrooms are fresh and bright and decorated with original artwork, in keeping with the relaxed, friendly atmosphere. The hosts provide services ranging from massage and craniosacral therapy (gentle manipulation of the skull to relieve pain and tension) to yoga classes and weddings. Their flourishing garden has a picnic table for guests' use, as well as a room on the second floor where children can play when meditation and yoga are not in session. Besides the green space outside the Museum of Nature (complete with life-size models of a woolly mammoth family), there's a park within walking distance with a children's playground and wading pool. For even more physical activity, get a day pass to the facilities at the YMCA across the street.

263 McLeod St., Ottawa, ON K2P 1A1. © **888/346-9642** or 613/563-4399. www.vegybnb.com. 3 units. C$70 (US$43) double; C$85–$125 (US$56–$83) per family depending on number of guests, including breakfast. Rollaway free. MC, V. Limited free parking. Pets C$10 (US$6). **Amenities:** Massage and other services available. *In room:* Ceiling fans, no phone.

2 Downtown (East of the Canal)

This downtown sector is bordered by the Ottawa River to the north, the Rideau River to the east, the Queensway to the south, and the Rideau Canal to the west. You'll find the lively and exciting ByWard Market area in this district, as well as a number of large high-rise hotels, Major's Hill Park, Strathcona Park, the University of Ottawa, the National Gallery, the Canadian War Museum, and the Royal Canadian Mint. On the quiet residential streets, embassy residences and B&Bs are interspersed among elegant Victorian and Edwardian homes.

VERY EXPENSIVE

Fairmont Château Laurier ★★★   One of Ottawa's premier landmarks, this grand hotel, built in 1912 in the same Loire Valley Renaissance style as Quebec City's Château Frontenac, has an imposing stone façade and copper-paneled roof. If you're looking for luxury, tradition, and attentive service, this is the place to stay—royalty and celebrities have always been attracted to the Château Laurier's graceful beauty. You'll pay for the pleasure, but the surroundings are exceptional. The spacious public areas display the grandeur of another era, as they are gradually being refurnished with the hotel's original furniture, rescued from a storeroom and meticulously restored. The less expensive rooms are rather small but just as elegant as the larger rooms and suites; nine rooms are equipped for guests with disabilities. The upper floors offer impressive views over the Ottawa River toward the Gatineau Hills. The extensive health club and pool area, built in 1929 in Art Deco style, has been admirably preserved. The two dining areas, Wilfrid's and Zoe's, named for Sir Wilfrid Laurier and his wife, who were the first guests at the hotel, offer a sumptuous dining experience.

1 Rideau St., Ottawa, ON K1N 8S7. ℂ **800/441-1414** or 613/241-1414. Fax 613/562-7032. www. fairmont.com. 429 units. C$309 (US$192) and up double; C$429(US$266) and up suite. Children 17 and under stay free in parents' room. Rollaway/crib free. AE, DC, DISC, MC, V. Valet parking C$23(US$14), self-parking C$16 (US$10). Pets C$25 (US$16) per day. **Amenities:** 1 restaurant, 1 outdoor terrace, 1 bar/tea room; large indoor pool; health club; sauna; bicycle and in-line skate rental; unsupervised children's playroom; small video arcade; concierge; business center; 24-hour room service; massage; same-day dry cleaning/laundry; executive floor. *In room:* A/C, TV w/ pay movies, dataport in some rooms, minibar, fridge available on request, coffeemaker, hair dryer, iron.

The Westin Ottawa ★★   The lobby is grand and the staff are obliging and exceedingly well-mannered at this upscale hotel. All rooms feature floor-to-ceiling windows to provide the best possible views of the city. A business center in the main lobby offers everything from paperclips to computer rental and is open daily 7am to 7pm. When you're ready for exercise, go for a challenging game of squash on one of the three international standard courts or take a dip in the indoor pool, which has an adjacent outdoor sundeck. For those who live to shop, the third floor of the hotel provides direct access to the stores and services of the Rideau Centre.

11 Colonel By Dr., Ottawa, ON K1N 9H4. ℂ **888/625-5144** or 613/560-7000. Fax 613/234-5396. www. westin.com. 487 units. C$339 (US$210) double. Children 18 and under stay free in parents' room. Rollaway/crib free. AE, DC, DISC, MC, V. Valet parking C$25 (US$16); self-parking C$10 (US$7). Pets accepted. **Amenities:** 1 restaurant, 2 bars; indoor pool; exercise room; hot tub; sauna; concierge; tour/activities desk; shopping arcade; 24-hour room service; massage; babysitting; same-day dry cleaning/laundry; executive floors. *In room:* A/C, TV w/ pay movies, dataport, minibar, coffeemaker, hair dryer, iron.

EXPENSIVE

Les Suites Hotel Ottawa ★★ (Value)   An all-suite property, Les Suites was originally built as a condominium complex in 1989. As a result, the one- and two-bedroom suites are spacious and well equipped, with a full kitchen in every unit. Elevators are situated away from the rooms and bedrooms are located at the back of the suites, away from potential hallway noise. For an even quieter environment, ask for a suite overlooking the garden courtyard. The health club and indoor pool are shared with guests of Novotel Ottawa. The Rideau Centre and the ByWard Market area are on the hotel's doorstep.

130 Besserer St., Ottawa, ON K1N 9M9. © **800/267-1989** or 613/232-2000. Fax 613/232-1242. www. les-suites.com. 243 units. C$210 (US$130) 1-bedroom suite; C$235 (US$146) 2-bedroom suite. Children 18 and under stay free in parents' room. Rollaway/crib free. AE, DC, DISC, MC, V. Parking C$14 (US$9). Pets C$25 (US$16) flat fee. **Amenities:** 1 restaurant; indoor pool; exercise room; hot tub; sauna; concierge; secretarial services; shopping arcade; limited room service; massage; babysitting; washers and dryers; same-day dry cleaning/laundry; executive suites. *In room:* A/C, TV w/ pay movies, dataport, kitchen, coffeemaker, hair dryer, iron.

Novotel Ottawa ⊙ This hotel is right in the middle of it all—the Rideau Centre, Parliament Hill, Rideau Canal, ByWard Market, and many of the museums are only a short walk away. With refurbishments completed in 1999, the public areas and rooms are decorated in Mediterranean hues of blue, orange, and yellow. The result is striking and sunny and a welcome change from the carefully neutral shades common to many hotels. High-speed Internet service was installed in 60 units in 2001, with plans to expand availability. Staff are cheerful and attentive.

33 Nicholas St., Ottawa, ON K1N 9M7. © **800/668-6835** or 613/230-3033. Fax 613/760-4765. www. novotel.com. 281 units. C$195 (US$129) and up double. Children 16 and under stay free in parents' room. Rollaway/crib free. AE, DC, DISC, MC, V. Parking C$12–$14 (US$7–$9). Pets accepted. **Amenities:** 1 restaurant, 1 bar; indoor pool; exercise room; hot tub; sauna; tour/activities desk; secretarial services; limited room service; massage; same-day dry cleaning/laundry. *In room:* A/C, TV w/ pay movies, dataport, minibar, hair dryer, iron.

MODERATE

Auberge McGee's Inn ⊙ Nestled in the heart of the historic Sandy Hill district, the inn was built in 1886 as a residence for John J. McGee. The guest rooms are individually decorated and amenities vary. Some rooms have fireplaces; others have private balconies. There are two suites designed for romantic couples—the Egyptian Room and the Victorian Roses Suite, both with fireplaces and double Jacuzzis. The second floor has a laundry room, ironing board and iron, and kitchenette with small stove and microwave for guest use. Special packages are often available; check the website or call for details.

185 Daly Ave., Otttawa, ON K1N 6E8. © **800/262-4337** or 613/237-6089. Fax 613/237-6201. www. mcgeesinn.com. 14 units. C$98 (US$61) and up double; C$198 (US$123) romantic suite. Rates include breakfast. Children under 6 stay free in parents' room. Rollaway C$20 (US$12). AE, MC, V. Free parking. **Amenities:** Washers and dryers; same-day dry cleaning. *In room:* A/C, TV, dataport, coffeemaker, hair dryer.

Benner's Bed & Breakfast ⊙⊙ A comfortable stroll from the ByWard Market, University of Ottawa, and downtown shopping, Benner's B&B encompasses two elegant Edwardian brownstone houses in the historic residential district of Sandy Hill. The interior is a seamless blend of the original architectural features of the home with sleek contemporary decor. That may sound like an almost impossible achievement, but the result is stunning. Features include exposed brick, artful lighting, thoughtfully placed sculptures, and a polished maple staircase. Guest rooms have been decorated with simple, clean lines and restful colors. There's a beautiful loft suite with a king-size bed and solarium. In the breakfast room, a striking arrangement of brilliant orange flowers creates a splash of color against the deep blue walls. For C$200 (US$124) a night, the entire third floor of one of the buildings can be yours—two bedrooms, an adjoining bathroom, and sitting area. This property is best suited to adults; well-behaved children 9 years and older are welcome.

539–541 Besserer St., Ottawa, ON K1N 6C6. © **877-891-5485** or 613/789-8320. Fax 613/789-8320. www.bennersbedandbreakfast.com. 8 units. C$85 and up (US$53) double; C$120 (US$74) loft. Rates include breakfast. MC, V. Limited street parking. *In room:* A/C, TV, phone in some rooms.

Gasthaus Switzerland Inn (★   A restored heritage property constructed of limestone in 1872, this family owned and operated inn features Swiss-style beds with cozy duvets and Swiss buffet breakfast. Each room is individually decorated and amenities vary. There are two specialty suites that are popular with couples. Each suite has a poster canopy bed, double Jacuzzi, CD stereo player, and ensuite bathroom. Efforts have been made to reduce allergens—windows can be opened, hardwood flooring has been used where possible, and non-allergenic duvets can be arranged if requested when making your reservation. The non-smoking rule is strictly enforced throughout the building. The property is best suited for adults and children over age 12.

89 Daly Ave., Ottawa, ON K1N 6E6. ℂ **888/663-0000** or 613/237-0335. Fax 613/594-3327. www.gasthaus switzerlandinn.com. 22 units. C$88 (US$55) economy double; C$158 (US$98) large double; C$228 (US$141) suite. Rates include breakfast. AE, DC, MC, V. Limited free parking. **Amenities:** Same-day dry cleaning/ laundry. *In room:* A/C, TV, dataport, hair dryer.

Quality Hotel Ottawa Downtown   Almost 40% of the rooms in this hotel are business class and plans are under way to further upgrade amenities for business travelers. Tourists can and do stay here quite comfortably, though. The location is prime for downtown and the parking is less expensive than at many other hotels in the area. Located on the southwest corner of King Edward Avenue and Rideau Street, it's easy to find. For the best view of the city and the Gatineau Hills, ask for a corner room or one facing northwest. The adjoining restaurant serves roadhouse-style Canadian and Continental meals with generous portions.

290 Rideau St., Ottawa, ON K1N 5Y3. ℂ **800/228-5151** or 613/789-7511. Fax 613/789-2434. www. qualityhotelottawa.com. 212 units. C$150 (US$93) double. Children 18 and under stay free in parents' room. Rollaway C$12 (US$7), crib free. AE, DC, DISC, MC, V. Parking C$9 (US$6). Pets accepted. **Amenities:** 1 restaurant/bar; secretarial services; limited room service; same-day dry cleaning/laundry; executive rooms. *In room:* A/C, TV w/ pay movies, dataport, coffeemaker.

INEXPENSIVE

Auberge "The King Edward" B&B (★   Conveniently situated close to the Rideau Canal and within easy walking distance of the ByWard Market, the Rideau Centre, and many downtown attractions, the King Edward is a distinguished Victorian home. The front parlor has been turned into a peaceful oasis of tropical plants, accented by a trickling fountain. A second sitting room offers comfortable chairs and sofas, suitable for reading or listening to music. Throughout the home you'll find many period details, including fireplaces, plaster moldings, pillars, and stained-glass windows. The elegant bedrooms, with turn-of-the-century furnishings, are generously proportioned. One room is large enough to accommodate a cot, and two other rooms have private balconies. At Christmas, a 3.6-m (12-ft.) high tree trimmed with Victorian decorations is a sight to behold. The owner also displays his collection of Christmas village pieces on the main floor of the property, which attracts much local interest. Children are welcomed at the discretion of the owner.

525 King Edward Ave., Ottawa, ON K1N 7N3. ℂ **800/841-8786** or 613/565-6700. www.bbcanada. com/kingedward. 3 units. C$75–$80 (US$50–$53) double; C$95 (US$63) large double with cot. Rates include breakfast. MC, V. Free parking. *In room:* A/C, TV, no phone.

Bella Notte B&B   The hosts of this fairly new B&B are charming and welcoming. Amenities are basic, but the hospitality of the owners and the care and attention given to the preparation and presentation of breakfast are worth experiencing. Bella Notte is well-positioned for reaching downtown on foot.

108 Daly Ave., Ottawa, ON K1N 6E7. ✆ **613/565-0497**. www.bellanottebb.com. 3 units. C$88 (US$55) and up double. Rates include breakfast. Limited street parking. *In room:* No phone.

Lampman House B&B   This Victorian heritage property, constructed of limestone, features 4-m (12-ft.) high ceilings and original interior trim. The front veranda, library with TV, and rooftop deck are all available for guests to enjoy. Rooms are not always available out of peak tourist season, so it's wise to call ahead. Lampman House is in a quiet residential district, within 15 to 30 minutes' walking distance of major tourist attractions.

369 Daly Ave., Ottawa, ON K1N 6G8. ✆ **877/591-4354** or 613/241-3696. Fax 613/789-8360. 3 units. C$85 (US$53) double. Rates include breakfast. MC, V. Limited free parking. **Amenities:** Business services. *In room:* Hair dryer, no phone.

Ottawa International Hostel   Before becoming a hostel, the building was the Carleton County Gaol (1862–1972). Guided tours of the former prison are available. Your bed for the night is a bunk in a jail cell or one of the dorms. Enjoy a quiet night's sleep behind bars—if the ghost of the last prisoner to be publicly hanged in Canada doesn't disturb you. If you are a Hostelling International member, you'll receive a discounted room rate. There is a daily charge of C50¢ (US30¢) per towel and C$2.50 (US$1.70) for bed linens. In 2001, the cozy TV lounge was updated with new leather couches and a big-screen TV. The communal kitchen was also updated, with new appliances, tables, and chairs. Lockers for storing food are available for guests. The dining room is housed in the former prison chapel, and in the summer, guests may use the barbecue in the garden. Washroom facilities, with washbasins, toilets, and showers, are unisex. Families may opt for a private room with bunk beds, which accommodates up to five people, but most likely your kids will want to sleep in the jail cells. Although the space is cramped and the beds are narrow, the experience will be authentic.

75 Nicholas St., Ottawa, ON K1N 7B9. ✆ **613/235-2595**. Fax 613/235-9202. www.hostellingintl.on.ca. 154 units. C$24 (US$15) per adult in dormitory; C$54 (US$33) private room (max. 5 people); children 9 and under free. AE, MC, V. Parking C$5 (US$3). **Amenities:** Game room; washers and dryers. *In room:* Tabletop fans, no phone.

3 The Glebe & South Central

The Glebe is a trendy, upper-middle-class family neighborhood lined with turn-of-the-century redbrick homes and a number of larger, elegant houses. Although the area's main street, Bank Street, has wonderful restaurants and shops, hotels and motels are scarce in this district. But some of the nicest B&Bs are to be found here, and many people prefer to be on a quiet back street than in the high-rises of downtown. Just south of the Glebe lies another quiet neighborhood, where you'll find the Carleton University campus, bordered by Dow's Lake, Bronson Avenue (one of the main arteries to downtown), and the Ottawa River.

MODERATE

Alanbury House ★★   Alanbury House is an elegant and welcoming B&B. The owners have meticulously redecorated the interior with chic Montreal style and taste. Furnishings and fabrics have been carefully selected to complement this beautiful three-story Victorian home. In the warmer months, a comfortable sunroom is the perfect place to relax and read. When the weather turns cold, snuggle up by the fireplace in the living room. If you're traveling as a family or would like a private sitting room, stay in the one-bedroom suite. The adjoining room can be used as a TV lounge or extra bedroom. The property is best suited for adults and children ages 8 and up.

119 Strathcona Ave., Ottawa, ON K1S 1X5. ✆ 613/234-8378. Fax 613/569-5691. alanbury@magma.ca. 3 units. C$119 (US$74) and up double; C$169 (US$105) 1-bedroom suite. Rates include breakfast. AE, DC, MC, V. Free parking. *In room:* A/C, TV, dataport, hair dryer.

Brighton House ⭐⭐   Brighton House is actually two neighboring houses, each the mirror image of the other. A splendid pair of Edwardian homes, Brighton House offers a choice of six rooms, each with its own personality and amenities. One suite has an adjoining sunroom with a pretty view of the garden, another suite has two bedrooms, and a third has an antique brass bed draped with lace and an adjoining sitting room with fireplace. Each house has a comfortable main-floor lounge with a fireplace. Breakfast is served to guests from both houses in one dining room. This property is beautifully decorated in keeping with the graceful and elegant period in which the homes were built. Rooms are tastefully furnished. The property is best suited for adults and children over age 12.

308 First Ave., Ottawa, ON K1S 2G8. ✆ 613/233-7777. www.brightonhouse.com. 6 units. C$109 (US$68) and up double; C$149 and up (US$92) 1-bedroom suite. Rates include breakfast. AE, DC, MC, V. Free parking. **Amenities:** Same-day dry cleaning. *In room:* A/C, TV, hair dryer, iron.

INEXPENSIVE

Bye-The-Way B&B   Situated on a quiet residential street in the Glebe, Bye-The-Way is a 1960s-era house tucked in the midst of century-old homes. This is basic accommodation at a reasonable price, and the hosts are pleasant and affable. The owners have thoughtfully created a lower-level suite suitable for families, so you'll get the friendliness of a B&B along with the independence of a separate entrance, kitchenette, phone, and TV. This open-plan suite contains one single and one double bed, and a cot can be arranged to allow a maximum occupancy of four people. The kitchenette is equipped with a fridge, microwave, two-ring hot plate, dishes, and utensils, but no dishwasher. A 10-minute walk will take you to the nearest park along leafy, shaded sidewalks.

310 First Ave., Ottawa, ON K1S 2G8. ✆ 613/232-6840. Fax 613/232-6840. www.byetheway.com. 4 units. C$85 (US$53) double. C$100 (US$62) 4 people sharing lower-level suite. Rate includes breakfast. Rollaway free. AE, DC, MC, V. Free parking. *In room:* A/C, TV, kitchenette, iron.

A Rose on Colonel By ⭐⭐ *Finds*   This cozy Edwardian-style home, built in 1925, is just steps from the Rideau Canal on a quiet residential street. Before becoming a B&B, the property was leased for many years by the American and French embassies as a diplomatic residence. The atmosphere is warm and friendly. The breakfast room is decorated with a collection of blue glass, strikingly displayed along the windowsills to catch the sunlight. The two bathrooms are shared among three guest rooms, but bathrobes have been thoughtfully supplied. A comfy lounge on the second floor is equipped with a fridge, microwave, coffeemaker, and phone. A short walk away is Brewer Park, bordered on its southern edge by the scenic Rideau River. The owner of the B&B will be happy to supply you or your children with crusts of bread to feed the ducks and swans on Brewer Pond.

9 Rosedale Ave., Ottawa, ON K1S 4T2. ✆ 613/291-7831. www.rosebandb.com. 3 units. C$88–$126 (US$55–$78) double. Rate includes breakfast. Rollaway/crib free. AE, V. Free parking. **Amenities:** Washer and dryer. *In room:* Ceiling fans, dataport, no phone.

Carleton University Tour and Conference Centre The student residences at Carleton are available between early May and late August. There are about 2,000 beds available in eight residence buildings. Most bedrooms are either single or double (two single beds) occupancy with shared bathrooms. The new Leeds building, which opened in 2001, offers two- and four-bedroom suites, all with double beds and one or two bathrooms per suite. These accommodations are ideal for families, priced at C$120 (US$74) per night for two adults and two children under 12. Rates include an all-you-can-eat breakfast in the large cafeteria. Athletic and recreational facilities on campus include an indoor pool, squash and tennis courts, a fitness center with sauna and whirlpool, a game room and video arcade. You can walk, bike, or in-line skate all the way downtown on canal-side pathways. At nearby Dow's Lake you can rent canoes, kayaks, and bicycles.

1125 Colonel By Dr., Ottawa ON K1S 5B6. ✆ **613/520-5611** late Aug–early May; ✆ **613/520-5609** early May–late Aug. Fax 613/520-3952. www.carleton.ca/housing/tourandconf. 2,000 units. C$67 (US$42) double, dorm style; C$95(US$59) double, new suite building; families of 2 adults and 2 children under 12 C$100–$120 (US$62–$74). Rates include breakfast. MC, V. Parking C$5 (US$3) per day Mon–Fri; free on weekends. **Amenities:** 1 cafeteria, 1 fast-food outlet, 1 food court; indoor pool; health club; tennis courts; hot tub; sauna; watersports/bicycle rental at Dow's Lake; game room; video arcade; washers and dryers. *In room:* A/C in some units, no phone.

4 Ottawa East

Just off the Queensway near St. Laurent Boulevard lies a little cluster of hotels. It may be too far to walk downtown, but don't let that deter you from staying in this district, because it offers lots of entertainment. St. Laurent Shopping Centre, with over 230 stores and services, is within walking distance. Several family entertainment venues, including the Silver City movie theater, the Gloucester Wave Pool, and the high-tech adventures of Cyberdome Entertainment, are in easy reach. Take in a game of AAA baseball at Jetform Stadium in season. A couple of minutes' drive north on St. Laurent Boulevard will bring you to the Canada Aviation Museum and the Musical Ride Centre, RCMP Rockcliffe Stables, and a couple of minutes in the opposite direction will take you to the Museum of Science and Technology. For those traveling by train, the hotels listed here are all a short cab ride from the station.

MODERATE

Comfort Inn East Most major cities and urban areas across Canada sport at least one of these moderately priced, comfortable hotels. Amenities are sparse, but the rooms are of a consistently good standard, and reliability is important when you're choosing somewhere to spend the night. Some units were redecorated in 2001, with new carpets, draperies, and bed linens.

1252 Michael St., Ottawa, ON K1J 7T1. ✆ **800/228-5150** or 613/744-2900. Fax 613/746-0836. www.choice hotels.ca. 69 units. C$120 (US$74) double. Children 18 and under stay free in parents' room. Rollaway C$8 (US$5). AE, DC, DISC, MC, V. Free parking. **Amenities:** Secretarial services; same-day dry cleaning/laundry. *In room:* A/C, TV w/ pay movies, coffeemaker, iron.

Hampton Inn ✪✪ *Value* A brand-new hotel that opened in 2000, the Hampton Inn has large guest rooms with high-quality furnishings and oversize bathrooms. Each room is equipped with a kitchenette that includes a microwave, sink, and small fridge (dishes and utensils are not supplied). The indoor pool area is spotless and spacious. A complimentary continental breakfast is served in the lobby lounge, and light fare is available in the evenings. As a result of its new and comfortable accommodations, indoor pool, and competitive pricing, the Hampton Inn has an edge over other options in the area.

100 Coventry Rd., Ottawa, ON K1K 4S3. ℂ **877/701-1281** or 613/741-2300. Fax 613/741-8689. www.hamptoninn.com. 179 units. C$125 (US$78) studio. Rate includes breakfast. Children 17 and under stay free in parents' room. Rollaway C$15 (US$9); crib free. AE, DC, DISC, MC, V. Free parking. **Amenities:** 1 breakfast room/lounge; indoor pool; exercise room; hot tub; secretarial services; massage; babysitting; washers and dryers; same-day dry cleaning/laundry. *In room:* A/C, TV, dataport, kitchenette, coffeemaker, hair dryer, iron.

WelcomINNS   A clean and comfortable room awaits you here. Some rooms have coffeemakers and small fridges. Facilities are basic, but the location near the rail station and close to the 417 (Queensway) may be an advantage for some travelers.

1220 Michael St., Ottawa, ON K1J 7T1. ℂ **800/387-4381** or 613/748-7800. Fax 613/748-0499. www.welcominns.com. 109 units. C$125 (US$78) double. Rates include continental breakfast. Children 17 and under stay free in parents' room. Rollaway C$10 (US$6). AE, DC, DISC, MC, V. Free parking. **Amenities:** Exercise room; hot tub; sauna; same-day dry cleaning/laundry. *In room:* A/C, TV w/ pay movies, dataport, fridge, hair dryer, iron.

5 Ottawa West

The hotels listed here are all good bets if you want to be a little closer to the Corel Centre or plan to explore the countryside west and south of Ottawa. Retail stores and family-style restaurants are within walking distance, and although you'll need to drive to downtown attractions, all of these hotels provide comfortable rooms and pools. If you find the downtown hotels a little pricey, or if they're full, consider staying in this area. Bayshore and Carlingwood are the two major shopping centers.

MODERATE

Best Western Barons Hotel ★ *Kids*   Although the location is a little far from the city center, the family-friendly nature of this hotel and its competitive pricing make it a worthwhile place to stay. Its proximity to the Queensway means that you can drive into the city in 15 minutes. The large regional shopping mall, Bayshore, is 5 minutes away, and the Corel Centre is only 10 minutes west. If you need to rent a car, there is a Budget car rental desk in the lobby. Staff are cheerful, knowledgeable, and polite. In the summer, ask them about the "Family Fun Deal," which may include anything from free comic books to museum and arcade passes or a disposable camera. Families also will enjoy the clean and bright indoor pool. In the summer, a patio and grassy area out back are popular with guests, who are welcome to use the barbecue. Rooms are larger than average, and most of the bathrooms have recently been retiled. Families may opt for the convenience of a limited number of one-bedroom suites, which have a sink, small fridge, and microwave but no dishes or utensils. The two largest suites have a two-ring hot plate, dishes, and utensils, in addition to the standard kitchenette fittings. Jacuzzis have recently been added to three suites.

3700 Richmond Rd., Ottawa, ON K2H 5B8. ℂ **800/528-1234** or 613/828-2741. Fax 613/596-4742. www.bestwestern.com/ca/baronshotel. 83 units. C$135 (US$84) double; C$175 (US$109) 1-bedroom suite; Children 17 and under stay free in parents' room. Rollaway C$10 (US$6); crib free. AE, DC, DISC, MC, V. Free parking. Pets C$10 (US$6). **Amenities:** 1 restaurant, 1 bar; indoor pool; exercise room; hot tub; sauna; secretarial services; limited room service; washers and dryers; same-day dry cleaning/laundry; executive rooms. *In room:* A/C, TV w/ pay movies, dataport, kitchenette in some units, coffeemaker, hair dryer, iron.

Best Western Macies Hotel ⚡ Macies is one of Ottawa's largest family-run hotels. Now in their third generation of family management and with more than 60 years of hospitality experience, the Macies staff are skilled at dealing with both tourists and business travelers. Enjoy the large outdoor pool in the summer. Video games available in all rooms. Westgate Shopping Centre, with around 45 stores and services, is directly opposite the hotel. A 10-minute drive will take you to the foot of the Peace Tower on Parliament Hill, or you can use the services of a shuttle bus in the peak tourist periods.

1274 Carling Ave., Ottawa, ON K1Z 7K8. ⓒ 800/268-5531 (Canada), 800/528-1234 (U.S.), or 613/728-1951. Fax 613/728-1955. www.macieshotel.com. 123 units. C$104–C$140 (US$64–US$87) double. Children 12 and under stay free in parents' room; C$5 (US$3) ages 13 and up. Rollaway C$9 (US$6); crib free. AE, DC, DISC, MC, V. Free parking. Domestic, house-trained pets accepted but cannot be left alone. **Amenities:** 1 restaurant, 1 lounge; large heated outdoor pool; health club; Jacuzzi; sauna; business services; limited room service; washers and dryers; same-day dry cleaning/laundry. *In room:* A/C, TV w/ pay movies, dataport, fridge, coffeemaker, hair dryer, iron.

Travelodge Hotel Ottawa West Refurbishment of guest rooms began in 1999, and by the end of 2001, 80% of the 200 units had been fully renovated, and now feature two queen-size beds and new bathrooms. Guest services have been enhanced, with the addition of room service and Web TV. Express check-out service is offered. The older tower is currently closed and will undergo renovations at a later date.

1376 Carling Ave., Ottawa, ON K1Z 7L5. ⓒ 800/578-7878 or 613/722-7600. Fax 613/722-2226. www.travelodge.com. 200 units. C$145 (US$90) double. Children 12 and under stay free in parents' room; C$10 (US$6) ages 13 and up. Rollaway C$10 (US$6); crib free. AE, DC, DISC, MC, V. Free parking. **Amenities:** 1 restaurant, 1 lounge; heated outdoor pool; secretarial services; limited room service; same-day dry cleaning/laundry. *In room:* A/C, TV w/ pay movies, dataport, fridge, coffeemaker, hair dryer, iron.

6 The Airport

Ottawa has a shortage of hotel rooms close to the airport, and the two places listed here are much in demand by business travelers. The problem is finally being addressed, with the completion of Southway Inn's expansion in late 2001 and plans under way for at least one new hotel to be built near the airport. Nevertheless, if you are traveling to Ottawa by air and would like a room close to the airport on arrival or prior to departure, these hotels are both comfortable. The Southway Inn has more amenities for families and business travelers than does the Airport Inn.

MODERATE

The Southway Inn ⚡ If you're seeking accommodations far from the high-rise jungle of downtown, this property in the south end of the city will suit. There are chain restaurants and services, including a bank and drugstore, nearby, and if you avoid traveling during rush hour, it's only a short drive from the action of downtown Ottawa. It's a short drive to the airport too. The indoor pool is bright and pleasant. The Southway Inn recently completed a major expansion that almost doubled its number of guest rooms, increased meeting/banquet space, and added a courtyard. Five new suites are available, all with full kitchens.

2431 Bank St. S., Ottawa, ON K1V 8R9. ⓒ 877/688-4929 or 613/737-0811. Fax 613/737-3207. www.southway.com. 170 units. C$145 (US$90) double; C$185 (US$115) suite with kitchen. Rollaway/crib C$15 (US$10). AE, DC, DISC, MC, V. Free parking. Pets C$15 (US$10) first day, C$5 (US$3) each additional day. **Amenities:** 1 restaurant/bar; indoor pool; exercise room; hot tub; sauna; secretarial services; limited room service; washers and dryers; same-day dry cleaning/laundry; executive rooms. *In room:* A/C, TV, dataport, kitchen in some units, fridge, coffeemaker, hair dryer, iron.

INEXPENSIVE

Adam's Airport Inn ★ *Value*   A 7-minute drive from the airport, this hotel is a good bet for a night's rest at either end of your vacation if you're traveling by air, especially if you have a late arrival or early-morning start. The rates are spot-on for what's on offer, which is a clean and comfortable bed, friendly desk staff, and free parking. Just the basics, nicely delivered. Although the building is set back a little way from busy Bank Street, ask for a room at the back overlooking the quiet residential neighborhood. A complimentary continental breakfast and 24-hour coffee are available in the lobby. There is one luxury suite available with king-size bed and in-room double Jacuzzi at C$135 (US$84).

2721 Bank St., Ottawa, ON K1T 1M8. (✆ **800/261-5835** or 613/738-3838. Fax 613/736-8211. 62 units. C$79 (US$49) double; C$89 (US$55) family rate (4 people) in a room with two double beds. Rollaway C$10 (US$6), crib free. AE, DC, MC, V. Free parking. Pets C$10 (US$7) per day. **Amenities:** Exercise room; washers and dryers. *In room:* A/C, TV, dataport, fridge, hair dryer.

7 On the Quebec Side

For some reason, the perception exists that Hull is "way over there," when in fact you're only a few minutes from the major attractions in Ottawa. Hull has its share of good-quality places to stay, ranging from B&Bs to upper-end hotel chains. I've listed three here, but you could also consider the **Best Western Hotel Jacques Cartier** ✆ **800/265-8550** or the **Four Points by Sheraton Hull–Ottawa** ✆ **800/567-9607.** If you're a nonsmoker, remember that you're likely to run into a lot of smokers in hotels, restaurants, and bars on this side of the Ottawa River.

EXPENSIVE

Hilton Lac Leamy ★★★   This fabulous hotel complements the urban resort of Casino de Hull, standing between two bodies of water—Lac Leamy and Lac de la Carrière, with its majestic fountain. The rooms are all larger than standard and you have a choice of view: the Ottawa skyline or Gatineau Hills. The ostentatious public areas are designed to impress. Extensive use of wood and marble in the interior convey warmth and luxury. A series of remarkable blown-glass sculptures adorn the lobby and main public areas. The luxurious spa offers a wide range of treatments. Truly a world-class hotel.

3 boulevard du Casino, Hull, PQ J8Y 6X4. (✆ **866/488-7888** or 819/790-6444. Fax 819/790-6408. www.lacleamy.hilton.com. 349 units. C$275 (US$171) double; C$600 (US$372) suite. Children 18 and under stay free in parents' room. Rollaway/crib free. AE, DC, MC, V. Free parking. **Amenities:** 2 restaurants; 2 lounges; indoor and outdoor pools; tennis courts; fitness center; spa; Jacuzzi; sauna; bike/ in-line skate rental at nearby Lac Leamy; children's center; theater room; concierge; business center; salon; 24-hour room service; massage; babysitting; same-day dry cleaning/laundry; executive rooms. *In room:* A/C, TV w/ pay movies, dataport, minibar, coffeemaker, hair dryer, iron, safe.

Holiday Inn Plaza la Chaudière ★   A convenient and pretty location opposite a city park where the Theatre de l'Ile (Island Theatre) performs in the summer. A couple of minutes' walk will link you up with bike and walking pathways along the Ottawa River and you're only a short drive or bike ride away from the entrance to Gatineau Park. RentABike operates an outlet at the hotel, so you can arrange your bike or in-line skate rental right on the premises. Rentals include helmets, locks, and maps. The lobby has a beautiful display of indoor plants and a waterfall. Two rooms are accessible for guests with disabilities.

2 rue Montcalm, Hull, PQ J8X 4B4. 🕿 **800/567-1962** (Canada) or 819/778-3880. Fax 819/778-3309. www. rosdevhotels.com. 238 units. C$200 (US$124) double; C$275 (US$171) 1-bedroom suite. Children under 18 stay free in parents' room. C$15 (US$9) per extra person 18 and over. Rollaway C$10 (US$6). AE, DC, MC, V. Parking C$10 (US$6). Pets accepted under 30 lb. weight. **Amenities:** 1 restaurant; one lounge; indoor pool; exercise room; Jacuzzi; sauna; bike/in-line skate rental; concierge; business center; limited room service; babysitting; same-day dry cleaning; executive floors. *In room:* A/C, TV w/ pay movies, dataport, minibar in some rooms, coffeemaker, hair dryer, iron.

Château Cartier Resort ⚘⚘⚘　　A luxuriously comfortable resort set in 62 hectares (152 acres) of rolling countryside on the north shore of the Ottawa River, just a few minutes' drive from downtown Ottawa and Hull. The majority of the guest rooms are junior suites, with a comfortable sitting room and separate bedroom with French doors. Leisure and recreational facilities are outstanding. There's an 18-hole golf course on the property with teaching professionals on hand. Two outdoor tennis courts, indoor racquetball and squash courts, fitness center with top-quality equipment, and full-service spa are just some of the activities available for guests. In the winter, there's a skating rink, tobogganing, tubing, cross-country skiing, snowshoeing, and horse-drawn sleigh rides. Downhill skiing is nearby and seasonal packages range from golf getaways to ski weekends. Public areas and guest rooms are extremely well-appointed and furnished.

1170 chemin Aylmer, Aylmer, PQ J9H 5E1. 🕿 **800/807-1088** or 819/777-1088. Fax 819/777-7161. www.chateaucartier.com. 129 units. C$199 (US$123) and up double (junior suite). Children under 18 stay free in parents' room. Rollaway free. AE, DC, MC, V. Free parking. Pets accepted C$25 (US$16). **Amenities:** 1 restaurant/lounge; indoor pool; golf course; 2 tennis courts; health club & spa; Jacuzzi; sauna; bike/in-line skate rental; other sports equipment rental; seasonal children's programs; concierge; business center; limited room service; babysitting; same-day dry cleaning/laundry. *In room:* A/C, TV w/ pay movies, dataport, minibar, coffeemaker, hair dryer, iron.

5

Dining

Dining out is one of life's great pleasures—a sensual blend of terrific food, memorable setting, and expert service. In this chapter, I've listed some of the best places to eat in Ottawa and Hull. The region is multi-ethnic and the population is large enough to support a wide range of excellent restaurants.

You can dine by candlelight at a lace-covered table in a traditional dark-wood-and-burgundy room, soak up the atmosphere in an Italian pasticceria while you sip an espresso, or chomp pancakes and bacon in a diner accompanied by a bottomless mug of coffee. If you want to kick it up a notch, head for a cafe and order *café au lait dans un bol* (European-style coffee made with warm milk and served in a large bowl) or experience the creations, featuring Canadian ingredients, of talented local chefs. Or if British afternoon tea, pad thai, or fresh mussels are more what you're looking for, you'll be more than satisfied.

Whenever the weather permits, go alfresco. Whether it's morning coffee on a busy sidewalk, a leisurely lunch on the banks of the Rideau Canal, or a romantic evening under the stars, eating outdoors heightens the experience.

Out-of-towners who stroll around the city will sooner or later come face to face with an Ottawa institution—the chip wagon. Their offerings hold no appeal for me, but I cannot deny their popularity in this part of the country. As well as the usual deep-fried sliced potatoes, many wagons serve poutine, a Québécois concoction of fries topped with cheese curds and smothered in gravy. As in most Canadian cities, sausage and hot dog carts edge their way onto downtown sidewalks once the weather begins to warm up in the spring.

The following listings are by no means the only places to enjoy good food in the Ottawa area. Rather, the idea is to give you a sampling of the broad range of excellent cuisine that awaits you there. Bon appétit!

DINING NOTES Dining out in Ottawa does not have to be an expensive venture, but be aware that taxes are high. Meals are subject to 8% provincial sales tax and 7% GST, so when you factor in an average tip, a whopping 30% is added to the bill. Tipping is usually left to the diner's discretion, although some establishments add 15% to the bill for parties of six or more. Wine prices in restaurants are quite high—don't be surprised to find your favorite vintage at double the price you'd pay at the liquor store. Save a little money by ordering an Ontario wine. Niagara vineyards produce some distinguished wines that are increasingly gaining international respect.

1 Restaurants by Cuisine

AFTERNOON TEA
Zoe's at the Fairmont Château Laurier ★★★ (Downtown East of the Canal, $$$, *p. 80*)

AMERICAN
Hard Rock Café ★ (Downtown East of the Canal, $$, *p. 80*)

ASIAN
Shanghai Restaurant ★ (Chinatown, $$, *p. 88*)

BAGELS
Kettleman's Bagels ★ (the Glebe, $, *p. 86*)
Ottawa Bagelshop & Deli (Wellington Street West, $, *p. 87*)

BAKERY
The French Baker/Le Boulanger Français (Downtown East of the Canal, $, *p. 82*)
Le Moulin de Provence (Downtown East of the Canal, $, *p. 83*)
Wild Oat Bakery and Natural Foods (the Glebe, $, *p. 86*)

BISTRO
The Black Tomato ★★★ (Downtown East of the Canal, $$$, *p. 79*)
Von's Bistro (the Glebe, $$, *p. 85*)

CAFE
La Brûlerie ★ (Hull, $, *p. 92*)

CANADIAN
Domus ★★★ (Downtown East of the Canal, $$$, *p. 79*)

CHINESE
Yangtze (Chinatown, $$, *p. 88*)

CREPES
Crepe de France ★ (Downtown East of the Canal, $$, *p. 80*)

DELI
Dunn's Famous Delicatessen (Downtown West of the Canal, $, *p. 75*)

DESSERTS
Oh So Good Desserts Café (Downtown East of the Canal, $, *p. 83*)

DINER
Elgin St. Diner (Downtown West of the Canal, $, *p. 78*)

ECLECTIC
Infusion ★★ (the Glebe, $$, *p. 84*)
Marchélino ★★ (Downtown East of the Canal, $, *p. 82*)

FRENCH
Bistro 115 ★ (Downtown East of the Canal, $$$, *p. 79*)
Le Pied de Cochon ★★★ (Hull, $$, *p. 91*)
Le 1908 ★ (Hull, $$, *p. 91*)

FUSION
Savana Café ★★ (Downtown West of the Canal, $$, *p. 75*)

ICE CREAM
Cow's Ottawa (Downtown East of the Canal, $, *p. 82*)
Pasticceria Gelateria Italiana Ltd. ★ (Little Italy, $, *p. 89*)
Piccolo Grande (Downtown East of the Canal, $, *p. 83*)
Pure Gelato ★★ (Downtown West of the Canal, $, *p. 78*)

INDIAN
Haveli (Downtown East of the Canal, $$, *p. 81*)
The Roses Café (Downtown West of the Canal, $$, *p. 75*)

ITALIAN
The Canal Ritz ★ (the Glebe, $$, *p. 85*)
Ciccio (Little Italy, $$, *p. 89*)
La Roma ★★★ (Little Italy, $$$, *p. 89*)
Mamma Grazzi's Kitchen ★ (Downtown East of the Canal, $$, *p. 81*)
Oregano's Pasta Market (Downtown East of the Canal, $$, *p. 81*)

MEDITERRANEAN
Bravo Bravo ★★ (Downtown West of the Canal, $$$, *p. 73*)

PIZZA
Café Colonnade ★ (Downtown West of the Canal, $$, *p. 74*)

SEAFOOD
The Fish Market ★★ (Downtown East of the Canal, $$$, *p. 80*)
Flippers ★ (the Glebe, $$$, *p. 84*)
The Pelican Fishery and Grill ★ (Farther Out, $$, p. 90)

TAKEOUT
L'Amuse Gueule ★★ (the Glebe, $, *p. 85*)
BeaverTails (Downtown East of the Canal, $, *p. 82*)
Fettucine's (Downtown West of the Canal, $, *p. 78*)
Luciano's ★★ (Little Italy, $, *p. 89*)

Parma Ravioli (Wellington Street West, $, *p. 87*)
Thyme & Again ★★ (Wellington Street West, $, *p. 87*)

TEX-MEX
The Lone Star Cafe (Farther Out, $$, *p. 90*)

THAI
Coriander Thai (Downtown West of the Canal, $$, *p. 75*)

VEGETARIAN
The Green Door (Farther Out, $, *p. 90*)
Peace Garden Café (Downtown East of the Canal, $, *p. 83*)
The Table ★ (Wellington Street West, $, *p. 87*)

VIETNAMESE
New Mee Fung ★ (Chinatown, $$, *p. 88*)

---

2 Downtown (West of the Canal)

You'll find loads of delightful restaurants tucked in the side streets and squeezed in between the high-rise buildings of the downtown core. Office workers and "suits" with cell phones grafted onto one ear fill these eateries at lunchtime on weekdays, but you can beat the crowd if you arrive before noon. Elgin Street is quite lively in the evening because of the plethora of bars and restaurants, but further west the foot traffic can be pretty light after around 6pm—it can seem too quiet in some spots. Parking may be a challenge around noon on weekdays so allow extra time to hunt for an empty meter.

EXPENSIVE

Bravo Bravo ★★ MEDITERRANEAN   The main dining area at the front of this large restaurant is bright and airy with plenty of space between tables. A warm Mediterranean sunset palette, scuffed wooden floors, and a faux stone archway complete the picture. Check out the display of authentic hand-painted Venetian masks on one of the walls. If you're a risotto fan, have a taste of Bravo Bravo's offerings. The mushroom, pancetta, and onion risotto is creamy smooth and al dente. It will stick to your ribs—and even feed two or three kids from one serving. After dinner, play a game of pool or sit at the granite bar and sip a drink or two. A narrow alley at the side of the restaurant has been turned into a summer Mediterranean paradise, with bright wall murals and tables for dining. If you want to savor Bravo Bravo at home or in your hotel suite, pick up some antipasto and rich, gooey desserts from the takeout section at the entrance.

292 Elgin St. © 613/233-7525. Reservations recommended weekends only. Main courses C$12–$20 (US$7–$12). AE, DC, MC, V. Mon–Sat 11am–2am, Sun 10:30am–2am.

Gourmet to Go

Ottawa must have a lot of enthusiastic resident foodies because the number of top-quality upper-end food retailers and specialty shops is satisfyingly high. For visitors looking for a quick but delicious meal to take home to their hotel suite or portable food for a picnic, this is good news. The obvious place to head to first is the **ByWard Market**. In spring, summer, and fall, local farmers proudly sell their produce. The quality is exceptional. An abundance of fresh flowers in season adds color and fragrance to the market atmosphere. Here are a few more destinations for food and wine lovers: **Godiva Chocolatier Inc.** in the Rideau Shopping Centre © **613/234-4470** has exquisite chocolate confectionery. You'll pay dearly for the experience, but it's worth every penny. **L'Amuse Gueule,** 915 Bank St. © **613/234-9400** has a French chef/owner and it shows. Pick up French and Québécois cheeses here and traditional French dishes including boeuf bourguignon and coq au vin. **Le Cordon Bleu Ottawa Culinary Arts Institute** at 453 Laurier Ave. E. © **613/236-2433** offers a variety of cooking classes or you can dine in the gastronomic restaurant featuring fine French cuisine. **Liquor Control Board of Ontario (LCBO)** has an incredible retail outlet at 275 Rideau St. © **613/789-5226,** including two floors of wines, beers, and liquors from around the world. Gifts and accessories are also available. Educational programs and demonstrations include Tuscan cuisine, tutored Scotch tastings, wine appreciation, and cocktail preparation. **Loblaw's Vanier Market,** 100 McArthur Ave. © **613/ 744-0705,** opened in 2001. This is your best bet for grocery staples. **Luciano's** at 106 Preston St. © **613/236-7545** has a wide range of homemade pasta and delectable sauces. Oven-ready lasagna and cannelloni, plus gelato, olive oil, bread—it's a gourmet must-go. **Nicastro's,** the specialty food supermarket, has a European flavor to its range of products. You'll find them at 1558 Merivale Rd. © **613/744-0705.** If you're a fan of fresh fish and seafood, pay a visit to **Pelican Fishery** (also a restaurant) at 1500 Bank St. in the Blue Heron Mall © **613/526-0995. Thyme & Again** at 1255 Wellington St. W. © **613/722-6277** is a take-home food shop and catering establishment. You can choose soups, salads, side dishes, main courses, and desserts from an ever-changing menu.

MODERATE

Café Colonnade ⋆ PIZZA   Pizzas almost fly from the oven onto tables and out the door at this place because Ottawans love Colonnade's pizza. And there's a lot to like—the thick crust with a sprinkling of cheese around the edge, the generous smear of tangy tomato sauce, and the gooey mozzarella that holds the toppings in place. Personal pizzas will fill most grown-up tummies or two kids at lunchtime, or you can order a medium or large and let everyone dig in. Although you really should go there for the pizza, the menu offers pasta, veal, chicken, manicotti, cannelloni, and other dishes. North American fare, including sandwiches and burgers, is also listed. The dining room is spacious and plainly furnished—the focus is clearly on the food. An outdoor terrace stretches along one side of the building, providing a place to hang out on warm summer days and evenings.

280 Metcalfe St. ℂ **613/237-3179.** Pizza C$7–$19 (US$4–$12); main courses C$7–$11 (US$4–$7). AE, DC, MC, V. Sun–Thurs 11am–10pm or 11pm; Fri–Sat 11am–11pm or midnight.

Coriander Thai THAI   A small restaurant tucked away a couple of blocks from the big hotels and office blocks of downtown, Coriander Thai offers a variety of Thai dishes. To begin your meal, choose from spring rolls, stuffed mussels, pork or chicken satay, or classic Thai soups prepared with fresh lime juice, lemongrass, chilies, coriander, coconut milk, and ginger. Salads, curries, seafood, and vegetable dishes abound for the main course. To adjust the heat in any dish, just mention to your server whether you want it turned up a notch or down a notch. The tables are close together and a lack of background noise makes it a little too easy to overhear other diners' conversations, but the service is quietly courteous and the food is fresh tasting.

282 Kent St. ℂ **613/233-2828.** Main courses C$9–$15 (US$6–$9). AE, DC, MC, V. Mon–Thurs 11:30am–2:30pm and 5pm–10pm; Fri 11:30am–2:30pm and 5pm–10pm; Sat 5pm–11pm; Sun 5pm–10pm.

The Roses Café INDIAN   East Indian cuisine is always a culinary adventure because everyone can spoon as much or as little of each dish onto their plate as they like. Typically, there are a lot of meatless choices and vegetables are presented with delicately spiced sauces. The appetizers and accompanying dishes are lots of fun to eat. Try the pappadums—thin, crispy chip-like disks that melt in your mouth. With a focus on South Indian cuisine, the Roses menu features the *dosa,* a rice and lentil flour crepe filled with a variety of Indian-style vegetables. Their butter chicken curry is mildly spiced and has earned a reputation for excellence in the city. Takeout is available. The success of the Gladstone Avenue location prompted the owners to open two more: Roses Café Too, at 3710 Richmond Rd., and Roses Café Also, at 349 Dalhousie St.

523 Gladstone Ave. ℂ **613/233-5574.** Reservations recommended on weekends. Main courses C$6–C$12 (US$4–$7). AE, DC, MC, V. Mon–Fri 11:30am–2pm and 5–10pm; Sat–Sun 11:30am–2:30pm and 5–10pm.

Savana Café ★★ FUSION   The walls of the Savana Café are warm, vivid, and tropical. Intense Caribbean blue, brilliant green, and exquisite sunset colors put you in the mood for fun and the food makes you want to sing (reggae, possibly?). West African–style vegetable stir-fry and sweet basil shrimp are two absolutely divine dishes. Or try the two-potato fries, coconut rice, pad thai, satay, or curry chicken—there's something for everyone. Servers are enthusiastic and knowledgeable. Don't be shy to ask for the ingredients of a particular dish or for a recommendation for younger taste buds. Come hungry because the portions are generous and you won't be able to stop yourself from cleaning your plate. Savana is a popular spot and fills up quickly on weekdays at lunchtime. There's a small terrace out front in the shade of mature trees.

431 Gilmour St. ℂ **613/233-9159.** Reservations recommended. Main courses C$10–$15 (US$6–$9). AE, DC, MC, V. Mon–Thurs 11:30am–3pm and 5–10pm; Fri 11:30am–10pm; Sat 5–10pm.

INEXPENSIVE

Dunn's Famous Delicatessen DELI   If you want to sample an authentic Montreal smoked meat sandwich without making the 2-hour trip from Ottawa, dive into Dunn's and sink your teeth into a stack of hand-carved smoked meat, brought in fresh from the Dunn's smokehouse in Montreal. Dunn's opened for business in Montreal in 1927, and the first Ottawa restaurant opened in 1990.

Ottawa Dining

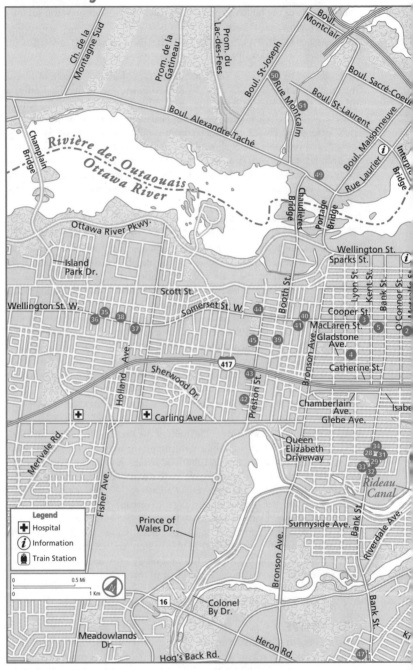

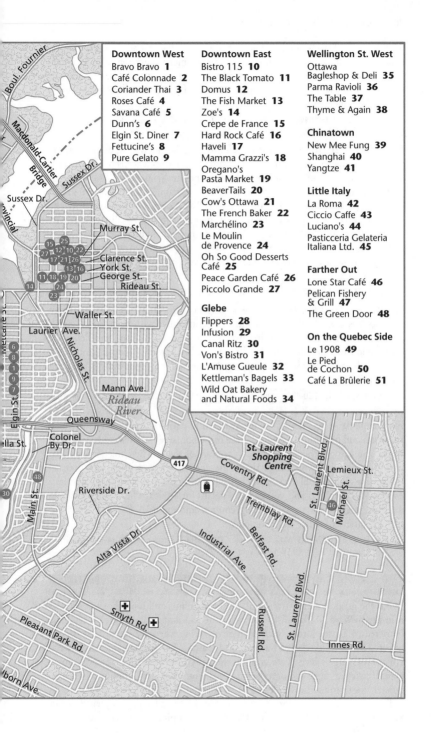

Downtown West
Bravo Bravo **1**
Café Colonnade **2**
Coriander Thai **3**
Roses Café **4**
Savana Café **5**
Dunn's **6**
Elgin St. Diner **7**
Fettucine's **8**
Pure Gelato **9**

Downtown East
Bistro 115 **10**
The Black Tomato **11**
Domus **12**
The Fish Market **13**
Zoe's **14**
Crepe de France **15**
Hard Rock Café **16**
Haveli **17**
Mamma Grazzi's **18**
Oregano's
Pasta Market **19**
BeaverTails **20**
Cow's Ottawa **21**
The French Baker **22**
Marchélino **23**
Le Moulin
de Provence **24**
Oh So Good Desserts
Café **25**
Peace Garden Café **26**
Piccolo Grande **27**

Glebe
Flippers **28**
Infusion **29**
Canal Ritz **30**
Von's Bistro **31**
L'Amuse Gueule **32**
Kettleman's Bagels **33**
Wild Oat Bakery
and Natural Foods **34**

Wellington St. West
Ottawa
Bagleshop & Deli **35**
Parma Ravioli **36**
The Table **37**
Thyme & Again **38**

Chinatown
New Mee Fung **39**
Shanghai **40**
Yangtze **41**

Little Italy
La Roma **42**
Ciccio Caffe **43**
Luciano's **44**
Pasticceria Gelateria
Italiana Ltd. **45**

Farther Out
Lone Star Café **46**
Pelican Fishery
& Grill **47**
The Green Door **48**

On the Quebec Side
Le 1908 **49**
Le Pied
de Cochon **50**
Café La Brûlerie **51**

The decor is a little scuffed around the edges, but that just adds to its comfortable, mom's-kitchen kind of appeal. With customers chattering, dishes clattering, and servers dashing around, it's an unpretentious place. The Elgin Street location never closes, so whether you're hungry for breakfast, lunch, or dinner, Dunn's is ready for you.

220 Elgin St. ✆ **613/230-6444**. Most items under C$10 (US$6). AE, DC, MC, V. Daily 24 hours. Also at 57 Bank St. ✆ **613/230-4005**. Mon–Fri 7am–9pm, Sat–Sun 8am–9pm.

Elgin St. Diner DINER   This is a comfy, neighborhood kind of place where you can saunter in, flop into a chair, and hang out with a coffee while the kids slurp milk shakes and chomp peanut butter and jam sandwiches. The breakfast special features two eggs, your choice of bacon, ham, or sausage, home fries, baked beans, toast, and coffee for C$4.50 (US$3), or you can choose from the variety of omelets or pancakes with real maple syrup on the all-day breakfast menu. There are plenty of old-fashioned dinners, including meat loaf, shepherd's pie, and liver and onions. Folks who live for traditional comfort food will feel right at home. Servers are cheerful, and you can drop in any time—they never close.

374 Elgin St. ✆ **613/237-9700**. Most items under C$10 (US$6). AE, DC, MC, V. Daily 24 hours.

Fettucine's TAKEOUT   If you're staying in a downtown suite with kitchen facilities, pay a visit to Fettucine's and stock your fridge with fresh pasta, sauces, and ready-to-eat salads. The spinach-and-cheese ravioli is filling and delicious. Other good bets are chicken parmigiana and basil pesto. Lasagna, cannelloni, pasta salad, and Caesar salad are also regular menu items. Everything is made on the premises.

280C Elgin St. ✆ **613/230-4723**. Most items under C$10 (US$6). AE, V. Mon–Sat 11am–8pm, Sun 11am–7pm.

Pure Gelato ★★ *Finds* ICE CREAM/CAFE   You can never have too much ice cream and it's handy to know a place or two outside the ByWard Market area where you can get the good stuff. Here's one of them. The choice is dizzying, with lots of fruit flavors, more than nine chocolate concoctions, and unusual flavors like ginger, Toblerone, and chestnut. Hot, golden malted Belgian waffles are only C$5 (US$3) and you can add gelato for a buck. Plunk yourself down on shiny metallic stools at the long counter and enjoy. A European-style bar serves a variety of coffee-based beverages.

350 Elgin St. ✆ **613/237-3799**. Most items under C$10 (US$6). V. Summer daily 11am–midnight; winter Sun–Wed 11am–11pm, Thurs–Sat 11am–midnight.

3 Downtown (East of the Canal)

By far the greatest concentration of good restaurants and food shops in Ottawa is in the ByWard Market district. East of the Rideau Canal, the area is officially bordered by Sussex Drive, St. Patrick Street, King Edward Avenue, and Rideau Street. The ByWard Market building and seasonal farmer's market run between York and George streets. Late at night the bar crowd makes its presence known here. If you're a night owl or a party animal, you'll feel right at home. There are quieter, more romantic venues to sip a cocktail or indulge in a good meal as well—there's something for everyone in the Market. Parking is plentiful, but because of the popularity of the dining and shopping here, spaces are scarce. If you don't luck out on the first or second pass, bite the bullet and park in one of the open-air or underground lots. It may cost a little more, but you're saved the time and stress of driving around in circles, and you can leave your vehicle for hours for a flat fee of C$10 (US$6) or less, whereas most meters in the market allow a maximum of 1 or 2 hours at certain times of the day.

EXPENSIVE

Bistro 115 ✯ FRENCH   This restaurant, housed in an Edwardian property in the heart of the ByWard Market district, is everything a romantic restaurant should be: dark wood, deep burgundy walls and linens, candlelit tables, lace cloths, and formal, attentive service. In winter, a cozy fireplace adds warmth to the dining room. Summer diners often retreat to the rear courtyard, shaded by grapevines and a maple tree. The food doesn't have the lively personality that the kitchens in The Black Tomato and Domus inject into their creations, which makes the prices here a bit hard to swallow. Best value is the mid-day table d'hôte, which gives you a choice of three appetizers, five main courses, and dessert for C$19 (US$12).

110 Murray St. ℭ **613/562-7244.** Reservations recommended. Main courses C$14–$26 (US$9–$16). AE, MC, V. Mon 11:30am–9pm; Tues–Fri 11:30am–9:30pm; Sat 10:30am–10pm; Sun 10:30am–9pm.

The Black Tomato ✯✯✯ BISTRO   This is one of the best places to eat in the ByWard Market area, with top marks for the food and the surroundings. The kitchen has heaps of culinary talent, so prepare yourself for a hedonistic evening. If the weather is warm, you can retreat to the back patio in the picturesque courtyard. Make the scrumptious Sunday brunch a family event. Three courses (granola or soup; egg special or French toast; dessert or sorbet; and coffee, tea, or juice) are yours for C$14 (US$9). My daughter polished off a wedge of French toast (cut from a round loaf) with strawberries and mango whipped cream, sautéed potatoes, and bacon, while I savored every spoonful of my black bean and corn chowder. Arrive early because the place gets extremely busy, especially in the evening.

11 George St. ℭ **613/789-8123.** Reservations accepted only for parties of 8 or more. Main courses C$16–$24 (US$10–$15). AE, MC, V. Mon–Sat 11:30am–10pm or 11pm; Sun 11:00am–10pm or 11pm.

Domus ✯✯✯ CANADIAN   Extremely popular with Ottawans and visitors alike, Domus's chef John Taylor creates menus that feature Canada's freshest available regional, seasonal, and often organic products. You can watch Taylor and his team at work in the shiny stainless-steel open kitchen at the rear of this compact restaurant. The decor is simple, with worn wooden floors, polished wood tables, and unfussy wrought-iron chairs—the message seems to be that the food is what shines here. Lovers of fine cuisine will delight in the menu, which changes daily. At lunch you might find grilled sausage, red onion, and aged Canadian cheddar cheese frittata with roasted potato and cress; Ontario Bosc pear and Quebec endive salad; or shallot, mushroom, and Blue Island mussel chowder with smoked trout, Yukon gold potato, fresh thyme, and leeks. (This last dish is rich, flavorful, and wonderfully aromatic.) For dinner, savor organic beetroot borscht, Quebec foie gras, Ontario bobwhite quail, or pan-roasted Mariposa Farm duck breast. Vegetables are imaginative—poached celery root, Chanterelle mushrooms, grilled radicchio, and wok-seared bok choy. Service is friendly and efficient. Next door is Domus kitchenware store; enter through the restaurant or from the street. It's a gourmet's delight.

87 Murray St. ℭ **613/241-6007.** Main courses C$9–$23 (US$6–$14). AE, DC, MC, V. Mon–Sat 11:30am–2pm and 6pm–9:30pm; Sun brunch 11am–2:30pm.

The Fish Market ★★ SEAFOOD   Ottawa's original fresh fish restaurant, established in 1979, has an astounding array of fish and seafood from around the world. Seafood lovers will find the menu a delight, with fresh oysters, salmon or shrimp pasta, lobster, Alaskan crab legs, scallops, tuna, marlin, and any number of other sea-dwelling creatures to choose from. The menu is refreshed twice a day as supplies ebb and flow in the kitchen. My daughter, who has eaten her fair share of fish and chips in England, declared the battered cod and chips the best she'd tasted this side of the Atlantic. I'm also a fan of fresh fish, having lived by the sea for a number of years, and the steamed mussels with white wine, garlic, and fresh vegetables met with my approval. Upstairs is the more casual Coasters Seafood Grill, with a central fireplace and open kitchen. There are more non-fishy menu choices here than downstairs and prices are a little lower.

54 York St. ✆ 613/2413474. Fish Market main courses C$13 (US$8) and up; Coasters main courses C$9–$13 (US$6–$8). AE, DC, MC, V. Main restaurant Mon–Thurs 11:30am–2pm and 5–10pm; Fri 11:30am–2pm and 5–11pm; Sat 11:30am–2:30pm and 5–11pm; Sun 11:30am–3pm and 5–10pm. Coasters daily 11:30am–midnight.

Zoe's ★★★ AFTERNOON TEA   There is nothing more civilized than afternoon tea, and the Château Laurier does it very well, from the white linen to the silver tea service and waiters in waistcoats and bow ties. Tea is served in the late afternoon in the glass-enclosed terrace of Zoe's restaurant (on the right side of the main hotel lobby). Have a good breakfast on the day you plan to visit and skip lunch because British afternoon tea is a substantial offering. The full tea at the Château Laurier consists of fresh fruit cup, seasonal fruit tartlets, afternoon tea cake, Victorian scones with Devonshire cream and strawberry jam, dainty finger sandwiches (English cucumber and cream cheese, smoked turkey with raspberry mayonnaise, and salmon and dill herb), and tea, coffee, or juice. No less than nine teas are listed and there's not a teabag in sight. Instead, waiters supply you with a silver-plated strainer that rests on your china cup to catch the tea leaves. You can almost see the ghosts of Edwardian ladies reaching for the teapot.

Fairmont Château Laurier, 1 Rideau St. ✆ 613/241-1414. Reservations recommended. C$20 (US$12) for full afternoon tea. AE, DC, MC, V. Afternoon tea Mon–Fri 3–5:30pm.

MODERATE

Crepe de France ★ CREPES   With red-and-white checkered tablecloths and tables for two, Crepe de France offers an intimate setting for a meal. Dishes are traditional French cafe style, with steak and *frites* and all-you-can-eat mussels (the latter on Tuesdays only) starring as two of their house specialties. The crepes are generously proportioned; come hungry because you won't want to leave anything on your plate. Both savory and sweet crepes are delicious.

76 Murray St. ✆ 613/241-1220. Reservations recommended Tues, Fri, and Sat evenings and Sun brunch. Main courses C$10–$18 (US$6–$11). AE, DC, MC, V. Mon–Thurs 11am–late, Fri 11am–1am, Sat–Sun 10am–1am.

Hard Rock Café ★★ AMERICAN   If you're a rock music fan, you'll find the collection of memorabilia from rock's most legendary performers jaw-dropping. Make sure you take the time to stroll around the place and don't miss upstairs. There are posters, jackets, records, instruments, and other bits and pieces on display. I was impressed by signed guitars from Brian May of Queen and David Bowie, but there are others if your taste in music runs in a different direction. No matter what your age, you'll recognize at least some of the bands.

Rock videos blare from TV screens, and when the restaurant is busy, the atmosphere is charged. There are two outdoor patios for summer toe-tapping and tabletop drumming. But stop singing along long enough to eat. Burgers, steaks, fajitas, chicken breast, and pot roast are all menu favorites. And how good is their hot-fudge sundae, made with Hard Rock Café's unbelievably rich signature ice cream? You'll just have to try it for yourself. For Hard Rock Café merchandise, including the legendary T-shirts, stop into the shop just inside the entrance on the left.

73 York St. © 613/241-2442. Reservations accepted only for parties of 6 or more. Main courses C$8–$25 (US$5–$16). AE, DC, MC, V. Daily 11:30am–late.

Haveli INDIAN   Popular with Ottawans, Haveli specializes in authentic North Indian cuisine, prepared by a team of chefs from various regions of India. The dining room reflects traditional Indian decor, with high-back chairs in intricately carved dark wood, and brass plates on the tables. The buffet, served for lunch every day except Saturday (when they are closed for lunch) and on Sunday evenings, allows novice and experienced samplers of Indian cuisine to taste a variety of dishes, from meat curries to tandoori chicken, naan, rice, samosas, vegetables, and salads, plus those little extras that we all love to order: raita, pappadums, pickles, and chutneys. Takeout is available.

39 Clarence St. © 613/241-1700. Reservations recommended weekends only. Main courses C$10–$16 (US$6–$10). AE, MC, V. Mon–Wed 11:45am–2:15pm and 5:30–9:30pm; Thurs 11:45am–2:15pm and 5:30–10pm; Fri 11:45am–2:15pm and 5:30pm–10:30pm; Sat 5:30–10:30pm; Sun noon–2:30pm and 5–9pm. Other location: 194 Robertson Rd. © 613/820-1700.

Mamma Grazzi's Kitchen ✦ ITALIAN   Mamma Grazzi's is one of those rare places that serves up consistently good food in a knock-out location. Whether you like your pasta dressed with tomato, cream, or olive oil, you'll have several combinations of ingredients to choose from. Housed in a heritage stone building, Mamma Grazzi's is especially delightful in the summer, when you can enjoy the old, cobblestone courtyard out back. The quaint courtyard is flanked by the terraces of a couple of other eateries, creating a European atmosphere. Because they make everything to order, you may have to wait a little, but it's worth it. Try the Italian sodas, infused with orange or lemon. They beat sickly sweet North American soft drinks hands-down. The entrance to the restaurant is in a little alleyway off George Street, and you'll have to negotiate stairs wherever you eat—up to the second floor, or down to the ground floor or outdoor terrace. Arrive early for lunch or dinner if you want to avoid lineups.

25 George St. © 613/241-8656. Reservations not accepted. Main courses C$8–$14 (US$5–$9). AE, MC, V. Sun–Wed 11:30am–10pm, Thurs–Sat 11:30am–11pm.

Oregano's Pasta Market ITALIAN   In an historic building in the heart of the market at the corner of William and George streets, Oregano's features a large dining room and two outdoor patios where you can watch the hustle and bustle of the ByWard Market while you eat. As you would expect, there's lots of pasta on the menu, including seashell pasta with shrimp, cannelloni, manicotti, tortellini, and grilled chicken with fettucine. Servings are generous and some pasta dishes can be ordered as half-portions (my half-portion of spaghettini Bolognese was plenty big enough and kept hunger pangs at bay for the entire afternoon). Pizzas with traditional toppings are under C$10 (US$6). You can order pasta with butter, tomato sauce, meat sauce, or, for the fussy bunch, just plain. The all-you-can-eat buffet, served at lunch and dinner, is an extravagant selection of appetizers, salads, pastas, and pizza. Opens at 10:30am on Sundays for brunch.

74 George St. ✆ **613/241-5100**. Reservations recommended for dinner. Main courses C$10–$14 (US$6–$9); buffet C$9 (US$6) lunch, C$10 (US$6) dinner. AE, DC, MC, V. Mon–Sat 11am–11pm, Sun 10:30am–11pm.

INEXPENSIVE

BeaverTails TAKEOUT   This fast-food treat, first served in 1978 in the ByWard Market, enjoys a loyal following in Ottawa. Beaver Tails are flat, deep-fried pastries shaped like a beaver tail, with toppings like drizzled chocolate, cinnamon and sugar, garlic, and cheese (but not all on the same tail!). They sell well in all seasons, but we like them best outdoors on a cold, crisp, sunny winter day when we've worked up an appetite from skating or skiing (you'll find locations at Blue Mountain ski resort in Ontario and Mont-Tremblant in Quebec). If you're more of an indoor kind of person, the St. Laurent Shopping Centre in Ottawa also has a stall. The opening and closing times are somewhat weather and crowd dependent, and may vary by an hour or so from the times listed below.

87 George St. ✆ **613/241-1230**. Most items under C$10 (US$6). Summer daily 10am–late. Winter Mon–Wed 10am–6pm; Thurs 10am–11pm; Fri–Sat 10am–midnight; Sun 10am–9pm.

Cow's Ottawa ICE CREAM   Cow's hails from Prince Edward Island in Canada's Atlantic provinces. Their secret recipe using natural ingredients, combined with a mixing process that minimizes the amount of air added to the product, results in a smooth, creamy, premium ice cream. They keep inventing new flavors, so you never know what you'll find when you drop in. Our family's favorite is vanilla studded with miniature filled chocolates. The company has created a unique retail store jam-packed with clothing and all kinds of small, kid-appealing knick-knacks that sport the black-and-white cow. You'll find lots of T-shirts with images of cows in humorous situations. The clothing is good quality and washes well.

43 Clarence St. ✆ **613/244-4224**. Most items under C$10 (US$6). AE, MC, V. Jan–Apr Mon–Fri 10am–5pm, Sat–Sun 10am–6pm; May–Sept 10am–10pm, mid-Sept–Dec 10am–6pm.

The French Baker/Le Boulanger Français BAKERY/CAFE   Reputed to have the flakiest, richest, most buttery croissants in the city, the French Baker also has authentic baguettes and other bread and pastry items. If you venture down the long corridor to the back of the small bakery, you'll find a chic gourmet food shop. Selection is limited but delicious. French and Québécois cheeses are available, and you can sit and sip a coffee or sample the light fare. In 2001, this small space was dubbed Benny's Bistro and began offering lunches and snacks between 8am and 4pm.

119 Murray St. ✆ **613/789-7941**. Most items under C$10 (US$6). AE, MC, V. Mon–Fri 7am–6:30pm, Sat–Sun 7:30am–5:30pm.

Marchélino ✦✦ ECLECTIC   This unique restaurant, situated just inside the east entrance of the Rideau Centre, offers an eclectic mix of gourmet fast food served up at various market-style stalls. It's an assault on the senses to wander among the colorful displays of fruits, salads, breads, and pastries, and watch the staff at work rolling out dough, baking bread, roasting chickens, sliding pizzas in and out of the stone hearth oven, and assembling sushi. The extensive selection of food to eat in or take out includes chocolate croissants, muffins, cinnamon buns, scrambled eggs with ham and chives, at least seven varieties of soup, custom-made sandwiches with five kinds of bread and a dozen fillings, grain-fed roasted chicken, pizza with classic or adventurous toppings, Yukon Gold fries, and pasta. Try the *rösti*, a Swiss dish of shredded potato, pan-fried golden brown and topped with smoked salmon, chicken, or sour cream. The crepes are highly recommended. Just tell the cook your choice of fillings and toppings—try bananas, vanilla ice cream and chocolate sauce, or fresh strawberries and *crème anglaise*. Portions are extremely generous. Even the coffee is upscale here—each cup is ground and brewed individually.

50 Rideau St. (in the Rideau Centre, ground floor). ℂ **613/569-4934**. Most items under C$10 (US$6). AE, MC, V. Mon–Thurs and Sat 7:30am–9pm, Fri 7:30am–10pm, Sun 7:30am–7pm.

Le Moulin de Provence BAKERY/CAFE At the north end of the ByWard Market building lies this wonderful mix of bakery, cafe, and pâtisserie. The atmosphere is comfy and cozy. Your only problem will be deciding what to choose from the gleaming display cases of artfully crafted baked goods, pastries, salads, and delicatessen items. Warm your hands around a bowl of café au lait and nibble on a delicate French pastry while you watch the shoppers bustle past the windows in the midst of the market. Then grab some cheese or paté, tuck a baguette under your arm, and head home for lunch in the true European manner.

55 ByWard Market. ℂ **613/241-9152**. Most items under C$10 (US$6). V. Daily 7am–7pm.

Oh So Good Desserts Café DESSERTS You can't miss the delectable desserts here, since the shiny glass showcase is front and center when you enter the door. The rest of the place is dark. Black tables, black chairs, black walls. Large chalk murals featuring a jazz theme give some color to the room. The cakes are displayed on three shelves in the well-lit showcase. Kids get the best view—they can look the peanut butter fudge buster right in the eye. On the day we visited, we counted 34 different cakes. There's only one serving size, which is huge, so bring a friend along unless you have a hefty appetite. If you order ahead, you can take the whole cake home. Selections include raspberry white-chocolate cheesecake, Dutch apple pie, lemon meringue torte, and a chocoholic's dream, "Truckload of Chocolate." Evenings tend to be busy, since it's a popular spot to hang out after dinner. In the summer you may be lucky enough to nab a table on the rear patio. Takeout is available.

108 Murray St. ℂ 613/241-8028. Most items under C$10 (US$6). AE, V. Mon–Thurs 9am–11pm, Fri 9am–midnight, Sat 11am–midnight, Sun 11am–11pm.

Peace Garden Café VEGETARIAN A tiny oasis in the leafy inner court of the Times Square Building, Peace Garden is a great place to retreat when you feel the need to escape from noisy city streets. There are a few small tables in the courtyard next to a tinkling fountain and a counter with stools. If you're hungry, soup, salads, sandwiches, and a variety of Indian, Malaysian, Italian, and Greek specialties will fit the bill. It's also a great place just to sip a spicy Indian chai tea or a cool, fresh mango *lassi* (yogurt drink). To boost your energy after a day of sightseeing, ask the server to recommend one of their power juices. Closing hours sometimes vary seasonally.

47 Clarence St. ℂ **613/562-2434**. Most items under C$10 (US$6). MC. Mon–Wed 7:30am–8pm, Thurs–Fri 7:30am–8:30pm, Sat 9am–9pm, Sun 10am–8pm.

Piccolo Grande ICE CREAM "Gelato is your fantasy," says Piccolo Grande. Dream up any flavor of gelato and Piccolo Grande will do their best to make it for you, although you may have to give them a few days to work on it. If it's one of their regular flavors (they have almost 80, so they can't keep them all in the store at once) and you'd like a liter (quart) or more, they will try to get it for you within 48 hours. Of course, they may already make your ultimate ice cream. Close your eyes and think of amaretto, mochaccino, pear, or zabaglione. If you want to appeal to the inner child, what about caramel chocolate chip, banana peanut butter, pumpkin, cinnamon, or strawberries and cream? Like fruit? Try apple, grape, or tangerine sorbet, or cranberry, mango, or honeydew melon sherbet. You can eat a tasty and inexpensive lunch here, too. Homemade soups, salads, Italian sandwiches, pasta, and lasagna are all available to eat in or take out. There are only 40 seats inside and lunchtime can get very busy. After 7pm they serve only gelato. You can order Piccolo Grande's wonderful product for dessert at three restaurants—Vittoria Trattoria, at 35 William St., Bravo Bravo, at 292 Elgin St., and Pub Italia at 434½ Preston St. Grande's ice cream is also on the shelf at Nicastro's Groceteria, at 1558 Merivale Rd. Now start dreaming.

55 Murray St. ℂ **613/241-2909**. Most items under C$10 (US$6). AE, MC, V. Summer Mon–Sat 9am–midnight, Sun 9am–11pm. Winter Mon 9:30am–5pm, Tues–Thurs 9:30am–7pm, Fri–Sat 9:30am–11pm, Sun 11am–6pm.

4 The Glebe

Strung along Bank Street between the Queensway and the Canal lies the trendy shopping and dining district known as the Glebe. Have your plastic ready because there will be lots of treasures to tempt you. When you need a break from all that frenzied shopping, take refuge in a cafe, restaurant, or gourmet food shop until your energy levels begin to rise once more.

EXPENSIVE

Flippers ⊛ SEAFOOD   "Look up!" says the recorded phone message. "We're on the second floor." Find the discreet doorway at 819 Bank St., and climb the stairs to a fresh fish restaurant that has been serving Ottawans since 1980, a long time in the fickle restaurant business. Seafood restaurant staples (bay scallops, salmon, shrimp, and mussels) are treated with respect and prepared with style. Specials include Alaskan king crab legs, Arctic char, and bouillabaisse. For the less adventurous, the menu includes English-style fish and chips, grilled Atlantic salmon, and pasta. A papier-mâché mermaid perches in one corner of the room, and glass fish mobiles hang from the ceiling.

819 Bank St. (Fifth Avenue Court). ℂ **613/232-2703**. Reservations accepted only for parties of 6 or more. Main courses C$11–$18 (US$7–$11) and up. AE, DC, MC, V. Mon–Sat 11:30am–2pm and 5pm–10pm; Sun 11:30am–2pm and 5pm–9pm.

Infusion ⊛⊛ ECLECTIC   A relative newcomer to the neighborhood (2001), Infusion has heaps of talent in the kitchen. Their objective is to carefully turn the spotlight on individual flavors and aromas in their dishes, rather than rushing the cooking process to serve diners quickly. Happily, they score high marks for exceptional presentation as well, making a meal at Infusion a very satisfying experience. The imaginative menu stimulates the appetite. Dishes include portabella, shiitake, and oyster mushroom strudel with Gruyère and fresh herb cream sauce, grilled lamb and baby spinach salad, and house-made Jamaican jerk pork tenderloin. The scrumptious weekend brunch is excellent value with a choice of ten entrees at C$10 (US$6) a plate. No bacon and eggs here; these dishes will blow your taste buds away. If you like seafood, what about blue crab, ice shrimp, and Nova Scotia lobster with mascarpone cheese and fresh chives? Or for a little sophistication, order the sautéed chicken, leeks, and mushrooms with champagne Dijon velouté and wild rice pilaf. If you have a sweet tooth, you just can't pass on the baked French toast, stuffed with roasted bananas, pecans, and mascarpone cheese, dipped in Kahlúa batter and served with fresh fruit. Close to heaven!

825 Bank St. © **613/234-2412**. Reservations recommended. Main courses C$12–$22 (US$7–$14). AE, DC, MC, V. Mon 5pm–11pm, Tues–Thurs 11:30am–10pm, Fri 11:30am–11pm, Sat 10am–3pm and 5pm–11pm, Sun 10am–3pm and 5pm–9pm.

MODERATE

The Canal Ritz ⭐ ITALIAN   With its converted boathouse setting, the Canal Ritz offers a constantly changing view of the Rideau Canal. In summer, boats sail past the tables on the spacious terrace, and in winter, skaters glide past on the world's longest skating rink. For lunch, try the Canal Ritz salad with fresh salad greens, herb-marinated shrimp, feta, cucumber, and tomatoes. The bread here is wonderful—loaves are satisfyingly dense, with a hint of sweetness and a crisp but not crumbly crust. Thin-crust designer pizza offers a choice of unusual toppings such as pears, dried figs, and smoked Gouda. The restaurant perches on the edge of the canal, with the Queen Elizabeth Driveway sweeping past the front door. You'll find the parking lot on the southwest corner of Fifth Avenue and Queen Elizabeth Driveway, directly opposite the restaurant.

375 Queen Elizabeth Dr. © **613/238-8998**. Reservations recommended. Main courses C$10–$15 (US$6–$9). AE, DC, MC, V. Daily 11:30am–11pm.

Von's Bistro BISTRO   Local residents are fond patrons of this centrally located Glebe eatery. Subdued, neutral decor with caramel walls, bisque table-cloths, and an abundance of dark wood is accented with chalkboard-covered pillars adorned with amusing and thought-provoking quotations. Lunch fare is light and quick—bagels, wraps, pasta, quiches, and omelets. In the evening, indulge in homemade ravioli, grain-fed chicken, *moules and frites* (mussels and french fries) with a choice of six broths, or several smoked salmon dishes. The smoked salmon also appears on the weekend brunch menu, and it's very good. A blackboard propped up at the entrance announces evening specials such as pan-seared sea bass and roast duck.

819 Bank St. © **613/233-3277**. Reservations accepted only for parties of 6 or more; reservations not accepted for weekend brunch. Main courses C$12–$18 (US$7–$11). AE, DC, MC, V. Mon–Fri 11:30am–3pm and 5pm–10pm; Sat–Sun 8:30am–3pm and 5pm–10pm.

INEXPENSIVE

L'Amuse Gueule ⭐⭐ TAKEOUT   Having spent many vacations in France, I can attest that the wonderful dishes coming from the French chef/owner's kitchen at this gourmet food shop are as good as any you'll get on the Continent. If boeuf bourguignon or carrot salad appear in the display case, snap them up. Takeout dinner entrees change weekly and feature a different dish every day. You might find herb-roasted grain-fed chicken, fillet of sole, coq au vin, or lobster-filled crepes. There are a few tables and chairs inside, but this is mainly a takeout and catering shop. Order a gourmet picnic basket packed with delights that may include Rosette de Lyon salami, pissaladiere, cornichons, olive tapenade, and clafouti. If you want to keep it simple, choose a couple of local or imported cheeses and a baguette or two, then head to the banks of the canal (you can walk from here; just ask for directions) for a leisurely picnic.

915 Bank St. © **613/234-9400**. Main courses C$10–$12 (US$6–$7). MC, V. Mon–Fri 9am–7pm, Sat 9am–6pm.

Kettleman's Bagels ⭐ BAGELS   I love coming here as much for the entertainment of watching the bakers at work as for the bagels. From the mounds of dough, bakers cut off strips, shape them into circles, and slide them into the open wood-burning oven on long planks. The freshly baked bagels are delicious simply spread with cream cheese, but Kettleman's doesn't stop there. There's a choice of 19 sandwiches, including two classics—smoked salmon, cream cheese, tomato, and onion, and the house special with hot Montreal smoked meat and sweet mustard. There are two additional locations: Carling Avenue in the west end and Place d'Orléans Drive in the east end. They never close, so you can satisfy hunger pangs at any time of the day or night.

912 Bank St. ☎ **613/567-7100.** Most items under C$10 (US$6). Daily 24 hours. Other locations: 2177 Carling Ave. ☎ **613/722-4357;** 1222 Place d'Orléans Dr. ☎ **613/841-4409.**

Wild Oat Bakery and Natural Foods BAKERY   If you need a break while trolling the cool shops along Bank Street in the Glebe, this is a good spot to dash in and grab a bite. Lots of folks must agree, because Wild Oat expanded into the space next door in 2001, moving the grocery and produce into one side, and keeping the bakery in the other. There's a doorway between the two, and limited seating is strung along a counter facing the shop-front windows. Ready-to-eat small pizzas, samosas, soups, or chili make a good light lunch, and you can follow them with brownies, squares, or one of the large cookies lined up in wicker baskets on the counter. I've sampled chocolate chip, peanut butter, ginger, maple and hemp seed, and oatmeal raisin and haven't found a dud among them. Wheat-free, yeast-free, and naturally sweetened baked goods are available. Browse the shelves for organic pasta, 100% organic fresh produce, and other healthy food items.

817 Bank St. ☎ **613/232-6232.** Most items under C$10 (US$6). Mon–Fri 8:30am–8pm, Sat 9am–6pm, Sun 10:30am–6pm.

 Coffee Break

Old-fashioned coffee and donut shops still abound in small-town Ontario, but in the big cities, chains with a more sophisticated (and expensive!) twist dominate downtown street corners. In Ottawa, **Second Cup, Starbuck's,** and **Grabbajabba** are the names you're most likely to see downtown. The coffee-based drinks in these trendy cafes tend to be tasty, but by the time you've downed your double decaf mocha latte with extra foam and a biscotti, the bill for your much-needed jolt of caffeine may be a little hard to swallow. Keep your eyes open for **Tim Horton's,** a more down-to-earth chain in terms of coffee selection and prices. There are a couple of downtown locations, but most branches are out in the suburbs, where they attract drive-thru business in droves. Tim's serves great donuts and reliable coffee, as well as inexpensive sandwiches, soup, and chili.

---

5 Wellington Street West

This residential neighborhood west of downtown is quieter than the Glebe, but there are also some interesting little shops to be found here (see chapter 9,

"Shopping"). Spend some time strolling the street and refuel at the eateries below. Watch for the seasonal farmer's market on Parkdale Avenue, where you can browse for local fresh produce.

INEXPENSIVE

Ottawa Bagelshop & Deli BAGELS   Here you'll find bagels and much much more. This is a retailer of many hats—it's a bakery, deli, cafe, and gourmet food shop. The food shop is a warren of shelves jam-packed with a bewildering variety of ethnic goodies. Venture toward the back and you'll discover the bagel counter, where you can buy bags of many-flavored bagels to take home. Turn right and up the steps to enter the eat-in section. A European coffee counter, a buffet table with hot and cold food, and a sandwich counter round off the eatery. If you choose the buffet, which includes BBQ chicken, Italian sausages, rice, and lots of salads, the cashier will weigh your plate and charge you an amount based on C$7.25 (US$4.50) per pound. Try the cheese blintzes—they're light and creamy with just a touch of sweetness. The place is a real neighborhood haunt for locals, catering to everyone from school children to mothers and babies and seniors.

1321 Wellington St. W. ⓒ **613/722-8753**. Most items under C$10 (US$6). AE, MC, V. Mon–Thurs and Sat 6:30am–7pm, Fri 6:30am–8pm, Sun 6:30am–6pm.

Parma Ravioli TAKEOUT   With its spacious open kitchen behind the retail counter, Parma Ravioli is an entertaining place. You're likely to see something different each time you visit. Cooks in white jackets and tall hats knead dough, mix pasta fillings, and assemble ravioli right before your eyes. After you've finished watching the show, take home oodles of Italian goodies—bread, rolls, focaccia, fresh pasta, ravioli, lasagna, manicotti, pasta sauces, and Italian desserts.

1314 Wellington St. ⓒ **613/722-6003**. Most items under C$10 (US$6). Mon–Fri 9:30am–6:30pm, Sat 9am–6pm, Sun 10am–5pm.

The Table ⭐ *Value* VEGETARIAN   In a large, bright cafeteria-style dining room with a generous number of country kitchen pine tables and chairs, you can eat for health and still enjoy the food. The Table has a wide selection of tasty vegetarian dishes arranged buffet-style. Grab a tray and sample soups, salads, meatless main courses, baked goods, and more. Vegan and gluten-free items are available. Whenever possible, organic ingredients are used. Whole grains are emphasized, and maple syrup, molasses, and honey are used in place of refined sugar. You can also fill takeout containers if you fancy a picnic or want to stock up your fridge. Two locations serve the needs of shoppers along Wellington St. W. and local residents and the crowd in the ByWard Market district.

1230 Wellington St. W. ⓒ **613/729-5973**. Also at 261 Dalhousie St. ⓒ **613/244-1100**. Price by weight C$17 (US$11) per kg (US 2.2 lb). AE, MC, V. Mon–Fri 11:30am–9pm, Sat–Sun 11:30am–9pm.

Thyme & Again ⭐⭐ *Finds* TAKEOUT/CAFE   Thyme & Again is a delightful place to browse, shop, and debate over which delectable dishes to take home and enjoy. At the front of the shop there's a small but select display of gifts and home accessories. If you're around over the Christmas season, you must drop in to see their unique selection of decorations. The take-home menu changes weekly and every week there is a choice of seasonal soups, three salads, four side dishes, five main courses, and a dip and vinaigrette of the week. The list reads like a fine dining menu—orzo salad with tomatoes, toasted pine nuts and kalamata olives, roasted garlic risotto with lemon and basil, pan-seared beef tenderloin with rosemary Stilton sauce, and pasta with white wine cream sauce, chives, and locally smoked salmon. Dreamy desserts include Tuscany cream cake, chocolate Grand Marnier cheesecake, caramel walnut tart, and mascarpone rice pudding. You can also savor the pleasure of an espresso and biscotti at one of the tiny tables tucked into the front corner of the shop. When skies are clear, sunlight streams through the windows.

1255 Wellington St. W. © **613/722-6277**. Most items under C$10 (US$6). AE, DC, MC, V. Mon–Fri 8am–8pm, Sat 9am–6pm, Sun 10am–5pm.

6 Chinatown

Ottawa's Asian community has settled primarily around Somerset Street West. The main street is lined with Asian grocery stores and restaurants. Highlighting just a few eateries is a difficult task because there are so many good places to eat Asian food in the city, and not all are in Chinatown.

MODERATE

New Mee Fung ⭐ VIETNAMESE   Meticulous attention to detail in the composition and presentation of the dishes results in a memorable dining experience. This small restaurant is clean, simply furnished, and casual. Lots of finger foods, dishes that require assembly (you can roll up your chicken in rice paper), and chopsticks to master. Each dish on the extensive menu is coded. Just jot down the numbers on the scrap of paper the smiling server gives you and wait for a splendid feast to arrive. Many dishes feature grilled chicken, beef, and pork, and there's a good selection of soups, spring rolls, salads, and noodles. Our grilled marinated chicken was accompanied by fresh mint, basil, and lettuce; soft, paper-thin disks made from rice flour for wrapping morsels of food; glass noodles sprinkled with chopped peanuts, carrots, bean sprouts, and cucumber salad; and delicately flavored dipping sauce. Takeout is available.

350 Booth St. © **613/567-8228**. Main courses C$5–C$12 (US$3–$7). MC, V. Wed–Mon 10am–10pm.

Shanghai Restaurant ⭐ ASIAN   Serving a mixture of Cantonese, Szechuan, and Asian dishes, Shanghai is one of the top restaurants in Ottawa's Chinatown. You'll find some familiar Canadian-Chinese dishes on the menu, but allow yourself to be tempted by spicy Thai chicken with sweet basil, ginger-teriyaki vegetable fried rice, Shanghai crispy beef, or shrimp with bok choy and roasted garlic. The coconut-curry vegetables in a spicy peanut sauce go well with a bowl of steamed rice. On Thursday evenings after 8pm the menu switches to finger foods and light snacks as a twenty-something crowd moves in to listen to a DJ spin tunes until 1am. Takeout is available.

651 Somerset St. W. © **613/233-4001**. Reservations recommended weekends only. Main courses C$7–$15 (US$5–$10). AE, MC, V. Tues–Wed 11am–2pm and 4:30pm–11pm, Thurs–Fri 11am–2pm and 4:30pm–1am, Sat 4:30pm–1am, Sun 4:30pm–11pm.

Yangtze CHINESE   Both Cantonese and Szechuan cuisine are served in this spacious dining room. Large, round tables will seat 8 to 10 comfortably, and a Lazy Susan in the center of the table allows everyone to help him- or herself from the communal dishes. Families and groups are welcome here for all-day dining. Many dishes familiar to North American diners are on the menu—kung po shrimp, sweet-and-sour chicken, broccoli with scallops, beef with snow peas, chow mein, and fried rice. House specialties include chicken in black-bean sauce, pepper steak, and Imperial spareribs. Takeout is available.

700 Somerset St. W. © **613/236-0555**. Reservations recommended. C$7–$15 (US$5–$10). AE, MC, V. Mon–Thurs 11am–12:30am, Fri 11am–1am, Sat 10am–1am, Sun 10am–12:30am.

7 Little Italy

Preston Street, also known as Corso Italia, is the heart of Ottawa's Little Italy. Food is the soul of Italy, and when you stroll up one side of Preston Street and down the other, you'll pass by plenty of ristorantes, trattorie, and caffès. Many of them have outdoor patios, and all offer a warm Mediterranean welcome. I've selected a formal fine-dining restaurant, a smart–casual restaurant with a summer terrace, a neighborhood cafe, and a pasta shop to give you a taste of Corso Italia. Explore on your own and you'll discover many more treasures.

EXPENSIVE

La Roma ★★★ ITALIAN   A well-established Preston Street ristorante, La Roma has a solid reputation for good-quality traditional Italian cuisine. The elegant ivory and burgundy dining room is sophisticated and charming. Service is impeccable. Choose from a wide variety of chicken, veal, pasta, and other Italian specialties, accompanied by Italian bread. The recently expanded all-Italian wine list is impressive in both its length and variety. I recommend the breast of chicken with lemon sauce, with a light, creamy, and dreamy tiramisu to follow and a robust espresso as the grand finale.

430 Preston St. © **613/234-8244.** Reservations recommended. Main courses C$12–$20 (US$7–$12). AE, DC, MC, V. Mon–Thurs 11:30am–2pm and 5–10pm, Fri 11:30am–2pm and 5pm–11pm, Sat 5pm–11pm, Sun 5pm–11pm.

MODERATE

Ciccio Caffè ITALIAN   Ciccio takes pride in its traditional Italian menu featuring fresh pasta (lasagna, cannelloni, and linguine) and desserts made on the premises. Signature dishes include rabbit with mushrooms in white wine, osso buco, and roast veal. In the summer, patrons love the ambience of the outdoor terrace.

330 Preston St. © **613/232-1675.** Reservations recommended. Main courses C$10–$19 (US$6–$12). AE, DC, MC, V. Mon–Tues 11am–10pm, Wed–Fri 11am–11pm, Sat noon–11pm, Sun 4pm–10pm.

INEXPENSIVE

Luciano's ★★ TAKEOUT   Near the top of Preston St., just north of Somerset St. W., you'll find Luciano's. Park behind the building (enter the parking lot off Somerset), and stock up on ravioli, agnolotti, and tortellini stuffed with yummy fillings like sun-dried tomato, spinach and ricotta, and butternut squash. Choose fresh spaghetti, fettucine, linguine, or rigatoni and homemade sauces—Bolognese, clam, tomato, putanesca, mushroom, pesto, or roasted red pepper. Buy oven-ready portions of lasagna or cannelloni, a baguette, olive oil, balsamic vinegar, and a tub of gelato, and you have an instant Italian dinner—home-cooked meals should always be so easy. Next door to the take-home food shop there's Luciano's supermarket.

106 Preston St. © **613/236-7545.** Most items under C$10 (US$6). MC, V. Mon 1–6pm, Tues–Thurs 9am–6pm, Fri 9am–8pm, Sat 9am–5:30pm.

Pasticceria Gelateria Italiana Ltd. ★ ICE CREAM/CAFE   A decidedly European atmosphere prevails in this mix of pastry shop, ice-cream store, and neighborhood cafe. You'll hear Italian spoken as older-generation local residents come for the social hour to exchange news over their espressos. The beautifully sculpted Italian pastries are a feast for the eyes as well as the stomach. For a filling and inexpensive lunch, help yourself at the hot pasta bar for C$5 (US$3).

The homemade gelato is superb. Try the mandarin orange. In fine weather, you can while away an hour or two on the large sheltered terrace.

200 Preston St. © **613/233-6199.** Most items under C$10 (US$6). V. Mon–Sat 7am–11pm, Sun 8am–11pm.

8 Farther Out

Here are a few more places to try. They're all no more than a 10-minute drive from downtown.

MODERATE

The Lone Star Café TEX MEX   If you're staying at one of the hotels near the St. Laurent Shopping Centre or live in the east end of Ottawa, soak up a little southern hospitality and down-home cooking at the newest location of the Lone Star Café. The owner, a native of Houston, Texas, played for the Ottawa Roughriders football team a number of years ago before opening a restaurant to remind him of home. Now part of a chain of 11 restaurants across Canada, the original restaurant remains at 780 Baseline Road in Ottawa. Corn tortilla chips are cooked up fresh in the kitchen every morning and afternoon, and their taste far exceeds the store-bought variety. Service is brisk and cheerful, with servers sporting cutesy names like Moonshine and Chili Pepper. Try mesquite-grilled chicken, which has a lovely smoky BBQ flavor. If you're into country music, mosey on down on Thursday, Friday, or Saturday after 9:30pm and check out the live bands for a stomping good time. A cover charge applies for the music; this is waived for patrons ordering a minimum of C$15 pre-tax from the restaurant menu.

1211 Lemieux St. © **613/742-9378.** Reservations accepted for parties of 8 or more, except Fri and Sat evenings and Sun. Main courses C$8–$19 (US$5–$13). AE, DC, MC, V. Mon–Wed 11:30am–10pm, Thurs 11:30am–11pm, Fri 11:30am–midnight, Sat noon–midnight, Sun noon–10pm. Other location: 780 Baseline Rd. (Ottawa West) © **613/224-4044.**

Pelican Fishery & Grill ★ SEAFOOD   You know the fish is fresh at this place—you walk right by the eye-catching display of fresh fish and seafood on the way to your table. The premises operate as a fishmonger on one side and restaurant on the other. Decor is simple and casual. The menu changes every day, depending on what's available. Grilled trout with wasabi and dill cream sauce, accompanied by herbed potatoes and mixed vegetables was featured the day we were there, and the fish was expertly cooked. In the evening, main courses are a little fancier. Paella, steamed sea bass, broiled scallops, and cedar-roasted Atlantic salmon fillet are often listed.

1500 Bank St. (in the Blue Heron Mall). © **613/526-0995.** Reservations recommended. Main courses C$8–$19 (US$5–$12). AE, DC, MC, V. Mon 11:30am–8:30pm, Tues–Fri 11:30am–9pm, Sat noon–9pm, Sun 5pm–8:30pm.

INEXPENSIVE

The Green Door VEGETARIAN   This casual eatery has tables set up cafeteria-style and a U-shaped buffet with a dessert station in the middle. Grab a tray, wander past hot vegetable stir-fries, tofu dishes, pasta, salads, breads, fresh fruit, cakes, and pies. If you're not a dedicated vegetarian but you've always wanted to try tofu or soy milk, here's your chance. A lot of the offerings are certified organic. You won't see meat anywhere, and if dairy products are contained in dishes, there's a sign to let you know. Pricing is easy—just hand your plate to the cashier and you'll be charged by weight. With prices set at C$17 (US$11) a kilogram (2.2 lb.), your stomach will be full before your wallet is empty. If you're heading out to a park, put together a picnic lunch. Servers will supply takeout containers and paper bags.

198 Main St. ℂ 613/234-9597. C$17 (US$11) per kg (2.2 lb.). AE, MC, V. Tues–Sat 11am–9pm, Sun 11am–3pm.

9 On the Quebec Side

While you may find hotels pretty much the same on one side of the Ottawa River or the other, if you have an affection for French cuisine, you really must cross over to the Quebec side. I've singled out three places here: a solid example of authentic French country cooking, a small cafe serving European-style beverages, and a classy bistro. You may also like to try the following places for French cuisine: **Café Henry Burger** ℂ 819/777-5646 (fine dining in elegant surroundings), **Café Jean Sébastien** ℂ 819/771-2934 (romantic setting), **Laurier sur Montcalm** ℂ 819/775-5030 (French regional cuisine), and **Le Tartuffe** ℂ 819/776-6424 (formal fine dining).

MODERATE

Le 1908 ⍟ FRENCH   When you enter Le 1908, there's a small wine bar overlooking the large sunken dining room. The ceiling is extremely high, making the room open and spacious. Wood is everywhere: cherry trim, blond wood floors, functional wooden chairs. Crisp white table linens complete the picture. Diners can watch the chefs at work in the open kitchen at the rear. A huge chalkboard hangs above the kitchen with the day's specials listed. Classic French dishes include boeuf bourguignon, steak tartare, duck breast with onion confiture, and snails flambéed with Pernod. For dessert, sample profiteroles or tarte au fromage. There is a pay parking lot next door to the restaurant. Service is commendable.

70 promenade du Portage, Hull. ℂ 819/770-1908. Reservations recommended. Main courses C$12–$19 (US$7–$12). AE, DC, MC, V. Mon–Wed 11:30am–10pm, Thurs 11:30am–11pm, Fri 11:30am–midnight, Sat 5:30pm–11pm.

Le Pied de Cochon ⍟⍟⍟ FRENCH   This is as close as you'll get to France without hopping on a plane to Paris. Begin with a simple green salad, moules marinière, or rabbit terrine. Progress to roast leg of lamb, grilled steak with tarragon, or veal medallions with Chanterelles. Complement the remains of your bottle of wine with a fine selection of cheese. Indulge in a fine, rich, crème brûlée and above all, linger. Eating in France (and Quebec!) is a serious business and must not be rushed. The three-course table d'hôte offers a choice of eight appetizers, five main courses, and around half a dozen desserts for under C$30 and is excellent value for the money. The decor is comfortable but unremarkable and the atmosphere is smart–casual. Service is satisfyingly attentive; your needs will be anticipated but the intimacy of your meal is not intruded upon. Free parking available beside the restaurant. In summer, there is a terrace in front. Book ahead to avoid disappointment.

248 rue Montcalm, Hull. ℂ 819/777-5808. Reservations required Fri–Sat; recommended at all times. Main courses C$7–$18 (US$7–$11; three-course table d'hôte C$27 (US$17). AE, ˙MC, V. Tues–Fri noon–2:30pm and 6pm–10pm, Sat 6pm–10pm.

INEXPENSIVE

Café La Brûlerie CAFE   For expertly prepared European-style coffee-based drinks, pay a visit to La Brûlerie. More than three dozen beans and blends are available and they are roasted on site. The roaster is a bit noisy when in operation but it's worth putting up with the racket just to experience the aroma of the roasting coffee beans. Take home whole beans or have them ground to your specifications. Specialty teas, cafetières, and coffee mugs also for sale. Soups, sandwiches, and salads are available daily until 6pm. Chocolate-dipped biscuits and cakes go well with a latte or café au lait.

152 rue Montcalm, Hull. © **819/778-0109.** Most items under C$10 (US$6). MC, V. Mon–Wed 7:30am–10pm, Thurs 7:30am–11pm, Fri 7:30am–midnight, Sat 8am–midnight, Sun 10am–10pm.

Chow-Down at Family-Friendly Chains

Chains thrive because they deliver a consistent product in a reliable manner. The menu is generally the same at every location, so you can order quickly and be pretty certain of what you'll get. It's all middle-of-the-road fare designed with North American palates in mind. If you have kids with you, hosts will supply everything from balloons and crayons to high chairs and booster seats. Keep an eye out for these chains when you're out and about. Some have more locations than I've listed here—let your fingers do the walking if your favorite isn't listed below in your neighborhood.

Boston Pizza, 1055 St. Laurent Blvd. (© **613/746-1039**) and 521 West Hunt Club Rd. (© **613/226-3374**), serves pizza, pasta, salads, ribs, and sandwiches for dine-in, takeout, or delivery. **Denny's** is a family-style restaurant at 2208 Bank St. (© **613/731-4828**). You'll find **East Side Mario's** American Italian fare at 1200 St. Laurent Blvd. (© **613/747-0888**). If you crave a good steak, try **The Keg,** 75 York St., (© **613/241-8514**).There's a **Kelsey's** roadhouse-style family restaurant close to the Canada Science and Technology Museum at 1910 St. Laurent Blvd. (© **613/733-2200**). **Mexicali Rosa's** serves up their California-style Mexican food at 895 Bank St. (© **613/ 236-9499**), 200 Rideau St. (© **613/241-7044**), and Dow's Lake Pavilion at 1001 Queen Elizabeth Dr. (© **613/234-8156**). Seafood is on the menu every day at **Red Lobster,** 1499 St. Laurent Blvd. (© **613/744-7560**). For good old-fashioned food, go to **Rockin' Johnny's Diner,** 1301 Carling Ave. (© **613/761-7405**) and 1129 St. Laurent Blvd. (© **613/744-5666**). A popular BBQ chicken restaurant in Quebec, **St-Hubert** has three locations in the Ottawa area, including one at 1754 St. Laurent Blvd. (© **613/526-1222**). And last but not least, every grandparent's favorite BBQ chicken restaurant is **Swiss Chalet,** 1910 Bank St. (© **613/733-7231**), 96A George St. (© **613/562-3020**), 675 Kirkwood Ave. (© **613/729-1789**), and 540 Montreal Rd. (© **613/746-1777**).

6

What to See & Do
in Ottawa

The nation's capital and the surrounding region has so many attractions, museums, parks, pathways, and festivals that you could jam-pack every day of your vacation in Ottawa and still not see and do everything. But be realistic and scale down your expectations. It's better to spend quality time on a few attractions than to dash madly around trying to experience it all. You can always come back for a second visit. When you do, schedule your trip for a different season of the year, so you can enjoy all that the region has to offer.

Visit some of the world-class attractions and experience Ottawa's green-space in one of the area's many beautiful parks. You can run, walk, bike, or in-line skate along the network of pathways throughout the region (see chapter 7, "Active Ottawa"). In winter, lace up your skates and glide along the canal. If you like to shop, stroll through one of the large indoor malls, the pedestrian Sparks Street downtown, or one of the neighborhood shopping areas (see chapter 9, "Shopping").

If you're only in Ottawa for a short break, concentrate your sightseeing in and around the downtown area. You'll find that many of the major attractions are within walking distance of each other along Wellington St. and Sussex Dr. or on streets leading off these two roads. Visit **www.virtualmuseum.ca** for a listing and brief description of some of Ottawa's museums and heritage attractions.

Don't forget that Ottawa hosts a wide variety of festivals and events ranging from Winterlude in February, to the Canadian Tulip Festival in May, Canada Day celebrations, and lots of summer festivities. See chapter 2, "Planning a Trip to Ottawa," for a list of annual events.

If this is a family vacation, keep in mind that many museums put on special programs and workshops for children and families on weekends and during school holidays (one week in mid-March, the months of July and August, and two weeks surrounding Christmas and New Year's Day). Call the **Capital Infocentre** *①* **800/465/1867** or *①* 613/239-5000 for exact dates as they vary slightly from year to year.

SUGGESTED ITINERARIES

If You Have 1 Day

In the **summer,** start the day with a parade. Head for the **Changing of the Guard** parade route along Elgin St. north of Laurier Ave., then west on Wellington St. to Parliament Hill, if you want to watch them march past. If your priority is watching the ceremonial guard change rather than the parade, stake your place on Parliament Hill before 10am, which is when the ceremony commences. Drop by the **Info Tent** on the Hill and reserve a spot on the free **tour of the Parliament Buildings** for later in the day.

The rest of the day will have to be planned around your allocated tour time. The interior of the Parliament Buildings and the accompanying commentary are highly recommended, but if you don't want the rest of your day's plans revolving around returning to the Hill, you can forgo the tour. After the Changing of the Guard is over, head east on Wellington St. Stop on the north side of **Plaza Bridge** and look down to see the **Ottawa Locks.** You may be lucky enough to watch a boat or two making its way through the lock system. Continue east to the magnificent **Fairmont Château Laurier Hotel.** If you're interested in period architecture and design, take a few minutes to peek inside the lobby and other public areas on the main level. Turn left along MacKenzie Ave. and take a stroll around **Major's Hill Park.** Cross the **Alexandra Bridge** using the pedestrian walkway to the **Canadian Museum of Civilization.** Enjoy the spectacular view of the Parliament Buildings, the Ottawa skyline, and the Ottawa River. Explore the main exhibition halls, which will take a couple of hours or more. Enjoy an evening meal in one of Hull's excellent French restaurants (reservations recommended), or head back across the Alexandra Bridge and browse the **ByWard Market** district, which is packed with boutiques, restaurants, and cafes.

In the **winter,** begin the day with a tour of the **Parliament Buildings** (prior reservations usually not required in the winter). Take a cab to the **Canadian Museum of Civilization** or walk if you're dressed warmly. For lunch, **Les Muses** in the museum offers fine dining and

an impressive view of the Ottawa River and Parliament Hill. **Café Henry Burger,** an elegant fine dining restaurant, is directly opposite the museum. Reservations are recommended for both venues. After lunch, head for the **National Gallery of Canada.** The architecture is stunning and the exhibits of Canadian art are admirable. Later in the afternoon, lace up a pair of rental skates and take a spin on the **Rideau Canal Skateway.** If you'd rather shop, wander the **ByWard Market** district or head for the **Rideau Centre Shopping Centre.**

If You Have 2 Days

On the first day, follow the itinerary above. On day 2, in the **summer,** buy a day pass for one of the city tour buses—either a double-decker bus or an old-fashioned trolley bus. The buses run every 45 minutes and a day pass allows you hop-on-and-off privileges along the way. Allow a couple of hours to explore the **Museum of Nature** or **Museum of Science and Technology,** both of which have fascinating exhibits for all ages. Get back on the bus and enjoy an alfresco lunch at one of the many restaurants in the **ByWard Market.** In the afternoon, take a **boat tour** of the Ottawa river or a **Rideau Canal cruise.** If you have energy to burn, **rent in-line skates or bikes** and follow the multi-use pathways along the banks of the Rideau Canal (see bike tours listed in chapter 7). In the **winter,** visit another museum—the **War Museum** and **Aviation Museum** are both good choices. Or explore **the Glebe** shopping district along Bank Street —just make sure you wrap up well in cold weather.

If You Have 3 Days

On your third day in the Capital Region, check out any of the suggested destinations in day 1 and 2 that you haven't had time to fit in yet. If you'd rather get out of the city, head for **Gatineau Park.** You can hike, swim, and bike in the summer, enjoy the autumn leaves in September and October, or ski and snowshoe in the winter.

If You Have 4 Days or More

With a longer visit, you can build in a couple of day trips. Enjoy a day out on the **Hull–Chelsea–Wakefield Steam Train,** explore the towns and villages of the **Rideau Valley,** or head to Quebec for downhill skiing, waterparks, or golf, depending on the season.

If You Have Kids with You

See the section "Especially for Kids" later in this chapter for suggestions for different age groups from toddlers to teens.

1 The Top Attractions

PARLIAMENT HILL ★★★

The Parliament Buildings, with their grand façade of steeply pitched copper roof panels, multiple towers, and sandstone block construction, are an impressive sight, especially on first viewing. In 1860, Prince Edward (later King Edward VII) laid the cornerstone for the buildings, which were finished in time to host the inaugural session of the first Parliament of the new Dominion of Canada in 1867. As you approach the Centre Block with its stately central Peace Tower through the main gate on Wellington Street, you'll pass the Centennial Flame, lit by then prime minister Lester B. Pearson on New Year's Eve 1966 to mark the passing of 100 years since Confederation. In June, July, and August, you can meet the Royal Canadian Mounted Police (affectionately called the Mounties) on Parliament Hill. They're friendly—and love to have their photo taken. If you're visiting the capital between mid-May and early September, your first stop on Parliament Hill should be the Info Tent, where you can pick up free information on the Hill and free same-day tickets for tours of the Parliament Buildings. Tickets are limited, though, and there is no guarantee in the busy summer months or weekends in spring and fall that you will get tickets for your first choice of time, or even day. If you arrive between 9am and 10am, you can usually select a tour time of your choice. Between September and May, get same-day tickets from the Visitor Welcome Centre, directly under the Peace Tower. All visitors to the buildings are required to go through a security screening system similar to that used in airports.

Where to eat: Parliament Hill is in the center of Ottawa off Wellington Street, so stroll along Sparks or Elgin streets or visit the ByWard Market area for a variety of restaurants. From late June to early September, the West Block Courtyard is open for light refreshments (weather permitting).

 Tips

During the busy summer months, drop by the information tent on the lawn in front of the Parliament Buildings between 9am and 10am. You can reserve a spot on the free tour of the Centre Block for later in the day and avoid the long lineups.

Canada's Government: The Basics

Canada functions as a parliamentary democracy, which means its government consists of elected representatives chosen by its citizens. Based upon the British structure of federal government that was established when Canada became self-governing, the **Parliament of Canada** consists of the head of state (**Queen Elizabeth II,** who is represented by the **Governor General**), the **Senate** (equivalent of the British House of Lords), and the **House of Commons.**

The parliamentary duties of the **Governor General** include summoning **Parliament** following each general election, announcing the current government's objectives at the beginning of each session of **Parliament** through the Speech from the Throne, and approving all bills passed by the **Senate** and the **House of Commons.**

The **Senate** is made up of 104 **Senators,** who represent regions and provinces. They are appointed by the **Governor General** on the advice of the **Prime Minister.**

The **House of Commons** has 301 seats. **Members of Parliament (MPs)** are elected to represent their constituents in each of these 301 ridings, or political districts, for up to five years. The party that wins the greatest number of seats in the House of Commons in a federal election usually forms the government, and the party's leader becomes **Prime Minister.**

The Prime Minister appoints **Cabinet Ministers,** who are responsible for a specific portfolio, for example, health, finance, industry, the environment, or immigration.

A Parliament is made up of one or more sessions during its lifetime. Parliament sits about 27 weeks of the year, beginning in September and usually lasting until June. Breaks are scheduled to allow **Senators** and **MPs** to spend time working in their regions and ridings.

The **Senate** and the **House of Commons** each meet on a regular basis to deal with issues of national concern and to debate bills (legislative proposals) that are introduced by **Cabinet Ministers, Senators,** or **private Members. Question Period** is often the most lively part of each sitting day. During **Question Period, Cabinet Ministers** are held accountable for their department's activities and also for the policies of the **government.**

To oversee the proceedings of the **Senate** and the **House of Commons,** to maintain order, and to enforce parliamentary rules and traditions, each House has a **Speaker,** who sits on a ceremonial chair at one end of the Chamber, with the **Government** on the right and the **Opposition** on the left. The **Speaker of the Senate** is appointed on the advice of the **Prime Minister.** The **Speaker of the House of Commons** is a current **MP,** elected by peers.

Besides the federal government, whose seat is Ottawa, Canada's 10 provinces and 3 territories elect representatives to deal with matters of provincial and territorial concern. The provinces and territories combine to make a federation in which the power is distributed between the **federal government** and the **provincial legislatures.**

THE PARLIAMENT BUILDINGS ✶✶

Centre Block, East Block, and West Block   The Parliament Buildings consist of three blocks of buildings—the **Centre Block,** with its central Peace Tower, and the flanking **West Block** and **East Block.** This is the heart of Canadian political life, the workplace of the **House of Commons** and the **Senate.** When the House of Commons is sitting, you can sit in the public gallery and observe the 301 elected members debating in their grand green chamber with its tall stained-glass windows. Parliament is usually in recess from late June until early September and occasionally between September and June, including the Easter and Christmas holidays. Otherwise, the House usually sits on weekdays. The 104 appointed members of the Senate sit in a stately red chamber. A fire destroyed the original Centre Block in 1916; only the **Library of Parliament** at the rear was saved. The West Block, containing parliamentary offices, is closed to the public, except for the Courtyard, which serves light refreshments in the summer months. You can tour the **East Block,** which has four historic rooms restored for public viewing: the original **governor general's office,** restored to the period of Lord Dufferin (1872–1878); the **offices of Sir John A. Macdonald and Sir George-Étienne Cartier** (the principal fathers of Confederation); and the **Privy Council Chamber** with anteroom.

(Fact

There are hundreds of gargoyles, grotesques, bosses, and other unusual animal shapes carved into the sandstone of the outer walls of the Parliament Buildings. Keep your eyes open for these entertaining sculptures!

Library of Parliament ✶✶✶   A glorious 16-sided dome, hewn from Nepean sandstone, supported outside by flying buttresses, and paneled inside with Canadian white pine, the library is designed in the Gothic Revival style and was opened in 1876. Inside, a variety of textures, colors, and hand-crafted detail is evident. The floor is an intricate parquet design of cherry, walnut, and oak. The pine paneling features thousands of carved flowers, masks, and mythical beasts. The center of the room is dominated by a white marble statue of the young Queen Victoria, created in 1871. Major repair work that may take a number of years is scheduled for the Library, during which time it will be closed to the public. Call ℂ **613/992-4793** to find out whether the Library will be open during your visit.

(Fact

Concerts of the 53-bell Carillon of the Peace Tower are presented weekdays in July and August at 2pm (1-hour concert). From September to June, there is a 15-minute noon concert most weekdays.

The Peace Tower ✶✶   The imposing 92-m (302-ft.) campanile of the **Peace Tower** is one of the most easily recognizable Canadian landmarks and dominates the Centre Block's façade. It houses a 53-bell carillon, a huge clock, an observation deck, and the Memorial Chamber, commemorating Canada's war dead. A 10.5-m (35-ft.) bronze mast flying a Canadian flag is on top of the tower. When Parliament is in session, the tower is lit. The elevator in the tower is unusual. See if you can sense the 10-degree angle off vertical that the elevator travels for the first 29m (98 ft.) of the journey. It's well worth the trip—the views from the Observation Deck are marvelous in every direction.

 Tips

Visit the Peace Tower and enjoy the view from the Observation Deck, but be aware that it closes half an hour before the last Centre Block tour of the day.

Guided Tour of Centre Block ★★★   Free guided tours of the Centre Block, which may include the House of Commons, the Senate, the Hall of Honour, and the Library of Parliament, are available in English and French all year. Guides tell animated stories and interesting anecdotes about the buildings and the people who have worked there. When Parliament is sitting, the tours do not visit the House of Commons or the Senate, but visitors are invited to sit in the public galleries and watch the proceedings. Please note that the Library of Parliament will be closing, possibly for several years, to allow repairs to be undertaken. To find out if the Library will be open during your visit, call ☎ **613/ 992-4793.** Tour times vary throughout the year; call the Capital Infocentre at ☎ **800/465-1867** or 613/239-5000 for information.

Self-Guided Tour of the Grounds   With the help of an outdoor self-guiding booklet called **Discover the Hill,** available from the Capital Infocentre across the street from the Parliament Buildings, you can wander around Parliament Hill and explore the monuments, grounds, and buildings on your own. Stroll the grounds clockwise around the Centre Block—they're dotted with statues honoring such prominent historical figures as Queen Victoria, Sir George-Étienne Cartier, William Lyon Mackenzie King, and Sir Wilfrid Laurier. Behind the building is a promenade with sweeping views of the river. Here too is the old Centre Block's bell, which crashed to the ground shortly after tolling midnight on the eve of the 1916 fire. At the bottom of the cliff behind Parliament (accessible from the Ottawa Locks on the Rideau Canal), a pleasant pathway leads along the Ottawa River. In July and August, you may be lucky enough to meet one or two of the historic characters from early Confederation times and exchange a word or two with them.

Guided Outdoor Walking Tour   Between late June and early September, you can get free same-day tickets at the Info Tent for a guided tour of the grounds. Visitors will get an introduction to some of the historic figures who have shaped Canada's past and present.

Changing of the Guard ★★★   On Parliament Hill's lawn, a colorful Canadian ceremony is held every morning (weather permitting) between late June and late August. Two historic regiments—the Governor General's Foot Guards and the Canadian Grenadier Guards—make up the Ceremonial Guard of the Armed Forces. The daily parade includes 125 soldiers in busbies and scarlet tunics. The Guard assembles at Cartier Square Drill Hall (Laurier Avenue by the Rideau Canal) at 9:30am and marches north on Elgin Street, sweeping west along Wellington Street and timed to reach the Hill at 10am. On arrival at the Hill, the Ceremonial Guard splits, with the old and new guard positioning itself on opposite sides of the Parliament Hill lawn. The dress and weaponry of both groups are inspected. The colors are then marched before the troops and saluted, and the guards present arms to each other. In true military fashion, sergeant-majors bark commands that prompt the soldiers to perform their synchronized maneuvers. The final symbolic act is the transfer of the guard-room key to to the incoming guard commander, signifying that the process has been completed. The relieved unit marches down Wellington Street and back to the Drill Hall to the beat of the military band.

Sound and Light on the Hill   Every evening between early July and early September, Canada's history unfolds and the country's spirit is revealed through music, lights, and giant images projected on the Parliament Buildings. This dazzling half-hour display of sound and light is free of charge and limited bleacher seating is available.

Moments

If you're a Canadian citizen, take a moment or two to look up at the Canadian flag on top of the Peace Tower and reflect on how proud and thankful you feel to be part of the great country that is Canada.

Test Your Knowledge of Parliament Hill

1. How many female speakers of the House of Commons have there been?
2. How tall is the Peace Tower?
3. How was the Library saved during the terrible fire of 1916 that destroyed the rest of the Parliament Buildings?
4. What color is the carpet in the Senate Chamber?
5. What or who stands in the center of the Parliamentary Library?
6. How many bells are there in the Carillon of the Peace Tower?
7. When was Canada's now-familiar red-and-white flag raised for the first time on the Peace Tower?
8. Who carved the frieze in the House of Commons foyer which depicts the History of Canada and how long did it take to complete?
9. What stone is primarily used on the exterior and interior of the Parliament Buildings?
10. What images can be seen in the stained-glass windows of the House of Commons?
11. Who lit the Centennial Flame in 1967?
12. How long does it take for the copper roof panels to turn green?

ANSWERS: *1. 2. 2. 92.2m (302.5 ft.). 3. A quick-thinking employee closed the iron doors to prevent the fire from spreading there. 4. Red. 5. A white marble statue of Queen Victoria. 6. 53. 7. February 15, 1965. 8. Sculptor Eleanor Milne took 11 years to create the beautiful stone frieze. 9. Nepean sandstone from Ontario is used on the exterior and Tyndall limestone from Manitoba is used inside. 10. The floral emblems of Canada's provinces and territories. 11. Prime Minister Lester B. Pearson. 12. About 30 years.*

Ottawa Attractions

The Top Attractions
Parliament Hill **1**
Canadian Museum
of Civilization **2**
National Gallery **3**
Canadian Museum
of Nature **4**
Canada Science &
Technology Museum **5**
Canada Aviation Museum **6**
RCMP Rockcliffe Stables **7**
Canadian War Museum **8**
Canada Agriculture
Museum & Central
Experimental Farm **9**

Ottawa's Waterways
Rideau Canal **10A**
Rideau River **10B**
Rideau Falls **10C**
Ottawa River **10D**
Dow's Lake **10E**
Ottawa Locks **10F**
Hartwells Locks **10G**
Hog's Back
Locks & Falls **10H**

Museums & Galleries
Canada and
the World Pavilion **11**
Canadian Museum of
Contemporary Photography **12**
Canadian Postal Museum **13**
Canadian Children's Museum **14**
Canadian Ski Museum **15**
Currency Museum
of the Bank of Canada **16**
Logan Hall,
Geological Survey of Canada **17**
National Library of Canada/
National Archives **18**
Royal Canadian Mint **19**
Lester B. Pearson Building **20**
Supreme Court of Canada **21**

Heritage Attractions
Billings Estate Museum **22**
Bytown Museum **23**
ByWard Market **24**
Laurier House **25**
Rideau Hall **26**
Turtle Island
Aboriginal Village **27**

Historic Churches
Cathedral Basilica
of Notre-Dame **28**
Christ Church Cathedral **29**
St. Andrew's
Presbyterian Church **30**

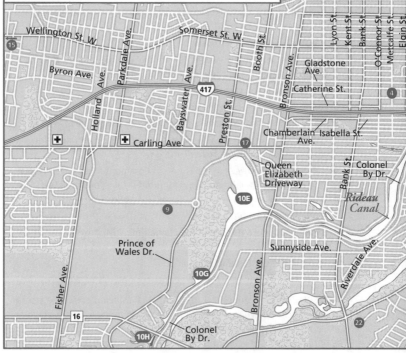

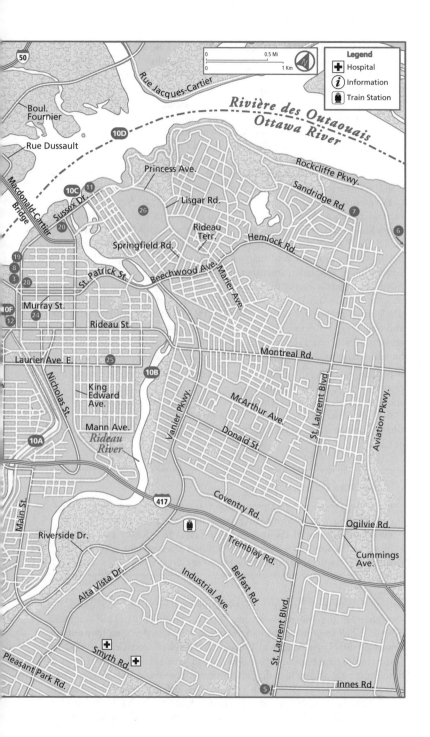

CANADIAN MUSEUM OF CIVILIZATION ✶✶✶

The largest of Canada's cultural institutions, the Canadian Museum of Civilization (CMC) attracts almost 1.5 million visitors each year. The museum is a combination of permanent and temporary exhibits that explore human history with special, although not exclusive, reference to Canada. The museum is located on the north shore of the Ottawa River in Hull, its stunning award-winning architecture clearly visible from downtown Ottawa. The building's flowing curves appear to have been sculpted by the forces of nature. Inside the museum, the impressive design continues to delight visitors as they make their way around the exhibition halls. Added attractions within the building are the Canadian Children's Museum, the Canadian Postal Museum, and the IMAX theater.

You'll enter the building at street level, where you can buy your museum entrance tickets and IMAX tickets. It's also the level that the **Canadian Children's Museum** is on. You can register for a 45-minute guided tour of the Grand Hall or the Canada Hall for an extra C$2.50 (US$1.70) per person or just wander on your own. Before you begin your exploration of the museum, be sure to drop off coats, umbrellas, and other outdoor gear at the complimentary cloakroom and collect a stroller or wheelchair if needed. There is pay underground parking with an inside entrance to the museum. You could easily spend the whole day here, especially if you take in an IMAX show. For **visitors with disabilities,** there are designated bays on level 1 of the parking arcade, elevator access to all floors, and access ramps installed where necessary. Spaces are reserved for wheelchairs in the IMAX theater and the performance/lecture theater.

Where to eat: There is a fine-dining restaurant, **Les Muses,** and a spacious cafeteria on site. Both facilities enjoy a spectacular view of the Ottawa River and Parliament Hill. Reservations recommended at **Les Muses;** call ✆ **819/776-7009.** If the weather's nice, you can take a picnic to Jacques-Cartier Park which is on the banks of the Ottawa River right beside the Canadian Museum of Civilization.

⎛ *Tips* Buy Two and Save

If you want to see an **IMAX** presentation (about 45 minutes in length) the same day, buy your tickets when you pay the museum entrance fee at the **Canadian Museum of Civilization.** You'll save a few dollars and you will also ensure a seat in the theater. **IMAX** shows often sell out in advance of showtime, particularly in the peak tourist season.

Grand Hall ✶✶   From the street-level lobby, descend the escalator to the showpiece of the museum—the magnificent Grand Hall. This enormous exhibition hall features a display of more than 40 totem poles, representing the culture of the Native peoples of Canada's Pacific Northwest Coast. Six Native house façades have been constructed in the hall, based on architectural styles of different coastal nations over the past 150 years. The Grand Hall also has a performance stage where storytelling sessions, demonstrations, and performances are held regularly. At the far end of the Hall, a forest setting has been created in a room displaying prehistoric artifacts and articles from the Tsimshian people of British Columbia.

Canada Hall ★★★   This impressive exhibit, set under a dramatically lit 17-m (56-ft.) high dome, takes visitors on a journey through 1,000 years of Canada's social, cultural, and material history. The Canada Hall is a presentation of full-scale tableaux and buildings that have been constructed in the architectural style of specific periods in history using materials (solid wood beams and planking, plaster, stucco, stone, and so on) and methods in use at the time. The sights and sounds of the country's past unfold before you, beginning with the landing of the Norsemen on Newfoundland's coast in A.D. 1000. As you move through the hall, you move west through the country and forward in time. Look below deck in a full-scale stern section of a 16th-century Basque whaling ship, see the crude process of rendering whale blubber into oil in a Labrador whaling station, and peer into a farmhouse in the St. Lawrence Valley in 18th-century New France. You'll walk into the public square of a town in New France and have the liberty of opening doors and peeking through windows into the lives of the inhabitants. You may be lucky enough to meet one of the colorful historic characters who roam the exhibits from time to time, interacting with the public and adding a new dimension to the museum experience. A lumber camp shanty, a Conestoga wagon, and the main street of a small Ontario town in the Victorian era are a few more sights you'll see during your exploration of Canada's heritage.

First Peoples Hall   The purpose of the First Peoples Hall is to provide a venue to showcase the cultural, historical, and artistic accomplishments of Aboriginal peoples in Canada. Exhibits include an Art Gallery dedicated to contemporary Aboriginal art.

Special Exhibitions   A large hall with three distinct exhibition spaces is dedicated to short-term displays encompassing all museum disciplines—archeology, ethnology, folk culture, and history. Call the museum to see what's on in the **Special Exhibitions Hall,** the **Arts and Traditions Hall,** and the **Gallery,** or just drop in and be surprised.

Canadian History Galleries   Special exhibitions in this space change on a regular basis. Recent exhibitions include The Story of Glass and Glass-Making in Canada. Until March 30, 2003, The Story of Dolls in Canada is on display. Over 400 dolls, including Inuit and First Nations dolls, rare antiques, and a collection of contemporary dolls made by Canadian artists are included in the exhibition.

Canadian Postal Museum   This museum is housed within the Canadian Museum of Civilization and admission is included with the main museum ticket. Discover the story of postal communications from coast to coast and around the world. Interactive displays and a high-tech station teach visitors about the world of stamps. All kinds of memorabilia are on display, from toys and quilts to mailboxes and mailbags. A new permanent exhibition was opened in 2000 that shows the role the post has played in Canada's history and features a complete post office from Quebec. Temporary exhibits range from an introduction to stamp-collecting and an opportunity to design your own stamp to displays of postage stamps from around the world with specimens from the Canadian Museum's International Philatelic Collection.

(Kids **Let Them Play**

If you have children with you when you visit the **Canadian Museum of Civilization,** I recommend visiting the **Children's Museum** first. Let them run around and play there, take a break for a drink and a snack or lunch (you can choose from formal dining or a cafeteria; both offer spectacular views over the Ottawa River toward the Parliament Buildings, or brown-bag it in the Lunch Box), and then walk through the **main exhibition halls.**

(Value

Admission to the **Children's Museum** is included with the main entrance ticket for the **Canadian Museum of Civilization,** although the hours may vary slightly from the main museum hours. You can just visit the Children's Museum if you wish, but the price will be the same.

Canadian Children's Museum ⭐⭐ Kids absolutely love to play in this hands-on just-for-kids museum. Every exhibit is child-size and the layout of the museum strongly encourages exploration. Hands-on activities and programs use real materials from the museum's collection. Visitors touch, climb, build, manipulate, move, and create. Through this highly interactive learning, children explore the world and its many cultures. For example, they can step inside a child-size Japanese family home. In the tatami (straw-matting) room kids are invited to try the art of origami (Japanese paper folding) or write their own haiku poetry in the garden. Other exciting adventures include exploring an Egyptian pyramid, crawling into a Bedouin tent, putting on an Indonesian shadow puppet show, sitting astride a camel, driving a Pakistani tour bus, or building a brick wall. Because of the scale of the interactive buildings and stations, kids immediately feel comfortable here and they do tend to zip around from place to place like an out-of-control pinball if you don't exercise a little parental guidance. Kids from 0 to 14 are the target group, but the kids who will get the most out of the museum (and may want to stay all day) are probably 4- to 11-year-olds. Programs, workshops, and theater performances are scheduled all year around. Call ahead to find out about upcoming special events. During the summer months, you get double the fun because the outdoor exhibition park **Adventure World** is open. Play chess on a giant chessboard, hop along with hopscotch, or shoot some marbles. The Art-rageous Adventure exhibit area hosts visual arts activities for children. The Waterways exhibit has a boat-making yard where you can design, build, and launch your own model watercraft. Kids can climb on a log-pulling tugboat or take an imaginary tour in the floatplane.

Where to eat: See Canadian Museum of Civilization.

100 Laurier St., Hull, QC. Within the Canadian Museum of Civilization (CMC). ✆ **819/776-7001.** Admission included with CMC ticket. For directions see listing information for Canadian Museum of Civilization.

IMAX Theater ⭐⭐ This amazing theater combines the technology of IMAX and IMAX DOME. The feeling is one of being wrapped in sight and sound. The IMAX screen is amazing enough—it's seven stories high and ten times the size of a conventional movie screen. To experience the full effect, a 23-m (76-ft.) diameter hemispheric IMAX DOME moves into place overhead once the audience is seated. All 295 theater seats tilt back to give the audience a comfortable and clear view of the dome. Not all films use the entire screening system. Advance ticket purchase is recommended as shows often sell out in advance. Tickets can be purchased in person at the museum box office (discount if purchased with a museum entrance ticket) or through Ticketmaster. All ages admitted. Plan to arrive 20 minutes before show time, as latecomers will not be admitted. Films are approximately 45 minutes in length.

100 Laurier St., Hull, QC. (C) **800/555-5621** or 819/776-7000. www.civilization.ca. IMAX Theatre information (C) **819/776-7010**. IMAX tickets at museum box office or call Ticketmaster (C) **613/755-1111**. Museum admission (prices subject to change) C$8 (US$5) adult, C$7 (US$4) senior, C$6 (US$4) student, C$4 (US$2.50) child, C$20 (US$12) family (max 5 members). Sunday half price. Free every Thurs 4pm–9pm, the Sunday before Heritage Day, Museums Day, Canada Day (July 1), Remembrance Day (Nov 11). Admission free for members. IMAX ticket sold separately. May 1–June 30 daily 9am–6pm, Thurs until 9pm (Children's Museum closes 6pm). July 1 to first Tues in Sept, Sat–Wed 9am–6pm, Thurs and Fri 9am–9pm (Children's Museum closes at 6pm). First Wed in Sept to second Tues in Oct daily 9am to 6pm, Thurs until 9pm (Canadian Children's Museum closes at 6pm). Second Wed in Oct to April 30, Tues–Sun 9am–5pm, Thurs until 9pm (Canadian Children's Museum until 6pm). IMAX Theatre hours may differ from museum hours. Pay parking on site in underground lot with inside access to museum. From the Ottawa River Parkway or Wellington St. downtown, take the Portage Bridge to Hull and turn right onto rue Laurier. The museum is on your right, just a couple of minutes' drive. From the east side of the canal, take Sussex Dr. and cross the Alexandra Bridge into Hull. The museum is on your immediate left as you exit the bridge.

(*Fact*

Did you know that Ottawa has the highest concentration of museums in Canada?

NATIONAL GALLERY OF CANADA

One of the most attractive buildings in the city, the **National Gallery** glitters and gleams from a promontory overlooking the Ottawa River. Moshe Safdie, who designed the Habitat apartment block and Musée des Beaux-Arts in Montreal, was the architect for the building, the permanent home of the largest collection of Canadian art in the world since 1988. The public entrance to the Grand Hall is along a cavernous sloped glass concourse that offers splendid views of Parliament Hill. Ingeniously designed shafts with reflective panels maximize the amount of natural light that floods the galleries. More than 800 paintings, sculptures, and decorative works by Canadian artists are regularly on display, a sampling of the 10,000 works in the permanent collection. Among the highlights are a comprehensive collection of works by Tom Thomson and the Group of Seven, early Québécois artists, and Montreal Automatistes. European masters are also represented, form Corot and Turner to Chagall and Picasso, and contemporary galleries feature pop art and minimalism, plus abstract works from Canadians and Americans. Admission is free to the permanent collections. Fees vary for special exhibitions, including a major summer exhibition held annually. Advance tickets may be purchased for some exhibitions—if you particularly want to see a certain exhibition, get tickets ahead to avoid disappointment. Call (C) **888/541-8888** for information. Families can visit the Artissimo kiosk weekends and during school vacations 11am to 4pm, where kids age 3 and up accompanied by an adult can create their own masterpieces.

Family workshops are designed for parents and kids to learn more about art, its interpretation, and its origins. For information or registration for these programs, call ℰ **613/990-4888.** Programs also available for guests with special needs, including occasional tactile workshops and tours for visually impaired visitors. Free guided tours of the permanent collections for the public are held daily at 11am and 2pm. Facilities include two restaurants and a gift and bookstore, which is well worth a visit. Wheelchairs and strollers available.

380 Sussex Dr. ℰ **800/319-2787** or 613/990-1985. http://national.gallery.ca. Admission free to permanent collection. Admission price varies for special exhibitions. May–mid-Oct daily 10am–6pm, Thurs until 8pm. Mid-Oct–Apr Wed–Sun 10am–5pm, Thurs until 8pm. From the Queensway, take Nicholas St. exit (exit 118). Turn left on Rideau St., right onto Sussex Dr. The Museum is on your left. Pay parking available on site in underground lot with inside entrance to museum.

CANADIAN MUSEUM OF NATURE ⟨★⟨★⟨★

This is a superb place to explore the wonders of the natural world and merits either a full day (with a good break halfway through) or a couple of visits to see all the exhibits—and everything is worth seeing, all four floors of it. The architecture of the historic building is remarkable. Built of local sandstone, the design includes towers, arched windows, magnificent stained-glass windows, and a grand central staircase.

The first place that most visitors head for is the **Dinosaur Exhibit.** All of the museum's skeletons date from 90 to 65 million years ago and were discovered in the Badlands of southern Alberta and Saskatchewan. Real fossilized bones are on display, augmented by plaster and fiberglass pieces where necessary. The **Creepy Critters Gallery** is alive with insects, rodents, and reptiles. It's not for the squeamish—only a pane of glass separates you from the hundreds of crawling, scurrying, and slippery creatures. See cockroaches, slugs, rats, snakes, leeches, spiders, and toads in habitats that replicate their natural living conditions. If you prefer cuddly, furry creatures, pay a visit to the galleries on the second floor east, which display preserved specimens of **Canadian birds and mammals** in highly detailed dioramas. Have a seat at the listening post and have fun trying to identify different birdcalls. Next, drop in to the **Viola MacMillan Mineral Gallery** and feast your eyes on glittering gemstones and precious metals. Move along to the Activity Centre, where you can take the helm of a deep-sea research submarine, visit a gold mine, and travel in an experimental time machine to learn about the **evolution of the Earth.** The **Plant Gallery** has hundreds of living plants, everything from ferns and mosses to coniferous plants and flowers. Between June and September, a colony of bees collect pollen to make honey. An exhibit on obtaining medicines from plant sources rounds out the "green" gallery.

⸩ Fun Fact

Do you know how the head gardener at the Museum of Nature keeps the plants looking so green and lush? Look up at the ceiling. When the museum is closed, these lights are switched on to simulate bright daylight at a greater intensity than would be possible naturally in the relatively dark conditions of the museum during the day.

Highly entertaining and educational nature films are on show in the recently installed **high-definition cinema,** the highest quality digital video technology available. Movies change frequently and are all approximately 45 minutes long. Generally there are two screenings daily in each official language and admission is included with your entrance fee to the museum.

Where to eat: There's a cafeteria on site with a brown-bag area. There's a grassy area with picnic tables in front of the museum, as long as you don't mind sharing the space with a life-size replica of a woolly mammoth family.

Victoria Memorial Museum Building, 240 McLeod St. ⓒ **800/263-4433** or 613/566-4700. Admission C$6 (US$4) adult, C$5 (US$3) senior and student, C$2.50 (US$1.55) child 3–12, children 2 and under free. Thurs half-price until 5pm; free 5pm–8pm. Mid Oct–Apr Tues–Sun 10am–5pm, Thurs until 8pm. May–Labour Day (first Mon in Sept) daily 9:30am–5pm, Thurs until 8pm. Labour Day–mid-Oct daily 10am–5pm, Thurs until 8pm. Located between O'Connor and Elgin streets, one block south of Gladstone Ave. Note that McLeod St. is a one-way street running west, so enter off Elgin St.

(**Fact**

Following the fire that destroyed the Parliament Buildings in 1916, emergency quarters were set up for the government in the building that is now the home of the Canadian Museum of Nature. The House of Commons sat in the Auditorium for four years, and the Senate occupied the Hall of Invertebrate Fossils (no joke intended). In 1919, the body of Sir Wilfrid Laurier lay in state in the Auditorium.

OTTAWA'S WATERWAYS

Ottawa's origins are inextricably linked to its waterways, since it was the settlement that grew up around the canal construction site that eventually became Ottawa. Modern-day Ottawa enjoys the canal and river primarily for leisure and pleasure. The city's beauty is enhanced by the extensive network of parkways, pathways, and parks that follow the shores of the Rideau Canal, Rideau River, and Ottawa River.

Rideau Canal 🌟   The **Rideau Canal** is actually a continuous chain of beautiful lakes, rivers, and canal cuts, stretching 202km (125 miles) between Ottawa and Kingston, and often described as the most scenic waterway in North America. The **Rideau Canal** waterway has been designated a National Historic Site and is one of nine historic canals in Canada. Parks Canada has the responsibility of preserving and maintaining the canal's natural and historic features and providing a safe waterway for boats to navigate. The canal and locks that link the lakes and rivers of the Rideau Valley were constructed between 1826 and 1832 to provide a safe route for the military between Montreal and Kingston in the wake of the War of 1812. Colonel By, the British engineer in charge of the project, had the foresight to build the locks and canal large enough to permit commercial traffic to access the system rather than building the canal solely for military use. As things turned out, the inhabitants of North America decided to live peaceably. The canal became a main transportation and trade route and communities along the canal grew and thrived. With the introduction of railroads in the mid–19th century, the commercial traffic subsided and the canal gradually became a tourist destination due to its beauty and tranquility. The locks have operated continuously since they first opened. In the **winter,** the canal freezes over and turns into the world's longest and most famous skating rink, the **Rideau Canal Skateway.** The season usually runs from late December to late February or early March. For current information on ice conditions during the season, call the **Skateway Hotline** © **613/239-5234.** Heated shelters, skate and sled rentals, boot-check and skate-sharpening services, rest areas, food concessions, and toilets are located at various points along the Skateway. Main access points are by the National Arts Centre, Fifth Avenue and Queen Elizabeth Drive, and Dow's Lake.

Rideau River   The Ottawa section of the Rideau River bisects the city, with the Rideau Canal running roughly parallel for the final 8km (5 miles) leading to the Rideau Falls. The Rideau River is part of the Rideau Waterway, a collective name for the entire system of lakes, rivers, and canal cuts that make up the route between Ottawa and Kingston. In 2000, the river gained the designation of a Canadian Heritage River. Many city parks are located along its banks, including Rideau Falls Park, New Edinburgh Park, Strathcona Park, Rideau River Park, Brewer Park, Vincent Massey Park, Hog's Back Park, and Mooney's Bay Park.

Rideau Falls ★   Located just off Sussex Drive where the Rideau River empties over a cliff into the Ottawa River, Rideau Falls is surrounded by a beautifully landscaped park. A footbridge spans the Rideau River and the 30-m (98-ft.) falls are illuminated in the evening. Canada and the World Pavilion, which re-opened in 2001 as a permanent attraction, is located here in the park.

Ottawa River   Historically, the Ottawa River was a major transportation corridor for moving people and goods. When the Europeans settled in the area, the water was harnessed to generate power for the lumber industry. This majestic river is now enjoyed by canoeists, white water enthusiasts, and other outdoor adventurers.

Dow's Lake ★   The pretty lake that adjoins the Rideau Canal in central Ottawa was once a mosquito-infested swamp and outbreaks of malaria were common amongst canal construction workers in the early 1800s. No one wanted to cut a canal through the swampland. Colonel By, the British engineer in charge of the canal construction, solved the problem by damming a branch of the Rideau River that used to run where Preston Street is now, and flooded the swamp. If you visit Dow's Lake when the water levels are low, you may see tree stumps here and there. These stumps are all that remain of the old white pines that grew in the area before the basin was flooded. Dow's Lake is a popular site in the summer. Pedal boats and canoes are available for rental and the Pavilion has restaurants with terraces overlooking the lake. In winter you can rent skates and go for a twirl on the ice.

Tips   **Tiptoe Through the Tulips**

The tulip beds in Confederation Park at the northern tip of Dow's Lake attract thousands of visitors during the Canadian Tulip Festival in May. An amazing 300,000 bulbs bloom in the park, making it the largest tulip display in the region.

Get on the Water

There are several companies operating river and canal tours. Reservations are recommended for all of them. **Ottawa Riverboat Company** (© 613/ 562-4888) offers a 90-minute tour on the 280-passenger *Sea Prince II,* the largest tour boat in Ottawa. Bilingual guides provide commentary as you tour past famous buildings and landmarks as seen from the Ottawa River. **Paul's Boat Lines** (© 613/225-6781) cruises the Ottawa River and the Rideau Canal. On the Ottawa River, the 150-passenger *Paula D* takes visitors on a 90-minute cruise, with spectacular views of the Parliament Buildings, Rideau Falls, and other sites. On the canal, you can glide along in one of three low-profile tour boats for a 75-minute cruise. For a unique tour of the city, hop on an amphibious bus (**Amphibus** © 613/223-6211 or **Canada Ducks** © 613/792-3825), a hybrid vehicle that cruises on the water and tours on land. The tours last between 1 and 1½ hours, driving along city streets past historic sites and city landmarks, then plunging into the Ottawa River for a cruise. If what appeals to you is nothing more than just "messing around in boats," then rent a paddleboat or canoe at **Dow's Lake.** For more detailed information on boat tours, see "On the Water" later in this chapter.

Locks ⓕ   Rivers often have rocky sections with shallow, fast-flowing water. Naturally this presents a challenge to navigation, and locks were devised to enable boats to safely move uphill and downhill through the water in a controlled manner. There are **45 locks** manned by **24 lock stations** along the main channel of the 202-km (125-mile) **Rideau Canal.** The waterway rises a total of 50m (164 ft.) from Kingston on Lake Ontario to Upper Rideau Lake, then drops 83m (273 ft.) to the Ottawa River in Ottawa, ending in the 30-m (98-ft.) Rideau Falls. In Ottawa there are three places where you can watch the locks in action. The most popular spot is in downtown Ottawa at the point where the first locks were built. If you stand on the north side of the **Plaza Bridge** (between Parliament Hill and Château Laurier) and look down, you'll have a wonderful view of the eight **Ottawa Locks,** which connect the canal to the Ottawa River, a drop of 24m (80 ft.). Travel time through the locks is about 1½ hours. You can go down a stairway beside the bridge (or go down a ramp from the south side of the bridge) right to the level of the locks and watch them in operation. If you have children with you, be extremely careful to keep them away from the lock side because there are no safety barriers next to the water. The **Bytown Museum** is alongside the locks. Upstream along the canal, the next two locks are **Hartwells Locks,** which take about half an hour to navigate. The entrance to the locks is off Prince of Wales Drive south of **Dow's Lake.** The **Central Experimental Farm** borders this section of the canal and there's an extensive network of paved and gravel bike paths. A little farther upstream are the **Hog's Back Locks,** reached by road at 795 Hog's Back Road. An interpretive trail links the locks with Hog's Back dam. There's a bonus at Hog's Back—a swing bridge is part of the lock system, designed to accommodate vessels requiring a clearance greater than 2.8m (9.4 ft.). The bridge swings on demand except during peak traffic periods on weekdays. The parkland in this area surrounds the spectacular **Hog's Back Falls,** situated at the point where the Rideau Canal meets the Rideau River. They're named after rocks that are said to resemble the bristles on a hog's back. A refreshment pavilion, parking, and washroom facilities are available.

The Rideau Canal joins the Ottawa River with a series of eight locks just east of the Parliament Buildings. The canal winds south for approximately 8km (5 miles), opening out into Dow's Lake roughly two-thirds of the way along, and eventually joins the Rideau River at Mooney's Bay on the west side of Riverside Dr. at Hog's Back Rd. The canal is bordered by Prince of Wales Dr. and Queen Elizabeth Parkway on the west side and Colonel By Dr. on the east side. The Rideau River follows a similar course to the east of the canal.

CANADA SCIENCE & TECHNOLOGY MUSEUM ⊛⊛⊛

This excellent museum has eye-catching interactive exhibits at every turn. One of the most intriguing long-term exhibits is **Canada in Space.** Discover the story of Canada's role in space. Various tools such as Radarsat, MSAT, the Canadarm, and the International Space Station Alpha can be explored. A space flight simulator will take you on a virtual voyage in a six-seat cinema pod that moves to the action on the huge screen. You need to purchase tickets for this ride and it's easiest to do that when you first enter the museum. Take note of the ride time so you don't miss your trip to outer space. The **Locomotive Hall** holds four huge steam locomotives, meticulously restored and maintained. You can climb in the cabs of some of them and you can also see a caboose, business car, old number boards, and hear sound effects that give you the feeling of riding in a live locomotive. Designed especially for kids, the **Energy Discovery Hall** helps young visitors to learn about energy as they explore dozens of interactive displays set in familiar environments such as a city park, nature trail, house, and amusement park. A major exhibition on **communications** is one of the largest of its kind in Canada and illustrates the history of electric and electronic communications in Canada. Lively, short **demonstrations** on different topics are held frequently during the day, so ask at the desk when you arrive and take in a show or two during your visit. Lots of programs and workshops are scheduled, so call ahead if you want to take part. Plan at least a half-day visit here. In the summer, have a picnic in the **Technology Park** out front. Visit the Cape North Lighthouse, radar antenna, pump jack, Convair Atlas rocket, telescope, windmill, and steam locomotive. A cafeteria indoors serves light meals and snacks. The museum's gift shop, located close to the main entrance, is a wonderful place to shop, with a science/technology/educational theme running throughout. The museum is fully wheelchair accessible and parking is free.

Where to eat: There's a cafe on site. In front of the museum there is a small park with picnic tables. On St. Laurent Boulevard there are a number of family restaurant chains.

1867 St. Laurent Blvd. ⓒ 613/991-3044 (general information), ⓒ 613/991-3053 (reservations and program information). www.science-tech.nmstc.ca. Admission C$6 (US$4) adult, C$5 (US$3) senior and student, C$2 (US$1.25) children 6–14, children 5 and under free, C$12 (US$7) family (max 2 adults and 2 children). Simulator ride C$5 (US$3) per person. Summer daily 9am–5pm. Winter Tues–Sun 9am–5pm. From the Queensway (Hwy 417), take the St. Laurent Blvd. South exit. Go south on St. Laurent Blvd. to Lancaster Rd. and turn left. The museum entrance is on your left.

CANADA AVIATION MUSEUM ⊛⊛

One of the best collections of vintage aircraft in the world is on display here. Whether you're young or old, you'll find something to catch your interest, as you stroll through the huge **exhibition hall** and trace the history of aviation from its beginning to the jet age. You can come close (but not enough to touch;

aircraft are fragile machines) to more than 50 aircraft inside the building and around half a dozen more outside in the summer months. A Silver Dart hangs from the ceiling as you enter. From that point, as you move through the museum, you'll see such famous aircraft as the Sopwith Camel, Messerschmitt, Spitfire, and Lancaster Bomber. The post-war exhibits include manufacturers such as Lockheed, de Havilland, and Sikorsky. Examples of the Beaver and Otter bush planes are on display and in the post-1960 section there are aircraft from the jet age. Video terminals dot the hall, showing short documentaries about aspects of flight. Several interactive displays, designed to teach the principles of flight, are simple enough for children to operate and understand. On weekends, Thursday evenings, and daily in the summer, the **Helicopter Studio** runs fun activities for families. Take a virtual flight through the Grand Canyon on the **Hang Glider Simulator,** only C$3 (US$2) a ride. Entertaining demonstrations are scheduled throughout the day—everything from wind tunnels to flying a Cessna 150. If you're looking for something a little different, try an **evening program** with scheduled events and dinner, or an **overnight stay** where you can explore the museum by flashlight and sleep under the wings of an airplane. If you are an aviation buff, or just love to fly, take advantage of a rare opportunity and splurge on a **vintage aircraft flight,** available from May to autumn. A 15-minute ride in an **open cockpit bi-plane** costs C$75 (US$46) per adult or C$110 (US$68) for an adult and child. You can also choose to fly in a two-seater de Havilland Canada **Chipmunk** with a canopy that allows clear views as you soar in the sky; price is C$75 (US$46) for a standard 15-minute ride. When you're back on terra firma, don't forget to take a turn through the **Aeronautica Boutique,** which stocks scale models of aircraft, books, posters, prints, toys, clothing, and kites. Free strollers and wheelchairs are available at the front entrance, plus a thoughtful addition: electric vehicles for visitors with physical disabilities and seniors. There's also a library specializing in the history of aviation with an emphasis on the Canadian experience. The library is primarily open by appointment for visitors with a special interest in aviation.

Where to eat: There is a small snack bar on site and an outdoor picnic area. Nearby St. Laurent Blvd. has a number of family restaurant chains.

11 Aviation Pkwy. (Rockcliffe Airport). © **800/463-2038** or 613/993-2010. www.aviation.nmstc.ca. Admission C$6 (US$4) adults, C$4 (US$2.50) seniors and students, C$2 (US$1.25) children 6–15, children under 6 free; C$12 (US$7) family (1 or 2 adults with children). Admission free to all Thurs 5pm–9pm. May 1–Labour Day (first Mon in Sept) daily 9am–5pm. After Labour Day to April 30 Tues–Sun 10am–5pm. All year Thurs until 9pm. Closed Mon in winter except holidays and school breaks. From downtown, travel northeast on Sussex Dr. (changes name to Rockcliffe Pkwy.) to Aviation Pkwy. Follow signs; museum is on the left.

RCMP MUSICAL RIDE AND STABLES ★★

The **Mounties** are beloved by Canadians and renowned the world over for their courage, integrity, and poise. They are also well known for their personable manner with the public, and this courtesy extends to their open invitation to the public to visit the **Training School and Stables** of the **RCMP Musical Ride.** The Musical Ride is a visual display by specially trained officers and horses who perform intricate riding drills and figures set to musical accompaniment. Free tours are available all year around. In the summer months, you'll find larger groups and more frequent tour schedules. In the winter, it's advisable to call ahead and set up a time with the coordinator, although it's not essential. When we called to ask about tours, we found out that there was a full dress rehearsal scheduled for the indoor arena in two days' time. We had the rare treat of watching the complete **Musical Ride** from a comfortable glassed-in gallery—in the company of the Irish Ambassador and his family, no less, which was an unexpected pleasure. We also had a tour of the stables and met several horses, including one who pulls the Queen's carriage when she's in town. Tour guides are friendly and willing to answer questions about the Musical Ride or the Mounties in general. If you don't happen to visit on a day when a practice is in session, or if the Ride is away on tour (which happens often during the summer), try to get tickets to one of their shows. They're always in Ottawa for the annual Sunset Ceremony in late June and they perform their Musical Ride on July 1 (Canada Day). Between May and October, they're on tour, but there are always some Eastern Ontario venues. There's a boutique at the Stables, open in the main tourist season, which stocks a variety of Mountie souvenirs.

Where to eat: St. Laurent Blvd. has a number of family restaurant chains, or head back downtown for a wider range of eateries.

Corner of Sandridge Rd. and St. Laurent Blvd. ✆ **613/993-3751** or **613/998-8199**. Free admission. Donations accepted. May–Oct daily 9am–4pm. Nov–Apr Mon–Fri 10am–2pm. From downtown, follow Sussex Dr. (changes name to Rockcliffe Pkwy.) to Aviation Pkwy. Follow signs; the Musical Ride Centre is at the northeast corner of Sandridge Rd. and St. Laurent Blvd.

 All About the Mounties

The Royal Canadian Mounted Police (RCMP) is Canada's national police force. Their mission is to preserve the peace, uphold the law, and provide quality service in partnership with the communities they serve.

The idea of a mounted police force was conceived by Sir John A. Macdonald, Canada's first prime minister and minister of justice. In order to open the western and northern frontiers of the young country for settlement and development in an orderly manner, law enforcement officers were needed. In 1873, the North-West Mounted Police was created, inspired by the Royal Irish Constabulary and the mounted rifle units of the United States Army. A year later, approximately 275 officers and men were dispatched to northwestern Canada.

Over the years, the force expanded and developed into the present-day organization, which numbers around 20,000 employees in total. The RCMP is unique in the world because it provides policing services at the national, federal, provincial, and municipal levels. A federal policing service is provided to all Canadians, plus three territories and eight provinces (Ontario and Quebec are the exceptions) are policed at the provincial level. Under separate agreements, the RCMP serves almost 200 municipalities and more than 190 First Nations communities.

Today the RCMP's role is multifaceted. Here's a list of the programs and services.

- Prevent and investigate crime
- Maintain order
- Enforce laws
- Contribute to national security
- Ensure the safety of state officials, visiting dignitaries, and foreign missions
- Provide vital operational support services to other police and law enforcement agencies.

RCMP Musical Ride: Facts & Figures

- The choreography of the Musical Ride is based upon traditional cavalry drill movements.
- The horse, scarlet tunic, and lance of the Ride are symbols of the Force's early history.
- The first Musical Ride was performed at Regina Barracks in Saskatchewan in 1887.
- The Ride is performed by 32 regular member volunteers (male and female) who have at least two years' police experience and who have taken a training course to qualify for the Ride.
- When on tour, the Ride team consists of 36 horses, 36 constables, 1 farrier, and 4 officers.
- The requirements for the horses' eligibility are very specific. They must be black, 16 to 17 hands high, and weigh between 523kg (1,150 lbs.) and 635kg (1,400 lbs.). Stallions must be registered Thoroughbred and broodmares are part Thoroughbred.
- Young horses, called remounts, begin training at 3 years of age. At 6 years old, they begin training specifically for the Musical Ride and take their first trip with the Ride.
- The saddle blankets feature the Force's regimental colors (blue and yellow) and bear the fused letters MP.
- The maple leaf pattern you can see on the horses' rumps is made with a metal stencil. Using a damp brush, the horses' hair is brushed across its natural lie to make it stand up.

CANADIAN WAR MUSEUM ★★

The Canadian War Museum is the country's military history museum and serves as a living memorial to men and women who have served in Canada's armed forces. Three floors of permanent exhibits tell the story of Canada in conflict, from the days of New France, through the two devastating world wars of the 20th century, to Canada's role as peacekeeper today. The personal stories of people whose lives have been affected by war are told and many exhibits feature authentic artifacts and memorabilia. Special events, concerts, war films, and historical re-enactments are frequently scheduled. Your ticket includes entry to **Vimy House** at 221 Champagne Avenue North, about a 15-minute drive from the War Museum. Vimy House is the museum's research and collections facility where military vehicles, tanks, artillery, weapons, war art, uniforms, and much more can be seen. Opening hours vary, so inquire at the War Museum before you set off to visit. Plans are under way for the construction of a new museum in the heart of downtown Ottawa on LeBreton Flats, an area of land bordering the Ottawa River about 2km (1.25 miles) west of Parliament Hill. The current museum artifacts and exhibits plus the contents of Vimy House will be displayed in the new complex. Construction is slated to begin in fall 2002, with the official opening in spring 2005.

330 Sussex Dr. ☎ **800/555-5621** or 819/776-8600. Admission C$4 (US$2.50) adult, C$3 (US$2) senior and youth, C$2 (US$1.30) child 2–12, C$9 (US$6) family (max 3 adults, 2 children or youth). Free admission for Canadian veterans, retired military personnel, and accompanying families. Free admission for members of the

Canadian Forces with identification and for cadets in uniform. Summer daily 9:30am–5pm, Thurs until 8pm. Winter Tues–Sun 9:30am–5pm, Thurs until 8pm. From the Queensway, take Nicholas St. exit (exit 118). Turn left on Rideau St., right onto Sussex Dr. The museum is on your left.

Tips

The Canadian Virtual War Memorial is being built as an electronic tribute to the Canadians and Newfoundlanders who have lost their lives in major conflicts since 1884. The website also serves as a searchable database so people can look for men and women in their own families who have given their lives for their country. Canadians are invited to submit digitized images of photos, letters, postcards, medals, and other war memorabilia. Visit **www.virtualmemorial.gc.ca** for instructions on how to add your family's war memorabilia to the Virtual War Memorial.

Kids   Playing at Soldiers

The Discovery Room on the third floor of the Canadian War Museum has interactive areas for kids and parents. Try on kid-size uniforms, peek through a trench periscope, or decipher the messages hidden in the beat of a military drum.

CANADA AGRICULTURE MUSEUM & CENTRAL EXPERIMENTAL FARM

In the heart of south central Ottawa lies one of the many greenspaces that contribute to Ottawa's reputation as the "green capital." More than 400 hectares (1,000 acres) of farmland make up the **Central Experimental Farm** (CEF). The major tenant of the CEF, occupying more than three-quarters of the property, is a crop research center, part of the federal government department of Agriculture and Agri-Food Canada. Within the vast CEF complex there are four public areas. Plants are the focus of the **Arboretum, Ornamental Gardens,** and **Tropical Greenhouse,** all with free admission. The Canada **Agriculture Museum,** which charges a modest entrance fee, features animal barns, special exhibits, and a chance to experience a traditional farm in action. The **Arboretum** covers about 35 hectares (88 acres) of rolling land near the Prince of Wales Drive roundabout. Open from sunrise to sunset daily, the Arboretum is a popular place for families to picnic and play in the summer. In the winter, the hills are used for tobogganing. Well over 2,400 distinct species and varieties of trees and shrubs grow here, with some dating from the 1880s. If you're a gardener or just love to wander among beautiful gardens, the 3.2-hectare (8-acre) **Ornamental Gardens** are a must-see. They were created by the government in the late 19th century to assist European immigrant farmers to test imported flowers, shrubs, and trees in the Canadian environment. There is a perennial collection, annual garden, rose garden, sunken garden, and rock garden. Some of the specimens in the hedge collection date from 1891. Approximately 100 types of iris and 125 strains of lilac are on display. The **Tropical Greenhouse** holds 500 different plants and is open daily 9am to 4pm. The **Agriculture Museum** offers city slickers (and country bumpkins, for that matter) a chance to get up close and personal with all things agricultural. The 2-hectare (5-acre) site is a unique blend of modern working farm and museum. Several heritage buildings are on the site, including a **dairy barn.** The **small animal barn** houses goats, sheep, pigs, and poultry. There's always something going on at the Agriculture Museum, whether it's a festival, special exhibit, day camp, or demonstration. If you're planning a visit, call ahead so you can catch one of the special days on the farm. Activities are planned with kids in mind and everyone from babies to grandparents will enjoy meeting the animals and learning about the farm. Programs and special events focus on how science and technology meshes with modern agriculture and show visitors the processes by which Canadians get their food, fibers, and other agricultural products.

Where to eat: Bring a picnic in summer and enjoy your lunch in the extensive grounds of the Central Experimental Farm. Dow's Lake Pavilion and Preston St. (Little Italy) are close by if you have a car.

Corner of Experimental Farm Dr. and Prince of Wales Dr. © **613/991-3044.** www.agriculture.nmstc.ca. Admission to Arboretum, Ornamental Gardens, and Tropical Greenhouse free. Admission to exhibits and animal barns of Agriculture Museum C$5 (US$3) adult, C$4 (US$2.50) students and seniors, C$3 (US$2) children 3–15, children under 3 free, C$12 (US$8) family (max 2 adults and 3 children). Animal barns daily 9am–5pm except Dec 25; exhibits and barn boutique daily 9am–5pm Mar 1–Oct 31. Take Prince of Wales Dr. and follow the signs. The museum is just west of Prince of Wales Dr. between Carling Ave. and Baseline Rd.

WHAT'S ON AT THE AGRICULTURE MUSEUM
This calendar of events will give you a good idea of the oodles of activities going on. Events are subject to change; please call ahead to avoid disappointment.

Spring
- Special exhibits re-open for the season. In 2001, the exhibits were "Bread: The Inside Story," which demonstrated how wheat is sown, grown, harvested, and made into bread. The "Barn of the 1920s" exhibit links with the bread theme by displaying the machinery of a wheat farm from that era.
- During the school break periods in Ontario and Quebec in March, special programs are scheduled that include feeding the animals, grooming calves, churning butter, and baking bread.
- Easter weekend features lots of family fun with rabbits to pet, newborn lambs and goats to visit, and hatching chicks. Join the Easter egg hunt on the grounds of the museum.
- Mother's Day and Museums Day are celebrated together with special family-oriented activities to acknowledge the important role of mothers on the farm.
- The annual sheep-shearing festival features demonstrations of sheep shearing, hoof trimming, Border collies herding sheep, wool crafts, and children's activities.
- Visit the farm on Spring Planting Day and help to plant oats, beans, barley, and wheat.

Summer
- Father's Day is marked with a day of activities to enjoy with Dad.
- Canada Day at the farm. Celebrate Canada's birthday with a day of family events, crafts, games, hayrides, and ice-cream making.
- One-week summer day camps are held in July and August for kids ages 4 to 14. They'll learn all about farming and food production through barn visits, daily

chores, crafts, and games. For information call ✆ **613/991-3053.**

Fall

- Labour Day weekend has special events scheduled. Maybe you'll see farm machinery, learn about organic farming, see rare breeds of farm animals, or meet horses, ponies, and donkeys.
- Fall Harvest Celebration takes place on Thanksgiving Weekend. Make apple cider, sample apple varieties, wander through a maze, take a hayride, or enjoy the entertainment.
- Barnyard Halloween. Decorate pumpkins and discover how they grow, and take part in a trick-or-treat scavenger hunt in the barns. You're invited to come in costume for this one.

Winter

- The barns are open daily 9am to 5pm except Christmas Day throughout the winter, but the exhibits and shop are closed.
- Between Christmas and New Year, special holiday activities are scheduled.

Ongoing

Barnyard Buddies is a series of one-hour workshops for 3- to 5-year-olds and their caregivers. Each week the fun includes a craft, story, songs, and a snack. Registration required. Call ✆ **613/991-3053.**

2 Museums & Galleries

MUSEUMS

Canada and the World Pavilion   Designed to celebrate and demonstrate achievements of individual Canadians on the international scene, this 1,104 m² (12,000 ft.²) pavilion opened as a permanent exhibition in 2001. Discover the unique stories of Canadians who have made an impact on the world in the fields of sports, the arts, international relations, and science and technology. Learn about filmmakers, comedians, the game of hockey, Olympic athletes, and the International Space Station. Operate a myoelectric arm or maneuver a wheelchair just like Rick Hansen's. Find out what Canadians are doing throughout the world to promote social justice, sustainable development, and basic human rights. Located in Rideau Falls Park on Sussex Drive, only a short walk from downtown. Free admission and on-site parking. While you're there, visit Rideau Falls (also in Rideau Falls Park) and Rideau Hall, whose main entrance is just a little farther north along Sussex Drive on your right.

50 Sussex Dr. (in Rideau Falls Park). For information call the Capital Infocentre at ✆ **800/465-1867** or 613/239-5000. Free admission. May–late June Wed–Mon 10am–5pm; late June–Labour Day (first Mon in Sept) daily 10am–6pm; Labour Day–late Oct Wed–Mon 10am–5pm. Parking on site. From downtown, travel northeast along Sussex Dr. The Pavilion is adjacent to Rideau Falls on your left.

Canadian Museum of Contemporary Photography   This museum is an affiliate of the National Gallery and the collection complements that of Canada's premier art gallery. On show is the best of documentary and art photography produced by Canada's most dynamic photographers, changing on a regular basis. The museum also organizes traveling exhibitions and educational programs.

1 Rideau Canal. ✆ **613/990-8257.** Admission free. May–Oct daily 10am–6pm, Thurs until 8pm. Oct–May Wed–Sun 10am–5pm, Thurs until 8pm. The museum is sandwiched between the Ottawa Locks and the Fairmont Château Laurier, just east of the Parliament Buildings.

Canadian Postal Museum   Tracing the history of mail delivery across the vast landscape of Canada, the Postal Museum is housed within the Canadian Museum of Civilization. For details, see the Canadian Museum of Civilization entry earlier in this chapter.

Canadian Ski Museum   Winter sports enthusiasts will enjoy a visit to the Canadian Ski Museum to learn about the history of skiing and how it evolved into the high-tech, high-speed sport of today. A large collection of photographs, memorabilia, and ski equipment is on display, aiming to preserve the memory of Canada's skiing history. The evolution of downhill skiing is explained, with credit for the world's first ski tow going to an enterprising Quebecer in the 1930s. Handmade wooden skis with strips of sealskin on the base to prevent back-slipping are a long way from the parabolic skis of today. After visiting the museum, you can browse the outdoor adventure equipment and supplies in **Trailhead,** the retail store on the main floor of the building. There are a number of other outdoor stores in the neighborhood of Westboro to explore as well—**Bushtukah** at 206 Richmond Road, **Mountain Equipment Co-op** at 366 Richmond Road, and **The Expedition Shoppe** at 369 Richmond Road. The Canadian Ski Museum entrance is at the side of the building housing Trailhead. Look for a blue door that opens to a stairway leading to the second floor.

1960 Scott St. ✆ **613/722-3584.** www.skimuseum.ca. Free admission. Mon–Sat 9am–5pm, Sun 11am–5pm. Guided tours are available.

Currency Museum of the Bank of Canada   Tracing the development of money over the past 2,500 years, the Currency Museum offers eight galleries to wander through and a spacious, light-filled atrium in the entrance hall of the center block of the Bank of Canada on Wellington Street, a couple of minutes' walk from Parliament Hill. Some unusual articles have been used as currency, including teeth, grain, cattle, glass beads, shells, fish hooks, and cocoa beans. Six of the galleries are devoted to history, the seventh holds special exhibits, and the eighth gallery showcases the most comprehensive display of Canadian numismatic material in the world. The collection puts particular emphasis on Canadian currency and its history. You can visit on your own or pre-register for a guided tour.

245 Sparks St. ✆ **613/782-8914.** For guided tour reservations call ✆ **613/782-8852.** www.bank-banque-canada.ca/museum. Free admission. May–Labour Day (first Mon in Sept) Mon–Sat 10:30am–5pm, Sun 1pm–5pm; Labour Day–April Tues–Sat 10:30am–5pm, Sun 1pm–5pm.

Logan Hall, Geological Survey of Canada   Logan Hall serves as an exhibition hall for a selection of the Geological Survey of Canada's vast collection of Canadian rocks, minerals, fossils, meteorites, and ores. Interactive displays and videos test visitors' knowledge of geology and even teach you how to pan for gold. An extensive fossil collection shows examples of bacteria, plants, and invertebrate and vertebrate animals, as well as fossils of specific historical interest. Logan Hall is named after Sir William Logan, who founded the Geological Survey of Canada in 1842 and was its first director.

601 Booth St. ✆ **613/995-4261.** Free admission. Mon–Fri 8am–4pm.

National Archives   The National Archives collect original unpublished material pertaining to Canada. They care for and share millions of documents of all types—diaries, artwork, maps, films, treaties, journals, and more. Access to these materials is provided to private researchers and government departments by appointment and there is a protocol to learn and follow. The public may visit the building to view special exhibitions that display a selection of archival materials. There is a permanent exhibition that tells the story of more than 400 years of Canadian history through approximately 100 original maps, paintings, photographs, and manuscripts. Temporary exhibitions change regularly and vary widely in their subject matter. Guided tours are available.

395 Wellington St. © 866/578-7777 or 613/995-5138. www.archives.ca. Free admission. Daily 9am–9pm.

National Library of Canada   The National Library is a federal cultural agency whose main focus is to collect and preserve works in all subjects written by, about, or of interest to Canadians. Anyone who registers at the Library can use the resources to find information on Canadian literature, music, history, genealogy, literary manuscripts, artists' books, and rare books. There are also tapes, records, and CDs in the Music Collection and personal papers and memorabilia in the Literary Manuscript Collection. Exhibitions and displays are staged regularly. Lectures, book launches, readings, films, storytelling workshops, musical concerts featuring pianists, medieval ensembles, folksingers, and cellists, and other events are held throughout the year.

395 Wellington St. © 877/896-9481 or 613/995-9481. www.nlc-bnc.ca. Admission free; some events require tickets and fee. General hours Mon–Fri 8:30am–5pm. Public programs weekdays 9am–4pm; reference services weekdays 10am–5pm; reading room daily 7am–11pm; exhibitions daily 9am–10:30pm.

Royal Canadian Mint ✦   Established in 1908 to produce Canada's **circulation coins,** the **Royal Canadian Mint** enjoys an excellent reputation around the world for producing high-quality coins. Since 1976, when a plant was built in Winnipeg, Manitoba, for the high-speed, high-volume production of circulation coins, the **Royal Canadian Mint** has concentrated on producing **numismatic (commemorative) coins.** The **Royal Canadian Mint** is also the oldest and one of the largest gold refineries in the Western Hemisphere and is known and respected around the globe as a premier **gold refinery.** Just gaining entry to the building is an experience at the **Royal Canadian Mint.** First you peer into the ticket booth beside a huge pair of iron gates to buy your tour tickets (you can also visit the boutique without taking the tour). As a security guard watches the entrance (also equipped with a surveillance camera), one of the gates swings open momentarily to allow you to step inside the compound, and then clanks shut behind you. When you enter the stone "castle," you find yourself in a foyer with a set of stairs leading upward on your left and an elevator straight ahead. Both will take you to the **boutique,** which displays the many coins and souvenirs available for purchase in well-lit glass showcases around the room. When it's time for the tour, you're ushered into a small theater to watch a short film on a selected aspect of the mint's activities. Next your guide accompanies you to the **viewing gallery,** which winds its way through the factory. There is a lot to see here, and the tour guide outlines the process of manufacturing coins as you move along the corridor above the factory floor. The process is fascinating, from the rollers that transform the cast bars into flattened strips, to tubs of blanks that have been punched from the strips, to workers hand-drying the blanks after washing, right to the final inspection and hand-packaging of the finished coins.

Where to eat: The ByWard Market area is your best bet for somewhere to grab a snack or meal. It's only a short walk southeast of the Mint.

320 Sussex Dr. © 800/276-7714 or 613/993-8990. Admission C$2 (US$1.25) adults and children 7 and over, free for children 6 and under, C$8 (US$5) family. Weekends half-price. Victoria Day (third Mon in May)–Labour Day (first Mon in Sept) Mon–Fri 9am–8:30pm, Sat–Sun 9am–5:30pm. Rest of the year daily 9am–5pm. Call for advance reservations for guided tours. From the Queensway, take the Nicholas St. exit (118). Turn left on Rideau St. and right onto Sussex Dr. The Mint is on your left.

FEDERAL BUILDINGS

Lester B. Pearson Building This building with its award-winning granite-aggregate-covered tiered towers is the home of the federal department of Foreign Affairs and International Trade. More than 7,000 people work within this department to manage Canada's relations with the world, both here in the capital and stationed at 250 missions around the globe. You are welcome to enter the main lobby and view the flags of more than 170 countries on display. Former prime minister Lester B. Pearson's Nobel Peace Prize medal, which he was awarded for his peacekeeping efforts during the Suez crisis in 1956, is also on display. Free guided tours (for groups only) may be arranged by calling © **613/992-9541.** Advance reservations required. Canada and the World Pavilion and Rideau Falls are just a few steps farther along Sussex Drive.

125 Sussex Dr. © **613/992-9541** (group tour inquiries). From the Queensway, take the Nicholas St. exit (118). Turn left on Rideau St. and right onto Sussex Dr. The Lester B. Pearson Building is on your right, just past the Macdonald–Cartier bridge to Quebec.

Supreme Court of Canada The Supreme Court is a general court of appeal for both criminal and civil cases and is the highest court of appeal in the country. Three sessions are held through the year between October and June and an average of 120 cases are heard annually. Weekdays 9:45am to 12:30pm and 2pm to 4pm are the usual times to hear appeals. Law students take members of the public on free guided tours, which take about half an hour and are recommended for all ages. From May to August, tours are held daily on a continuing basis, and the rest of the year tours are available by prior arrangement on weekdays. The architecture of the building is impressive to behold and the grand entrance hall is magnificent. If you'd like the experience of witnessing an appeal, take a seat in the public gallery when court is in session.

301 Wellington St. © **613/995-4330.** For tour reservations, call © **613/995-5361.** May–Aug daily 9am–5pm, Sept–Apr Mon–Fri 9am–5pm.

GALLERIES

Carleton University Art Gallery Principally showing Canadian art with a small but growing collection of European prints.

1125 Colonel By Dr., St. Patrick's Building, Carleton University Campus. © **613/520-2120.**

Gallery 101 This nonprofit artist-run center focuses on professional presentation of visual and media art from Canadian and international contemporary artists.

236 Nepean St. © **613/230-2799.**

Ottawa Art Gallery The Ottawa Art Gallery is an independent nonprofit public gallery showing contemporary art from the local arts community.

Arts Court Building, 2 Daly Ave. © **613/233-8699.**

Ottawa School of Art Gallery The Ottawa School of Art holds courses and workshops by professional artists for all levels of student. Work is on display at the school gallery.

35 George St. © **613/241-7471.**

SAW Gallery This contemporary art center focuses on new media arts, performance visual art that reaches beyond traditional forms of expression, and art that openly declares its political and social position.

67 Nicholas St. © **613/236-6181.**

3 Heritage Attractions

Ottawa has an unusually high number of **designated heritage properties** and districts. This is partly due to a keen interest in local architecture and history expressed by citizens and politicians. The sophisticated system of heritage planning that protects many of Ottawa's most interesting and beautiful structures is a relatively recent phenomenon, however. It began in 1975, the year that the Ontario government passed the *Ontario Heritage Act,* which gave power to municipal governments to designate properties of heritage significance. As a result of efforts by the Local Architectural Conservation Advisory Committee, the City of Ottawa's official policy on encouragement of heritage preservation was accepted in 1995. Approximately 3,000 properties in Ottawa are designated under the *Ontario Heritage Act.* About 10% of these have individual designation; the rest lie within 15 heritage conservation districts.

If you're looking for a **stroll through a heritage district,** wander the streets in the following neighborhoods, easily accessible from downtown: **ByWard Market and Lowertown** (bounded by Sussex Drive, Bolton Street, King Edward Avenue, and Rideau Street) or **Sandy Hill** between Waller Street, Besserer Street, Cobourg Street, and Laurier Avenue. **Centretown** (bounded by Kent Street, Lisgar Street, Elgin Street, and Arlington Avenue), although a heritage district, is not as pleasant for walking, since there is a lot of road traffic and there are high-rise buildings on the major roads. **Somerset Village,** a stretch of Somerset Street between Bank and O'Connor streets, is characterized by a cluster of historic redbrick buildings. You can also enjoy the leafy residential streets of **the Glebe.** Streets leading off Bank Street between the Queensway and the Rideau Canal are lined with Victorian and Edwardian homes. The village of **Rockcliffe Park,** a residential neighborhood just northeast of Rideau Hall, has numerous gracious properties, many of which have been transformed into ambassadors' residences.

MUSEUMS & ATTRACTIONS

Billings Estate Museum   This historic Georgian estate home, which was completed in 1829, is one of Ottawa's oldest properties. Built for Braddish and Lamira Billings, who settled on the land in 1813, the Billings Estate includes several outbuildings on the 3.4-hectare (8.4-acre) site and was home to five generations of the Billings family, spanning two centuries. Browse the collections of family heirlooms, furnishings, tools, paintings, and documents on your own or take a guided tour. Hands-on activities, special events, and workshops are scheduled on a regular basis. Stroll the lush lawns, colorful flower beds, wooded slopes, and old pathways. Enjoy tea on the lawn in the summer months, served several afternoons each week.

2100 Cabot St. ✆ 613/247-4830. Admission C$2.50 (US$1.70) adult, C$2 (US$1.30) senior, C$1.50 (US$1) children 5–17, under 5 free. May–Oct, Tues–Sun noon–5pm. Closed Thanksgiving weekend. Hours subject to change; call ahead.

Bytown Museum   Housed in Ottawa's oldest stone building (1827), which served as the Commissariat during the construction of the Rideau Canal, this museum is operated by the Historical Society of Ottawa. Articles belonging to Lieutenant-Colonel By, the canal's builder and one of Ottawa's (then known as Bytown) most influential citizens, are on display. In addition, artifacts reflect the social history of local pioneer families in four period rooms and a number of changing exhibits. The rooms depict an 1850s Bytown kitchen, a French-

Canadian lumber camp shanty, a Victorian parlor, and an early toy store. The museum is situated beside the Ottawa Locks, sandwiched between Parliament Hill and the Fairmont Château Laurier Hotel.

Beside Ottawa Locks. ✆ **613/234-4570.** Admission C$5 (US$3) adult, C$2.50 (US$1.60) senior & student. Dec–Mar by appointment. Apr–mid-May daily 10am–2pm. Mid-May–mid-Oct daily 10am–4pm. Mid-Oct–Nov 10am–2pm.

History of the ByWard Market

The ByWard Market area is the oldest part of Ottawa. Following the War of 1812, the British were looking for an alternative navigable waterway between Montreal and Kingston as a precaution against renewed hostilities with the Americans. The Rideau River was chosen, despite the fact that a canal would have to be built to bypass the Rideau Falls, the only point of contact between the Ottawa and Rideau Rivers. Wrightsville was a thriving lumber town on the north shore of the Ottawa River, but a settlement was needed for canal workers on the south shore adjacent to the construction site. Accordingly, a shantytown grew up in the area between the Rideau River and the canal and came to be known as Lowertown, which has today's ByWard Market district as its heart. The opening of the Rideau Centre shopping mall adjacent to the Market led residents and visitors to rediscover the district, and the ByWard Market is now one of the trendiest places in Ottawa for shopping, dining, and entertainment.

ByWard Market ★★   In a compact area bordered by St. Patrick Street on the north, King Edward Avenue on the east, Rideau Street on the south, and Sussex Drive on the west, there is a lively district known as the ByWard Market. In the heart of the area, one block east of Sussex Drive between York and George streets, lies the ByWard Market building and the outdoor stalls of the farmer's market, where you can buy outstanding fresh local produce, flowers, and other products such as maple syrup. Outdoor markets are wonderful places to stroll. The activity and bustle of the market and the fun of choosing a selection of fresh fruit and vegetables to take home and enjoy is a world away from trudging up and down supermarket aisles. To complement the fresh produce, you'll find gourmet food vendors inside the Market building. There are dozens of excellent food retailers in the district, and I urge you to venture inside and taste what's on offer. Here's a few places to keep a look-out for, just to get you started: Le Boulanger Français/The French Baker, 119 Murray St.; Chilly Chilies, 55 ByWard Market; House of Cheese, 34 ByWard Market; International Cheese & Deli, 40 ByWard Market; L'Ami des Gourmets, 55 Murray St.; Lapointe Fish, 46 ByWard Market; Le Moulin de Provence, 55 ByWard Market; The Tea Party, 119 York St. Throughout the year, the ByWard Market hosts family-oriented events on weekends as a thank-you to their customers and to make the community surrounding the market a little brighter. Events include a Mother's Day celebration with special restaurant menus, an outdoor fashion show, a jazz band, free hayrides, and farm animals on display. On the first Sunday in June, a display of 150 vintage, classic, and high-performance cars is held. Annual events later in the year include Bytown Days when 19th-century Ottawa is revisited, a search for the world's biggest pumpkin, and an old-fashioned Christmas with carolers riding around the Market district in a horse-drawn carriage adorned with sleigh bells.

From the Queensway, exit at Nicholas St. (exit 118). At Rideau St., turn right and then left on King Edward Ave. From King Edward Ave., turn left onto George, York, Clarence, or Patrick streets. Or you can turn left onto Rideau St., right on Sussex Dr., and then turn right onto George, York, Clarence, or Murray streets.

Laurier House   This fine Victorian residence, built in 1878, has been home to two prime ministers and is a designated National Historic Site. A tour of this home helps to put a human face on Canada's politics and history. Prior to 1896, there was no official residence provided for the prime minister. Sir Wilfrid Laurier, Canada's first French-Canadian prime minister, was the first resident of Laurier House, purchased by the Liberal Party to house their leader. Several rooms contain furnishings and mementos of Laurier's, but the majority of the house is restored to the era of William Lyon Mackenzie King, Canada's longest serving prime minister and the second occupant of the house. Apparently King held seances in the library, and his crystal ball is on display. The Pearson Gallery contains former prime minister Lester B. Pearson's study, which was moved here from his home in Rockcliffe Park. The gallery displays photographs and artifacts from the Pearson years, including a replica of Pearson's Nobel Peace Prize medal, which he was awarded for his role in the 1956 Arab–Israeli dispute. Wander over to Strathcona Park after visiting the museum. It's just across the street from Laurier House. Stroll the pathways in summer and watch the swans glide along the Rideau River. If you have children with you, take them to the delightful playground.

335 Laurier Ave. E. ✆ **613/992-8142.** Admission C$2.50 (US$1.70) adult, C$2 (US$1.30) senior, C$1.25 (US$.80) youth, free for children 5 and under. Apr–Sept Tues–Sat 9am–5pm, Sun 2pm–5pm; Oct–Mar Tues–Sat 10am–5pm, Sun 2–5pm. From the Queensway, take the Nicholas St. exit (exit 118). Turn right on Laurier Ave. E. The museum is on your left.

Rideau Hall ✮✮   Rideau Hall has been the official residence and workplace of Canada's Governor General since 1867 and is considered to be the symbolic home of all Canadians. The public is welcome to wander the 32 hectares (79 acres) of beautiful gardens and forested areas and visit the greenhouse. Outdoor concerts and cricket matches are held in the summer and there's ice-skating on the pond in winter. **Free guided tours** of the staterooms of the residence are offered. The **Governor General's Awards** are presented here annually, honoring Canadians for extraordinary accomplishments, courage, and contributions to science, the arts, and humanity. Two receptions are held annually for the public—the **Garden Party** in June and the **New Year's Day Levee.** The Ceremonial Guard is on duty at Rideau Hall during July and August. The first **Changing of the Guard Ceremony,** held in late June, features a colorful parade led by a marching band. **Relief of the Sentries** is a ceremony performed hourly 9am to 5pm during the summer. The **Visitor Centre,** operating daily between May and September, has family activities, a play structure, and hands-on activities for children. The **Governor General's Summer Concerts** are held on the beautifully landscaped grounds. Set up your lawn chairs, spread out the picnic blanket, and enjoy the sunshine. The six free concerts are usually scheduled for late Sunday afternoons. Past performers include children's performers Sharon, Bram, and Friends, country musicians Farmer's Daughter, and East Coast fiddler Natalie MacMaster. Wheelchairs, washroom facilities, and picnic tables are available at Rideau Hall.

1 Sussex Dr. ℭ **800/465-6890** or 613/991-4422. www.gg.ca. Admission to all tours and activities is free. Grounds are generally open daily 9am–sunset; subject to change without notice. From the Queensway, take the Nicholas St. exit (exit 118), turn left on Rideau St., right on Sussex Dr. The entrance to Rideau Hall is on your right, just after you cross the Rideau River.

 ## The Role of the Governor General

The governor general's role is to represent the Crown in Canada, promote Canadian sovereignty, celebrate Canadian excellence, and encourage national identity, national unity, and moral leadership.

Canada is both a parliamentary democracy and a constitutional monarchy. Since Canadians recognize Her Majesty Queen Elizabeth II as the Head of State, a representative of the Queen is required in Canada. This is one of the roles of the governor general—to carry out Her Majesty's duties in Canada on a daily basis.

Various trophies and awards, including the Stanley Cup, Grey Cup, and the Governor General's Literary Awards, have been created by past governors general and serve to recognize and celebrate Canadian achievements.

Governors general are appointed by the Queen on the advice of the prime minister.

The current governor general of Canada is Her Excellency the Right Honourable Adrienne Clarkson.

Turtle Island Aboriginal Village   On historic Victoria Island in the Ottawa River, just west of Parliament Hill, Turtle Island Tourism Company operates an Aboriginal village in the summer months. Live demonstrations of traditional and contemporary Native singing, drumming, and dancing are staged. Listen to an ancient legend or story in an authentic tipi, enjoy traditional Aboriginal foods and visit the cultural displays. On show are tipis, birch bark canoes, totem poles, and Cree Hunt Camps. Fun for all ages. The Trading Post craft shop stocks arts and crafts made by the local Aboriginal community. Take advantage of special programs that take you to the Gatineau Hills for a three-hour visit. Sit around a fire with Native guides, walk through the woods, and learn about the First Peoples' relationship with nature. Wilderness survival retreats and outdoor adventure programs are held—one to five days in length. You can reach Victoria Island from the Chaudières Bridge by car or via the Portage Bridge if you're walking or cycling.

Victoria Island ℭ **877/811-3233** or 613/564-9494. www.aboriginalexperiences.com. Victoria Island is just west of the Parliament Buildings, and lies below the Chaudières and Portage bridges.

PLACES OF WORSHIP
Cathedral Basilica of Notre-Dame ⭐   The splendid Notre-Dame Cathedral Basilica is Ottawa's oldest church. A wooden structure was first erected on the site in 1832, and construction of the current building began in 1841. The exterior stonework has a plain, flat façade but this is offset by the magnificent French-Canadian tin steeples that house the church bells. The late-Victorian interior is typically ornate. Details include two vaulted ceilings, side galleries,

extensive carved woodwork, carved altars, and 30 life-size carved figures. A 3-m (10-ft.) high wooden gilded statue of the Madonna and Child, created by Italian sculptor Cardona in 1865, stands above the apex of the front façade gable between the two steeples.

385 Sussex Dr.

Christ Church Cathedral   The original church on this site was completed in 1833. In 1872, the growing congregation required a larger church, and a new building was constructed on the site between 1872 and 1873. When the Diocese of Ottawa was formed in 1896, Christ Church became the seat of the Anglican bishop of Ottawa. The architectural style is that of English Gothic Revival and the building's exterior has survived in its original form. Some changes have been made to the interior over the years. A number of state funerals have been held here, including those of governor general Vincent Massey, prime minister John Diefenbaker, and prime minister Lester B. Pearson.

439 Queen St.

St. Andrew's Presbyterian Church   St. Andrew's predates Christ Church as the oldest Protestant congregation in Ottawa, with worship held on the site since 1828. When the construction of the new Christ Church began in 1872, it prompted St. Andrew's, which was also suffering from overcrowding, to build a new church on the site. Also constructed in Gothic Revival style, the new St. Andrew's was built of rock-faced gray limestone, which distinguished it from the golden sandstone of Christ Church. Then prime minister Mackenzie King attended services at St. Andrew's. During World War II, when the Dutch Royal family was in exile in Ottawa, the daughter of Queen Juliana of the Netherlands was baptized at this church.

82 Kent St.

Other downtown churches you may like to visit, which all date from the 19th century and are designated heritage properties, include **St. Patrick's Basilica,** 240 Kent St., **First Baptist Church,** 140 Laurier Ave. W., **St. Alban the Martyr Church,** 125 Daly Ave., **St. Paul's–Eastern United Church** (originally St. Paul's Presbyterian Church; the United Church was not created until 1925), 90 Daly Ave., **St. Paul's Evangelical Lutheran Church,** 210 Wilbrod St., **All Saints Anglican Church,** 315–317 Chapel St., and **Eglise Ste-Anne,** 528–530 Old St. Patrick St.

 The Lives and Times of Canada's PMs

As you tour around the city, you will notice public buildings, streets, and bridges named after some of Canada's most prominent past political leaders. There are plenty of places to visit where you can learn more about the country's prime ministers and how they shaped Canada's identity, political structure, and social fabric.

You can visit the office of **Sir John A. Macdonald,** Canada's first prime minister, in the East Block of the Parliament Buildings. His statue stands on the Hill between Centre Block and East Block. A visit to **Laurier House** at 334 Laurier Ave. E., will give you a glimpse into the lives of three prime ministers. **Sir Wilfrid Laurier** was the first prime minister to reside there.

Several rooms contain items pertaining to Laurier, but the majority of the house has been restored to the era of **William Lyon Mackenzie King,** who inherited the house from the Lauriers. Churchill and Roosevelt both visited King at this residence. King had an estate in the midst of **Gatineau Park,** which was bequeathed to the Canadian people upon his death in 1950. It's open from mid-May to mid-October. Also at Laurier House is **Lester B. Pearson's** study, which was moved here from his home in Rock-cliffe Park. On Parliament Hill, Laurier's statue stands at the southeast corner of East Block, King at the northwest corner of East Block, and you'll find Pearson just north of West Block. To learn more about the times of **John Diefenbaker,** take a tour of the **Diefenbunker Cold War Museum,** an underground bunker built to shelter the Canadian government in the event of nuclear attack during the period of the Cold War. Diefenbaker's statue stands on the northeast corner of West Block. Finally, if you want to catch a glimpse of Canada's current head of government, Prime Minister **Jean Chrétien,** keep your eyes open around the **Langevin Block** at 50 Wellington St., across from Parliament Hill. The offices of the prime minister are housed in this magnificent olive sandstone building. You can also drive or stroll past the gates of **24 Sussex Drive,** the official residence of the prime minister.

4 Organized Tours

ON WHEELS

Amphibus   For a unique tour of the city, hop on the "Amphibus," a hybrid vehicle that cruises on the water and tours on land. The 90-minute tour begins at the corner of Sparks and Elgin streets, motoring past historic sites and city landmarks, then plunges into the Ottawa River for a cruise. Reservations recommended.

Sparks St. and Elgin St. ✆ **613/223-6211.** Seasonal.

Canada Ducks Inc.   Operated by the same tour company that owns Capital Double Decker and Trolley Tours, Canada Ducks offers a lively and humorous amphibious trip around Ottawa by land and water.

Sparks St. and Metcalfe St. ✆ **613/792-3825.** Seasonal.

Capital Double Decker and Trolley Tours ⭐   This locally owned and operated tour company offers authentic open-top double decker buses and historic replica trolley buses. Fully narrated tours. Free hotel pickup and return. The most popular ticket is a three-day pass that allows you to hop on and off at any of the 20 designated stops at your leisure. Cost for a family three-day pass is C$56 (US$37). Other tours are available. There are discounts on other attractions when you buy your tickets. Tickets available from the main kiosk at the corner of Sparks and Metcalfe streets downtown and the Capital Infocentre. Call for more information.

Kiosk at corner of Sparks St. and Metcalfe St. ✆ **800/823-6147** or ✆ **613/749-3666.** Seasonal.

Grayline Sightseeing Tours ⭐   Choose an open-top double decker bus or vintage trolley bus. Step on or off the bus any time you wish at these stops:

Parliament Hill, Museum of Civilization, Notre-Dame Basilica, Rideau Hall, RCMP Rockcliffe Stables, Canada Aviation Museum, National War Museum, Royal Canadian Mint, National Gallery of Canada, ByWard Market, Rideau Canal, Dow's Lake, Central Experimental Farm, Museum of Nature. If you call ahead, they'll pick you up at your downtown hotel. Tours operate from May to October. Tickets are valid for three days and prices are reasonable —a family of four can get a three-day, on-off-privilege ticket for C$54 (US$36).

For departure locations and times and other information call Grayline ✆ 800/297-6422 or 613/565-5463. Seasonal.

Orient Express Rickshaws   Although we're not in the Orient, traveling by rickshaw in the summer is a convenient way to get around downtown and it's lots of fun. The rickshaws carry two or three people, pulled by strong and friendly young men or women. You can take a half-hour tour of the cobblestone ByWard Market courtyards and enjoy entertaining stories of days gone by, or use the rickshaws as a taxi service. They're on a cellular dispatch system and you can book ahead by phone. You can also usually find them on George Street in the ByWard Market area.

George St., ByWard Market. ✆ 613/860-SHAW(7429). www.rickshaws.net. Mid-May to Labour Day (first Monday in Sept).

ON FOOT

Aside from the tours listed here, see the walking tours described in chapter 7, "Active Ottawa."

Art Walk (Self-Guided)   The National Capital Commission has produced a guide describing seven public art walking tours in Ottawa and Hull. You will see statues of prominent historic figures, contemporary sculptures made of wood, stone, papier-mâché, metal, and fiberglass, war memorials, statues of Canadian heroes, totem poles, murals, and monuments. Tours vary from 35 minutes to 1 hour in length. Available free from the Capital Infocentre, 90 Wellington Street.

Blue Umbrella Tours   The daytime arm of Haunted Walks, Blue Umbrella Tours operates a variety of walking tours—gardens, pubs, crime and scandal, and even a scavenger hunt.

Call for tour meeting place. ✆ 613/232-0344. Tickets C$12 (US$7) adult, C$8 (US$5) senior and student, children 10 and under with an accompanying adult are free. May–October.

Haunted Walk of Ottawa   For an entertaining evening, follow a black-cloaked storyteller, lantern in hand, through the city streets and hear the darker side of Ottawa's history. They welcome families on the tour and claim that many of their fans are in fact children. There aren't any nasty surprises or theatrical incidents on the tour, as the guides prefer to tell the stories and take you to the sites of hauntings and ghost sightings—they leave the rest up to your imagination. The walks take place entirely out of doors, so dress for the weather. The tour takes about 1½ hours and the total distance covered is about 1.6km (1 mile). Call for information on French-language tours and Halloween tours. Tickets may be purchased in advance by phone with a major credit card or within the hour before the tour begins from the tour guide.

Tour departs from D'Arcy McGee's Irish Pub, 44 Sparks St. at Elgin St. ✆ 613/730-0575.Tickets C$12 (US$7) adult, C$8 (US$5) senior and student, children 10 and under with an accompanying adult are free. May–October.

The Terry Fox Statue: A Symbol of Hope and Courage

Across from the Centre Block of Parliament Hill, in front of the Capital Infocentre, stands a proud memorial to a courageous young Canadian. In 1977, 18-year-old **Terry Fox** was given the devastating news that he had bone cancer and his right leg would have to be amputated six inches above the knee. Terry wanted to do something to give hope to people living with cancer, and he decided to run across Canada to raise money for **cancer research.** After many months of training, during which he ran more than 5,000km (3,000 miles), Terry dipped his artificial leg in the Atlantic Ocean on April 12, 1980 and began his **"Marathon of Hope."** He traveled courageously through six provinces and over 5,370km (3,330 miles) before being forced to retire near Thunder Bay, Ontario. The cancer had spread to Terry's lungs and he was flown home to British Columbia. Ten months later, in June 1981, Terry died at the age of 22. The country was in mourning.

An annual fundraising event was established in his memory and the first **Terry Fox Run,** held at more than 760 sites across Canada and around the world in 1981, raised C$3.5 million. By the year 2000, the total amount of money raised in Terry's name was close to C$270 million. Terry is a true Canadian hero and has become a symbol of hope and courage to people living with cancer and their families and friends.

 Take Time for a Scenic Drive

Enjoy a leisurely drive along Ottawa's parkways and scenic driveways.

HEADING EAST Head east on Wellington Street past **Parliament Hill,** through Confederation Square. You'll pass the grand **Fairmont Château Laurier** on your left. Turn left at the lights (north) onto Sussex Drive. After passing the **American Embassy** on your left, glorious views open up across the islands.

Continue along Sussex Drive to St. Patrick Street, turning left into **Nepean Point.** Here you can share a fine view of the river with a statue of French explorer **Samuel de Champlain,** one of the first Europeans to arrive in the region almost 400 years ago. Adjacent to Nepean Point is **Major's Hill Park,** where there are wonderful views of the canal locks, the Ottawa River, and the striking architecture of the **National Gallery.** Rejoin Sussex Drive, traveling northeast. You'll cross the Rideau River via Green Island. **Rideau Falls** are on your left. The road passes **24 Sussex Drive,** the **residence of the prime minister,** which is not open to the public. Just ahead on your right is **Rideau Hall.** In summer, a brief **Changing of the Guard** ceremony is held at noon at the main gate. Tours of the grounds and the interior public rooms are available. For information, stop at the Visitor Centre (open daily 9:30am to 5:30pm) or call ✆ **613/991-4422.** Continuing, the drive becomes **Rockcliffe Parkway,** a beautiful route along the Ottawa River and through **Rockcliffe Park.** Watch for a right fork to Acacia Avenue, which leads to the **Rockeries,** planted with spring blooms. If you wish, continue along the Parkway to the **Musical Ride Centre, RCMP Rockcliffe Stables** and the **Aviation Museum,** or return to the Parkway and head west toward downtown Ottawa.

HEADING WEST Head west on Wellington St., past **Parliament Hill,** the **Supreme Court of Canada,** and the **National Library** on your right. The road opens up into the **Ottawa River Parkway.** Continue through the parkland to **Island Park Drive** and turn left. This road will take you under the Queensway (Hwy 417) and through the grounds of the **Experimental Farm and Arboretum.** When you reach a European-style "roundabout," you have two choices. Turn **right,** and you can take **Prince of Wales Drive** to **Hog's Back Rd.** Turn left here, by the locks and **Hog's Back Falls.** Turn left again onto **Colonel By Drive** and follow this picturesque route along the east bank of the **Rideau Canal** back downtown. If you decide to turn left (north) at the roundabout, you'll take a slightly shorter but just as pretty route back downtown along **Queen Elizabeth Driveway,** on the west bank of the **Rideau Canal.**

Ottawa Walks   Guided walking tours of the ByWard Market, Rideau Canal, historic Ottawa, and more.

1536A Beaverpond. © 613/744-4307. Tickets C$5.75 (US$3.60) adult, C$4 (US$2.50) senior and student, children free. Operates year-round with tours scheduled daily 9am–9pm. Call for more information.

Parliament Hill (Self-Guided)   A free booklet available from the Capital Infocentre gives a detailed description of a self-guided walking tour of Parliament Hill. See entry under "Parliament Hill" earlier in this chapter.

Path of Heroes (Self-Guided)   The Government of Canada has produced a guide with seven walking tours around the heart of the National Capital Region. The walks vary in length from 15 minutes to one hour. Each tour has a different theme: The Heroic Heart, Remembrance, Culture, and Honour, Pictures and Visions, Canada and the World, Bridges and Meeting Places, Across Space and Time, and finally Lore, Law, and Money. The guide suggests places to stop along the way at designated buildings, vistas, and statues that tell the stories of Canadian heroes. Available free from the Capital Infocentre, 90 Wellington Street.

ON THE WATER

Amphibious Transport   Your choice of **Amphibus** or **Canada Ducks.** Take a tour beginning on land and then plunge into the Ottawa River for a relaxing cruise. See entry above "On Land."

Ottawa Riverboat Company ⟨★   Take a 90-minute narrated tour on the 280-passenger *Sea Prince II,* the largest tour boat in Ottawa. Refreshments are available on board. Reservations recommended. Cruise tickets available at the ticket booth in Confederation Square, Ottawa Riverboat Dock (at the foot of the Ottawa Locks just west of the Fairmont Château Laurier Hotel), Jacques-Cartier Park and Marina in Hull, and selected hotels. A family-oriented Sunday Brunch tour is offered mid-June to mid-September on the *Sea Prince II.* An evening cruise featuring a four-course dinner catered by Café Henry Burger, a renowned Hull restaurant, is offered in July, August, and selected dates in

September. Host ship is the 130-passenger *MV Senator.* Dinner is served in an elegant Edwardian-style deck salon with arched mahogany windows. Reservations are required for brunch and dinner cruises.

335 Cumberland St., Suite 200. ℂ 613/562-4888. Tickets for 90-minute tour C$16 (US$10) adult, C$14 (US$9) senior/student, C$8 (US$5) child 6–12, under 6 free, C$40 (US$25) family (max 2 adults and 2 children). Three to five departures daily in season from Ottawa dock at the foot of the Ottawa Locks and from the Jacques-Cartier Park marina in Hull; call for departure times and information on brunch and dinner cruises.

Paul's Boat Lines 🖈   Paul's Boat Lines cruises the Ottawa River and the Rideau Canal. On the Ottawa River, the 150-passenger *Paula D* takes visitors on a 90-minute cruise, with spectacular views of the Parliament Buildings, Rideau Falls, and other sites. On the canal, you can glide along in one of three tour boats for a 75-minute cruise.

219 Colonnade Rd. ℂ 613/225-6781 (Office), 613/235-8409 (Summer Dock). Tickets C$14 (US$9) adult, C$12 (US$7) senior, C$10 (US$6) student, C$7 (US$4) child under 15, C$30 (US$19) family (max 2 adults and 2 children). Four to seven departures daily in season from Ottawa dock at the foot of the Ottawa Locks, from the Jacques-Cartier Park marina in Hull, and from the Conference Centre on the Rideau Canal; call for departure times.

Kids Cruises for Kids

If you have young children (under age 10 or so), then an Ottawa River cruise is the better choice. You can stroll around the deck or have a snack, and the open design is perfect on a hot summer's day, as you can catch the cool breeze off the water. In contrast, the canal boats have a single enclosed deck and are more confined.

IN THE AIR

Hot Air Ballooning   If you fancy floating in the sky at a leisurely pace with the city spread out below you and you're not afraid of heights, you might like to splurge on a trip in a hot air balloon. For many people it's a once-in-a-lifetime experience. There may be restrictions on the minimum age for passengers, so call ahead. Or go to a launching and watch the balloons being prepared for flight and then takeoff. Everyone from babies to grandparents will enjoy the sight of the huge, colorful silken spheres as they gracefully rise into the sky. In the Ottawa area, the main operators are **High Time Balloon Co. Inc.,** ℂ 613/521-9921, www.hightimeballoon.com, **Skyview Ballooning,** ℂ 613/724-7784, www.skyviewballooning.com, **Sundance Balloons,** ℂ 613/247-8277, www. sundanceballoons.com, and **Windborne Ballooning,** ℂ 613/739-7388.

Private Small Aircraft   View the Ottawa area from the sky in a 5-passenger plane and have fun identifying the major landmarks on a flight with **Air Conquest,** 1 Crownhill St. ℂ 613/745-6747. Twin-engine plane. Operates February to December daily from 9am to 9pm. Rates vary. Sightseeing tours are available by seaplane with **Air Outaouais,** which takes off from the Ottawa River. Prices start at C$35 (US$23) per person depending on the tour. Air Outaouais operates from May to November, sunrise to sunset. Reservations required. Flights are accessible for **travelers with disabilities.** P.O. Box 511, Aylmer, QC. ℂ 819/568-2359.

5 Spectator Sports

Ottawa Lynx   Take me out to the ball game! For fun and affordable family entertainment, visit **JetForm Park,** where the Ottawa Lynx, Ottawa's Triple-A affiliate of the Montreal Expos, play 72 home games from April to September. JetForm Park, which opened in 1993, is a state-of-the-art building that combines the old-time ballpark experience with modern facilities and services. The stadium boasts an award-winning natural grass and clay field, comfortable seats, and excellent sightlines. The open-air stands hold 10,000 spectators, most of whom are families. Facilities include a picnic area, barbecue terrace, and parking for 800 cars. Since the team's inception in 1993, the Ottawa Lynx Baseball Club has set two attendance records in the league and has won the International League Championship. JetForm Park is close to Highway 417 (the Queensway), at the corner of Vanier Parkway and Coventry Road. Tickets are available at the park or by phone. 300 Coventry Rd. © 800-663-0985 or 613/747-LYNX (5969). www.ottawalynx.com. Tickets C$6.50–$8.50 (US$4–$6); C$1 (US66¢) off for seniors and children 14 and under.

Ottawa Rebel   The popularity of lacrosse is on the rise and the Ottawa Rebel, playing at the **Corel Centre,** is one of 12 National Lacrosse League teams in a league that includes teams from Canada and the northeastern United States. Come and watch the Ottawa Rebel take on the Toronto Rock, Washington Power, New York Saints, Philadelphia Wings, Rochester Knighthawks, and more. The 16-game regular season runs during the winter months. 1000 Palladium Dr. © 613/599-0123. www.ottawarebel.com. For tickets, visit any Ticketmaster outlet or the Corel Centre box office (Gate 1), or call Ticketmaster Sportsline at © 613/755-1166. Tickets C$15 (US$9) and up.

Ottawa Senators   Experience all the excitement of true National Hockey League (NHL) action at the **Corel Centre,** home of the Ottawa Senators. Limited family and alcohol-free seating is available in the Coca-Cola Family Fan Zone, sections 314, 315, and 316. More than 1,000 seats are available in the Family Fan Zone at the bargain price of C$21 (US$13). These tickets are released a couple of months at a time and they sell out fast. A **Hard Rock Café** and other restaurants and bars are on site for meals and snacks before or after the game. For all your Sens souvenirs, visit **Sensations,** the official merchandise outlet of the Ottawa Senators Hockey Club in the Corel Centre at Gate 1. To order Game Day tickets online or check available seating for all home games, visit www.ticketmaster.ca. 1000 Palladium Dr. © 613/599-0123. www.ottawasenators.com. For tickets, visit any Ticketmaster outlet or the Corel Centre box office (Gate 1), or call Ticketmaster Sportsline at © 613/755-1166 or the Sens ticket office at © 800/444-7367 or 613/599-0300. Tickets C$21–$165 (US$13–$102).

Ottawa 67's   For up-close and personal Ontario Hockey League (OHL) action, visit the **Civic Centre,** in Lansdowne Park, home of the **Ottawa 67's** since their inception in 1967. With a seating capacity exceeding 10,000 and 47 luxury suites, it is reputed to be one of the best homes in Junior hockey. Free parking and family packages are available. 1015 Bank St. © 613/232-6767. Tickets C$11 (US$7) adults, C$8 (US$5) children.

University Sports Teams   Check out the variety of varsity sports at **Carleton University** (© 613/520-7400; www.carleton.ca), including basketball, fencing, field hockey, golf, indoor hockey, rowing, rugby, skiing, soccer, swimming, and water polo. The **University of Ottawa** (© 613/562-5700; www.geegees. uottawa.ca) has inter-university teams for badminton, basketball, cross-country, fencing, football, golf, hockey, rowing, rugby, soccer, skiing, swimming, volleyball, and water polo.

6 Especially for Kids

When you're traveling with children, put their needs first when planning your itinerary and everyone will have a more enjoyable vacation. You're on a family vacation, so plan activities that all ages will enjoy. Be sure to schedule in plenty of time for relaxation (and naps if your children are very young). The best advice you can follow is not to over-schedule. Don't expect your kids to act like adults—young children have short attention spans. When they start to wiggle and fidget, let them have 20 minutes in a playground, sit on a park bench and eat an ice-cream cone or take them to a movie. Here's a lineup of the best things for kids to see and do in the Ottawa area. Please don't feel restricted by these lists. The intention is to guide you to the best attractions for these age groups. No matter what their ages, your kids will still enjoy visiting places not mentioned under their age group (and so will you!). You should also check out chapter 7 "Active Ottawa" and chapter 10 "Exploring the Region" for other family-oriented activities.

All Ages   Museum of Nature, Museum of Science and Technology, Changing of the Guard, Aviation Museum.

5 and under   Children's Museum, Agriculture Museum.

6- to 9-year-olds   Children's Museum, Agriculture Museum, Musical Ride Centre, RCMP Rockcliffe Stables, Canadian Museum of Civilization, Rideau Skateway and bikepaths.

9- to 12-year-olds   Children's Museum, Agriculture Museum, Musical Ride Centre, RCMP Rockcliffe Stables, Canadian Museum of Civilization, Rideau Skateway and bikepaths, Changing of the Guard, Rideau Hall.

Teens   Canadian Museum of Civilization, National Gallery, Parliament Hill tour, Musical Ride Centre, RCMP Rockcliffe Stables, Canadian War Museum, Rideau Skateway and bikepaths, ByWard Market, Diefenbunker Cold War Museum, Rideau Hall.

7 For Visitors with Special Interests

Adventure   Downhill skiing, snowboarding, caving, white water rafting and kayaking, and even bungee jumping are all within driving distance of Ottawa. Have a look at chapter 10, "Exploring the Region."

Animals   To see farm animals at close range and perhaps get a chance to handle small ones or even help to milk a cow or shear a sheep, visit the **Canada Agriculture Museum.** A tour of the **Musical Ride Centre, RCMP Rockcliffe Stables** takes you right into the stables where you can pat the horses' noses and feed them carrots. At the **Museum of Nature,** most of the creatures are of the preserved variety, but they are extremely well displayed.

First Nations   The **Canadian Museum of Civilization** has excellent exhibits on Native peoples and an impressive collection of giant totem poles. For a first-hand experience and the opportunity to meet First Nations people at work and play, visit Victoria Island in the summer months to see the **Turtle Island** summer village with tipis, canoes, storytelling, and Native foods, or the annual **Odawa Spring Pow Wow,** held at Nepean Tent and Trailer Park in late May.

Fitness You can bike, hike, jog, walk, in-line skate, snowshoe, ski, and probably a few other things on the trails and pathways in Ottawa and Hull's extensive **greenspace.** Skate on the longest ice rink in the world, the **Rideau Canal.** Experience the beauty of the wilderness in **Gatineau Park.** Join in one of the annual events, such as the **Keskinada Loppet** cross-country ski competition or the **National Capital Race Weekend** that features a world-class 42-km (26-mile) marathon.

Flight The obvious choice here is the **Canada Aviation Museum,** where you can get close to dozens of real aircraft and sit in cockpit sections, fly a hang glider simulator, or go up for a ride in a vintage airplane. Visit the **Ottawa Airport's** Observation Deck and watch the big guys take off and land. The second weekend in September, enjoy the annual **National Capital Air Show.** And every Labour Day weekend (first weekend in September), there's the **Gatineau Hot Air Balloon Festival.** For commercial flights in small aircraft and hot air balloons, see "In the Air," earlier in this chapter.

Food & Wine Head first for the **ByWard Market.** Also worth a visit is the extensive **Liquor Control Board of Ontario (LCBO)**'s two-level retail outlet at the corner of Rideau St. and King Edward Ave. See also "Gourmet to Go" in chapter 5, "Dining," for more food destinations. And don't forget to have at least one meal at a French restaurant in **Hull.**

Ghosts Those with nerves of steel can visit the ghost of **Watson's Mill** in Manotick or the ghost that haunts the **Ottawa International Hostel** (the site of Canada's last public hanging in this former jail). Enjoy an evening of entertainment on the **Haunted Walk of Ottawa** or check out the gravestones in **Beechwood Cemetery,** the final resting place of many famous Canadians, including politicians, writers, poets, and 12 Hockey Hall of Fame members.

History Visit the **Canadian Museum of Civilization, National Archives, Billings Estate Museum, Bytown Museum, Laurier House, Rideau Hall,** and the **Diefenbunker Cold War Museum.**

The Military Visit the exhibits at the **Canadian War Museum** and the collection of artillery, weapons, and military vehicles at **Vimy House.** Watch the colorful **Changing of the Guard** ceremony at Parliament Hill in the summer.

Music The **National Arts Centre** features live musical performances all year around. Popular musical artists appear at the **Corel Centre, Centrepoint Theatre,** and the **Civic Centre. Theatre du Casino du Lac-Leamy** focuses on musical entertainment. There are dozens of live music venues as well: bars, clubs, and restaurants, some of which are listed in chapter 8, "Ottawa After Dark." Summer music festivals include the **Ottawa Chamber Music Festival, Ottawa International Jazz Festival, Bluesfest,** and the **Ottawa Folk Festival.** Concerts are also held throughout the year at various downtown churches.

Numismatics Visit the **Royal Canadian Mint** where you can purchase commemorative coins and take a guided tour of the factory along an enclosed walkway above all the action. Check out the **Currency Museum** in the center block of the Bank of Canada on Wellington St.

Photography   For the most comprehensive showing of works by contemporary Canadian photographers, the **Canadian Museum of Contemporary Photography** is the place to go. The museum also runs workshops on topics related to photography. There are also some photographs exhibited in the **National Gallery.**

Politics/Law   In addition to the obvious **(Parliament Hill),** pay a visit to the **Supreme Court of Canada.** If you'd like to learn more about Canada's past prime ministers, see the special section earlier in this chapter, "The Lives and Times of Canada's PMs."

Philately   The **Postal Museum,** housed within the Canadian Museum of Civilization, traces the history of Canadian postal communications.

Rocks and Minerals   For those with an interest in rocks, minerals, fossils, meteorites, and ores, the small museum at **Logan Hall** is a good choice to spend an hour or two. The **Ecomuseum** in Hull and the **Museum of Nature** also have excellent displays of rocks and minerals.

Science and Nature   Best bets for the sci-and-tech crowd are the **Canada Museum of Science and Technology** and the **Canadian Museum of Nature.** They'll be occupied for hours.

Trains   Train buffs will enjoy the locomotive collections at the **Museum of Science and Technology** and the **Smiths Falls Railway Museum.** If you want to really blow their whistle, take eager train-spotters for a trip on the **Hull–Chelsea–Wakefield Steam Train.**

Visual Arts   The **National Gallery** has an impressive collection of art, with an emphasis on Canadian artists. Plan to spend several hours here if you have a passion for art. You'll also enjoy the **Canadian Museum of Contemporary Photography.** Local galleries always have something of interest—see the listings earlier in this chapter under "Museums & Galleries."

7

Active Ottawa

Ottawa is one of the greenest capital cities in the world. Beautifully groomed city parks are complemented by vast expanses of protected wilderness, and waterways flow gracefully through the center of the city and along its northern borders.

Much of the credit for the establishment of Ottawa's physical beauty goes to Jacques Gréber, a French urban planner, and former prime minister William Lyon Mackenzie King. In the late 1930s, King invited Gréber to Ottawa initially as an advisor for the planning of the War Memorial and Confederation Square. World War II interrupted these plans, but following the war, Gréber returned and prepared a report with recommendations for extensive urban renewal. The report outlined several major changes to the urban landscape.

The National Capital Greenbelt, a swath of greenery that stretches around the city like an emerald necklace, can be largely attributed to Gréber's design. Stretching from Gatineau Park in Quebec across the Ottawa River, through Nepean in the west end, around the southern city limits, through Gloucester, and back up to the Ottawa River in the east, the Greenbelt encircles Canada's capital.

It's no accident that the logo, flag, and coat of arms created for the new City of Ottawa feature green and blue. The colors were chosen to represent the abundant greenspace and picturesque waterways and to symbolize the connection between the natural environment and quality of life that citizens of Ottawa enjoy.

Ottawans appreciate the beauty of their surroundings, and you'll see hundreds of them cycling, walking, jogging, in-line skating, ice skating, and cross-country skiing to work or school or just to enjoy the outdoors in their leisure time. In fact, Ottawa residents have one of the highest participation rates in the country for golf, skiing, and cycling. With the expanse of waterways that meander around the city, boating, hanging out on the beach, and playing water sports are popular as well.

Since Ottawa is a major urban center, there are also more citified ways to be physically active. You can splash in a wave pool, scale a rock-climbing wall, or experience the thrill of high-tech arcade games. If you enjoy sports, you'll find plenty of places to play tennis or golf, go skiing, or swim.

1 City Strolls

So many of Ottawa's famous landmarks, museums, and attractions are located within walking distance of each other in the downtown areas east and west of the Rideau Canal that you are bound to spend a fair amount of time on foot when you visit the city. The three walking tours in this section will cover most of the places of interest in the center of the city. The fourth tour takes you on a cycling route on pathways alongside the Rideau Canal and offers several options for the

Active Ottawa Maps

To take full advantage of Ottawa's parks, pathways, and waterways, get hold of some specialized maps that clearly mark routes for cycling, walking, skating, or skiing. Some maps have suggested routes with information on the length and the level of difficulty. Good hunting grounds for maps are the **Capital Infocentre,** 90 Wellington St. (© **800/465-1867** or 613/239-5000); **Place Bell Books,** 175 Metcalfe St. (© **613/233-3821**), which specializes in maps, travel guides, and travel literature; and **A World of Maps,** 1235 Wellington St. (© **800/214-8524** or 613/724-6776), which carries topographic maps, nautical maps, and travel guides for the local region and the rest of the world. For maps of **Gatineau Park**, including highly detailed trail maps, visit the **Gatineau Park Visitor Centre,** 33 Scott Rd., Chelsea (© **800/465-1867** or 819/827-2020).

Here's a rundown of a few maps to get you started. **Explore the Recreational Pathways of Canada's Capital Region,** produced by the National Capital Commission, details pathways in **Gatineau Park** and other sites in Quebec, as well as pathways in Ottawa. There are 17 routes marked on the map, ranging from 1.5km (1 mile) to 31km (20 miles) in length. Descriptions of the terrain, level of difficulty, and points of interest are listed for each route. Five tours are highlighted. For the more adventurous, Environment Canada Parks Service provides a cycle touring map of the **Rideau Canal,** detailing routes along the 202-km (125-mile) waterway between Ottawa and Kingston. One of the **Gatineau Park** maps available at the Gatineau Park Visitor Centre is a scale map that includes hiking trails, cycling paths, bridle paths, seasonal trails, and sections of the Trans Canada Trail. A new winter trail map for Gatineau Park includes contour lines, magnetic north, and exact drawings of ski trails, winter hiking trails, and snowshoe trails, with huts and shelters also marked. For trails in the **National Capital Greenbelt,** which encircles Ottawa from Kanata in the west, along the entire southern edge of the city, and around to Cumberland in the east, refer to the **Greenbelt All Seasons Trail Map.**

return journey, making a pleasant morning or afternoon outing. There are other pleasant areas of the city to wander at leisure. The leafy residential streets leading off Bank Street in the Glebe are fairly quiet. The area bounded by King Edward Avenue, Rideau Street, Laurier Avenue, and Charlotte Street has some interesting older properties and the streets are reasonably traffic free during the day. The extensive grounds of Rideau Hall are also enjoyable for a leisurely stroll.

WALKING TOUR 1 ■ THE HEART OF IT ALL

Start:	Ottawa Locks
Finish:	Canadian Museum of Civilization or Jacques-Cartier Park
Distance:	Approximately 2.5–4.5km (1.5–3 miles); 1–2 hours
Best Time:	Anytime when the weather is reasonably fine.
Worst Time:	It won't be much fun crossing Alexandra Bridge if the weather is very cold, windy, or wet. Rush-hour traffic will also detract from the pleasure of this walk.

This tour will take you past symbols of Ottawa's history from its earliest days to modern-day national endeavors. Begin your tour at the site of Ottawa's birth—the Ottawa Locks.

❶ Stand on the north side of the Plaza Bridge and look down onto the eight **Ottawa Locks,** which connect the canal to the Ottawa River, a drop of 24m (80 ft.). Travel time through the locks for canal traffic is about 1½ hours. You can go down a stairway beside the bridge (or go down a ramp from the south side of the bridge) right to the level of the locks and watch them in operation. Next make your way to the stone building on the west side of the locks, the **Commissariat.**

❷ The **Bytown Museum** is housed in the Commissariat, the oldest building still remaining from the original settlement of Bytown. Lieutenant-Colonel John By had the Commissariat built in 1827 to be used as offices during the construction of the Rideau Canal. Articles belonging to Colonel By are displayed here, as are artifacts reflecting the social history of the pioneer families of the area. Opening hours vary; they are longer in summer, limited in winter. ℭ **613/ 234-4570.**

❸ South of Plaza Bridge lies **Confederation Square,** a triangular concrete pedestrian precinct, bound on each side by several lanes of traffic, but graced with the **National War Memorial,** inaugurated by King George VI in 1939. From the Rideau Canal, a broad set of stairs leads up to the center of the Square. Every year, crowds gather in the Square on November 11, Remembrance Day.

❹ Walk south on the east side of Elgin Street, passing the **National Arts Centre** on your left, and the **British High Commission** and the elegant **Lord Elgin Hotel** on your right.

❺ Stroll through **Confederation Park.** Rest on a park bench or wander past the sculptures and artwork on display. The central **fountain** is a belated tribute to **Colonel John By,** who met with disapproval upon his return to England because of overspending on the construction of the Rideau Canal. During his lifetime, Colonel By did not receive the credit he deserved for his monumental achievement.

❻ Leave the park at the south end and walk east along Laurier Street until you see **Cartier Square Drill Hall** on your right. This is the oldest armory in Canada still in use and also the starting point of the daily **Changing of the Guard** ceremony, which takes place in the summer months. The Governor General's Foot Guards and the Canadian Grenadier Guards, accompanied by drums and a brass military band, march up Elgin Street, timed to reach Parliament Hill promptly for the 10am ceremony.

❼ Walk back along Laurier Street to Elgin Street. If you're ready for a break, walk farther south along Elgin until you reach the beginning of the commercial district with its shops and restaurants. Otherwise, head north on Elgin and cross over Rideau Street to the **Château Laurier.**

❽ Admire the imposing façade, then enter the lobby and wander through the main public areas on the ground floor. Rich wood paneling and opulent decor is evident throughout. For a special treat, make reservations for **afternoon tea** at **Zoe's,** the cafe enclosed by glass above the main entranceway.

❾ As you leave the hotel, you will see the distinctive columns of the old **Union Station** on the opposite side of the street, once the main railway station and now host of government conferences, conventions, and exhibitions.

Walking Tours

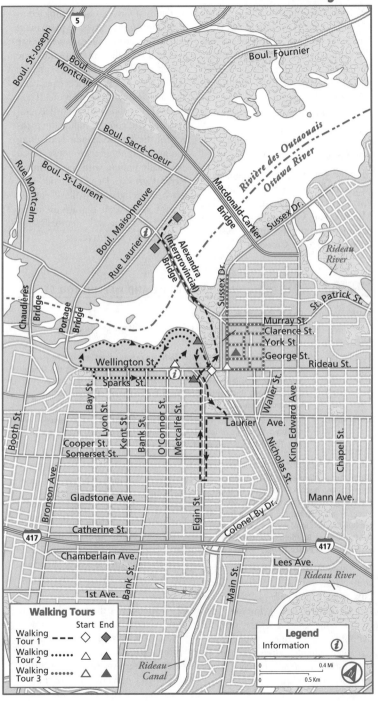

⑩ Turn immediately left past the Château Laurier (along Mackenzie Street) to **Major's Hill Park.** From this park you'll get great views of the Parliament Buildings, the Rideau Canal, the Ottawa River, Hull, and the National Gallery.

⑪ Cross the **Alexandra Bridge** on the pedestrian walkway. This bridge was built at the turn of the 20th century for two railway lines.

⑫ Now you have a choice of how to spend the next few hours. You can visit the spectacular **Canadian Museum of Civilization,** Canada's national museum of human history, or enjoy Jacques-Cartier Park. The Museum of Civilization, completed in 1989, features impressive permanent and temporary exhibits, as well as the Canadian Children's Museum, the Canadian Postal Museum, and the IMAX theater. There is a cafeteria and an up-scale dining room on site. If you decide to wander through Jacques-Cartier Park, you can follow the pathway of the **Trans Canada Trail** along the north shore of the Ottawa River, eventually linking with the **Gatineau River Pathway.** Jacques-Cartier Park has been designated "Mile 0" of the Trans Canada Trail, a multi-use recreational trail that will eventually link Canada from coast to coast.

WALKING TOUR 2	PARLIAMENT HILL AND WELLINGTON STREET
Start:	Capital Infocentre
Finish:	D'Arcy McGee's pub, Capital Infocentre, or Ottawa Locks
Distance:	3–3.5km (2 miles); 1½ hours
Best Time:	Weekdays during the day, when there are plenty of walkers on the river trail and Sparks Street is filled with pedestrians. August during the Sparks Street Mall International Busker Festival. December when more than 200,000 lights shine in celebration of the beginning of winter and the Christmas season.
Worst Time:	Evenings or weekends November to March, Christmas and Winterlude excepted. Once the office workers go home for the day at this time of year, the district is very quiet.

Begin your outdoor exploration of Parliament Hill and historic Wellington Street at the **Capital Infocentre,** 90 Wellington Street. If you stand in the square in front of the building and look north, you're facing the **Parliament Buildings' Centre Block** with its central **Peace Tower.**

① You will also see a statue of a courageous young Canadian, **Terry Fox,** who attempted to run across Canada despite having lost his right leg to bone cancer. Every year, in memory of this brave young man, Canadian schoolchildren take part in a sponsored run/walk to raise funds for cancer research.

② Cross Wellington Street and enter Parliament Hill through the gates. Note the elaborate stone and iron **Parliamentary Fence,** built between 1872 and 1874. Some modifications have been made to accommodate changes in traffic flow over the years, but its characteristics have changed little since its construction.

③ At the foot of the central pathway to the Centre Block is a fountain with a natural gas flame, the **Centennial Flame,** which burns through the water flowing over the bronze shields of Canada's provinces and territories.

Former prime minister Pearson lit the flame at one second after midnight on January 1, 1967, to commemorate Canada's 100th birthday—and the flame has been burning ever since.

④ The building to your right is the **East Block** of the Parliament Buildings. Its architecture is an outstanding example of Gothic Revival design. Several rooms, including Sir John A. Macdonald's office, have been restored to resemble their original state.

⑤ In front of the East Block, turn south and look across the street to admire the **Langevin Block** at 62 Wellington Street. It was built in the Second Empire style, similar to the New Louvre, built in Paris in 1852. The Langevin Block was constructed to accommodate the growing number of politicians and civil servants on the Hill, and today the offices of the prime minister are located here.

⑥ After circling the East Block building, walk north along the pathways to the rear of Centre Block. Here you will discover the imposing **Library of Parliament.** The library's design is based on the round medieval chapter house. The building features massive flying buttresses and the exterior is primarily local Nepean sandstone.

⑦ As you continue along the pathways on the west side of Centre Block and past the **West Block,** which houses government offices and is not open to the public, you will pass by many **statues and monuments.** For a detailed description of these tributes to Canadian people and events, obtain a free copy of "Discover The Hill," published by the National Capital Commission and available at the Capital Infocentre.

⑧ Walk west on Wellington Street to number 128, the **Union Bank** building. This building, made of olive-colored New Brunswick sandstone, is the only surviving bank building of its era on Wellington Street, which was once the banking center of the city.

⑨ Further west, between Bank Street and Kent Street, stands the **Bank of Canada** building. Originally constructed in 1937, a glass-towered addition appeared in the mid-1970s. The **Currency Museum** can be found inside.

⑩ As you cross Kent Street, you'll see **St. Andrew's Presbyterian Church** on the southwest corner, constructed of Ottawa Valley limestone between 1872 and 1874.

⑪ On the north side of Wellington just past Kent St. stands the impressive architecture of the **Supreme Court of Canada.** The plain, smooth-cut sandstone topped by the château-style roofing similar to the Parliament Buildings and the Château Laurier, makes a dramatic impression as you approach the building. The court is in session between October and June, and free half-hour guided tours of the building are available year-round. It's worth taking a peek at the grand entrance hall, even if you don't take a tour.

⑫ Next you will come to the **National Library and National Archives of Canada.** The Library is responsible for collecting and preserving Canada's published heritage. The National Archives holds a huge collection of maps, diaries, films, journals, official records, photographs, and documentary art. There are washrooms and a snack bar in the library.

⑬ At this point, you can decide whether to return to your starting point via the **Trans Canada Trail** along the south shore of the Ottawa River, or stroll back through **Sparks Street Mall,** Canada's first pedestrian mall. If you walk back along the river, you will end up at the **Ottawa Locks** and you can ascend the stairs or ramp to Plaza

Bridge (where Wellington Street becomes Rideau Street). If you walk back along Sparks Street, you can turn left on Metcalfe to return to the **Capital Infocentre,** or continue along Sparks Street to Elgin Street. On the corner you will find a jovial pub, **D'Arcy McGee's,** where you can enjoy a fine pint of Guinness after your long walk.

WALKING TOUR 3 | **SUSSEX DRIVE AND BYWARD MARKET DISTRICT**

Start:	Junction of Rideau St. and Sussex Dr.
Finish:	Clarendon Court
Distance:	2–4km (1.25–2.5 miles), depending on how many streets you wander up and down in the ByWard Market district; 1–2 hours or more.
Best Time:	This area always offers something interesting to see and do. It's a great place to stroll almost any time.
Worst Time:	Late at night when the bar crowd is out and about.

Sussex Drive is Ottawa's "other" famous roadway, aside from Wellington Street where the Parliament Buildings are located. Originally named Sussex Street, it was once the commercial center of Ottawa and was lined on both sides with handsome limestone buildings.

① Walk north on Sussex Drive on the left-hand side of the road so you can see the restored limestone and brick commercial buildings on the east side of the street. One of the finest remaining examples of these properties is **541 Sussex Drive,** on the northeast corner of Sussex Drive and George Street.

② Next you'll pass by **York Street,** which has a number of **designated heritage properties** along its length. Some buildings (on York Street as well as many other city streets) have a bronze plaque that gives a brief bilingual description of the heritage significance of the property.

③ Continuing north, keep an eye out for an original carved wooden signpost hanging on 449 Sussex Drive. The former **Castor Hotel** (*castor* is French for "beaver") depended on this sign to attract their illiterate customers. Other businesses in the area used the same strategy during the mid-1800s—the local hardware store, jeweler, shoe store, and tobacco shop all sported wooden symbols.

④ As you approach Murray Street, you'll see the roadway sweep to the left across Alexandra Bridge to Hull. In the center of the traffic lanes stands the **Peacekeeping Monument,** erected in 1992.

⑤ The grand glass and stone **National Gallery of Canada** stands on the northeast corner of Sussex Drive and Patrick Street. At this point, you might like to visit the gallery, or walk a few steps farther north on Sussex Drive to the **Canadian War Museum** or the **Royal Canadian Mint.**

⑥ If these attractions are scheduled for another day of your trip, cross Sussex Drive to **Notre-Dame Cathedral Basilica,** the oldest church in Ottawa. The exterior of this Roman Catholic church is rather plain on the front façade, contrasting with the ornate and elaborately detailed late-Victorian interior. Vaulted ceilings, side galleries, intricately carved woodwork, and 30 life-size figures are some of the most impressive features of the Basilica's interior.

⑦ Turn left (south) upon exiting the Basilica until you reach **Murray Street.** This is a most charming street on which to while away an hour or so. Unique retailers, restaurants, and cafes can be found here. One of the most picturesque buildings is the block at 47–61 Murray Street, the former Martineau Hotel. The round arched openings you can see once led to stable yards at the rear.

8 Continue along Murray Street and turn right (south) onto **Dalhousie Street,** the easternmost border of the **ByWard Market,** as defined for heritage district purposes in 1991.

9 Now, you can wander at will in the area bordered by Murray Street, Dalhousie Street, Rideau Street, and Sussex Drive. Within these few city blocks, there are dozens of shops, bars, cafes, and restaurants. At the heart of the district lies the **ByWard Market Building.** There has been a market on this site since the 1830s, but three market buildings were destroyed by fire before the current one was built in 1927. Between May and October, the

outdoor farmer's market clusters around the perimeter of the building, located between York Street, George Street, William Street, and a lane known as ByWard Market.

10 Your final glimpse into the colorful history of this district is the charm of two courtyards. **Tin House Court** is situated between York and Clarence streets and originally served as a tradesman's entrance to properties on Sussex Drive. Tin House Court is characterized by the preserved façade of an early Edwardian tinsmith's house, which has been mounted on one of the limestone walls enclosing the courtyard. **Clarendon Court** can be reached through a narrow alleyway on the north side of George Street, just east of Sussex Drive. This cobblestone courtyard is a romantic spot on a summer evening. Several restaurants have terraces facing into the courtyard, and the atmosphere is decidedly European.

CYCLING TOUR   CANAL, LAKE, AND LOCKS

Start:	Ottawa Locks
Finish:	Ottawa Locks
Distance:	Minimum 16km (10 miles); maximum 24km (15 miles) if you take the longest route back.
Best Time:	When tulips are in bloom in May; on a warm day when you can enjoy boating on Dow's Lake; in the summer when you can enjoy the beach at Mooney's Bay.
Worst Time:	Morning and evening rush hour in the event you decide to do some road travel; also there is more noise and fumes from adjacent roadways at those times.

Begin your tour at the head of the Ottawa Locks. There's a pathway under Plaza Bridge (the bridge overlooking the locks) which leads you to the Rideau Canal Western Pathway.

1 The first landmark you pass is the **National Arts Centre,** one of the largest performing arts complexes in Canada. A wide variety of performances can be seen on its four stages,

including English and French theater, dance, music, and community programming.

2 Next you'll pass by the edge of **Confederation Park,** site of many summer festivals and a popular spot during warmer weather for office workers and tourists to relax on a bench.

Cycling Tour

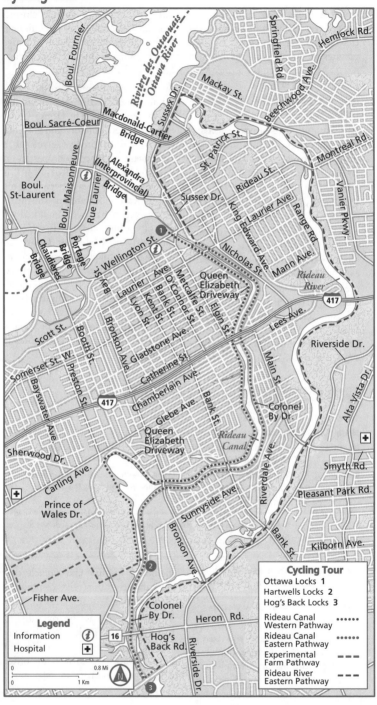

Cycling Tour
Ottawa Locks **1**
Hartwells Locks **2**
Hog's Back Locks **3**

Rideau Canal
Western Pathway ••••••

Rideau Canal
Eastern Pathway ••••••

Experimental
Farm Pathway ━ ━ ━

Rideau River
Eastern Pathway ━ ━ ━

Legend
Information 🛈
Hospital ✚

0   0.8 Mi
0   1 Km

❸ The pathway continues alongside the canal, with Queen Elizabeth Driveway on the west side. Keep an eye out for drinking fountains stationed along this stretch.

❹ At the intersection of Queen Elizabeth Driveway and Fifth Avenue, you'll see the **Canal Ritz.** Open 11:30am to 11pm daily, you can enjoy a drink, snack, or full meal. Sit on the terrace and watch the boats on the canal.

❺ **Dow's Lake** is a couple of kilometers (about 1.25 miles) farther along. There are restaurants, washroom facilities, and boat rentals here. Dow's Lake is adjacent to **Commissioner's Park,** which in the spring has the largest display of tulips in the capital—an amazing 300,000 bulbs burst into bloom in a colorful display.

❻ Continue past Dow's Lake for about 1km (just over half a mile) until you reach Hartwells Lock Station. At this point you have several options:

- Cross over the canal and return to Ottawa Locks at the head of the Rideau Canal via the **Rideau Canal Eastern Pathway.** This pathway has the canal on its west side and Colonel By Drive on its east side. This is the shortest tour, about **16km total (10 miles).**
- Turn west along the **Experimental Farm Pathway** and cycle through wooded and open scenic natural areas. If you wish, visit the **Canada Agriculture Museum,** **Arboretum,** and **Ornamental Gardens.** Return downtown on the **Rideau Canal Eastern Pathway** or **Rideau Canal Western Pathway.** Depending on how much cycling you do around the Central Experimental Farm area, this tour is a total of about **20km (12.5 miles).**
- Continue past Hartwells Lock Station for another 2km (1.25 miles) until you reach **Hog's Back Falls.** This is the point where the Ottawa section of the Rideau Canal ends. Refreshments and washroom facilities are available here. Enjoy the picturesque waterfalls, and, if there's any boating traffic, you can watch the locks and swing bridge in operation. A little farther along on the east bank of the Rideau River you can enjoy the beach at **Mooney's Bay Park.** Returning to your starting point via one of the canal pathways, this tour is about **20km (12.5 miles).** Or cycle back downtown via the **Rideau River Eastern Pathway.** This is the longest tour, about **24km (15 miles),** but it takes you on an entirely different route, through numerous city parks along the east bank of the Rideau River and across the bridge next to the **Rideau Falls.** From that point, you need to cycle west on Sussex Drive (which does not have a designated bike lane), to return downtown.

2 Green Ottawa

URBAN PARKS

Commissioner's Park Situated along Dow's Lake, Commissioner's Park attracts thousands of visitors during the Canadian Tulip Festival with the largest tulip display in the region. An amazing 300,000 bulbs bloom in the park flowerbeds. Bring your camera and snap away.

Confederation Park Major festivals are held in this downtown park at the intersection of Elgin Street and Laurier Avenue, including Winterlude and the Ottawa International Jazz Festival. There are memorials to Canadian history

Parks & Green Spaces

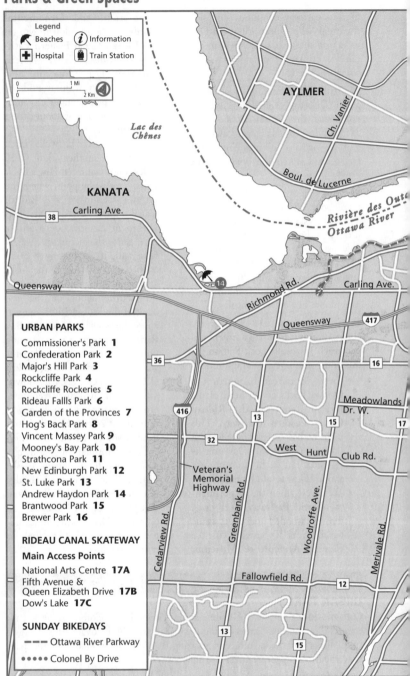

Legend

🏖 Beaches   ⓘ Information

✚ Hospital   🚆 Train Station

0   1 Mi
0   2 Km

Lac des Chênes

AYLMER

Ch. Vanier

Boul. de Lucerne

KANATA

Carling Ave.

38

Rivière des Outa
Ottawa River

Queensway

Richmond Rd.

Carling Ave.

Queensway

417

URBAN PARKS

Commissioner's Park **1**
Confederation Park **2**
Major's Hill Park **3**
Rockcliffe Park **4**
Rockcliffe Rockeries **5**
Rideau Fallls Park **6**
Garden of the Provinces **7**
Hog's Back Park **8**
Vincent Massey Park **9**
Mooney's Bay Park **10**
Strathcona Park **11**
New Edinburgh Park **12**
St. Luke Park **13**
Andrew Haydon Park **14**
Brantwood Park **15**
Brewer Park **16**

RIDEAU CANAL SKATEWAY

Main Access Points

National Arts Centre **17A**
Fifth Avenue &
Queen Elizabeth Drive **17B**
Dow's Lake **17C**

SUNDAY BIKEDAYS

– – – Ottawa River Parkway

••••• Colonel By Drive

36

416

32

13

Veteran's
Memorial
Highway

West Hunt Club Rd.

Meadowlands
Dr. W.

15

16

17

Cedarview Rd.

Greenbank Rd.

Woodroffe Ave.

Merivale Rd.

Fallowfield Rd.

12

13

15

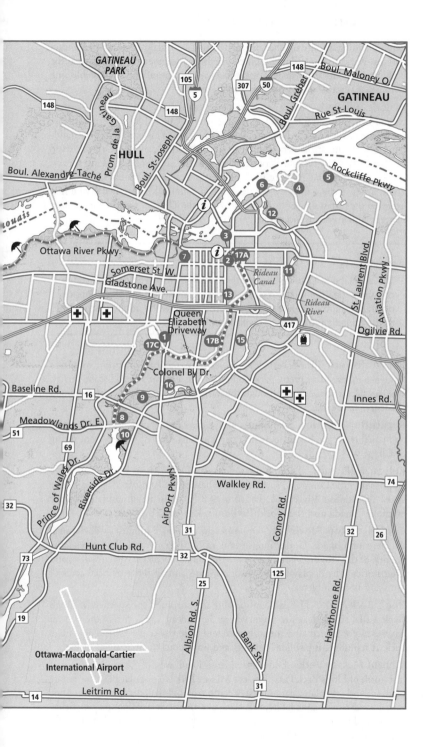

here, including a fountain that originally stood in Trafalgar Square in London and was dedicated to Colonel John By, the British engineer who supervised the building of the Rideau Canal. The colonel was a major influence in establishing Bytown, as Ottawa was formerly known.

Major's Hill Park   Ottawa's oldest park, established in 1874, is tucked in behind the Fairmont Château Laurier. A statue of Colonel John By stands close to the site of his house, which was destroyed by fire. This park offers outstanding views of the Parliament Buildings, the Rideau Canal, the Ottawa River, Hull, and the National Gallery. It's also a major site for many festivals and events, including the Tulip Festival. At the tip of the park, you'll find Nepean Point. You can share the view with a statue of Samuel de Champlain, who first explored the Ottawa River in 1613. The Astrolabe Theatre, a venue for summer concerts and events, is located here.

Fun Fact

The astrolabe (a 17th-century navigational instrument) held by the statue of Samuel de Champlain at Nepean Point was unwittingly placed upside down by sculptor Hamilton McCarthy. You can view the original astrolabe at the **Canadian Museum of Civilization.**

Rockcliffe Park   Travel east along Sussex Drive just past the prime minister's residence to reach this pretty park, complete with a picnic site and stone shelter. You can take a scenic drive through the park and catch a glimpse of the grand residences in the area.

Rockcliffe Rockeries   Continue a little farther east along Rockcliffe Parkway and you'll reach the Rockeries, with their gorgeous show of flowers from spring to fall.

Rideau Falls Park   Located just off Sussex Drive where the Rideau River empties into the Ottawa River, this park is beautifully landscaped. A footbridge spans the Rideau River and the 30-m (98-ft.) falls are illuminated in the evening. **Canada and the World Pavilion** is located in the park.

Garden of the Provinces   Opposite the National Library and National Archives of Canada at the intersection of Wellington and Bay streets, the Garden of the Provinces commemorates the union of Canada's 10 provinces and 2 territories. The display features two fountains and all the provincial coats of arms and floral emblems.

Hog's Back Park   The parklands in this area surround the spectacular **Hog's Back Falls,** situated at the point where the Rideau Canal meets the Rideau River. They're named after rocks that are said to resemble the bristles on a hog's back. A refreshment pavilion, parking, and washroom facilities are available.

Vincent Massey Park   Located on Heron Road, west of Riverside Drive and just north of Hog's Back Park, Vincent Massey Park is a popular place for family reunions and other large gatherings. Amenities include ball diamonds, horseshoe pits, a bandstand, picnic tables, fireplaces, a refreshment pavilion, playing fields, recreational pathways, drinking fountains, and public washrooms. A parking fee is charged from May to October.

Mooney's Bay Park   South of Vincent Massey Park and Hog's Back Park along Riverside Drive, you'll find Mooney's Bay. There's a supervised, sandy swimming beach, a playground, shade trees, a refreshment pavilion, and public washrooms. A parking fee applies in the summer months.

Strathcona Park   On the banks of the Rideau River, beautiful Strathcona Park beckons. Relax on a bench under the huge shade trees and watch the royal swans lazily swim past on a sunny summer afternoon. Odyssey Theatre holds its outdoor summer performances here. There are paved walking paths for easy stroller pushing and an elegant water fountain. Visit the children's play area.

Kids

Strathcona Park has a wonderful play area for children. The wading pool, playground, and castle ruins, complete with a slide and animal statuettes, are great fun to explore.

New Edinburgh Park   On the east side of the Rideau River, south of Sussex Drive, New Edinburgh Park provides yet another peaceful refuge from the city within a few minutes' drive of downtown. Walking trails weave along the banks of the river, and because much of the park has been preserved in its natural state, there's an abundance of wildlife, including groundhogs, turtles, muskrats, butterflies, and blue herons. Bring binoculars—and insect repellent. There's also a children's playground.

St. Luke Park   At the intersection of Elgin Street and Gladstone Avenue, this park is a great place to hang out after a bout of shopping on Elgin. Sugar Mountain (candy heaven) and Pure Gelato (Italian ice cream) are close by. There's a paddling pool, playground, and picnic tables.

Andrew Haydon Park   West of the downtown core, at the intersection of Acres Road and Carling Avenue, you'll find this park on the southern bank of the Ottawa River. There are picnic sites with barbecues, walking paths, and a small artificial lake. Lots of diversions for younger children: water sprinklers and jets, sand to dig in, and play structures, including a ship with rope ladders and swings. Refreshment pavilions and washrooms are on site.

 The Origin of Ottawa's Parkways and Pathways

In the 19th century, Ottawa's railways were an essential feature of the landscape. Vast networks of rail tracks crossed the city. Their existence, however, became a real challenge after World War II for the urban planners whose goal was to beautify Canada's capital while reclaiming and preserving the waterway shorelines. In 1950, work began on relocating the railway and converting old rail lines into Ottawa's parkways and pathways. Today, residents and visitors alike can enjoy the beautiful parks, pathways, and roadways of the Ottawa River shore, the Rideau Canal banks, and Dow's Lake. Most pathways are smooth asphalt on flat terrain, so they're easy to negotiate for all ages.

Brantwood Park   Turn east on Clegg Street off Main Street, and you'll soon come across Brantwood Park, on the west bank of the Rideau River. There's a wading pool and play structure. In winter, skaters can weave through a series of skating rinks joined by ice paths. For a delicious vegetarian snack or meal, visit the Green Door at 198 Main Street (see chapter 5, "Dining," page 90).

Brewer Park   Bordering the Rideau River and Bronson Avenue, Brewer Park is a good site for feeding waterfowl on the river, so bring along some crusts of bread. In the winter, a speed-skating oval is open to the public. There's a children's waterpark in the summer, with water sprays, jets, and slides. A specially designed tots' playground, a pool, an arena, baseball diamonds, picnic areas, and pathways along the river complete the scene.

SUBURBAN & RURAL GREEN SPACE

Gatineau Park   This beautiful wilderness area, covering 361km² (141 miles²) in the Gatineau Hills, is under the care of the National Capital Commission. The south entrance to the park is located just across the Ottawa River in Hull, a few minutes' drive from downtown Ottawa. Hiking trails, cycling pathways, mountain-bike trails, cross-country ski trails, sandy beaches, and campgrounds are all located within the park. Your first stop should be the **Gatineau Park Visitor Centre,** at 33 Scott Road in Chelsea (✆ **800/465-1867** or 819/827-2020), open every day of the year. For more information on Gatineau Park, see chapter 10, "Exploring the Region."

The Greenbelt   The National Capital Greenbelt covers 200km² (77 miles²) of crescent-shaped land bordering Ottawa to the west, south, and east. A mix of forests, agricultural land, and natural areas, the Greenbelt has several sectors open to the public and accessible from major highways. Moose, beavers, chipmunks, foxes, raccoons, deer, pygmy shrews, rabbits, and squirrels all call this wilderness area home. For directions to specific sites, call the Capital Infocentre (✆ **800/465-1867** or 613/239-5000). Better yet, pick up a copy of the Greenbelt All Seasons Trail Map, available at the Infocentre opposite Parliament Hill. If you're venturing into the Greenbelt during bug season, protect yourself with insect repellent or use a bug jacket. Always respect the Greenbelt rules—place all litter in the waste bins provided in parking areas, keep your dog on a leash and pick up after it, and don't walk or snowshoe on cross-country ski tracks in winter.

The **Pine Grove Sector** is a large urban forest with a mixture of natural woods and plantations extending southeast from Hunt Club and Conroy roads. Along the wide, level trails are interpretive panels to help visitors identify more than 20 species of native trees and to explain the principles of modern forest management. **Stony Swamp Sector** has been designated a provincially significant wetland and contains more than 700 species of plants and many types of animals. A recently constructed 5-km (3-mile) section of the **Trans Canada Trail** runs through **Stony Swamp.** The **Rideau Trail, a 300km (185 mile) footpath between Ottawa and Kingston,** also passes through this sector. In the summer months, the Sarsaparilla Trail in Stony Swamp is universally accessible.

The **Mer Bleue Conservation Area** on the southeastern edge of Ottawa is a unique ecological environment protected by an international treaty. The area contains a large peat bog more than 5-m (16-ft.) deep and a northern boreal forest, a type of forest that is typically found much farther north. If you visit on a cool morning in the spring or fall, you may be lucky enough to witness a bluish-tinged mist hanging over the bog, which gave the area its name (*mer bleue* is

French for "blue sea"). There are several trails crossing the area, but the easiest one to negotiate is the Mer Bleue Interpretative Trail, a walk of just over 1km (⅔ mile) with a boardwalk and information panels. To reach the Interpretative Trail, follow Innes Road to Anderson Road, then go south to Borthwick Ridge Road and follow the signs. Elsewhere in the Greenbelt, during the winter you can go **ice fishing** on the Ottawa River, accessible from Parking Lot 1 at **Shirley's Bay** (Range Road north off Carling Avenue). For family **tobogganing** fun, try **Bruce Pit** (Parking Lot 12, Cedarview Road off Hwy. 416 at Hunt Club Road) or **Conroy Pit** (Parking Lot 15, south of Hunt Club Road on Conroy Road).

(Kids) For Active Families: Where to Play Indoors

Since Ottawa is a major urban center, there are lots of indoor entertainment venues where kids can run, jump, and play. You can splash in a wave pool, scale a rock-climbing wall, or experience the thrill of high-tech arcade games. Many museums have organized activities for children and families on weekends and during school vacation periods, so you'll always have an answer when your kids get into one of those "There's nothing to do!" moods.

Gloucester Splash Wave Pool has a sloping entry to the wave pool, so running in and out of the waves is almost as exciting as being on a natural beach. There's a 34-m (112-ft.) high water slide with its own landing pool, a separate toddler pool, solarium, and plenty of deck chairs. Located at 2040 Ogilvie Road in Ottawa's east end; ℂ **613/748-4222.** For information on municipally owned and operated **indoor pools** around the city call ℂ **613/580-2400.** If you're looking for a place to tire out a high-energy kid or two, go to **Cosmic Adventures,** one of Canada's largest indoor playgrounds. Kids ages 12 and under can bounce, crawl, slide, climb, and swing in a four-level soft-play structure filled with tunnels, mazes, obstacle courses, ball pits, and slides. Located in east Ottawa at 1373 Ogilvie Road; ℂ **613/742-8989.** In the St. Laurent Shopping Centre at 1200 St. Laurent Blvd., there's a high-tech play space called **Cyberdome** ℂ **613/742-6540.** Kids ages 5 to 85 can play laser tag, race on downhill ski simulators, motorbikes, and Super GT racing cars, or climb the 13.5-m (45-ft.) Power Tower climbing wall. Play an old favorite like air hockey or test-fly a new top-secret jet. Across the road from the Canada Science and Technology Museum, you'll find **Midway Family Fun Park** at 2370 Lancaster Road ℂ **613/526-0343.** There's nine-hole mini golf, bumper cars, jungle gym, bowling lanes, arcade games, and a toddler play center.

---

3 Sports & Games

BEACHES

Along the banks of the Ottawa River and the Rideau River, there are a number of beaches where you can cool off on a hot summer's day. Sandy shores abound, and there are usually washrooms, changing rooms, and snack bars nearby. Supervised swimming is available at Britannia Bay, Mooney's Bay, and Westboro beaches in the city of Ottawa. Water quality is checked regularly, and beaches may occasionally be closed for a brief period, usually after heavy rainfall. For water-quality updates and general information on beaches within the city, call ⓒ 613/580-2400. You can get to **Britannia Bay,** on the Ottawa River, by following Richmond Road to Britannia Road or by traveling on the Ottawa River bike path. For **Mooney's Bay Park,** on the banks of the Rideau River, drive along Riverside Drive just north of Walkley Road, or take the Colonel By Drive bike path to Hog's Back, cross Meadowlands Drive, and take the path through the marina. You'll find **Westboro Beach** on the south shore of the Ottawa River, off the Ottawa River Parkway at Kitchissippi Lookout (west of the Champlain Bridge).

Just a short drive from the city you can visit **Baxter Conservation Area,** south of Kars on Dilworth Road (ⓒ 613/489-3592), which has a beach on the Rideau River. The refreshing lakes of **Gatineau Park** (ⓒ 819/827-2020) are open for public swimming from mid-June to early September. The park has five public beaches, located at Philippe, Meech, and La Pêche lakes. Lifeguards are on duty daily from 10am to 6pm; swimming in the park is prohibited at other times. Swimming is also available in **Lac Beauchamp,** at **Parc du Lac Beauchamp,** 745 bd. Maloney, Gatineau, PQ (ⓒ 819/669-2548).

BOATING

If you want to spend a lazy summer afternoon drifting around in a boat, visit Dow's Lake Pavilion, 1001 Queen Elizabeth Drive (ⓒ 613/232-1001 general information, or 613/232-5278 marina). A fully operational marina at the pavilion site on Dow's Lake rents out paddleboats and canoes. Dow's Lake is an artificial lake that provides a quiet place for water recreation away from the main traffic in the Rideau Canal. If you cross the Ottawa river to Hull Marina, you can rent personal water craft, jet boats, fishing boats, and pontoon boats by the hour, day, or weekend at Location Moto Marine Outaouais, 71-B rue Jean Proulx, Hull, PQ (ⓒ 819/595-0909). Boats are also available for rental at Gatineau Park. For boat rentals at Philippe Lake and Taylor Lake, call ⓒ 819/456-3555; for La Pêche Lake, call ⓒ 819/456-3494. If you like your outdoor activities wet 'n' wild, check out the white-water rafting adventure companies listed in chapter 10, "Exploring the Region."

CYCLING AND IN-LINE SKATING

Ottawa and its environs offer a comprehensive network of pathways and parkways where people can bike and in-line skate through beautiful natural scenery. In addition, there are designated bicycle lanes on a number of city streets. No wonder Ottawa has the highest per capita population of cyclists in Canada.

Fact

Did you know that there are more than 370km (230 miles) of major bike routes and 273km (170 miles) of minor routes in the new City of Ottawa?

If you didn't bring your own equipment, **Rent-A-Bike,** at 1 Rideau Street (in the underground parking lot of the Fairmont Château Laurier; ⓒ 613/241-4140), has a professionally equipped workshop, bicycle store, and rental service.

They have all kinds of bikes, including standard hybrid bikes designed for comfortable, leisurely touring, standard light-trail mountain bikes, on-road and off-road performance bikes, and on-road tandems. You can add a two-seat trailer for infants and toddlers or a one-seat trail-a-bike for 3- to 5-year-olds to your rental bike. In-line skates are also available. Daily bike rentals are C$23 to C$50 (US$15–$33). Prices include taxes, a helmet, a lock, and a map. Self-guided bicycle tours and escorted tours (for groups of six or more) are available. **Cyco's,** at 5 Hawthorne Avenue (by the canal at Pretoria Bridge; © **613/567-8180**), also rents out bicycles and in-line skates.

OC Transpo, Ottawa's public transit system, has installed **bike racks** on more than 150 buses—most buses on routes 2, 95, and 97 have racks. Each rack holds two bikes and is designed to make loading and unloading quick and easy. There's no cost to use the rack, other than regular bus fare. The program runs from spring through fall.

Use common sense when riding your bike or in-line skating, and be sure to follow the specific rules for cyclists. All cyclists under age 18 must wear a **bicycle helmet.** Cyclists cannot ride on the sidewalk and must not exceed speeds of 20km per hour (12.5 mph) on multi-use pathways. Pass only when it is safe to do so, and use your bell or voice to let others know you're about to pass. Be considerate of other road or pathway users, and whether you're skating or cycling, always keep to the right.

If you're in the vicinity of the Rideau Centre and the ByWard Market, you can **park** your bike at a supervised facility. Located at Rideau and William streets, the facility operates daily 8:30am to 5:30pm, from Victoria Day until Labour Day weekend (third Saturday in May to first Monday in September). The maximum charge is C$2 (US$1.30).

For **maps** of the pathways and more information, head to the **Capital Info-centre,** opposite Parliament Hill at 90 Wellington Street (© **800/465-1867** or 613/239-5000).

 Tips

If you're driving to the parkways to cycle, skate, or walk, here are a few good places to park.
- For the Rockcliffe Parkway, park at the Aviation Museum.
- For the Ottawa River Parkway, park at Lincoln Fields Shopping Centre, 2525 Carling Ave., or Kitchissippi Lookout off the Ottawa River Parkway.
- For the Rideau Canal, park along side streets in the Glebe.

 Sunday Bikedays

In the summer, Sunday mornings present a real treat for lovers of the outdoors in Ottawa. No less than 65km (41 miles) of parkways in Ottawa and Gatineau Park are reserved exclusively for walking, running, cycling, in-line skating, and other non-motorized recreational activities. Motor traffic is banned. In Ottawa the motor-free period runs from 9am to 1pm. In Gatineau Park, there are 40km (25 miles) of hilly roadways to hike, bike, or skate from 6am to noon. **Sunday Bikedays** are sponsored by local radio stations and businesses. Many local organizations provide volunteers to supervise start and end points and crossings every Sunday morning during the event.

In Ottawa, there are three motor traffic–free areas for the event, all of which are fully accessible to people with disabilities. The **Ottawa River Parkway,** located on the south side of the Ottawa River just west of downtown, has a 9-km (6-mile) stretch beginning at the Mill restaurant and continuing to Carling Avenue. If you drive to this section, park your vehicle at the Lincoln Fields Shopping Centre at Carling Avenue. Beginning at the Laurier Bridge, you can enjoy **Colonel By Drive** as it winds its way along the east side of the Rideau Canal to Hog's Back Bridge, a total distance of 8km (5 miles). Park your car on one of the side streets to access Colonel By Drive. **Rockcliffe Parkway** is another choice for the Sunday morning excursion. Just east of downtown, and running along the southern shore of the Ottawa River, is an 8-km (5-mile) section between the Canada Aviation Museum and St. Joseph Boulevard. Parking is available at the Canada Aviation Museum.

For information about the Sunday Bikeday program, visit the **Capital Infocentre** at 90 Wellington Street (✆ 800/465-1867 or 613/239-5000), or call the **Gatineau Park Visitor Centre** (✆ 819/827-2020).

CROSS-COUNTRY SKIING

You're spoiled for choice for cross-country skiing in the Ottawa area. If you want to use the trails throughout the extensive **Greenbelt,** consult the **Greenbelt All Seasons Trail Map.** Or come to **Mooney's Bay Park,** 2960 Riverside Drive (✆ 613/247-4883) and ski on 5km (3 miles) of groomed and well-lit trails. Classic and skate skiing are available for a mere C$2 (US$1.30) per day or C$25 (US$17) for a season's pass. Across the Ottawa River in the city of **Gatineau,** you'll find **Parc du Lac Beauchamp.** Winter activities in the park include outdoor ice skating and cross-country skiing. For information on Lac Beauchamp, call ✆ 819/669-2548.

For the ultimate cross-country ski experience, visit **Gatineau Park.** The park has earned a reputation as one of the greatest ski-trail networks in North America for its remarkable 200km (125 miles) of trails, which are well maintained using the latest technology. The level of difficulty is marked on each trail, enabling skiers of all abilities to enjoy the meadows, valleys, and forests of the park. Both skiing styles are accommodated throughout the park, so you can glide along in classic Nordic fashion or burn up energy with the skate-skiing technique. There are eight heated shelters where you can stop to rest and refuel with a snack from your backpack. Gatineau Park ski patrollers are on watch to assist skiers in difficulty. When you arrive at the park, you can buy a day pass at any of the 16 parking lots, which give direct access to the ski trails, or at the **Gatineau Park Visitor Centre,** 33 Scott Road, Chelsea, QC (✆ 819/827-2020), open throughout the year, daily from 9am to 5pm. Weekday pass prices for cross-country ski trails are C$7 (US$4) for adults, C$4.50 (US$3) for seniors and youths, free for children 12 and under, C$18 (US$11) per family

(2 adults and 3 teens). Weekend prices are C$8 (US$5) for adults, C$5 (US$3) for seniors and youths, and free for children 12 and under.

Always carry a map when in wilderness areas. When you arrive at the park, pick up the Gatineau Park official winter trail map from the visitor center. The map costs C$5 (US$3) and is available on waterproof paper for C$10 (US$6). A new winter trail map has recently been produced through GIS technology, drawn to scale and including contour lines, magnetic north orientation, and exact representation of the trails. Depicted on the map are ski trails, winter hiking trails, snowshoeing trails, huts, and shelters. Because skiing and weather conditions change frequently, Gatineau Park reviews and updates ski condition information three times daily. The trail conditions hot line is open 24 hours daily ✆ **819/827-2020.**

FISHING

Fishing with a **Quebec permit** is allowed in the **Gatineau Park** lakes (Philippe Lake, Meech Lake, and La Pêche Lake). **Mulvihill Lake,** near the Mackenzie King Estate, has a fishing jetty designed to accommodate wheelchairs. There are many classes of fishing license available, from a day to a year and longer. Maps and current regulations are available from the Ministry of the Environment and the Société de la Faune et des Parcs' regional office at 98 Lois Street, Hull, ✆ **819/772-3434.** To fish in Ontario, you need an Ontario license. Ontario residents, other Canadian residents, and nonresidents all receive different licenses. **Access Ontario,** in the Rideau Centre (✆ **613/238-3630**), provides licenses, as well as a list of Ottawa-area merchants that sell them.

GOLF

There are dozens of golf courses within an hour or so's drive of Ottawa, both in Ontario and Quebec. The varied countryside in the region provides excellent sites for courses. Most are open to the public. Green fees vary enormously, dependent upon the season, day of the week, time of day, and other factors. Most fees for 18 holes fall into the C$25 to $75 (US$16–$47) range. See individual listings in chapter 10, "Exploring the Region."

HIKING

Besides the pathways and trails through many of the city parks and the Greenbelt area, as discussed earlier in this chapter, you might wish to explore Gatineau Park, the Rideau Trail, and parts of the Trans Canada Trail, particularly if you're looking for more challenging, longer routes.

The **Rideau Trail** is a cleared and marked hiking trail, approximately 300km (185 miles) long, linking the city of Kingston, on the shores of Lake Ontario, with Ottawa. The trail path is indicated by orange triangular markers. To distinguish the two directions, Kingston-bound markers have yellow tips. The path crosses varied terrain, ranging from gentle agricultural land to the rugged Canadian Shield. The trail is designated for walking, cross-country skiing, and snowshoeing. You can pick up a guide book with maps and a description of the trail from the **Rideau Trail Association,** P.O. Box 15, Kingston, ON K7L 4V6 (✆ **613/545-0823**). You'll also find the guide book in major outdoor expedition stores in Ottawa, at the Scout Shop, 1345 Baseline Road (✆ **613/224-0139**) and at A World of Maps, 1235 Wellington St. (✆ **613/724-6776**). (See chapter 9, "Shopping," for details on these and other stores.) Call the store of your choice before you make a special trip, as they may not always have the book on hand.

The **Trans Canada Trail** is a recreational trail currently under construction that will traverse Canada from coast to coast, crossing every province and territory. In the Ottawa area, sections of the Trans Canada Trail can be found in **Gatineau Park, Hull,** the **National Capital Greenbelt,** and the **Ottawa River Parkway.** The trail is signposted with trail markers featuring the Trans Canada Trail logo. For more information, call 𝄐 **800/465-3636** or visit www.tctrail.ca.

For information on hiking in **Gatineau Park,** see "Hull, Gatineau & the Outaouais Hills" in chapter 10, "Exploring the Region."

 ## The Trans Canada Trail

The **Trans Canada Trail,** currently under construction, is a recreational trail that will link Canada from coast to coast. At approximately 17,250km (10,700 miles) in length when completed, it will be the longest trail of its kind in the world.

Where practical, the trail is designated as a shared-use pathway with five core activities permitted: walking, cycling, horseback riding, cross-country skiing, and snowmobiling. Wherever possible, existing trails are used, provided they can accommodate these multiple uses. In addition, some provincial and federal park property, Crown land, abandoned railway lines, and rights-of-way on private land will become part of the trail.

The trail truly belongs to Canadians. Local organizations in communities across the country own, operate, and maintain their own segments, and more than 1.5 million volunteers are taking part in the project.

About half of the trail is already accessible, and it's expected that it will be substantially complete by late 2005. In some areas, it's virtually completed, but other sections still require a significant amount of work, so you won't find a final set of maps yet. Atlantic Canada's trail network is quite advanced and this has been the first region to be mapped. Available from the Trans Canada Trail website for C$6 (US$4), this map details the route through the Atlantic provinces and includes points of interest along the way. Eventually, maps will be produced for each region of the country.

In the Ottawa area, you'll find sections of the trail in **Gatineau Park, Hull,** the **National Capital Greenbelt,** and the **Ottawa River Parkway—** you can spot them by the trail markers with the Trans Canada Trail logo. For more information on the Trans Canada Trail, call 𝄐 **800/465-3636** or visit www.tctrail.ca.

ICE SKATING

The number one place to skate in the nation's capital is the world-famous Rideau Canal. If you visit Ottawa during the skating season, you must take everyone for a glide along the canal—it's an experience not to be missed. The **Rideau Canal Skateway** is the world's longest skating rink, offering almost 8km (5 miles) of continuous skating surface. The ice is usually ready in late December, and the season lasts until late February or early March. During the first three weekends in February, the Rideau Canal becomes the heart of **Winterlude,** Ottawa's winter festival. Skating is free. Heated shelters, skate and sled rentals, boot-check and skate-sharpening services, rest areas, food concessions, and toilets are located at various points along the Skateway. There are 35 access points along the canal for skating, so it's easy to get on the ice. To find out about ice conditions on the Rideau Canal, call the **Skateway Hotline** at ✆ **613/239-5234.**

For a special treat, visit the grounds of **Rideau Hall,** residence of the governor general, and skate on the historic outdoor rink built by Lord and Lady Dufferin in 1873. The rink is open to the public on weekends from noon to 5pm and reserved for organized groups on weekdays from noon to 8pm and weekends from 5 to 8pm. The rink opens in early January each year (weather permitting).

In **Brewer Park,** accessible from Hopewell Avenue near Bronson Avenue, there's a speed-skating oval that is open to the public. **Brantwood Park,** at Onslow Crescent between Elliot Avenue and Clegg Street, has a series of outdoor rinks connected by paths of ice so you can skate from one to another. Across the Ottawa River in the city of Gatineau, you'll find **Parc du Lac Beauchamp.** Winter activities in the park include outdoor ice skating and cross-country skiing. For information on Lac Beauchamp call ✆ **819/669-2548.**

More than 70 outdoor skating rinks are scattered throughout the city. Pleasure skating, lessons, carnivals, and hockey are enthusiastically enjoyed at these sites. For the outdoor rink closest to you, and to find out the times of family recreational skating at indoor arenas throughout the region, call the **City of Ottawa Client Service Centre** ✆ **613/580-2400.**

THE RIDEAU CANAL SKATEWAY

 Did You Know?

- The Skateway is visited by more than 1 million skaters every year.
- Staff work around the clock to maintain the ice surface.
- Many residents use the Skateway to commute to work and school every day.
- The Skateway ice surface area is equivalent to 20 Olympic-size ice rinks.
- The average length of the skating season on the canal is 52 days.
- The shortest season to date was 30 days, and the longest was 90 days.
- A system of colored flags indicates the ice conditions: red = closed, yellow = fair to good, green = very good to excellent.

SWIMMING

You have a choice of riverbank beaches, municipal pools, and state-of-the-art wave pools. See "Beaches," earlier in this section, and "Where to Play Indoors" earlier in this chapter.

TENNIS

The following courts are open to the public. Call ahead to book a court time. **Elmdale Tennis Club** is located close to downtown at 184 Holland Avenue ✆ **613/729-3644.** The **Ottawa New Edinburgh Club** provides affordable sporting facilities for its members and the community. Seven European-style, red clay courts are available. The club is located at 504 Rockcliffe Parkway ✆ **613/746-8540.** Public tennis courts can also be found at the **RA Centre,** 2451 Riverside Drive ✆ **613/733-5100.** The **West Ottawa Tennis Club** is located in Britannia Park at the corner of Pinecrest Road and Carling Avenue (*C* **613/828-7622**). During the summer season (May 1–September 30), 10 clay courts and 3 hard courts are open. The rest of the year, play is available on 6 clay courts. Instruction for all levels is available.

 Tips

For loads of winter fun right in the city, visit **Carlington Snowpark,** at 941 Clyde Avenue *C* **613/729-9206.** Go tubing or snowboarding and get a comfortable ride back up the hill. There are 10 slides to choose from, with night illumination and machine grooming. Hourly passes are available.

8

Ottawa After Dark

Ottawa's colorful origin as a rowdy lumber town was substantially attenuated as merchants and white-collar civil servants gradually changed the face of the city's population during the last century. The city became decidedly more genteel. But the past decade or two has seen an upswing in the energy of Ottawa's nightlife. This has been partly due to the influx of young techies to "Silicon Valley North," but the efforts of the local tourism industry and members of Ottawa's arts community must also be credited.

In 1997, the downtown Rideau commercial area was given a new moniker—"Ottawa's Arts and Theatre District." Encompassing 23 downtown blocks bordered by the Rideau Canal, George Street, King Edward Avenue, Besserer Street, Waller Street, the Mackenzie King Bridge, and Elgin St., there are almost four dozen arts and culture organizations located in the zone. You'll find the National Arts Centre, Canadian Museum of Contemporary Photography, Odyssey Theatre, Ottawa Little Theatre, and Arts Court here. Retail stores, restaurants, clubs, bars, galleries, theatres, attractions, hotels, and services—it's all here, ready to entertain you.

The lion's share of annual events and festivals takes place during the summer months, when the weather is warm and the number of visitors peaks. All year round, however, you can attend theater productions, spectator sports, a variety of films, live musical performances, dance clubs, pubs, and the spectacular Casino du Lac-Leamy.

FINDING OUT WHAT'S ON Your best bet for finding out what's happening and where, for current live music, theater, and film, particularly for the under-40 crowd, is to pick up a copy of *Ottawa's Weekly Xpress,* a free publication distributed each Thursday, or visit online at www.ottawaxpress.ca. *Where Ottawa–Hull,* a free monthly tourist guide listing entertainment, shopping, and dining, is available at hotels and stores in the city. *Voir* is a French-language weekly arts and entertainment paper that lists some venues and events in Hull and Gatineau as well as Ottawa.

Visiting families should keep an eye out for *Capital Parent,* a free monthly newspaper, and *Ottawa Families,* a free bimonthly newspaper. The *Ottawa Citizen* has a comprehensive Arts section on Fridays with an emphasis on films; a special Going Out section on Saturdays, which lists upcoming live entertainment events; and a list of community activities for the coming week on the back page of Sunday's A section, with an emphasis on family events. For news and information about regional arts events and activities, drop in to **Arts Court,** 2 Daly Ave. (© **613/564-7240**), or call the **Council for the Arts in Ottawa (CAO)** (© **613/569-1387**).

GETTING TICKETS Tickets to events at the **Corel Centre** and the **National Arts Centre** are sold at the on-site box offices or through **Ticketmaster** (Sportsline © **613/755-1166;** other events © **613/755-1111; www.**

ticketmaster.ca). You can also visit the Ticketmaster box office at 112 Kent Street, Monday to Friday from 9am to 5:30pm and Saturday from 9:30am to 1:30pm. Ticketmaster handles ticket sales for numerous venues. Also see the individual listings in this chapter.

SPECIAL EVENTS Ottawa frequently hosts large sports and entertainment events, so check with the **Ottawa Tourism and Convention Authority** (www.tourottawa.org) or **National Capital Commission,** 40 Elgin Street, Ottawa ON, K1P 1C7 (© **800/465-1867** or 613/239-5555; www.capcan.com) for special events scheduled during your visit.

1 Major Venues

Centrepointe Theatre   Featuring a unique blend of community and professional programming, Centrepointe Theatre is home to the productions of many community groups, including the Nepean Choir, the Canadian Showcase Chorus, the Nepean All-City Jazz Band, Les Petits Ballets, the Nepean Concert Band, the Savoy Society, and the Orpheus Musical Theatre Society. Liona Boyd, Christopher Plummer, and Peter Ustinov have stood in the spotlight. Four spots are reserved for guests in wheelchairs on the orchestra level, and you can make special arrangements to accommodate larger groups. An audio-loop system for the hearing impaired is also available. To arrange for special seating, please specify your needs to the box-office attendant when purchasing tickets. Parking is free. Ben Franklin Place, 101 Centrepointe Dr. © **613/727-6650.**

The Corel Centre   This 18,500-seat multipurpose sports and entertainment complex, formerly known as the Palladium, opened its doors in January 1996. Home of the **Ottawa Senators** National Hockey League (NHL) team and the **Ottawa Rebel** lacrosse team, this complex hosts various sporting and entertainment events. There are 170 seating spaces for people with disabilities on the Club and Main Concourse levels, as well as four elevators. If you require special seating, mention this when purchasing your tickets. There are more than 140 concession stands on the two public concourses, plus a Hard Rock Café, Marshy's Bar-B-Q and Grill, the Penalty Box Restaurant, Rickard's Pub, and the Silver Seven Brew House. Official Ottawa Senators merchandise can be purchased at Sensations, located at Gate 1. **OC Transpo** (© 613/741-4390) provides direct bus service from Transitway stations across the city to all Senators games and most other events. Free parking is provided at five Park & Ride lots. The Corel Centre is a smoke-free building. For smaller events, the **WordPerfect Theatre** provides seating for 2,500 to 7,400 people. An automated retractable curtain system divides the arena in half. For sports tickets call Ticketmaster Sportsline at © **613/755-1166;** for other events call Ticketmaster at © **613/755-1111,** or visit any Ticketmaster outlet or the Corel Centre box office (Gate 1). 1000 Palladium Dr. © **613/599-0123.**

Lansdowne Park   This large facility hosts hundreds of events annually, including trade and consumer shows, family entertainment, rock concerts, Junior hockey tournaments, national and international athletic competitions, and the Central Canada Exhibition. A number of exhibition halls are on site, as is the 10,000-seat **Civic Centre,** home of the Ontario Hockey League **Ottawa 67's.** 1015 Bank St. © **613/580-2429** for general information; © **613/232-6767** for information on the Ottawa 67's.

Maison de la culture de Gatineau   The 652-seat Odyssée Hall is located here. Patrons enjoy francophone plays, music, songs, comedians, and dance performances. 855 La Gappe Blvd., Gatineau. ℭ **819/243-2525.**

National Arts Centre   Situated in the heart of the city, across from Confederation Square and Parliament Hill, the NAC is one of the largest performing arts complexes in Canada. Home to the internationally acclaimed 46-member National Arts Centre Orchestra, this center also stages a wide variety of performances, including English and French theater, dance, music, and community programming. Four performance halls are housed within the unique multi-level structure. The largest of the four performing halls with more than 2,300 seats, **Southam Hall** hosts Broadway musicals, ballets, operas, musical acts, lectures, ceremonies, films, orchestral music, and other entertainment and corporate events. Mega-musicals such as *Phantom of the Opera* and *Les Misérables* have been staged here. Ideal for plays, musicals, seminars, conferences, films, chamber music, and other musical events, **Theatre Hall** (just under 1,000 seats) also presents numerous Stratford Festival productions. Musicals such as *Crazy for You* have been showcased here. **Studio Hall** is a versatile venue that has a capacity of 250 to 300, depending on the seating arrangement, and hosts performances, corporate seminars, and presentations. **The Fourth Stage** is a multipurpose performance space for community programming, including dance, music, storytelling, choral singing, and theater. The Fourth Stage can accommodate various stage configurations and seats up to 150. The NAC's restaurant, **Le Café,** has views over the Rideau Canal, an outdoor terrace for summer dining, and a good local reputation for its cuisine. Enjoy lunch, pre-performance dinner, table d'hôte after 8pm, or post-theater dessert and coffee. The NAC is fully accessible to guests with disabilities and provides special tickets for patrons in wheelchairs. Underground parking is available; parking entrances are located on Elgin Street (at the corner of Slater Street) and on Albert Street. 53 Elgin St. ℭ **613/947-7000.** For tickets visit the NAC box office or call Ticketmaster at ℭ **613/755-1111.**

Ottawa Congress Centre   This meeting facility hosts large-scale conventions and trade and consumer shows. The center includes the 6,000-m^2 (66,000-ft.^{2}) Congress Hall and the Colonel By Salon, with floor-to-ceiling windows overlooking the Rideau Canal. Rooftop terraces also offer views of downtown Ottawa. Direct access to the Rideau Centre is provided. 55 Colonel By Dr. ℭ **613/563-1984.**

Theatre du Casino du Lac-Leamy   This state-of-the-art theater has been designed as an intimate space despite the 1,001 seating capacity. Opened in 2001, the theater is adjacent to Casino du Lac-Leamy. The entrance is separate from the Casino to allow theater patrons of all ages to enjoy performances. 1 Casino Blvd., Hull. ℭ **819/772-2100.**

2 Performing Arts

Because Ottawa serves two masters—the Canadian population as the national capital and the local citizens of the city of Ottawa—the arts and entertainment field includes a major federal arts presence and a vibrant and energetic local arts community. If you want to find out what's really happening on the local front, drop in to **Arts Court** at 2 Daly Avenue ℭ **613/564-7240,** Ottawa's center for performing, visual, media, and literary arts.

THEATRE

Astrolabe Theatre In the summer months, this outdoor theater on Nepean Point, built as part of the Centennial celebrations, stages entertainment for the whole family. Contact the National Capital Commission at © 800/465-1867 or 613/ 239-5000 for more information.

A Company of Fools Founded in 1990, the company's aim is to make Shakespeare entertaining and accessible. Initially, the troupe rehearsed and acted out Shakespearean scenes on the street. Audiences respond to their unique brand of high-energy performance, classical text, and modern slapstick. In 2001, the company performed at the Ottawa Fringe Festival and also presented "Shakespeare Under the Stars," featuring scenes, sonnets, and songs in various parks in the Ottawa region, beneath the night sky. Performing at various locations. © 613/ 863-7529 booking hotline. www.acompanyoffools.com.

Dramamuse Since 1989, this resident theater company in the Canadian Museum of Civilization has been entertaining visitors. Actors perform short plays and play colorful historical characters who mingle with visitors and "interpret" the museum exhibits. Dramamuse brings the museum to life for young and old. Performing at the Canadian Museum of Civilization, 100 Laurier St., Hull. © 800/ 555-5621 or 819/776-7000.

Festival 4–15 Part of the Ottawa Festival of the Arts for Young Audiences, Festival 4–15 brings in theater groups from around the world to entertain children in Ottawa during their summer and winter festivals. In 2001, the festival found a new home at the 500-seat theater in the Canadian Museum of Civilization. Visit their website at www.ottawachildrensfestival.ca and sign up for free updates on their programming. Call the Festival Office © 613/241-0999 for information and tickets. Tickets are not available at the museum. Performing at the Canadian Museum of Civilization, 100 Laurier St., Hull, QC. © 800/555-5621 or 819/776-7000.

Great Canadian Theatre Company The GCTC has provided bold, innovative, and thought-provoking theater to Ottawa audiences for more than a quarter of a century. The season runs from September to March. Performing at 910 Gladstone Ave. © 613/236-5196. Tickets C$16–$24 (US$10–$15).

Kanata Theatre This community theater group was established in 1968. Since then, they have staged more than 100 productions in their own theater in Kanata. 1 Ron Maslin Way. © 613/831-4435. Tickets C$12 (US$7).

NAC English Theatre The NAC English Theatre develops, produces, and presents an English-language theater program locally, as well as co-producing plays with theater companies in other Canadian centers. The season consists of a five-play Mainstage series; a three-play alternative Studio series; special presentations; family, youth, and education activities; and a new play development program. The plays that make up the season range from the classics to new Canadian works. The Family Theatre Series presents three plays in the studio with matinee and evening performances on weekends. During the Christmas season, the NAC stages a special holiday play, suitable for all ages. **NAC French Theatre** features a variety of French-language productions, including performances for children ages 4 to 11. Performing at the NAC, 35 Elgin St. © 613/947-7000. For tickets visit the NAC box office or call Ticketmaster at © 613/755-1111. Ticket prices vary.

Odyssey Theatre This professional summer theater company is noted for its imaginative use of masks, dance-like movement, and original music. Its open-air productions are based on Italian Renaissance street theater, known as *commedia dell'arte*. Odyssey specializes in productions of classic comic texts and original works. For 5 weeks in late summer, they perform in Strathcona Park on the banks of the Rideau River, close to downtown Ottawa. For youth and family audiences, the troupe also stages one-hour versions of the summer production, with demonstrations and a question-and-answer period. Performing in Strathcona Park. Office at 2 Daly Ave. ℃ **613/232-8407.**

Orpheus Musical Theatre Society Orpheus has been entertaining Ottawa audiences with their musical performances since 1906. The company performs three fully staged musical shows per season. Recent shows include *The Wizard of Oz, Man of La Mancha,* and *Anything Goes.* Performing at Centrepointe Theatre, 101 Centrepointe Dr. ℃ **613/727-6650.** Tickets C$12–$22 (US$8–$15).

Ottawa Little Theatre Since 1913, this amateur community theater has been producing plays in Ottawa. The comfortable 510-seat auditorium was redesigned after the original building was destroyed by fire in 1970. The company stages eight productions, with one per month from September through May, as well as one popular and entertaining musical each year as part of the summer series. Productions range from comedies to dramas, mysteries, farces, and musicals, and include the works of William Shakespeare, Agatha Christie, and Neil Simon. Performing at 400 King Edward Ave. ℃ **613/233-8948.** Tickets C$15–$18 (US$9–$11).

Savoy Society The Savoy Society of Ottawa is an organization of people who share a common interest in performing the comic operas of Gilbert and Sullivan. The society staged its first production, *The Pirates of Penzance,* in 1976, and now presents one play annually, running seven public performances (including a Sunday matinee) plus a benefit performance. You can obtain information on the society by calling ℃ **613/825-5855.** Performing at Centrepointe Theatre, 101 Centrepointe Dr. ℃ **613/727-6650** for tickets. Tickets C$10–$22 (US$7–$15).

Sock 'n' Buskin This theater company is student run and community based, performing at the 444-seat Alumni Theatre on the campus of Carleton University. 1125 Colonel By Dr. ℃ **613/520-3821** (Alumni Theatre) or ℃ **613/520-3770** (information on the theatre company).

The Tara Players The Tara Players stage classic, modern, and contemporary dramas and comedies from and about Ireland and written by playwrights of Irish heritage. Three productions are staged per season, from October to May. Performing at St. Patrick's Hall, 280 Gloucester St. ℃ **613/746-1410.** Call for current ticket prices.

Theatre de l'Ile This French-language theater actually is on an island in a beautiful park setting in downtown Hull. There is always a summer production, and other performances are scheduled at various times throughout the year. Dinner theater packages are available. 1 Wellington St., Hull. ℃ **819/595-7455.**

DANCE

Anjali Anjali (Anne-Marie Gaston) is a classically trained East Indian dancer, choreographer, teacher, lecturer, and photographer. Performances consist of East Indian temple dances and innovative, contemporary choreography based on traditional forms. Recitals are performed against a backdrop of images of temples, goddesses, and remote corners of Bhutan and the Himalayas. Call for performance schedule and venues. ℂ **613/745-1368.**

Le Groupe Dance Lab At the forefront of choreographic research, Le Groupe Dance Lab is an international center that focuses on the process of creating dance rather than the production of finished pieces of choreography. The group holds interactive public presentations of works-in-progress each season. 2 Daly Ave. ℂ **613/235-1492.**

Les Petits Ballets Les Petits Ballets, a nonprofit organization, was founded in 1976 to develop youth ballet talent. Professional guest dancers and young local talent share the stage in full-length ballets, including *Coppelia* and *Cinderella*. Performances are held twice yearly. Performing at Centrepointe Theatre, 101 Centrepointe Dr. ℂ **613/727-6650** box office, or 613/596-5783 studio.

NAC Dance Productions Throughout the year, the NAC hosts a variety of dance performances, ranging from classical ballet to contemporary dance. Guest dance companies include Les Grands Ballet Canadiens de Montreal, Toronto Dance Theatre, Iceland Dance Company, Ballet British Columbia, Brazilian Dance Theater, National Ballet of Canada, and Royal Winnipeg Ballet. 35 Elgin St. ℂ **613/947-7000.** For tickets visit the box office or call Ticketmaster at ℂ **613/755-1111.** Ticket prices vary.

CLASSICAL MUSIC, CHORAL MUSIC & OPERA

Cantata Singers of Ottawa One of the region's most popular choirs, the Cantata Singers perform regularly with the NAC Orchestra and also have their own annual concert series. Call ℂ **613/798-7113** for more information.

NAC Orchestra Offering more than 100 performances a year, this vibrant, classical-size orchestra draws accolades at home and abroad. In 1998 Pinchas Zukerman became the fifth conductor to lead the orchestra. The NAC Orchestra performs with Opera Lyra Ottawa and frequently accompanies ballets, including regular performances in Ottawa by Canada's three major ballet companies—the National Ballet of Canada, the Royal Winnipeg Ballet, and Les Grands Ballet Canadiens. The **Pops Series** combines popular songs and light classical music in a series of six evening performances. **NACO Young Peoples Concerts** are directed to 7- to 11-year-olds and feature music, storytelling, animation, and audience participation. Performing at the NAC, 35 Elgin St. ℂ **613/947-7000.** For tickets visit the box office or call Ticketmaster at ℂ **613/755-1111.**

Opera Lyra Ottawa Ottawa's resident opera company performs in the NAC, staging three operas between September and April. Recent main-stage productions include *Salome* and *La Bohème*. Their holiday-season production, presented in cooperation with the University of Ottawa and performed at Tabaret Hall, is suitable for all ages. Past productions include *The Magic Flute* and *Cinderella*. Performing at the NAC, 35 Elgin St., and Tabaret Hall, University of Ottawa, 550 Cumberland St. ℂ **613/233-9200.** www.operalyra.ca. For tickets call Ticketmaster at ℂ **613/755-1111.** Ticket prices vary.

Ottawa Chamber Music Society Concert Series Some of Canada's most accomplished chamber music artists perform in downtown Ottawa churches from October to April. A 2-week summer festival is also held. See www. chamberfest.com for concert schedules. Performing at various locations. ℂ **613/234-8008.** Tickets C$5–$30 (US$3–$19).

Ottawa Choral Society   This 135-voice symphonic chorus performs major works from every period of the choral repertoire. They perform regularly with the NAC Orchestra, Ottawa Symphony Orchestra, and Thirteen Strings. Call ℂ 613/725-2560 for more information.

Ottawa Symphony Orchestra   With 90 musicians, the Ottawa Symphony Orchestra is the National Capital Region's largest orchestra. A series of five concerts is held at the NAC from September to May, featuring the music of the 19th and early 20th centuries. Performing at the NAC, 35 Elgin St. ℂ 613/947-7000. For tickets visit the box office or call Ticketmaster at ℂ 613/755-1111 or the OSO ticket office at ℂ 613/747-3104. Tickets C$15–$45 (US$10–$30).

Thirteen Strings   One of Canada's foremost chamber music ensembles, Thirteen Strings has an annual subscription series of six concerts at St. Andrew's Presbyterian Church in Ottawa and performs a wide range of music for strings from the 15th to the 20th century. Performing at St. Andrew's Presbyterian Church, 82 Kent St. ℂ 613/745-1142. www.thirteenstrings.ca. Tickets at the door C$25 (US$16) adults, C$5 (US$3) ages 18 and under.

3 The Club & Live Music Scene

Dance clubs, bars, and live entertainment venues are often changing, trying to keep up with or keep ahead of their patrons' latest passions. By the time you visit some of the venues listed here, they may have changed the type of music they offer, the decor, the beer, or even their name. Your best bet for finding out what's happening, and where, is to pick up a copy of *Ottawa's Weekly Xpress,* a free publication distributed each Thursday. The *Ottawa Citizen* publishes a hefty Arts section on Fridays and a special section, Going Out, on Saturdays. *Voir* is a French-language weekly arts and entertainment paper that lists some venues and events in Hull and Gatineau as well as Ottawa. You can take potluck as well if you're willing to gamble on what you might stumble upon. Ottawa's live music scene is extensive, and there are lots of pubs and bars offering live music on one or more evenings a week—too many to list here. Drop by for a pint or two at one of Ottawa's watering holes and you just might be surprised.

COMEDY CLUBS

The Institution   A local group of comedians put on several regular shows. One of their most popular is *Laff Lines,* an improv show with audience participation. If you've ever seen the television show "Whose Line Is It, Anyway?" then you understand the concept. When we went to press, the group was still looking for a new location, probably in the ByWard Market area. You can call ℂ 613/563-2255 for information or visit their website www.theinstitution.cc.

Yuk Yuk's Komedy Kabaret   Stand-up comedians are featured in this club, which has a bar and restaurant service. Shows are generally Wednesday to Saturday evenings and last about 2 hours. Cover charge applies. 88 Albert St. ℂ 613/236-5233.

ECLECTIC

Barrymore's Music Hall   Whatever your musical preferences, you'll find a band scheduled to play here sooner or later that you just have to see. Rock, pop, blues, punk, alternative rock, metal, Celtic, swing, retro—just about everybody hits the stage here. On nights when there isn't a live band, resident DJs get everyone dancing up a storm. 323 Bank St. ℂ 613/233-0307.

Zaphod Beeblebrox This Ottawa institution is a combination of live music venue and dance club. Famous for their Pan Galactic Gargleblaster cocktail. Past performers include Alanis Morissette, Jewel, Ashley MacIsaac, and The Tea Party. The headline act is usually over by 11pm, and then a DJ spins tunes until very late. 27 York St. ✆ 613/562-1010.

FOLK & CELTIC

Rasputin's Rasputin's is a small but perennially popular venue featuring lots of variety—in addition to traditional and contemporary folk, you'll find Cajun country, Maritime tunes, storytellers, Celtic jams, and open-mike nights. 696 Bronson Ave. ✆ 613/230-5102.

JAZZ & BLUES

Jazz music is a natural accompaniment to dining, and several area restaurants feature live jazz on one or more evenings weekly. Try **Bourbons on Clarence,** 33 Clarence Street ✆ 613/241-4811, or **Vineyards Wine Bar & Bistro** at 54 York Street ✆ 613/241-4270. To find out what's playing in the blues vein around the city, call the Bluesfest Office at ✆ 613/247-1188.

Bayou Blues & Jazz Club They play it like the name says—jazz and blues. Recent bands include Mississippi Delta blues sensation Big Jack Johnson & The Oilers and metal–blues fusion with The Frank James Project. 1071 Bank St. ✆ 613/738-1709.

The Rainbow A reputation as Ottawa's legendary home of the Blues, The Rainbow has had the honor of opening their stage to Dan Ackroyd, Jim Belushi, and Matt Murphy, who performed their Blues Brothers routine. Live music is featured seven nights a week. During the summer music festivals in Ottawa, many of the musicians and spectators gather here. 76 Murray St. ✆ 613/241-5123.

LATINO

Ole Bistro Latino Music is an integral part of Ole. The dining menu offers lots of Spanish-, Caribbean-, and Latin American–influenced dishes. There's live entertainment nightly with an assortment of flamenco guitarists, other musicians, and dancers with an emphasis on Latin American and Afri-Cuban styles. Popular with the after-work crowd and also busy later in the evenings. 352 Somerset St. ✆ 613/569-6397.

PIANO BARS

Friday's Roast Beef House Pianists entertain nightly. 150 Elgin St. ✆ 613/237-5353.

Zoe's At the Fairmont Château Laurier Hotel, enjoy the sounds of a pianist from 5pm to 7pm on weekdays. Music to dance by is provided on Friday and Saturday evenings. 1 Rideau St. in the Château Laurier Hotel. ✆ 613/241-1414.

DANCE CLUBS

Atomic Nightclub A mostly young crowd dances the night away at this two-floor dance club. DJs spin different mixes different nights of the week, including disco, hip-hop, reggae, and house. 137 Besserer St. ✆ 613/241-2411.

Babylon Babylon features live reggae every Thursday, music they promise your parents would hate on Wednesdays, and a mixture of hip-hop, electronica, and guitar rock on the weekends. 317 Bank St. ✆ 613/594-0003.

China White   China White is aiming for a sophisticated ambience with its white decor accented with chrome. Music is electronica, Latin, and techno & industrial. Next door is the **Buddha Bar** martini lounge. Crowd is under 40. 104 Clarence St. ✆ **613/241-6581.**

Mercury Lounge   Targeting a professional clientele, the prices are a little higher here and the crowd a little older. This is a place to dance or listen to the music as you sip martinis on red velvet couches. A mix of live bands and DJs. NuJazz is currently in demand, but you'll also hear electronica, funk, soul, Latin, and world rhythms.

Maxwell's   A second-floor nightclub on lively Elgin Street, Maxwell's features a lounge singer on Wednesdays and retro '80s dance music on Fridays. 340 Elgin St. ✆ **613/232-5771.**

Rincon Latino   Hot nights are promised at this night club on Preston Street. Tango Tuesdays, free salsa lessons on Wednesdays, specialty cocktails, and 100% Latin music on Saturday nights. 412 Preston St. ✆ **613/233-7207.**

The Well   One of Ottawa's first underground dance clubs and one of the longest to stay alive, The Well is on George Street below the Market Station bar. Featuring house, trance, and techno beat tunes belting out to a young crowd. 15 George St. ✆ **613/860-1616.**

4 The Bar Scene

BARS

ARC Lounge   The lounge bar at ARC the.hotel is sleek, minimalist, and sophisticated. Membership is free but mandatory. (If you're not a guest at the hotel, you can fill out a form and join the first time you visit.) Try their signature martini, the Arctini. Nibble on stylish tapatizers (the menu might include spiced tuna sashimi, marinated salmon carpaccio, or duck confit) in the early evening. 140 Slater St. in ARC the.hotel ✆ **613/238-2888.**

Eighteen   One of Ottawa's newer bars, opened in summer 2001 in an historic building at 18 York Street. The 25+ crowd dresses up rather than dresses down. If you want to sample several wines from their extensive selection, order a cluster of four 2-ounce glasses. 18 York St. ✆ **613/684-0444.**

Empire Grill   Trendy and upscale, the Empire Grill has exciting cocktails and an extensive wine list. Outdoor patio, live jazz some nights, DJs after 10pm other nights. 47 Clarence St. ✆ **241-1343.**

Social   There's a bit of everything at this popular upscale evening destination. A fusion of French and Mediterranean cuisine is served in the restaurant. At night, enjoy jazz or blues. At weekends, a DJ revs up the music scene. 537 Sussex Dr. ✆ **613/789-7355.**

PUBS

The Arrow & The Loon   This comfortable neighborhood watering hole in the Glebe is filled with regulars. Ontario and Quebec microbrews are featured. They've also been known to pull a pint or two of cask-conditioned real ale such as Wellington's Arkell Best Bitter. 99 Fifth Ave. ✆ **613/237-0448.**

The Barley Mow   Cask-conditioned ales and almost 2 dozen microbrews and imported beers on tap, plus an extensive selection of single-malt Scotch earns this pub a nod from beer and whisky lovers. 1060 Bank St. ✆ **613/1279.**

Bytown Tavern　Their logo says "Shut up and drink your beer." If you factor in eight TVs plus two giant screens tuned to sports action, that kind of tells you it's a guy place. Yep, there's a wing night. 292 Elgin St. ✆ **613/233-0057.**

D'Arcy McGee's Irish Pub　Housed in a heritage building at the corner of Sparks Street and Elgin Street, D'Arcy McGee's has an authentically Irish interior (it was actually designed and handcrafted in Ireland and imported). The crowd includes a smattering of politicians, civil servants, and tourists. Live Celtic, Maritime, and folk music. The patio has a great view over Confederation Square, with the Château Laurier in the background. 44 Sparks St. ✆ **613/230-4433.**

Duke of Somerset　Four venues cover all the bases in the historic **Somerset House** at the corner of Somerset and Bank streets. Enjoy a drink on the **Village Green Patio,** head downstairs to the **Duke's Pub** for the best in British football and rugby television coverage, take a seat in the **Lockmaster Tavern** and watch your favorite North American pro sports team in action, or experience the energetic atmosphere of **Ole Tapas Bar & Bistro,** which features live entertainment nightly. 352 Somerset St. at Bank St. ✆ **613/233-7762.**

Earl of Sussex　Located right on the tourist track, the Earl of Sussex is an English-style pub, with wing-backed chairs, a fireplace, and a dartboard. The atmosphere is friendly and cozy, as tourists mix with regulars and business people. There are more than 30 beers on tap, including European and domestic. The sunny rear patio is very popular in warm weather. 431 Sussex Dr. ✆ **613/562-5544.**

 For Beer Lovers

True beer connoisseurs always appreciate a pint of the best. Ottawa has dozens of British-style pubs and North American–type bars where you can sample brews from Britain, Ireland, Germany, Belgium, and, of course, Canada.

There are several local **microbreweries** to keep an eye out for in Ottawa-area restaurants and pubs. The **Scotch Irish Brewing Co.** in Kinburn, Ontario, produces a British-style bitter called Session Ale and an Irish-style porter, Black Irish. **Hart Brewing Co. Ltd.** in Carleton Place, Ontario, produces a range of ales and stouts. And right in Ottawa itself, at 5459 Canotek Road, **Heritage Brewing Ltd.** brews Heritage Premium Lager.

If you want to sample the homemade draught of a **brew pub,** here are a couple to try. The **Clocktower Brew Pub** at 575 Bank Street ✆ **613/233-7849** features an ever-changing selection of seasonal brews, listed on a chalkboard menu. Two of the most popular are Bytown Brown, a heavy, dark beer to accompany a pub meal on a winter's night, and Indian Summer Ale, which is perfect in a pitcher on the large summer patio. **Master's Brew Pub & Brasserie,** at 330 Queen Street, brews a variety of lagers and ales on site. Decor is Art Deco and they're generally open Monday to Friday, early to late, to serve local office workers and downtown hotel residents. For more places to get a decent pint, check out the Pub listings earlier in this chapter.

Heart & Crown   Good range of beer available here. Live Celtic music several nights a week. Favorite British pub fare including shepherd's pie and fish 'n' chips. 67 Clarence St. ✆ **613/562-0674.**

Lieutenant's Pump   In the heart of the Elgin Street bar district, this large pub draws a big crowd. More than a dozen beers on tap, including Montreal microbrews. 361 Elgin St. ✆ **613/238-2949.**

The Manx   This British-style pub has a mix of young and older clientele. An impressive selection of Scotch—more than 50 single malts, plus 10 Irish whiskys. The pub occasionally holds Scotch tastings. Provides wall space for local artists. 370 Elgin St. ✆ **613/231-2070.**

Patty Boland's Irish Pub & Carvery   A spacious meeting place, with two floors of dark wood and brass. Pub fare available. Two fireplaces to warm your toes in winter, and two patios for summer sipping—one out front for people watching, and a quieter one at the back for conversation. 101 Clarence St. ✆ **613/789-7822.**

Royal Oak   You'll bump into Royal Oaks all over town—downtown, east end, west end, the Glebe; there are eight altogether. The original pub, dating from 1980, is at 318 Bank Street, where the crowd tends to reflect whatever band is head-lining at Barrymore's Music Hall across the street. The most recent addition is at 221 Echo Drive by Pretoria Bridge. The two-level patio has a nice view over the canal. 318 Bank St. ✆ **613/236-0190;** 221 Echo Dr. ✆ **613/234-3700;** and six other locations.

5 The Gay & Lesbian Scene

Social life and entertainment for the gay and lesbian community in Ottawa is clustered around Bank Street in the vicinity of Frank Street, Somerset Street W., and Lisgar Street. There are also a couple of venues in the ByWard Market district.

Centretown Pub   Located in a three-story Victorian house, this pub doesn't have a sign outside, but you can identify it by the brown awning that covers the main walkway. It's comfortable and friendly and frequented by regulars, mostly men. It has been described as a "gay Cheers." 340 Somerset St. W. ✆ **613/594-0233.**

Icon   There are three different venues to choose from at Icon. The main level lounge has a bar and cafe tables, plus pool tables, video games, and a dance floor with a screen showing music videos. Downstairs is the Twist Show Bar, which features female impersonators. Upstairs, the dance club pulses 'til the wee hours on Friday and Saturday nights and attracts a younger crowd. 366 Lisgar St., near Bank St. ✆ **613/235-4005.**

Lookout Bar & Bistro   Upstairs at 41 York Street in the ByWard Market, this bar attracts a diverse crowd of gays, lesbians, and straights of all ages. The bal-cony is popular in the summer. On DJ nights, tables are moved back to make room for dancing. 41 York St. (upstairs) ✆ **613/789-1624.**

Market Station   The Market Station Bar Bistro is one of a handful of restaurant/bars that overlook the Clarendon Courtyard, a romantic cobblestone courtyard in the ByWard Market district. Consequently, the large patio is extremely busy and popular in the warmer months. 15 George St. ✆ **613/562-3540.**

Club Polo Pub & Lounge   There are two bars here; the upstairs one has a dance floor. Theme nights are popular. 65 Bank St. ✆ **613/235-5995.**

Village Inn Pub   This restaurant/bar is relaxed and friendly. Food is inexpensive and weekly events are held. 313 Bank St. ℭ **613/594-8287.**

6 Film

If you love the silver screen, you'll have plenty of choice in Ottawa. Experience the latest in cinematic technology at the **IMAX** Theatre in the Canadian Museum of Civilization, cozy up at a budget family movie theater, or enjoy tiered seating and big sound at an urban monster megaplex.

HIGH-TECH CINEMA

IMAX Theatre   This amazing theater at the Canadian Museum of Civilization is the only one of its kind in the world. The technology of IMAX plus a giant dome gives you the feeling of being wrapped in sights and sounds. At seven stories high, the IMAX screen is amazing enough, but the real adventure begins when the 23-m (75-ft.) hemispheric dome moves into place overhead once the audience is seated. Not all films use the entire screening system. This theater is busy, so buy your tickets in advance and plan to arrive 20 minutes before show time—latecomers will not be admitted. All ages are welcome. Canadian Museum of Civilization, 100 Laurier St., Hull ℭ **819/776-7010** for show times. For tickets visit the museum box office or call Ticketmaster at ℭ **613/755-1111.**

REPERTORY CINEMAS

Bytowne Cinema   Ottawa's premiere independent cinema has been screening independent and foreign films in this large, locally owned and operated theater for more than 50 years. Get real butter on your popcorn and settle down in the comfy chairs to enjoy the big screen and Dolby sound. Two to four movies are screened every day, with the lineup changing every few days. 325 Rideau St. ℭ **613/789-3456.** www.bytowne.ca.

Canadian Film Institute Cinema   The Canadian Film Institute presents a regular public program of contemporary, historical, and international cinema in the auditorium of the National Archives of Canada. Festivals and special events are held. If you have an interest or expertise in the art of cinematography, check out their calendar of events. All screenings at the National Archives Auditorium, 395 Wellington St. ℭ **613/232-6727.**

Mayfair Theatre   Screening a mixture of relatively recent releases and older films, the Mayfair changes its bill almost daily. Two films are run every night. 1074 Bank St. ℭ **613/730-3403.** www.mayfair-movie.com.

Ottawa Family Cinema   Also known as Westend Family Cinema, this non-profit theater offers movies on the big screen with digital stereo sound, cartoons, and door prizes. A friendly, family atmosphere prevails, with special events and movie parties held throughout the season. Films include recent releases and older films that are suitable for family viewing. 710 Broadview Ave. ℭ **613/722-8218.** www.familycinema.org. Open Sat afternoons and every second Fri evening, Sept–May, except Christmas and Easter weekends.

MAINSTREAM NEW RELEASES

The city is well serviced by large multi-screen movie theaters. For current listings and prices, check the ***Ottawa Citizen*** (Friday has the most comprehensive Arts & Entertainment coverage), or visit **http://ottawa.film-can.com.** If you wince at the cost of taking the family out to a movie these days, check cinemas for special offers. Full-price tickets run as high as C$12.50 (US$7.75), but if you shop around and go at off-peak periods, you may pay up to 50% less.

AMC 24 Kanata is in the west end of the city at Highway 417 and Terry Fox Drive (© **613/599-5500**). **Rideau Centre Famous Players** is conveniently located at 50 Rideau St. in the Rideau Centre (© **613/234-3712**). **South Keys Cineplex Odeon** is in the south end at 2214 Bank St. S. at Hunt Club Road (© **613/736-1115**). **World Exchange Plaza Cineplex Odeon,** 111 Albert St., 3rd Floor (© **613/233-0209**), is in the heart of downtown and screens matinees daily. **Coliseum 12 Famous Players,** in Ottawa's west end, is just north of Bayshore Shopping Centre at 3090 Carling Ave (© **613/596-1812**). **Orleans Cinemas Cineplex Odeon** is at 250 Centrum Blvd. in Place d'Orléans shopping complex (© **613/834-0666**). **Silver City Gloucester Famous Players,** 2385 City Park Dr. (© **613/749-3029**), is situated in the big-box complex at the corner of Blair Rd. and Ogilvie Rd.

7 Gaming

CASINO DU LAC LEAMY

The extensive facilities of **Casino du Lac Leamy** have continued to grow since the complex first opened in 1996 on the shores of Lac Leamy (Leamy Lake).

Gaming Area   This huge entertainment and gaming destination can accommodate 6,500 visitors at a time. There are 2,557 gaming spaces, including 1,866 slot machines. Gaming tables number 64 and offer Blackjack, Roulette, Baccara, Poker Pai Gow, Mini Baccarat, Grand Baccarat, Caribbean Poker, Poker Grand Prix, SicBo, and Craps. Additional gaming facilities include a Keno salon, electronic horse race track, electronic bingo, a high-limits gaming area and lounge with personalized service, and a private gaming salon. The interior of the gaming area is vast. Thousands of tropical plants and the creative use of water features result in a unique atmosphere. The following customer services are complimentary: parking, valet service, admission, coat check, boat docking (reservations required), and nonalcoholic beverages (in gaming areas only). The Casino has been designed to accommodate guests with physical disabilities. Approximately two-thirds of the gaming area is nonsmoking. Dress code is in effect, but casual is okay—just make sure your blue jeans are neat and your running shoes aren't too scruffy.

Restaurant and Bar Services   Three dining areas, two bars, and two private reception facilities are on site. **Le Baccara** is an elegant fine-dining restaurant that has quickly established a reputation for its cuisine. **Banco** offers a choice of buffet-syle or a-la-carte dining. For a quick snack, drop into **Le Café.** A forest of tropical plants fills **Le 777** bar. Offering a selection of more than 70 imported beers, **La Marina** features a saltwater aquarium, an outside patio, and panoramic views over Lac de la Carrière, which has a 60-m (197-feet) high fountain as its focal point. Musical entertainment is provided in Le Baccara and La Marina in the evenings. **L'Executif** is a private salon accommodating up to 22 guests. For larger functions, **Le Salon Royal** banquet hall will seat 200 patrons, or up to 350 for cocktail receptions.

Theatre du Casino du Lac Leamy   This state-of-the-art live performance theater opened in the fall of 2001. With 1,001 seats, including 10 places for wheelchairs, the theater has been designed so that all seats in the house are 25m

(82 ft.) or closer to the stage, minimizing the distance between the audience and the performers. The space has been designed to give an impression of height and airiness despite the proximity of the seating to the stage. The theater has a separate entrance from the casino, so that audiences of all ages can enjoy performances. Theater and dinner packages available. To find out what shows are coming up, or to book a package or buy tickets, call the Casino du Lac-Leamy at ✆ 800/665-2274 or 819/772-2100. Tickets can also be purchased through **Admission Network** ✆ 800/361-4595 or www.admission.com.

Hilton Lac Leamy The magnificent Hilton Lac Leamy opened in October 2001. Bordering Lac Leamy and connected to the Casino du Lac-Leamy, this luxury hotel is equipped with first-class facilities and amenities. Call the hotel for information or reservations at ✆ 866/488-7888 or 819/790-6444, or visit online at www.lacleamy.hilton.com. See full listing details in chapter 4, "Accommodations," page 69. 1 boulevard du Casino, Hull. ✆ 800/665-2274 or 819/772-2100. www.casinos-quebec.com. Daily 11am–3am. Free admission. Free parking. Admittance restricted to persons ages 18 and over.

Rideau Carleton Racetrack Slots Less than a 10-minute drive south of the airport, this gaming complex features more than 1,000 slot machines and live harness racing. There's live entertainment and a buffet nightly. Take the Airport Parkway to Lester Rd., travel east to Albion Rd., turn south. You'll see Rideau Carleton Racetrack Slots on your left, between Leitrim Rd. and Mitch Owens Rd. 4837 Albion Rd. Ottawa. ✆ 877/870-7586 or 613/822-8668. Daily 11am–3am. Free admission. Free parking. Admittance restricted to persons ages 19 and over.

⟨Tips⟩ Gambling Should Be Fun, Not Obsessive

Many people enjoy playing games of chance for entertainment. But for a minority of people, gambling becomes a real problem and they find themselves unable to control the amount of money they spend. Information on dealing with a gambling problem can be obtained by calling ✆ **800/461-0140** in Quebec or ✆ **888/230-3505** in Ontario.

9

Shopping

With a regional population topping 1.1 million, shopping facilities in Canada's National Capital Region are excellent. Whether you prefer dazzling, multi-story, glass-and-steel malls, city streets lined with funky boutiques and cafes, or big-box discount stores, it's all here. Put on comfortable shoes, rev up your plastic, and get ready to shop 'til you drop.

HOURS Most stores in the Ottawa area are open Monday through Saturday from 9:30 or 10am to 6pm, and many have extended hours one or more evenings a week. Sunday opening hours are generally from noon to 5pm, although some malls open at 10am or 11am and some independent stores are closed. You should call ahead if you have a specific destination in mind.

TAXES Sales taxes add a chunk to your bill. The provincial retail sales tax in Ontario is 8% for most items—two exceptions are basic groceries and children's clothing, which are exempt. The federal Goods and Services Tax (GST) is 7%. In general, nonresidents may apply for a tax refund (see "Fast Facts" in chapter 3, "Getting to Know Ottawa").

1 The Shopping Scene

GREAT SHOPPING AREAS

BANK STREET PROMENADE

You'll find 15 blocks of stores and services in this area, beginning at Wellington Street in the heart of downtown and stretching south to Gladstone Avenue. About 500 businesses operate on this stretch of Bank Street, ranging from small, locally owned retailers, bargain stores, and souvenir shops to restaurants, bars, and cafes. Some of the shops are rather colorful. As the name suggests, the major banks established their first local offices on this street—in fact, the district is one of the city's oldest shopping areas.

BYWARD MARKET ★★

More than 100 boutiques jostle for position with restaurants, pubs, services, and food retailers in the warren of side streets that make up the vibrant ByWard Market area, bordered by Sussex Drive, St. Patrick Street, King Edward Avenue, and Rideau Street. Head for this district to be entertained, excited, and delighted by what's on offer in the diverse collection of shops. The ByWard Market building, located on the original site where farmers and loggers met to carry out their business in the 1800s, was restored in 1998 and now houses gourmet food shops and the wares of local and regional artisans. Excellent quality local fruit, vegetables, flowers, and other farm products are available at stalls surrounding the market building between April and October. Cheese shops, butchers, bakeries, and other food retailers complete the mix.

DOWNTOWN RIDEAU

The stores and restaurants continue as you stroll from the ByWard Market toward the Rideau Centre, the major downtown shopping mall, so you won't notice that you've stepped into the shopping area known as Downtown Rideau. Bordered by the Rideau Canal, King Edward Avenue, George Street, and the Mackenzie King Bridge, this 23-block section of the city is promoted as the city's Arts and Theater District—Arts Court, the National Arts Centre, and the Canadian Museum of Contemporary Photography are in the vicinity, in addition to many national chain retailers and unique independent stores.

THE GLEBE ⊛⊛

Farther south on Bank Street, between the Queensway and the Rideau Canal, is a stretch of trendy, higher-end stores, services, and eateries serving the upscale middle-class neighborhood known as the Glebe. It's well worth spending a morning or afternoon strolling up one side of the street and down the other. If you begin at the north end, take a break near the canal before making your return journey. Brown's Inlet and Park are tucked a couple of blocks west of Bank Street, north of Queen Elizabeth Drive. If you start at the canal end, take a break in Central Park, which straddles Bank Street in the vicinity of Powell Avenue and Clemow Avenue. For winter strolling, take refuge in the atrium at Fifth Avenue Court, about midway down this section of Bank Street.

SPARKS STREET MALL

Canada's oldest permanent pedestrian shopping street, Sparks Street Mall runs between Elgin and Lyon streets, 1 block south of Parliament Hill. Although it's busy during the working day because of the many office blocks that surround it, Sparks Street can seem deserted on evenings and weekends. In summer, restaurants set up patio tables and chairs and there's an annual Busker Festival (see chapter 8, "Ottawa After Dark.")

WELLINGTON STREET WEST ⊛

Not to be confused with Wellington Street in the downtown core, which runs in front of the Parliament Buildings, Wellington Street West is actually a continuation of Somerset Street West in the stretch between Parkdale Avenue and Island Park Drive, where it then changes name to Richmond Road. There's an interesting mix here, with fine-dining restaurants, neighborhood cafes, interior decorating retailers, and antique shops squeezed in beside the usual main street businesses.

WESTBORO VILLAGE

This traditional city neighborhood west of downtown has enjoyed a revitalization since the late 1990s. The addition of Richmond Road Mountain Equipment Co-op spurred retail growth in the west end of Westboro's commercial ribbon, and there is hope that the area will eventually link with Wellington Street West to form a shopping district much like the ByWard Market and the Glebe.

WHERE TO BROWSE THE BIG BOX STORES   Strategically placed clusters of big-box retailers have moved into the Ottawa area, as in other Canadian cities. Especially popular with consumers hunting for big-ticket items like electronics, furniture, and appliances, big-boxes attract shoppers with their promise of lower prices and wide selection. Multi-screen movie theaters and popular chain restaurants are often located within the complex. The Centrum in Kanata (take the Terry Fox exit from the Queensway) and South Keys (Bank Street north of Hunt Club Road) are two of the largest big-box sites. Bells Corners and Merivale Road in Nepean and Ogilvie Road in Gloucester are also worth a look.

MAJOR MALLS

Bayshore Shopping Centre   In Ottawa's west end, close to the Queensway, Bayshore Shopping Centre has three floors of shops and services, with three anchor stores—The Bay, Zellers, and the most recent addition, Les Ailes de la Mode, an upscale department store based in Quebec. The unisex clothing store Old Navy also arrived in 2001. Women's wear is well represented here and there are a number of better quality shoe stores. The customer service center, on the first level near the Gap, offers car unlocking, battery boosting, and other services in addition to stroller, wheelchair, and walker rental. 100 Bayshore Dr. ✆ 613/829-7491. Mon–Sat 9am–9pm; Sun 10am–6pm. Free parking.

Carlingwood Shopping Centre   Carlingwood offers one-floor shopping, which is a boon if you're a young parent or a shopper with physical disabilities. Anchored by Sears and Loblaws, this mall has a number of special services for families, plus coat and parcel check, free stroller and wheelchair rental, and a lounge area where you can take a break. There's a good range of shoe stores here and almost two dozen women's wear stores. One of the novelties here is a giant chess set—play a game or just watch, it's up to you. 2121 Carling Ave. ✆ 613/725-1546. Mon–Fri 9:30am–9pm; Sat 9:30am–6pm; Sun 10am–5pm. Free parking.

Place d'Orléans   Follow Highway 174 east to the suburb of Orleans and you'll find this large mall just on the edge of the highway. Anchored by The Bay, The Bay Home Store, and Wal-Mart, Place d'Orléans offers two levels of shops and services. With a large family market, Place d'Orléans provides excellent facilities for parents and children. Place Bébé has changing tables and private breastfeeding rooms. On the second floor, there's an indoor playground and play-care center run by the YMCA/YWCA. The guest services center is located right in the middle of the first floor beside the elevator. Stroller and wheelchair rental are free. In 2001, the mall welcomed the addition of American Eagle Outfitters, Campus Crew, and Mix Mix Leather. There's also about a dozen home furnishings and accessories stores, including Artworks, Beddington's, English Butler, McIntosh & Watts, and The Home Company. 110 Place d'Orléans Dr. ✆ 613/824-9050. Mon–Sat 9:30am–9pm; Sun 11am–5pm. Free parking.

Rideau Centre   In the heart of downtown, with direct access from the Ottawa Congress Centre and the Westin Hotel, the Rideau Centre has more than 180 stores, plus services, restaurants, and cinemas. You'll find a good selection of jewelers, leather goods stores, and better quality casual clothing. Try Marchelino for gourmet made-to-order fast food. Free stroller and wheelchair rental and a nursing room are available. 50 Rideau St. ✆ 613/236-6565. Mon–Fri 9:30am–9pm; Sat 9:30am–6pm; Sun 11am–5pm.

St. Laurent Shopping Centre   Situated at the junction of the Queensway and St. Laurent Boulevard, this mall has an entertainment wing with a climbing wall and high-tech arcade zone. The Cyberdome has motion simulators, virtual reality games, air hockey, a batting cage, and laser tag. Guest services are located in the entertainment wing and include free stroller and wheelchair rental, parcel check, and car boosts. Anchor stores are The Bay, Sears, Sportchek, and Toys "Я" Us. 1200 St. Laurent Blvd. ✆ 613/745-6858. Mon–Sat 9:30am–9pm; Sun 11 am–5pm. Free parking.

OTHERS In the west end, bordered by the Queensway, Carling Avenue, and Merivale Road, **Westgate Shopping Centre** focuses on independent merchants rather than mall chains and also has a cinema complex. Downtown, several smaller, upscale indoor malls serve office workers and tourists alike. **L'Esplanade Laurier,** at the corner of Bank Street and Laurier Avenue, features women's fashions, gift shops, banking, and postal services. At the corner of Sparks and Bank streets, **240 Sparks Shopping Centre** has a large food court and is anchored by Holt Renfrew, which stocks designer label men's and women's clothing plus Ottawa's only Tiffany boutique. **World Exchange Plaza,** at the corner of Metcalfe and Albert streets, combines movie theaters, boutiques, and a cafe.

2 Shopping A to Z

ANTIQUES

The Antique Shoppe This Glebe antique dealer specializes in 18th- and 19th-century furniture from Canada, England, and France. 750 Bank St. ✆ 613/232-0840.

Ottawa Antique Market Just south of the Glebe, more than 40 antique dealers display their wares in this indoor market. 1179A Bank St. ✆ 613/730-6000.

Yardley's Antiques On dry days, you'll see the pavement in front of this shop crammed with articles for sale. There's something for everyone here. Antiques rub shoulders with country pine furniture, old light fixtures, and pop memorabilia. 1240 Bank St. ✆ 613/739-9580.

BOOKS

Basilisk Dreams Books Specializing in classic and contemporary science fiction, horror, and fantasy, this store is a must for fans of these genres. Book signings and monthly meetings held. 857 B Bank St. ✆ 613/230-2474.

Benjamin Books Primarily general fiction and nonfiction are stocked here. Rideau Centre. ✆ 613/241-0617.

Books on Beechwood This independent store carries general fiction and nonfiction. Emphasis is on literary fiction rather than pulp. Also a large children's and young adult section, a number of British and military history books, and a small but select mystery section. 35 Beechwood Ave. ✆ 613/742-5030.

Chapters Dominating everything from big-box skylines to newspaper headlines, Chapters has become a familiar name with Canadian shoppers over the past few years. There are five locations to choose from in the Ottawa area, offering an extensive selection of books and magazines. Larger stores carry CDs and a growing selection of giftware. 47 Rideau St. ✆ 613/241-0073; 2735 Iris St. ✆ 613/596-3003; 2210 Bank St. ✆ 613/521-9199; 2401 City Park Dr. ✆ 613/744-5175; 400 Earl Grey Dr. ✆ 613/271-7553.

Coles This well-established bookstore chain carries a variety of mainstream titles and can be found in most malls in the city. 2269 Riverside Dr. ✆ 613/731-2444; Place d'Orléans ✆ 613/837-2312; and other locations.

Collected Works This independent store stocks general fiction and nonfiction, with an emphasis on literary fiction and children's books. It offers a comfortable browsing atmosphere. 1242 Wellington St. ✆ 613/722-1265.

Leishman Books Ltd. This independent store carries general fiction and nonfiction and French-as-a-second-language books. There's a large children's section at the back of the store. Westgate Shopping Centre. © 613/722-8313.

Librairie du Soleil Come here for the most extensive selection of French-language books in Ottawa. French/English dictionaries are available. 321 Dalhousie St. © 613/241-6999.

Nicholas Hoare *(Finds)* Specializing in British authors and publishers, this shop also offers a comprehensive children's section and a good selection of Canadian fiction. The atmosphere is restful and the background music soothing. Floor-to-ceiling bookshelves line the walls and elegant library ladders glide on rails to allow access to the top shelves. Enjoy the selection of literature, popular fiction, art books, hardcover coffee table books, travel books, and cookbooks. 419 Sussex Dr. © 613/562-2665.

Perfect Books An independent bookseller carrying general fiction and nonfiction, Perfect Books has a strong literary fiction section, plus a good chunk of politics and current events. Higher-end cookbooks are also stocked. 258A Elgin St. © 613/231-6468.

Place Bell Books Specializing in travel books and maps, this bookstore has a hefty selection of titles on vacation destinations around the world. Local guide books and books featuring scenic photography of the Ottawa region are also on hand, as are general interest titles. In the Place Bell mall, entrance on Metcalfe St. 175 Metcalfe St. © 613/233-3821.

Prime Crime Books As you just may have deduced, this bookstore specializes in crime and mystery fiction. Frequented by local authors and mystery fans. 891 Bank St. © 613/238-2583.

Smithbooks A large chain of bookstores primarily situated in malls, Smithbooks carries mainstream book titles in a variety of categories, including children's books for all ages. You can find Smithbooks at the following shopping centers: Bayshore, 240 Sparks, Carlingwood, Gloucester, Herongate, Merivale, Place d'Orléans, Rideau Centre, and St. Laurent.

CANADIAN FINE ARTS

The Carlen Gallery Work by almost 200 Canadian artisans is featured at this Bank St. showroom. 1171 Bank St. © 613/730-5555.

Galerie d'Art Vincent This gallery in the Château Laurier specializes in 20th-century Canadian paintings and original Inuit carvings and prints. 1 Rideau St. (inside Château Laurier Hotel). © 613/241-1144.

Inuit Artists' Shop This nonprofit enterprise offers a wide range of Inuit arts and crafts, including carvings, prints, dolls, and jewelry. Worldwide shipping service. 16 Clarence St. © 613/241-9444; 2081 Merivale Rd. © 613/224-8189.

Northern Country Arts The work of almost two dozen Canadian Native and Inuit artists are featured in this ByWard Market area gallery. 21 Clarence St. © 613/789-9591.

The Snow Goose Limited This Canadian arts and crafts shop specializes in Inuit and Native works in every price range. You'll find clothing, sculptures, prints, masks, totems, and jewelry. 83 Sparks St. © 613/232-2213.

CD'S, MUSIC

Larger shopping malls have at least one store specializing in music CDs. The two big chain stores in the Ottawa area are HMV and Music World. There are a number of stores that buy, sell, and trade music CDs. Some also deal in cassette tapes and vinyl records. Try **CD Exchange,** 142 Rideau St. ℂ **613/241-9864; The Turning Point,** 411 Cooper St. ℂ **613/230-4586;** or **Spinables,** 193 Rideau St. ℂ **613/241-1011.**

HMV Canada   Located at the corner of Bank and Sparks streets and in a number of malls, including Bayshore Shopping Centre, Merivale Place, Place d'Orléans, Rideau Centre, and St. Laurent Shopping Centre.

Music World   Located at Billings Bridge Plaza, Merivale Mall (different from Merivale Place), Rideau Centre, and St. Laurent Shopping Centre.

CHOCOLATES & SWEETS

Godiva Chocolatier Inc.   Go ahead, indulge in top-quality chocolate confections. This shop is highly recommended if you want to treat a loved one or yourself. Rideau Centre. ℂ **613/234-4470.**

Laura Secord   This chocolatier has been a Canadian favorite for more than 85 years. The chocolates and truffles are quite delicious. Try the white chocolate almond bark and the butterscotch lollipops. 85 Bank St. ℂ **613/232-6830;** Billings Bridge Plaza ℂ **613/737-5695;** Place d'Orléans Shopping Centre ℂ **613/837-7546;** Rideau Centre ℂ **613/230-2576;** St. Laurent Shopping Centre ℂ **613/741-5040.**

Rocky Mountain Chocolate Factory   This British Columbia–based company has lots of goodies—chocolate (of course!), cookies, fudge, candy apples, and other sweet treats. Located inside the ByWard Market building at the south end. 55 ByWard Market. ℂ **613/241-1091.**

Sugar Mountain *Finds*   Kids love this place. Adults are also known to be frequent visitors. Walls are lined with clear plastic bins at the right height for scooping the most outrageous colors and flavors of sugar-loaded confections into loot bags. Islands of boxed and wrapped candy and chocolates fill the two-level store. Looking for retro candy? Thrills gum (why *does* it taste like soap?), black licorice pipes, sherbet fountains, pink popcorn, and Curly Wurlys have all been spotted here. The selection changes frequently and there's often a good variety of British sweets. Get ready for a major sugar rush. 286 Elgin St. ℂ **613/230-8886.**

CHRISTMAS STORES

Christmas & Candles   This pretty gift store is worth a peek. Christmas decorations are nicely displayed on artificial trees. In addition to Christmas decorations for the home, you'll find a wide selection of candles and candleholders. Seasonal and holiday decorations for other festivals throughout the year are stocked at appropriate times. 481 Sussex Dr. ℂ **613/241-5476.**

Christmas in the Capital Inc.   High-quality Christmas ornaments and beautifully decorated trees fill the store. Collectibles such as Department 56 and Snowbabies also in stock. Decorations for other seasonal celebrations available. 231 Elgin St. ℂ **613/231-4646.**

COMPUTERS, CAMERAS & ELECTRONICS

Compusmart   Shop for major brand-names of computer hardware and software. Unit 18, 1547 Merivale Rd. ℂ **613/727-0099.**

The Focus Centre   Check out the new, used, and rental photographic equipment and supplies. There's also a large selection of digital cameras and accessories and a develop-and-print service. 254 Bank St. ✆ 613/232-5368.

Ginn Photographic Co.   This store sells and rents new and used photographic equipment and supplies, plus darkroom equipment and supplies. They also provide digital equipment sales and service and imaging services. 433 Bank St. ✆ 613/567-4686.

Radio Shack   Offering the latest in home electronics, computers, phones, and lots of neat accessories, Radio Shack has almost a dozen locations in the city, so check out the Yellow Pages. 286 Bank St. ✆ 613/238-6889; Rideau Centre, 1st floor ✆ 613/563-1156 and 3rd floor ✆ 613/241-2981.

DEPARTMENT STORES

Les Ailes de la Mode   An upscale department store based in Quebec, this is the first store opened outside the home province. One of Bayshore Shopping Centre's anchors, Les Ailes de la Mode features designer-label fashions for men, women, and children. Lines include Hugo Boss, Mexx, and Nautica. The store also carries home accessories, cosmetics, and lingerie. A beauty institute and hair salon complete the services. Bayshore Shopping Centre ✆ 613/721-4537.

The Bay   Established as a fur-trading post known as The Hudson's Bay Company in the Canadian north more than 300 years ago, The Bay carries standard department store collections of fashions and housewares. Sales are frequent and merchandise is good quality. The Bay occupies an anchor spot at four large Ottawa area malls—Bayshore Shopping Centre, Place d'Orléans Shopping Centre, Rideau Centre, and St. Laurent Shopping Centre.

Eatons   Rising from the ashes of the collapsed Eaton empire, Eatons in Ottawa is one of seven stores rescued by Sears Canada Inc. Targeting urban consumers, Eatons offers designer-label fashions and items for the home that appeal to the urban lifestyle. Rideau Centre. ✆ 613/560-5311.

Sears Canada Inc.   Offering a comprehensive range of consumer goods, Sears anchors Carlingwood Shopping Centre and St. Laurent Shopping Centre.

DRUGSTORES (24 HOURS)

Shopper's Drug Mart   Shopper's Drug Mart has a dispensary for prescription medicines and an extensive front shop with toiletries, books and magazines, groceries, greeting cards, gifts, vitamins, and over-the-counter medicines. You'll see their distinctive signs—red letters on a white background—all over the city, but only one location is open 24 hours. 1460 Merivale Rd. at Baseline Rd. ✆ 613/224-7270.

FASHION, CHILDREN'S

Gap Kids   Kids from grade 1 to high school and beyond want to be seen in Gap sweaters. Gap kid clothes are practical, the styles are fun, the colors are usually great, and they wash and wear well. Bayshore Shopping Centre ✆ 613/828-8131; Rideau Centre ✆ 613/569-4110; St. Laurent Shopping Centre ✆ 613/746-8787.

Glebe Side Kids   If you don't want to dress your kids in the same gear as your friends and neighbors, step into Glebe Side Kids for designer clothing in eye-catching colors and styles. You'll find casual and dressy clothing for boys and girls in sizes from infants to teens. Lines include Bleu and Deux Par Deux from Quebec and imports from Germany and France. High quality and prices to match. 793 Bank St. ✆ 613/235-6552.

Gymboree   This store provides colorful, sturdy clothing and helpful staff, plus a play area at the back of the store. Prices can be on the high side, but the store has frequent sales. Bayshore Shopping Centre ℂ 613/829-7236; Rideau Centre ℂ 613/565-3323; St. Laurent Shopping Centre ℂ 613/842-4716.

Jacob Jr.   This fashion-forward store sells clothing in scaled-down versions of adult styles, including separates and underwear for girls who just want to have fun. Bayshore Shopping Centre ℂ 613/828-4204; St. Laurent Shopping Centre ℂ 613/746-7095.

Laura Ashley Shops Ltd. *(Value)*   This excellent-quality British clothing shop stocks dresses and separates for little ladies ages 2 to 9, and the clothing for their mums is just as nice. 136 Bank St. ℂ 613/238-4882.

Northern Getaway   Younger school kids all seem to have something from Northern Getaway in their wardrobes. This is strongly themed clothing for boys (sports, wild animals; strong, dark colors) and girls (flowers, puppies; lilacs and pinks). Kids like the clothes and the prices are middle-of-the-road. Sales come up often. Colors are coordinated so that separates for each season mix and match throughout the store. Bayshore Shopping Centre ℂ 613/829-0385; Carlingwood Shopping Centre ℂ 613/722-6107; Rideau Centre ℂ 613/569-2225; Place d'Orléans ℂ 613/834-2377; St. Laurent Shopping Centre ℂ 613/746-6150.

Please Mum   Browse the bright, coordinated separates for active kids. Place d'Orléans Shopping Centre ℂ 613/830-1366; St. Laurent Shopping Centre. ℂ 613/820-5145.

Roots Canada Ltd.   This casual clothing, in infant to adult sizes, washes and wears well. Only selected stores carry kids' merchandise. In Ottawa, that's at Place d'Orléans. There's also a factory outlet location in the south end of the city; prices are slashed but the selection varies. Place d'Orléans ℂ 613/841-7164; factory outlet 2210 Bank St. ℂ 613/736-9503.

R.W. Kids *(Value)*   Ottawa's OshKosh store has perhaps Canada's best selection of OshKosh clothing. Most parents are familiar with OshKosh quality—kids just can't seem to wear it out and outfits still look good on the second or third child. The store is well laid out, with cascading hangers lining the walls so that styles and sizes are easy to find, and it's easy to navigate with a stroller. There's a play-room at the back and a rack of gently used OshKosh consignment clothing on display. An annual membership for a small fee entitles you to a 15% discount on all regular-price items. Hampton Park Plaza, Carling Ave. and Kirkwood Ave. ℂ 613/724-4576.

Tickled Pink *(Finds)*   Opened in spring 2001, this effervescent collection features lines from three Ottawa designers. Bright, intense colors, practical styling, and fun patterns. Yummy Mummy maternity wear from Toronto, locally made sheepskin hats, gloves, and slippers, and dress-up clothes (fairies, ballerinas, princesses). Worth a visit. 55 ByWard Market. ℂ 613/562-8350.

West End Kids *(Finds)*   If you're tired of mall wear, head here for top-quality upscale clothing for infants to teens. Labels include Mexx, Columbia, Tommy Hilfiger, Deux Par Deux, and Fresh Produce. 373 Richmond Rd. ℂ 613/722-8947.

FASHION, MENS & WOMENS

Buckland's Fine Clothing   Clothing and accessories for well-heeled clients. Top brand-names and designer labels include Anne Klein, Tommy Hilfiger, Arnold Brant, and Cambridge Suits. 722 Bank St. ℂ 613/238-2020.

Club Monaco   Favoring young styling with simple lines and neutral tones, mixed with black and white separates, Club Monaco attracts urban sophisticates. Bayshore Shopping Centre ℰ **613/596-4030**; St. Laurent Shopping Centre ℰ **613/ 745-0583**; Rideau Centre ℰ **613/230-0245**.

Guess   Brand-name casual wear for young men and women. Rideau Centre ℰ **613/569-4580**.

Holt Renfrew   Men's and women's fashions and accessories in the upper price range. Many designer labels. 240 Sparks St. ℰ **613/238-6223**.

Mexx   Men's and women's casual clothing and separates for work or play. Young but classy. Rideau Centre ℰ **613/569-6399**.

Roots Canada Ltd.   Although Roots has been a well-known Canadian label for many years, their sponsorship of the Nagano Winter Olympics catapulted their coats, sweaters, and caps into the world spotlight. Demand has grown for their clothing line since that time, particularly in the U.S. This casual clothing, in infant to adult sizes, washes and wears well. Only selected stores carry kids' merchandise. In Ottawa, that's at Place d'Orléans. There's also a factory outlet location in the south end of the city; prices are slashed but the selection varies. Roots has expanded their product line to include fragrances, jewelry, leather goods, and shoes. 787 Bank St. ℰ **613/232-3790**; Bayshore Shopping Centre ℰ **613/ 820-4527**, Place d'Orléans ℰ **613/841-7164**; Rideau Centre ℰ **613/236-7760**; factory outlet 2210 Bank St. ℰ **613/736-9503**.

FASHION, MEN'S

Harry Rosen   Pay a visit to this upper-end men's clothiers for top-quality service and the finest in menswear designers. Choose from Hugo Boss, Brioni, Versace, and others. Rideau Centre ℰ **613/230-7232**.

Moores   Mid–price range clothing for the average man on the street— although their sizes run from extra short to extra tall and oversize. Some of their merchandise is Canadian made, and includes suits, sport coats, and dress pants, as well as a good selection of casual wear. In addition to the downtown store at Bank St., there's one in the west end and one in the east. 162 Bank St. ℰ **613/235-2121**.

Morgante Menswear   Fine clothing from formal wear rental to casual and sportwear, with lines by Canali, Jeans Couture, Versace, and Hugo Boss. Professional tailoring available, and alterations while you wait. 141 Sparks St. ℰ **613/234-2232**.

FASHION, WOMEN'S

Eclection   Exclusively stocking Canadian designers hailing from Toronto through Quebec, Eclection has fascinating and unusual women's separates and accessories. Jewelry, hats, and scarves available. Check out their line of medieval street clothing. 55 ByWard Market. ℰ **613/789-7288**.

Richard Robinson   This exciting Ottawa-based fashion designer has a ready-to-wear collection available. 447 Sussex Dr. ℰ **613/241-5233**.

Sable Classics   Women's fashions and accessories, with an emphasis on dresses and sportswear. One of the featured designers is Canadian Linda Lundstrom. 206 Sparks St. ℰ **613/233-8384**.

Shepherd's   Canadian, American, and European designers are featured at this local boutique. Lines by Helen Kaminski and Linda Lundstrom. Good selection of accessories, including jewelry, handbags, belts, and purses. Bayshore Shopping Centre ✆ 613/596-0070; Rideau Centre ✆ 613/563-7666.

FLY FISHING

Brightwater Fly Fishing   Drop by Brightwater to pick up everything a fisherman could ever want. Rentals and fly-tying instruction are available. Fishing is permitted in designated areas of Gatineau Park, but don't forget to purchase a license (available in store) before casting your line. 336 Cumberland St. ✆ 613/241-6798.

FOOD

Lovers of fine wines and good food can check out the recommendations in "Gourmet to Go" in chapter 5, "Dining."

FURS

Dworkin Furs   Serving Ottawa for more than a century, this large boutique carries Canadian-made and imported furs, sheepskins, and leathers. Designer names include Nina Ricci, Oscar de la Renta, Valentino, and D'Arcy Moses. Ask about special discounts and terms for tourists. U.S. visitors may make duty and tax-free purchases. Worldwide shipping available. 256 Rideau St. ✆ 613/241-4213.

Pat Flesher Furs   This well-established furrier has a fine selection of Canadian-made furs and designer coats. Mink, beaver, fox, raccoon, sable, and other furs available. Services include custom design, made-to-measure, repairs, and remodeling. Duty and tax-free purchases for U.S. visitors. 437 Cooper St. ✆ 613/237-1700.

GIFT SHOPS

Abington's Animals   This store features many lines of collectibles, especially figurines. For kids, there are Beanie Babies, Beanie Kids, and Harry Potter merchandise. St. Laurent Shopping Centre. ✆ 613/744-7094.

Canada's Four Corners   Canadian fine crafts and quality Canadian souvenirs share space with a gallery of framed or matted prints. 93 Sparks St. ✆ 613/233-2322.

Giraffe the African Store   Authentic art from Africa. Handmade masks, statues, fabric wall hangings, jewelry, ebony, soapstone, musical instruments, and pottery. 19 Clarence St. ✆ 613/562-0284.

Hard Rock Café   This retail outlet in the restaurant sells souvenir Hard Rock Cafe merchandise featuring their logo, including T-shirts, caps, jackets, and pins. 73 York St. ✆ 613/241-2442.

O'Shea's Market Ireland   Family owned and operated for more than 25 years, O'Shea's is packed with goods imported from the Emerald Isle. Popular items include Celtic jewelry and woolen goods—especially sweaters, cardigans, blankets, and throws. Hundreds of family crests and coats-of-arms on hand. 91 Sparks St. ✆ 613/235-5141.

Oh Yes Ottawa!   This terrific Canadian-made souvenir clothing is also sold at the airport. Rideau Centre. ✆ 613/569-7520.

Ottawa Souvenirs and Gifts   Browse the selection of T-shirts, sweatshirts, mugs, plaques, spoons, and maple syrup products. Rideau Centre. ✆ 613/233-0468.

The Snow Goose Limited   This Canadian arts and crafts shop specializes in Inuit and Native works in every price range. You'll find clothing, sculptures, prints, masks, totems, and jewelry.   83 Sparks St. ℭ **613/232-2213.**

HOBBY & CRAFT STORES

Dynamic Hobbies   Model enthusiasts will love the radio-controlled model cars, airplanes, helicopters, and boats, on-site indoor and outdoor tracks, and the 45-m (150-ft.) slot car track.   21 Concourse Gate, Unit 6. ℭ **613/225-9634.**

Hobby House Ltd.   This store offers a wide variety of hobby supplies, including plastic model kits, model trains and accessories, military and aviation books, modeler's tools and supplies, rockets, kites, die-cast models, wooden ship kits, and puzzles.   80 Montreal Rd. ℭ **613/749-5245.**

Lewiscraft   Lots of materials and supplies for artistically inclined kids and grown-ups, plus knowledgeable and helpful staff.   Carlingwood Shopping Centre ℭ **613/729-8428;** Place d'Orléans ℭ **613/834-9039;** Rideau Centre. ℭ **613/230-7792.**

Lilliput *(Finds*   A delightful collection of dollhouse furniture, fixtures, and accessories is beautifully displayed. Dollhouse kits in several styles are available, with some completed models on show.   9 Murray St. ℭ **613/241-1183.**

Michael's Arts and Crafts   Following the big-box challenge of trying to carry everything under one roof, Michael's has row upon row of shelves crammed with arts and crafts supplies for the home crafter and decorator, including kid-friendly supplies and seasonal stuff.   2210-F Bank St. ℭ **613/521-3717;** 2685 Iris St. ℭ **613/726-7211.**

The Sassy Bead Co. *(Finds*   Browse the colorful jars, trays, and boxes filled with beads of every description. Make your selection, then sit at a table and create your own jewelry right in the shop. There's also a good selection of unique ready-made items. Workshops and kids' birthday parties are available. The Bank Street location carries a line of Sassy clothing for teens and women.   757 Bank St. ℭ **613/567-7886;** 11 William St. ℭ **613/562-2812.**

HOME DECOR

Belle de Provence   This store is deliciously French in its merchandise and atmosphere. Exquisite toiletries, linens, books, and items for the home. A delightful shop.   80 George St. ℭ **613/789-2552.**

Casa Luna   Featuring furniture and home accessories with a Southern flavor, Casa Luna carries Mexican-made furniture among others. Many unusual and one-of-a-kind items. Carved reproduction Spanish and French pieces and lots of wrought iron. Shop for the dining room, kitchen, bedroom, and bathroom.   1115 Bank St. ℭ **613/730-3561.**

Ikea   They advise you to wear comfortable shoes, and they mean it. This Swedish store has about 75 life-size rooms displaying their home furnishings, including kitchens, bedrooms, offices, and living rooms. Most furniture comes flat-packed and requires assembly at home, but many of Ikea's customers are in the family van category, so it's easy for them to load up their purchases. The fresh, young, urban image draws big crowds, especially on Saturdays. Free stroller rental, a baby–care room for feeding and changing, and a kids play area will make parents happy. On-site restaurant. Catalogue available.   Pinecrest Shopping Centre, 2685 Iris St. ℭ **613/829-4530.**

La Cache   Beautiful classic floral linens for dining rooms and bedrooms. 763 Bank St. ℂ **613/233-0412.**

Linen Chest   A big-box store that will make filling your bridal registry list a breeze. Aisle upon aisle of china, dinnerware, cutlery, houseware, linens, crystal, kitchenware, and gifts. After the honeymoon, go back for another visit to stock up on baby bedding, furniture, and accessories. 2685 Iris St., Pinecrest Shopping Centre. ℂ **613/721-9991.**

McIntosh & Watts Ltd.   Established in 1906, McIntosh & Watts deals in fine china, crystal, flatware, and giftware. In addition to the store on Sparks St. downtown, you'll find branches at Bayshore Shopping Centre, Place d'Orléans Shopping Centre, and St. Laurent Shopping Centre. 193 Sparks St. ℂ **613/236-9644.**

Varia   Home and kitchen accessories and gifts.   521 Sussex Dr. ℂ **613/244-1130.**

JEWELRY

Birks   Founded in 1879, Birks is a respected Canadian jewelry retailer. Carries a wide range of silver, crystal, and china as well as top-quality jewelry. Popular for engagement rings.   Bayshore Shopping Centre and Rideau Centre. ℂ **800/682-2622.**

Davidson's   Serving customers from their Glebe store since 1939, Davidson's is a full-service jewelers, offering design, repairs, appraisals, and gem prints. Member of the Canadian Jewellers Association. Stockists of Canadian Diamonds, Fabergé, Lladró, Movado, and other top brands.   790 Bank St. ℂ **613/234-4136.**

Howard   This family owned downtown business specializes in jewelry design and there's an artist on staff. Their diamond ring collection features platinum, 18K, and 14K gold settings. Wristwatches by Tag Heuer, Gucci, Da Vinci, and Rolex. Repairs and appraisals available.   200 Sparks St. ℂ **613/238-3300.**

La Maison d'Or   In the Place d'Orléans Shopping Centre, this jeweler specializes in diamonds from around the world, including Canadian diamonds. Rings can be custom designed, then set in their own studio. They also buy and sell estate and antique jewelry.   Place d'Orléans Shopping Centre. ℂ **613/837-1001.**

KITCHENWARE

Ottawa is blessed with fine kitchenware stores, and culinary enthusiasts will love the following five retailers. They're all at the top of their class; you'll just have to visit them all.

C.A. Paradis   Located near a gaggle of antique stores on Bank St. south of the Glebe, C.A. Paradis has some very classy merchandise. If a chef craves it, this place probably has it. Check out their cellaring equipment, tasting supplies, and Reidel stemware too.   1314 Bank St. ℂ **613/731-2866.**

Domus   It's a real dilemma—do you eat first in the delectable Domus restaurant (see chapter 5, "Dining") and shop afterwards in the kitchen store, or vice versa? Both are outstanding. Enjoy.   85 Murray St. ℂ **613/241-6410.**

Glebe Emporium   It's extremely tough to browse and not buy in this shop. You're bound to see something you just can't resist owning for yourself or buying as a gift for someone else. Kitchen gadgets, everyday dinnerware, table linens, gifts, and more.   724 Bank St. ℂ **613/233-3474.**

J. D. Adam Kitchen Co.   Walk slowly around this compact Glebe shop so that you don't miss anything. Space is at a premium here but they make good use of every inch. Great merchandise and helpful staff.   795 Bank St. ℂ **613/235-8714.**

Ma Cuisine   Spacious and gracious, Ma Cuisine has chic dinnerware, a good selection of glassware, pans, gadgets, cookbooks, linens, and lots more. Staff are courteous and welcoming.   269 Dalhousie St. ✆ **613/789-9225.**

LEATHER

Danier Leather   Leather clothing for men and women.   Bayshore Shopping Centre. ✆ **613/828-4200.**

Mix Mix Leather   Leather and suede clothing for men and women. Washable suede and leather available.   Carlingwood Shopping Centre ✆ **613/798-1999;** St. Laurent Shopping Centre ✆ **613/748-9876.**

LINGERIE

Femistique   In the shopping center at the corner of Sparks St. and Bank St., this upscale boutique carries high-fashion lingerie and a selection of fragrances, jewelry, and other feminine gifts.   240 Sparks St. ✆ **613/235-8306.**

La Senza   Lots of pretty undergarments, sleepwear, and gifts.   Carlingwood Shopping Centre ✆ **613/729-4481;** St. Laurent Shopping Centre ✆ **613/748-7611.**

La Vie en Rose   Feminine lingerie and a good selection of sleepwear.   Bayshore Shopping Centre ✆ **613/828-8383;** Rideau Centre ✆ **613/563-2959.**

MAGAZINES/NEWSPAPERS

For a great variety of international publications, visit **Mags & Fags** at 254 Elgin St. ✆ **613/233-9651** or **Planet News** at 143 Sparks St. ✆ **613/232-5500.**

MAPS/TRAVEL BOOK STORES

Place Bell Book Store   Specializing in city, country, and worldwide maps, including Michelin, Rand McNally, British Ordinance Survey, and Canadian Topographical, this shop also offers a wide selection of travel guides and literature.   175 Metcalfe St. ✆ **613/233-3821.**

A World of Maps   Situated where else but at the geographical center of Ottawa, A World of Maps is both a retailer and a mail-order company. They're a regional distributor for all Canadian government maps and charts produced by the Canada Map Office. Topographical, aeronautical, nautical, international, and world maps, atlases, globes, travel books, and other map-related items are available here.   1235 Wellington St. W. ✆ **800/214-8524** or **613/724-6776.**

MARKETS

ByWard Farmer's Market *(Value*   The quality of the produce is outstanding at this thriving outdoor farmer's market, with about 200 vendors. In spring and early summer, flower stalls abound. Lots of family-oriented events are scheduled on weekends throughout the year.   55 ByWard Market Square. May–Oct daily 6am–6pm, Nov–Apr daily 9:30am–5:30pm.

Ottawa Organic Farmer's Market   For fresh market produce grown without pesticides or other chemicals, head on down on a Saturday. The number of vendors varies from 8 to 17.   Kingsway United Church, 630 Island Park Dr. Year-round Sat 10am–2pm.

Parkdale Farmer's Market   This small open-air farmer's market, with 20 vendors on average, offers fresh, high-quality produce.   Parkdale Ave. at Wellington St. Apr–Dec 24 daily 7am–6pm.

MUSICAL INSTRUMENTS

Ottawa Folklore Centre   They repair, buy, sell, consign, trade, rent, and appraise just about any instrument you can think of—from guitars to amps, banjos, fiddles, Celtic harps, mandolins, recorders, folk flutes, hand drums, autoharps, accordions, and dulcimers. 1111 Bank St. ✆ **613/730-2887.**

Song Bird Music   Dealing in new, used, and rental instruments, Song Bird Music has guitars, woodwinds, percussion, brass, keyboards, amps, and more. They outgrew their original store and had to open a second location across the street. 388 Gladstone Ave. ✆ **613/594-5323.**

OUTDOOR STORES

Bushtukah Great Outdoor Gear   This store is well stocked with tents, camping gear, sleeping bags, and other assorted outdoor equipment. 203 Richmond Rd. ✆ **613/792-1170.**

The Expedition Shoppe   In the outdoor shopper's corner of Ottawa, along with Bushtukah, Mountain Equipment Co-op, and Trailhead, this store sells clothing and outdoor equipment for travel, hiking, and camping, as well as guide books and maps. 369 Richmond Rd. ✆ **613/722-0166;** 43 York St. ✆ **613/241-8397.**

Irving Rivers   If you like the great outdoors, hike over to this outdoor emporium, stuffed with rain gear, camping clothing, travel appliances, backpacks, heavy-duty footwear, and everything else for a back-to-nature vacation. 24 ByWard Market St. ✆ **613/241-1415.**

Mountain Equipment Co-op   While you're browsing the outdoor adventure stores in the area, stop in here for sound advice on good quality outdoor gear. Mountain Equipment Co-op has been in operation since 1971. 366 Richmond Rd. ✆ **613/729-2700.**

The Scout Shop Camping Centre   You can't miss the huge totem pole on the front lawn. Housed in the Scouts Canada Headquarters building, the Scout Shop has lots of practical, neat, and useful camping accessories, plus books, Scout uniforms, and small toys. 1345 Baseline Rd. ✆ **613/224-0139.**

Trailhead   Another outdoor adventure and hiking store, conveniently situated close to most of the others above, and not far from the bridge to Gatineau Park. Come here for canoes, kayaks, skis, snowshoes, travel clothing, and accessories. 1960 Scott St. ✆ **613/722-4229.**

SHOES

Armstrong Shoes   Better quality footwear can be found here. 79 Sparks St. ✆ **613/236-0551;** Bayshore Shopping Centre ✆ **613/829-8282.**

Dack's   Dack's has been supplying high-quality men's footwear to customers in the Ottawa area since 1834. 240 Sparks St. ✆ **613/233-4377.**

Kiddie Kobbler   For casual and dress shoes, boots, sandals, slippers, and dance shoes for your child, visit one of four Ottawa mall locations. Carlingwood Shopping Centre ✆ **613/722-5565;** Place d'Orléans ✆ **613/834-8876;** Rideau Centre ✆ **613/560-5311;** St. Laurent Shopping Centre ✆ **613/746-6411.**

Letellier   Specializing in walking and comfort shoes, Letellier is a well-established shoe retailer in Ottawa, serving customers since 1897. A large selection of widths and sizes in both men's and women's footwear, with lines from Clarks, Rockport, Ecco, Mephisto, and more. 146 Rideau St. ✆ **613/241-6557.**

Sports 4   Brand-name footwear includes New Balance, Birkenstock, Nike, Reebok, and more from this athletic and casual footwear specialist. A large range of widths and sizes available.   149 Bank St. ℭ **613/234-6562;** also in Kanata.

SPORTS EQUIPMENT & CLOTHING

Cyco's   Specializing in rental and sales of in-line skates, ice skates, bikes, and clothing and accessories for both sports, this store also sells used sports equipment.   5 Hawthorne Ave. (beside Rideau Canal) ℭ **613/567-8180;** 780 Baseline Rd. ℭ **613/226-7277.**

En equilibre   Come here for snowboards, skateboards, wakeboards, clothing, shoes, and accessories.   1071 Bank St. ℭ **613/730-8266.**

Figure 8 Boutique Ltd.   Whether you're skating in competitions or just gliding along the canal, Figure 8 has a skate for you. They offer new, used, and rental skates, as well as expert sharpening and skate mounting and hockey-skate blade replacement.   1408 Bank St. ℭ **613/731-4007.**

Fresh Air Experience   This is the store for bicycles (mountain, hybrid, road, and children's), cross-country skis, and specialty clothing.   1291 Wellington St. W. ℭ **613/729-3002.**

Kunstadt Sports   These ski, bike, snowboard, tennis, and hockey specialists offer equipment, clothing, and service.   1583 Bank St. ℭ **613/260-0696;** 462 Hazeldean Rd. ℭ **613/831-2059.**

Ritchie's Sports-Fan Apparel Shop   Sports fans will love the wide selection of licensed souvenirs, caps, and jerseys for all the major sports—hockey, baseball, football, basketball, and soccer.   134 Sparks St. ℭ **613/232-6278.**

Running Room Canada   Come here for footwear and apparel for running, walking, swimming, and fitness.   911 Bank St. ℭ **613/233-5617;** 260 Centrum Blvd. ℭ **613/830-7539;** 160 Slater St. ℭ **613/233-5165;** 1568 Merivale Rd. ℭ **613/228-3100.**

Sensations   If you're looking for Sens gear, this is the place to go. The official merchandise outlet of the Ottawa Senators Hockey Club is located in the Corel Centre at Gate 1 and is stocked with hats, jerseys, jackets, pucks, sweaters, shirts, T-shirts, and sticks.   Corel Centre, 1000 Palladium Dr. ℭ **888/688-7367** or 613/599-0333.

Tommy & Lefebvre   One of the city's best-known sporting goods retailers, in business since 1958, Tommy & Lefebvre has an extensive selection of goods for adults and children.   464 Bank St., 2206 Carling Ave., and locations in Orleans and Gatineau. ℭ **888/888-7547.**

STATIONERY

Paper Papier   A peek inside this little store will reward you with the discovery of unusual and inspiring gift wrap, pens, greeting cards, stationery, journals, and other paper-related items.   11A William St. ℭ **613/241-1212.**

The Papery (*Finds*)   This store sells delicate, pretty, and funky things made of paper—cards, wrapping paper, ribbons, invitations, stationery, journals, albums, and pens. During the holiday season, check out their selection of elegant Christmas crackers, remarkable gift wrap, and exquisite table-top angels. 850 Bank St. ℭ **613/230-1313.**

TOYS

The Disney Store   All kinds of products, ranging from videos to dress-up costumes, baby and preschool clothing, beach towels, and stuffed Disney character toys, will thrill your little ones. You can even buy passes to Disney theme parks here. Staff love children, and the customer service is good. Rideau Centre ℭ 613/569-5500; Bayshore Shopping Centre ℭ 613/721-4155.

Go Toys   For toys that really move, drop into this toy shop on trendy Sussex Dr., opened in 2001. 517 Sussex Dr. ℭ 613/562-4116.

Ikea *(Value*   In addition to home furnishings especially for younger family members, Ikea has a great selection of European-style toys, including puppets, dollhouses, musical instruments, bean bags, and china tea sets. Of course, they have lots of toy storage, cushions, tables, and chairs, too. See "Home Decor," earlier in this chapter.

Lost Marbles *(Finds*   Grown-ups and kids alike will find this store fascinating. Where else would you find a plush moray eel, a build-your-own set of shark's jaws, a table with human legs, or 16 different kinds of dice? 315 Richmond Rd. ℭ 613/722-1469.

Mrs. Tiggywinkles   This store stocks a wide variety of educational and high-quality toys and games for infants to teens. It's great place to browse. There's a two-floor emporium in the Glebe and several mall locations. A new location on Richmond Road in Westboro Village is set to open in 2002. 809 Bank St. ℭ 613/234-3836; Bayshore Shopping Centre ℭ 613/721-0549; Place d'Orléans ℭ 613/834-8988; Rideau Centre ℭ 613/230-8081.

Playvalue Toys   This is a full-line dealer for Little Tikes, Step 2, Brio, Play-mobil, Lego, and other quality toys. 1501 Carling Ave. ℭ 613/722-0175.

Scholar's Choice Retail Store   This store carries educational and high-quality toys for infants and up, as well as elementary teachers' resources. 2635 Alta Vista Dr. ℭ 613/260-8444; Carlingwood Shopping Centre ℭ 613/729-5665.

Toys "Я" Us   This big-box retailer has a large selection of mainstream toys and other products for children. If they've seen it on TV, this is the place to get it. 1683 Merivale Rd. ℭ 613/228-8697; 1200 St. Laurent Blvd. ℭ 613-749-8697.

TRAVEL GOODS

Capital City Luggage   Luggage, garment bags, computer bags, trunks, travel accessories, and briefcases. Repairs to handles, zippers, and locks. 1337 Wellington St. W. ℭ 613/725-3313.

Ottawa Leather Goods   Travel accessories, luggage, business cases, handbags, and small leather goods. Repair shop on premises. 179 Sparks St. ℭ 613/232-4656.

VIDEOS

Two major video stores in the Ottawa area are **Blockbuster Video** and **Rogers Video,** both with more than a dozen locations. DVD and VHS movies and games are available for sale and rental. Rental requires a membership.

Bestsellers   Just as the name says, you'll find the most popular videos and DVDs here, plus a small selection of the latest paperbacks. 2121 Carling Ave. ℭ 613/728-0689.

WINE & SPIRITS

Liquor Control Board of Ontario (LCBO)   Most of the province's wine, some beer, and all spirits are purchased through these outlets. There are locations all over the city. The Wine Rack (see below) and some individual winery boutiques are also licensed to sell wine, but you can't buy alcoholic beverages in a grocery or convenience store. Beer is also available at the Beer Store, with about 20 locations in Ottawa. Opening hours vary by individual store. The **LCBO's flagship retail store** is at 275 Rideau St. ✆ **613/789-5226.** This large store has two floors of fine products from around the world, as well as a Vintages section with a wide selection of high-quality products. Wine accessories are also available, and seminars and tastings are regularly scheduled.

Wine Rack   One of the few wine stores not under the banner of the Liquor Control Board of Ontario (LCBO), Wine Rack carries a variety of Ontario wines from Niagara vineyards. There are several locations around the city in addition to the ByWard market location. 70B George St. ✆ **613/562-0347.**

10

Exploring the Region

If you've read this far into the book, you'll know that there's enough to do in Ottawa itself for more than one vacation. But take some time to venture into the region surrounding the city. You'll discover a whole new side to Canada's capital. Scenic drives, picturesque towns and villages, summer and winter sports, artisans' studios, museums and heritage buildings, and more. Leisure activities and tourist attractions in eastern Ontario and western Quebec could fill another book, but in this chapter I've highlighted some of the best daytrips to destinations around Ottawa that you can reach in an hour or so by car.

1 The Outaouais Region of Quebec

VISITOR INFORMATION

To obtain information for visitors to Quebec, visit the **Association touristique de l'Outaouais,** 103 Laurier St., Hull, PQ J8X 3V8 (*©* **800/265-7822** or 819/778-2222; fax 819/778-7758; www.western-quebec-tourism.org). The office is open mid-June to Labour Day (first Monday in September) Monday to Friday 8:30am to 8pm, Saturday to Sunday 9am to 6pm. The rest of the year, it's open Monday to Friday 8:30am to 5pm, weekends 9am to 4pm. The building is wheelchair accessible and there is free parking on the west side. The easiest way to reach the tourist office from Ottawa is to walk or drive across the Alexandra Bridge, which leads off Sussex Drive just east of the Parliament Buildings and west of the National Gallery. You'll see the office facing you as you come to the end of the bridge.

URBAN EXPERIENCES

While 2001 heralded a new beginning for the city of Ottawa as it experienced amalgamation of a dozen local municipalities, 2002 ushered in the new city of **Gatineau.** Composed of the cities of **Hull** and **Gatineau** plus the neighboring communities of **Aylmer, Buckingham,** and **Masson–Angers,** the new city has a population of 225,000.

HULL

Hull was established in the early 1800s by Philemon Wright, an American Loyalist who shrewdly exploited the area's rich natural resources, primarily the forests of red and white pine. The forestry industry brought lumber camps and wood-processing factories to the region and attracted new residents—lumbermen, rafters, farmers, tradespeople, and merchants. Today, the pulp-and-paper mills of the Outaouais region still play an important role in the economy, with the federal government and the service industry as other major employers.

Hull is renowned for its excellent French cuisine. Reservations are recommended to avoid disappointment. **Café Henry Burger** has been preparing fine cuisine in elegant surroundings for its patrons since 1922. It's located across from the Museum of Civilization, at 69 rue Laurier (© **819/777-5646**). **Café Jean Sebastian Bar** has a more casual atmosphere, serving mussels, cassoulet, and filet mignon from its location at 49 rue St-Jacques (© **819/771-2934**). For dishes featuring local, seasonal produce, visit **Le Tartuffe,** at 133 rue Notre Dame (© **819/776-6424**). Housed in an old railway station, **Laurier sur Montcalm** is a small restaurant with a delicious menu. You'll find it at 199 rue Montcalm (© **819/775-5030**). See "On the Quebec Side" in chapter 5 for reviews of **Le 1908,** 70 promenade de Portage © **819/770-1908** and **Le Pied de Cochon,** 248 rue Montcalm © **819/777-5808.**

On the shores of the Ottawa River next to the Canadian Museum of Civilization, **Jacques-Cartier Park** has beautiful pathways for strolling or cycling. The small stone house at the western end of the park was built by Philemon Wright, the founder of Hull, in the late 1830s. At the opposite end of the park, you'll find an information booth, La Maison du Vélo, where you can obtain information on recreational pathways in the Outaouais region. **Jacques-Cartier Park** offers spectacular views of the Ottawa skyline and hosts **Winterlude** activities, as well as a **fireworks display** on Canada Day. **Lake Leamy Ecological Park** is bordered by Lake Leamy, the Gatineau River, and the Ottawa River. Vehicular access is via boulevard Fournier. The park offers a supervised beach, a refreshment pavilion, washrooms, and picnic tables. The **Casino du Lac-Leamy** is on the opposite shore of **Lake Leamy.** For park information, call © **819/239-5000.**

Tips **Walk in the Steps of History**

If you want to walk in the steps of history, seek out the Indian Portage Trail at Little Chaudière Rapids in **Brébeuf Park.** To reach the park, take boulevard Alexandre-Taché, turn left onto rue Coalier, opposite the south entrance to Gatineau Park, then continue to **Brébeuf Park.** At the eastern end of the park, where the trail continues beside the river, is the old portage route that was used by First Nations peoples, fur traders, and explorers. A statue of Saint Jean de Brébeuf stands as a memorial to this 17th-century French missionary. Look for the rock steps used by the voyageurs when they transported their goods and equipment by land to circumvent the rapids.

Canadian Museum of Civilization   The striking architecture of the Canadian Museum of Civilization simply cannot be missed as you gaze across the Ottawa River toward Hull. A short walk from Ottawa across the Alexandra Bridge will take you there, but you can also take a cab or drive if the weather is inclement. To explore the museum thoroughly, you need a full day, particularly if you want to spend time in the Children's Museum and the Postal Museum, which are in the same building (there's no extra charge for these attractions), and take in an IMAX film (you *do* need separate tickets for the IMAX Theatre). For detailed information on the Museum of Civilization, see chapter 6, "What to See & Do in Ottawa."

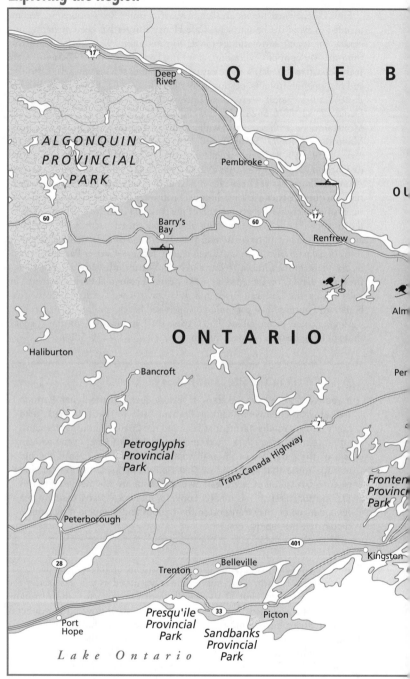

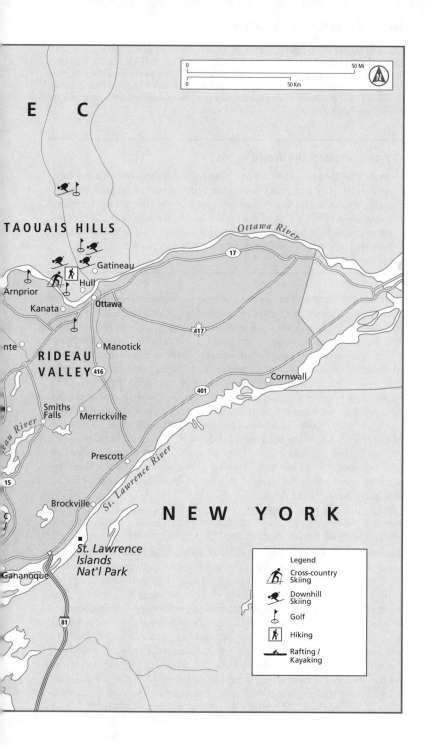

Legend
- Cross-country Skiing
- Downhill Skiing
- Golf
- Hiking
- Rafting / Kayaking

100 Laurier St., Hull, PQ. © **800/555-5621** or 819/776-7000. www.civilization.ca. Admission C$8 (US$5) adults, C$6 (US$) students, C$7 (US$4.50) seniors, C$4 (US$2.50) children 2–12, C$20 (US$12) family (max. 5 members). Sun half-price. Additional fee for IMAX theater. May 1–Thanksgiving (second Mon in Oct) daily 9am–6pm, Thurs until 9pm; July 1–Labour Day (first Mon in Sept) also open Fri until 9pm; Thanksgiving–Apr 30 Tues–Sun 9am–5pm, Thurs until 9pm. IMAX screenings do not always correspond with museum hours and extended evening hours do not apply to the Children's Museum.

(Kids) **Around the World in Play**

Inside the Canadian Museum of Civilization, there's a unique place for children to play and explore. Included with the admission price to the main exhibits, the Children's Museum is a trip around the world—kids can tour the pyramids of Egypt, listen to African drum beats, and take a ride on an Indian tour bus. The stimulating exhibits are kid-size and designed for maximum interaction. See chapter 6, "What to See & Do in Ottawa," for more details.

Ecomuseum (Ecomusée) (Kids) (Value)   Don't be fooled by the apparent size of this museum, housed in a quaint historic building. Good things come in small packages, and this museum is a fine place to spend a couple of hours. A huge sphere representing the planet Earth greets you as you wind your way down a curved pathway to the main exhibits, which trace the origins of life on Earth up to the arrival of modern humans. There are plenty of authentic fossils on display. Interactive exhibits demonstrate the formation of continents, volcanoes, earthquakes, and magnetic fields. If you've ever wondered what an earthquake feels like, step into the high-tech simulator and experience two quakes—the larger one reaches 7.0 on the Richter scale. More than 5,000 insect specimens are displayed in the Insectarium and along the sides of the main corridor. Don't worry, they don't crawl or creep around. There are spiders, beetles, moths, butterflies, and stick insects to marvel over, in myriad colors, forms, and sizes. Take a few minutes to watch the water clock in operation in the lobby. Free parking is available in the lot across the street.

170 Montcalm St., Hull, PQ. © **819/595-7790**. Admission C$5 (US$3) ages 16 and over, C$4 (US$2.50) students, seniors, and children 6 and over, C$13 (US$8) family (max. 4 members), free for children 5 and under. May 1–early Sept daily 10am–6pm; early Sept–Apr 30 Tues–Sun 10am–4pm.

Casino du Lac Leamy   The magnificent Casino du Lac Leamy is picturesquely situated between De la Carrière Lake and Lac Leamy. A sweeping tree-lined drive leads to ample parking in front of the main entrance. Once inside, you enter a different world. The enormous casino area boasts lofty ceilings, thousands of tropical plants, soothing waterfalls and reflecting pools, an abundance of natural cherry wood, and an ingenious catwalk suspended above the gaming area. Fifty gaming tables offer popular gambling games including Blackjack, Baccarat, Roulette, Pai Gow Poker, Let It Ride, and Caribbean Stud Poker. There's also a Keno lounge, Royal Ascot Electronic Track Horse Racing, and more than 1,400 slot machines. Admission is free, but restricted to persons ages 18 and over. Smoking is restricted to designated areas. There are three restaurants, including the award-winning fine-dining restaurant Le baccara, and two bars. See Chapter 8, "Ottawa After Dark," for more information.

1 boulevard du Casino, Hull, PQ. © **800/665-2274** or 819/772-2100. www.casinos-quebec.com. Free admission. Admission restricted to persons 18 and over. Daily 11am–3am.

GATINEAU

The city of **Gatineau,** across from Hull on the east side of the Gatineau River, was created in 1975 with the merger of seven smaller communities. Its population numbered around 105,000 until January 1, 2002, when a new city of Gatineau was established, which includes Hull, Aylmer, Buckingham, and Masson–Angers. One municipal government now serves 225,000 residents of the Outaouais region. Gatineau's Municipal Arts Centre features entertainment throughout the year. Every year on Labour Day weekend, the **Gatineau Hot Air Balloon Festival** draws large crowds. **Rue Jacques-Cartier** has numerous sidewalk cafes that offer a great view of Ottawa and the Ottawa River. **Lac-Beauchamp Park** is a large urban park where you can swim, picnic, canoe, bike, skate, and cross-country ski. For park information call ✆ **819/669-2548.** For more information on the city of Gatineau, call ✆ **819/243-2345,** or contact the **Association touristique de l'Outaouais,** 103 Laurier St., Hull, PQ ✆ **800/265-7822** or 819/778-2222.

SCENIC ADVENTURES

The Outaouais Region is blanketed in majestic outcroppings of rock, clear streams, and forested hills. The beauty of the countryside is irresistible. Get out of the city bustle for a day or two and experience rural Quebec. Travel on a scenic tour on an historic steam train or explore the wonders of Gatineau Park.

HULL–CHELSEA–WAKEFIELD STEAM TRAIN

Take a trip on an authentic steam train along one of the most scenic rail routes in eastern Canada—the banks of the Gatineau River bordering Gatineau Park. Railroad buffs might like to note that the star of the show is a 1907 Swedish-built type 2-8-0 locomotive, believed to be the only European steam train operating on Canadian tracks. Nine Swedish-built climate-controlled coaches, dating from the 1940s, can accommodate a total of 528 passengers. One car is accessible for passengers with disabilities, but if you want to take advantage of this service, you should request seating in this coach when you make your reservation. Each coach has two washrooms and there's a snack bar and souvenir shop on board the train. During the journey, you'll be entertained by strolling minstrels and bilingual tour guides, who will share stories and music from the region's history and the steam locomotive's colorful past.

A round trip from **Hull** to **Wakefield** and back is 5 hours—the journey is 1½ hours in each direction and there's a 2-hour stopover in the pretty village of **Wakefield.** After disembarking, watch the 93-ton steam locomotive pivot on Canada's only manually operated turntable. **Wakefield** has a number of boutiques, artists' studios, and outdoor terrace restaurants to help you pass the time until you hop back on the train. From Wakefield Memorial Park, in the heart of the village, you can see the historic **Wakefield covered bridge,** which has been rebuilt. The 1838 grist mill has recently been converted to a luxurious inn and conference center, the **Wakefield Mill.** Call ✆ **888/567-1838** or 819/459-1838 for rates and package information for the Wakefield Mill, or visit their website at www.wakefieldmill.com.

There are many special events and tourist packages available that include a trip on the steam train. Fall Foliage Tours, Sunday Brunch, Mother's Day Brunch, and Family packages featuring accommodations, museum admissions, and sightseeing tours are on offer. A special Sunset Dinner Train excursion features the renowned cuisine of Hull's **Café Henry Burger.** The dinner train can seat up to 356 guests and musical entertainment is provided on board.

165 Deveault St., Hull, PQ. ✆ **800/871-7246** or 819/778-7246. www.steamtrain.ca. Return ticket prices starting from C$29 (US$18) adults, C$26 (US$16) seniors, C$25 (US$16) students, C$14 (US$9) children, C$74 (US$46) family (max. 2 adults and 2 children). Price varies according to season and package. Reservations required. May–Oct on various days.

GATINEAU PARK

Just a short drive from downtown Ottawa lies a beautifully preserved wilderness park. Within the 361km² (141 miles²) of **Gatineau Park,** there are 200km (125 miles) of cross-country ski trails and 175km (115 miles) of hiking and biking trails. The park's landscape is carved from the Canadian Shield, and the exposed rocks, dating back to the Precambrian Era, are among the oldest exposed rocks on earth. More than 50 glacial lakes are scattered throughout the park. The forested areas consist mainly of maple and oak; spruce, white pine, and eastern hemlock cover only about 3% of the park's land. The large number of rare plant and animal species has stimulated many scientific research projects. **Gatineau Park** is open year-round and has something to offer in every season. Vehicle access fees are in effect in certain areas of the park during the peak summer period of mid-June to early September. Your first stop should be the **Visitor Centre,** at 33 Scott Rd., Chelsea, PQ (✆ **800/465-1867** or 819/827-2020), open every day of the year. It's a great source for all kinds of park maps and information on special events and festivals. The knowledgeable and friendly staff are available to answer questions and help you to plan your visit. The village of **Chelsea,** lying roughly halfway between Hull and Wakefield and close to Gatineau Park's Visitor Centre, has several restaurants serving French cuisine. **Café–Restaurant L'Agaric** has a rustic setting close to the Gatineau Park entrance and is located at 254 Old Chelsea Road ✆ **819/827-3030.** You'll find **L'Orée du Bois** at 15 Kingsmere Road ✆ **819/827-0332.** You could also try **Les Fougères** at 783 Hwy. 105, call ✆ **819/827-8942.**

WILDLIFE Lakes in the park are home to 40 species of **fish,** including trout, yellow perch, pike, and bass, which are all popular sport-fishing catches. Around 2,000 **white-tailed deer** also live in the park. They are most likely to be observed feeding in early morning or late afternoon, close to La Pêche Lake and Philippe Lake, or in open fields and alongside roads. In the far northwest corner of the park live one or two **timber wolf** packs. You are unlikely to see them because they avoid contact with humans, but you might be lucky enough to hear them howl. A wolf pack howls in a drawn-out, harmonious chorus, which is distinguishable from the short, high-pitched bark of a **coyote** pack.

When you're on the trails, keep an eye out for **bear** tracks on muddy sections of the trail and around beaver ponds. If you're unfamiliar with animal tracks, drop in to the Visitor Centre before your hike and ask the staff for information. Also watch for claw marks on the trunks of trees—bears love to climb.

Along the Gatineau Parkway, there are numerous **beaver** ponds, where you can observe these busy, furry creatures in action, especially at dawn and dusk. Other wildlife that make the park their home include the **bobcat, Canada lynx, wolverine, mink,** and **otter.** If you enjoy bird-watching, you're in for a treat. The waterways, fields, forests, wetlands, and rocky escarpments provide vital food and shelter for about 230 species of **birds.** A brochure listing dozens of species and hints for when and where to observe the park's feathered friends is available from the Visitor Centre. **Grass snakes, turtles, frogs, toads, bull frogs, tree frogs, salamanders,** and **newts** are also native park inhabitants.

Tips **What Should I Do If I Meet a Bear?**

The bear population in Gatineau Park is estimated at around 200. If you happen to see a bear on a trail, make loud noises and keep your distance. Never try to feed a bear or approach it, as you may make the bear feel threatened. Keep well away from a mother and her cubs, and never position yourself between them. Never try to outrun, outswim, or outclimb a bear, since the animal may interpret your actions as a sign of weakness.

CAMPING

Gatineau Park has three campgrounds, each offering a different outdoors experience. Philippe Lake is the largest campground, with 246 wooded campsites. Sandy beaches, a convenience store, and plenty of water taps and washrooms contribute to a comfortable vacation. If you don't mind fewer modern conveniences in exchange for being a little closer to the wilderness, try Taylor Lake, which offers rustic tent camping with only 33 sites, all close to the lake. If you want still more of a back-to-nature adventure, La Pêche Lake has canoe-in camping available at 35 individual sites in a dozen wooded areas around the lake. For all three sites, call © **819/456-3016** or fax © **819/456-3134** to make campsite reservations. To arrange boat and mountain-bike rentals for Philippe Lake and Taylor Lake, call © **819/456-3555.** To rent a boat for La Pêche Lake, call © **819/456-3494.** Note that alcoholic beverages are not allowed in the campgrounds or elsewhere in the park. Pets are not allowed in campgrounds, picnic areas, or on beaches, although dogs on a leash are permitted on hiking trails.

CYCLING/MOUNTAIN BIKING

Grab a map at the Visitor Centre to help you plan your route on the network of trails and paved bikeways in the park. The length and variety of mountain-bike trails are excellent. Trails are open from May 15 to November 30. The sport is restricted to designated trails to protect the natural environment; you may not use cross-country ski trails for winter biking. Mountain bikes are available for rental. Contact the Visitor Centre for more information.

Tips **Looking for a Smooth Ride?**

Because of its topography, the park's network of bike paths requires cyclists to be in good physical condition and experienced in cycling on challenging terrain. If you're looking for a leisurely cycle ride, you will find the relatively flat and smooth surface of the bikeways in the city of Ottawa easier and more enjoyable. You might also consider cycling in the park on Sunday mornings in the summer, when the main roadways are closed to motorized traffic.

HIKING

There are 175km (115 miles) of hiking trails in the park, including about 90km (56 miles) of shared-use trails (walkers and mountain bikers), with the remainder set aside exclusively for hiking. Some of the shorter trails feature interpretation panels and are suitable for wheelchair and stroller access. If you are considering hiking one of the longer trails, make sure you are sufficiently prepared, with appropriate clothing, food, water, and sturdy, comfortable footwear. The Gatineau Visitor Centre has an excellent map available (1:25,000 scale) for C$5 (US$3); it is strongly recommended for hikers and mountain bikers.

If you enter the park at the south entrance, off boulevard Alexandre-Taché in Hull, the first short trail you'll find is **Des Fées Lake,** a 1.5-km (1-mile) trail around a small lake; the trail should take about 1 hour to walk. A little farther along the Gatineau Parkway, **Hickory Trail** is a short trail, just under 1km (0.5 mile) long, which takes about 20 minutes to walk. The trail has been designed so you can comfortably push a stroller or wheelchair along the route, and a picnic area and interpretive panels provide diversion along the pathway.

As you drive deeper into the park, you'll pass **Pink Lake.** This site is exceptionally beautiful in the fall, when the many deciduous trees turn to red, orange, and yellow against a background of dark green firs. Pink Lake (it's green, by the way, not pink) is unusual because it is one of only a dozen or so meromictic lakes in Canada. Because there is no circulation between the different layers of water, the lake harbors prehistoric bacteria, 10,000-year-old sedimentary deposits, and saltwater fish that have adapted to fresh water. There is a 2.5-km (1.7-mile) trail around the lake, which takes about 1½ hours to walk.

(*Fun Fact* **Unique Waters**

A "meromictic" lake is an unusual body of water where there is no circulation between the different layers of water. It typically has a green color and is home to saltwater fish that have adapted to freshwater conditions. There are often sedimentary deposits dating back 10,000 years and prehistoric bacteria in its depths.

If you're looking for panoramic vistas, try one of the trails leading to the top of the **Eardley Escarpment.** A steep 2-km (1.25-mile) path called **King Mountain Trail** rewards hikers with a wonderful view of the Ottawa Valley. Farther into the park, the **Champlain Trail,** 1.3km (0.9 mile) long, has interpretive panels explaining how the site has evolved since the time of the last glaciers. From the **Champlain Lookout,** the valley view sweeps majestically for many miles. To reach the picturesque **Luskville Falls Trail,** travel west on boulevard Alexandre-Taché past the main south entrance to Gatineau Park, and continue west on Highway 148 to Luskville. Follow signs for Luskville Falls, where you'll find a parking lot and picnic site. The 5-km (3-mile) trail leads to the top of the Eardley Escarpment, where you will have a great view of the Ottawa Valley.

SWIMMING

There are five public beaches with lifeguard supervision within the park, located at Philippe, Meech, and La Pêche lakes. The beaches are open mid-June to early September daily 10am to 6pm. Swimming is prohibited in the beach areas outside these times, and at all times elsewhere in the park.

WINTER IN THE PARK

Gatineau Park has lots to offer winter visitors. An extensive network of cross-country ski trails and special trails for hiking, snowshoeing, and kick-sledding will keep you active and outdoors. The park has earned a reputation as one of the best ski-trail networks in North America because of its remarkable 200km (125 miles) of trails, which are well-maintained using the latest technology. Both classic Nordic-style cross-country skiing and the more energetic skate-skiing are accommodated. The park provides eight heated shelters. Ski patrollers travel the area, ready to assist skiers in difficulty. When you arrive at the park, you can buy a day pass for the trails at any of the 16 parking lots, which give direct access to the trails, or at the **Visitor Centre.** If you don't have a map, your first stop should be the Visitor Centre to buy the official winter trail map. An extremely accurate winter trail map has recently been produced using GIS technology, which includes contour lines, magnetic north orientation, and exact representation of the trails. Because skiing and weather conditions change frequently, Gatineau Park reviews and updates ski information three times daily. For downhill skiing and snowboarding, Camp Fortune ski resort is right in the park. Lessons and equipment rental are available. See "The Great Outdoors," later in this chapter. For more information, contact **Camp Fortune** at ✆ **819/827-1717.**

Tips **Sleepovers in the Park**

Skiers and snowshoers can experience the silence of nature in winter by spending the night in one of Gatineau Park's shelters located deep in the heart of the forest. Bunk beds and wood stoves are installed in each cabin. Reservations are required.

Mackenzie King Estate   The estate of William Lyon Mackenzie King, Canada's longest-serving prime minister, was bequeathed to the Canadian people upon his death in 1950. You can visit the restored cottages on the property and stroll through the gardens, which include formal flower beds, a hidden rock garden, and a collection of picturesque ruins. The estate screens short films describing the life and times of Mackenzie King, and guides are on hand to answer questions. There is a tearoom on the premises serving light refreshments. The estate is open mid-May to mid-October, weekdays 11am to 5pm, weekends and holidays 10am to 6pm. For more information call ✆ **819/827-2020.**

SPECIAL EVENTS IN GATINEAU PARK

Other events may be scheduled in addition to the ones listed below, and dates may change from year to year. For more information, contact the **Gatineau Park Visitor Centre,** 33 Scott Rd., Chelsea, PQ ✆ 819/827-2020.

January
The park celebrates winter with a weekend ski festival, including ski lessons for beginners and activities for the whole family.

February
The annual Keskinada Loppet has a cross-country ski event for every member of the family—there's even

a 2-km (1.25-mile) mini-Keski for children under age 12.

March
A spring celebration on the second Sunday of the month marks the end of winter.

May
The Mackenzie King Estate opens for the summer season.

The Canadian Tulip Festival is celebrated at Mackenzie King Estate.

Sunday Bikedays begin for the season.

July

Canada Day celebrations take place at Mackenzie King Estate.

The Mackenzie King Estate hosts the Flower Festival.

Learn about conservation and the natural and historic heritage of Gatineau Park on Parks Day.

September

The Mackenzie King Estate celebrates Labour Day weekend with festivities.

September/October

Fall Rhapsody, a celebration of nature's autumn colors, takes place in the park.

October

Thanksgiving weekend activities are held at the Mackenzie King Estate.

2 The Rideau Valley

The **Rideau Valley** lies southwest of Ottawa, following the path of the **Rideau Canal.** The canal is actually a continuous chain of beautiful lakes, rivers, and canal cuts, stretching a distance of 202km (125 miles) between Ottawa and Kingston, and often described as the most scenic waterway in North America. The **Rideau Canal Waterway** has been designated a national historic site and is one of nine historic canals in Canada. Parks Canada has the responsibility of preserving and maintaining the canal's natural and historic features and providing a safe waterway for navigation. You can explore the region by boat; drive along the country roads that wind their way through the towns and villages along the waterway; or hike a portion of the **Rideau Trail,** a cleared and marked footpath about 300km (185 miles) long that meanders between Ottawa and Kingston.

RIDEAU CANAL AND LOCKS

The canal and locks that link the lakes and rivers of the **Rideau Valley** were constructed between 1826 and 1832 to provide a safe route for the military between Montreal and Kingston in the wake of the War of 1812. Colonel By, the British engineer in charge of the project, had the foresight to build the locks and canal large enough to permit commercial traffic to access the system, rather than building the canal solely for military use. As things turned out, the inhabitants of North America decided to live peaceably. The canal became a main transportation and trade route, and communities along the canal grew and thrived. With the introduction of railroads in the mid–19th century, the commercial traffic subsided and the canal gradually became a tourist destination owing to its beauty and tranquility. The locks have operated continuously since they first opened.

 Rideau Canal Numbers

• Number of locks in the main channel	45
• Number of lockstations	24
• Length of canal (Ottawa–Kingston)	202km (125 miles)
• Length of man-made canal cuts	19km (12 miles)
• Minimum available water depth	1.5m (5 ft.)
• Size of locks	41m by 10 m (134 ft. by 33 ft.)
• Travel time, one-way	3 to 5 days

MANOTICK

Manotick is a quiet village about 24km (15 miles) south of Ottawa on the banks of the Rideau River. The original settlement grew around a water-powered gristmill, now known as **Watson's Mill,** on the west side of the river. The village expanded around the original buildings, which date from the mid-1800s, and now includes residences on Long Island, a 3.5-km (2-mile) long island in the river, and an area on the east side of the river. **Dickinson Square,** in the heart of the village, is a good spot for strolling and visiting local shops. Wander across the dam and feed the ducks on the millpond. **Watson's Mill** is open to visitors in the summer. Every second Sunday afternoon from June to October, the mill swings into operation, grinding wheat to make flour. You can wander through the five-story historic stone building or take a guided tour. Call ✆ **613/692-2500** for information on opening hours and tour times. To get to Manotick from Ottawa, take Riverside Drive south to the village. To reach the mill, cross the bridge to the west bank of the river.

Fun Fact **Watson's Mill**

Watson's Mill is reputedly haunted. Ghostly sightings have been reported of a tall, fair-haired young woman, believed to be the wife of Joseph Currier, one of the original mill owners. During a visit to the mill in 1861, the young bride's long skirts were accidentally caught in a revolving turbine shaft. She was thrown against a nearby support pillar and died instantly.

There are several places to eat in the village, ranging from tearooms to family-style restaurants and fast-food outlets on Mill Street, Main Street, John Street, and River Road. For a nice leisurely lunch or if you fancy quaffing a brew by the river on a warm summer day, head south on River Road. About 7km south of Manotick, you'll find **The Swan on the Rideau,** 2730 River Road, ✆ **613/692-4550** a pub/restaurant on the east banks of the Rideau River. Have a quiet drink, or enjoy a snack or meal—the menu lists steak, chicken, pasta, and seafood. The atmosphere is casual and friendly.

MERRICKVILLE

To reach **Merrickville,** continue south along the scenic route beside the **Rideau River** and past **Manotick.** If you travel along the west bank of the river on County Road 13, you'll pass **Baxter Conservation Area,** where you can stop for a picnic, stroll, or swim. Continue on County Road 13 to County Road 5. Turn left toward Becketts Landing, passing **Rideau River Provincial Park** on your left, another pleasant spot to stretch and enjoy the outdoors. Just after the park, the road changes to County Road 2 and takes you straight to Merrickville. For a more direct, faster route from Ottawa, use Highway 416 south (exit 42 or 43). The picturesque village of **Merrickville** is a popular tourist destination, especially in the summer months when the streets are decorated with flowers. One of Canada's best preserved and restored 19th-century villages, **Merrickville** has more than 100 historic and heritage properties. The community was chosen as Ontario's most beautiful village in 1996 and as Canada's most beautiful village in 1998. More than 50 professional artists make their home in the vicinity of

Merrickville, and their wares, ranging from paintings to leather crafts, wood carvings, blown glass, pottery, and other creations, are available in boutiques and shops in the village. The village, founded in 1793 by William Merrick, was originally a large industrial center on the Rideau River with a number of woolen mills, sawmills, and gristmills. The original blockhouse, overlooking the locks, is now a small museum. Several cafes and restaurants are dotted about the village. The **Baldachin Inn,** 111 St. Lawrence St. ✆ **613/269-4223** offers comfortable rooms for an overnight stay in addition to a fine-dining restaurant and a British-style pub, in an historic building that dates from the 1860s. Farther south on St. Lawrence Street at number 317, you'll find the **Goose and Gridiron English Country Pub** ✆ **613/269-2091.** Serving imported and domestic beer accompanied by English-style pub meals, this eatery does a smashing job of imitating the Brits. Try the steak and kidney pie with chips and peas. Overlooking the Rideau Canal at 118 Main Street East, **Sam Jakes Inn,** ✆ **800/567-4667** or 613/269-3711, is a heritage limestone property. Rooms and suites are furnished and decorated in period style. There is a restaurant on site serving breakfast, lunch, and dinner. Cozy fireplaces are lit in the winter and there's a garden patio for summer enjoyment. Packages are available for romantic getaways. Just west of the village is the **Rideau National Migratory Bird Sanctuary.**

SMITHS FALLS

The town of Smiths Falls, established in the mid-1800s, was built around the heart of the Rideau Canal. There are three small museums in town that chronicle the history of the canal, the railroads, and the pioneers who settled in this district. Check opening hours before visiting, since two of them are open by appointment only during the winter months. There's one other attraction that chocoholics will not let you drive by—the **Hershey Chocolate Factory.** To reach Smiths Falls, take County Road 43 west from Merrickville (exit 43 on Hwy. 416). An alternative route from Ottawa is to take Highway 417 west to Highway 7 west, then take Highway 15 south to Smiths Falls.

Hershey Canada Chocolate Factory Tour   Kids and grown-ups will love this free tour of the Hershey plant, where you can watch thousands of chocolate bars take shape right before your eyes. The tour is actually a self-guided walk along an enclosed gallery with windows looking down to the factory floor. You can see huge vats of melted chocolate being stirred, chocolate molds traveling along conveyor belts to be filled with chocolate, individual bars being wrapped and packed for shipping, and boxes moving along the conveyor belt around the factory. At the end of the tour, where else could you possibly end up but in the middle of a shop crammed with Hershey products? You may snag a bargain, but prices are not necessarily discounted. Be prepared to elbow your way past enthusiastic customers with bulging bags of calories as they line up at the cash registers. If you wish, you can shop at the store without taking the tour. The factory is easy to find by road, since it's well signposted once you reach the town of Smiths Falls.

Hershey Canada Inc., 1 Hershey Dr., Smiths Falls, ON. ✆ **613/283-3300.** www.hersheys.com. Free admission. Mon–Fri 9am–6pm, Sat 9am–5pm, Sun 10am–5pm. Closed on some holidays, so call before you go.

Smiths Falls Railway Museum   Railroad buffs will enjoy a visit to this museum, which has a collection of railway artifacts, including express train and passenger train memorabilia, archives, track tools, and old photographs and prints. Kids will love the full-size locomotives, passenger coaches, and cabooses.

90 William St., Smiths Falls, ON. ✆ **613/283-5696.** Call for admission fee. May–Oct daily 10am–4:30pm; Sept–April by appointment.

Rideau Canal Museum This museum has many hands-on displays for visitors to explore. You can operate a working lock model or test your skill as a canal skipper as you maneuver a model boat. Climb up to the lookout to get a bird's-eye view of the Rideau Canal and Smiths Falls. Lots of artifacts and historical displays share five floors with high-tech touch-screen computers and laserdisc mini-theaters. A guided tour of the Smiths Falls Combined Locks is available daily June to August or by request. The outdoor walking tour is about 1 hour and includes the modern hydraulic lock system and the original three-lift manual system built by Lt.-Col. John By in 1829.

34 Beckwith St. S., Smiths Falls, ON. © 613/284-0505. Call for admission fee. Mid-May–mid-Oct. daily 10am–4:30pm; rest of year open by appointment.

Heritage House Museum Adjacent to the Rideau Canal, Old Slys Lockstation, and a Victorian landscaped picnic area, this house has been restored to the time of Confederation. Seven period rooms are featured, reflecting the lifestyle of a wealthy mill owner. Special programs, tours, and events are scheduled throughout the year. There's an annual strawberry social, Victorian tea served on Thursday afternoons in July and August, and Christmas celebrations in the winter.

Old Slys Rd. (off Hwy. 43), Smiths Falls, ON. © 613/283-8560. Call for admission fee. Jan 2–Apr 30 Mon–Fri 10:30am–4:30pm; May 1–Dec 21 daily 10:30am–4:30pm.

3 The Great Outdoors

Blessed with excess energy? Burn up the ski slopes, golf courses, and white-water raft runs. Searching for a new experience? Bungee jump in a limestone quarry, descend into an underground anti-nuclear shelter, or go spelunking. The fun just never ends.

DOWN THE HILLS IN EVERY SEASON

Within a short drive of Ottawa are many ski centers that will thrill **downhill skiers and snowboarders.** Elevation at the ski hills near Ottawa ranges from 106 to 381m (350–1,250 ft.). The facilities and runs are compact compared to those in major resort destinations like Mont-Tremblant (about a 2-hour drive from Ottawa) and Mont–Ste-Anne (about a 4-hour drive from Ottawa), but they have the advantage of being close by. Equipment rental, lessons, facilities for children, terrain parks, and challenging downhill runs—it's all here on a small scale and you can be home in time for supper. A number of resorts have expanded their facilities to include activities for all seasons. **Water parks** have been included in this section. **Golf courses** are listed under "Along the Fairways" later in this chapter. For **mountain biking and hiking,** call resorts for information. **Cross-country skiing** is listed in chapter 7, "Active Ottawa."

Calabogie Peaks Reputed to have the highest vertical in Ontario, the resort offers 17 downhill runs and a snowboarding terrain park. Ice skating is available at the resort, and cross-country skiing, ice fishing, snowshoeing, and snowmobiling facilities are nearby. In the summer, you can swim, fish, canoe, windsurf, play tennis or beach volleyball, go mountain biking, or just lie on the beach. To get to Calabogie Peaks, travel on Highway 417 (the Queensway) west. Approximately 8km (5 miles) past Arnprior, turn left onto Calabogie Road and continue to Calabogie Peaks Resort.

Calabogie Rd., near Arnprior, ON. © 800/669-4861 or 613/752-2720. www.calabogie.com.

Camp Fortune   In the heart of Gatineau Park, Camp Fortune has 20 runs, a snowboarding park, a designated children's area, and several quad lifts. A new kids' park opened during the 2000–2001 winter season with a handle tow for little snowbunnies, a mini half-pipe and rollers so kids can learn skiing and boarding in a fun but safe environment. The supervised park is open on weekends and holidays. Camp Fortune recently made renovations to one of the main lodges. A new grooming machine was purchased in 2001 and more than 33 hectares (100 acres) of new ski slopes opened the same season. Mountain biking is offered in summer. A ski bus service is available from Ottawa; call the resort for details. To get to Camp Fortune, take Highway 5 north to exit 12, chemin Old Chelsea. Travel west on Meech Lake Road and turn left into Camp Fortune.

300 chemin Dunlop, Chelsea, PQ. ✆ **888/283-1717** or 819/827-1717. www.campfortune.com.

Edelweiss   Since 2000, Edelweiss has renovated the main lodge and added a new cafeteria with a great mountain view and twice the seating capacity of the old refreshment area. They've also installed a new magic carpet lift for children, purchased a fleet of new snow-making guns, and created a new snowboarding park to take advantage of the mountain's natural terrain. Plans are under way to increase the number of trails from the current 18. A ski bus runs on weekends and holidays; call the resort for details. On Saturday nights from 6pm to closing, a two-for-one deal is available on all categories of lift tickets. In Edelweiss Valley, you can also swoosh down the hills in the summer months at **Le Grand Splash Water Park.** This family water park features five water slides, a children's pool, a lounge pool, and an enormous 15m (50-ft.) hot tub. Picnic areas and tennis courts are also on site. To get to Edelweiss, take Highway 5 north to Route 105 toward Wakefield. Take Route 366 east (chemin Edelweiss) to the ski hill. It's about a half-hour drive from Ottawa.

540 chemin Edelweiss, Wakefield, PQ. ✆ **819/459-2328.** www.edelweissvalley.com.

Mont-Cascades   This resort offers plenty of activities in winter and summer. There are 6 lifts and 16 runs, with illuminated night skiing on 11 of those. Lessons and equipment rental are available. The six-slide **water park** has something for everyone. There's an area for kids under 121cm (4-ft.) tall, with water sprays, a small slide, and a wading pool. For older and braver kids, there's a tunnel slide, a six-story drop slide, and larger slides that several people can slip down together in a raft. When it's time to eat, visit the restaurant or bring your own lunch and munch at a picnic table in the shade. To get to Mont-Cascades from Ottawa, take the Macdonald-Cartier Bridge to Hull, then take Highway 50 east. Take the first exit, which is boulevard Archambault. Turn right onto Highway 307. Turn left on chemin Mont-Cascades, and proceed 7km (4.3 miles) to Mont-Cascades. It's about a half-hour drive from Ottawa.

448 chemin Mont-Cascades, Cantley, PQ. ✆ **888/282-2722** or 819/827-0301. www.montcascades.ca.

Mont–Ste-Marie   This resort has the highest vertical in the Outaouais region at more than 366m (1,200 ft.). Two peaks and two high-speed chairlifts give beginners and experienced skiers a choice of 24 runs in total. One of the longest beginner trails in western Quebec, snowboarding parks, a huge half-pipe, and a permanent boarder-cross course will provide the kids with plenty of thrills. Rentals and lessons are available. To reach Mont–Ste-Marie, take Highway 5 north through Hull and join Highway 105 north. Stay on 105 until you see the signs for Mont–Ste-Marie, a driving time of about 1 hour from Ottawa. A ski bus operates from Ottawa; call for details.

76 chemin de la Montagne, RR#1. Lac Ste-Marie, PQ. © **800/567-1256** or 819/467-5200. www.montstemarie.com.

Ski Vorlage   This resort offers a choice of 15 runs including a terrain park, with 12 runs illuminated for night skiing. Bring along your skates (there's no charge to use the rink) or try snowtubing. Fly down the slope on an inflatable donut and get towed back up the hill. Non-skiers might like to spend a couple of hours in the shops and restaurants of nearby Wakefield. Vorlage is about 25 minutes from Ottawa by car. Follow Highway 5 north to Highway 105 north and turn right into Wakefield. Turn onto Burnside Road and follow the signs to Vorlage.

65 Burnside Rd., Wakefield, PQ. © **877/867-5243** or 819/459-2301. www.skivorlage.com.

Mount Pakenham   West of Ottawa, Mount Pakenham offers downhill and cross-country skiing, snowboarding, and snowtubing. Pakenham is equipped with 7 lifts and 10 alpine runs. There's a snowboarding and terrain park, and night skiing is available. To get to Mount Pakenham, take the Queensway (Hwy. 417) west past Kanata. The road will reduce to two lanes and become Highway 17. Turn left on Road 20 across a stone bridge, and turn left at the stop sign onto Road 29/Highway 15. Drive through the village of Pakenham. Turn right on McWatty Road to a T-junction. Turn right to Mount Pakenham. It's approximately 25 minutes' drive from the Corel Centre exit on Highway 417.

Pakenham, ON. © **613/624-5290**. www.mountpakenham.com.

ALONG THE FAIRWAYS

There are dozens of golf courses within an hour's drive of Ottawa. A few suggestions are listed below, but there are many more excellent courses to visit. Check out **www.ottawagolf.com,** consult your golfing friends, or ask for a recommendation at the tourist information office in Ottawa or Hull.

Amberwood Village   Executive 9-hole course in a quiet suburban setting about a half-hour from Ottawa. Take Hwy. 417 (Queensway) west; exit at the Carp Road/Stittsville exit. Turn left onto Carp Road for approximately 2km (1.25 miles). Turn left onto Hazeldean Road, then right onto Springbrook Drive until you reach Amberwood.

54 Springbrook Dr., Stittsville, ON. © **613/836-2564**.

Calabogie Highlands Resort and Golf Club   Rated in the top 50 golf courses in Ontario, this resort features an 18-hole championship course and a 9-hole lakeview course. Accommodation available. Practice range, outdoor pool, and tennis. Take Hwy. 17 (Queensway) west past Arnprior. Turn left on Hwy. 508 to Calabogie (about 23km; 14 miles). Turn left onto Hwy. 511, then right onto Barryvale Rd. About an hour's drive from Ottawa.

1234 Barryvale Rd., Calabogie, ON © **613/752-2171**.

Capital Golf Centre   Situated in the south end of the city next to the Greenbelt, this 18-hole course is exclusively par 3, with the longest hole at 202 yards. The layout deliberately omits water and sand hazards as a benefit to beginning golfers. More experienced golfers can play the course to sharpen up their short game. There's also a championship miniature golf course and three practice ranges for all types of play—drives, short irons, bunkers, and chipping. Lessons available. Situated 2km (1.25 miles) south of Hunt Club Road on Bank Street.

3798 Bank St., Ottawa, ON. © **613/521-2612**.

Champlain Golf Club   Just 10 minutes from downtown Ottawa, this 18-hole championship course was established in 1929. There's a great practice center here where all levels of players can improve their game. Facilities include a driving range, two chipping greens, three practice sand traps, and two putting greens. Lessons available. Pro shop and refreshments. Cross the Champlain Bridge over the Ottawa River to Hull and turn left on Hwy. 148 (boul. Alexander Taché/chemin d'Aylmer). A mere 1.3km (0.8 mile) on your right you'll find the golf club.

1145 chemin d'Aylmer, Aylmer, PQ. © **819/777-0449.**

Château Cartier   A luxurious golf and conference resort, situated on 62 hectares (152 acres) on the north shore of the Ottawa River, Château Cartier is just a short drive from Ottawa. Château Cartier received an award from Canada's *Golf Ranking Magazine* in 2000 for Best Downtown Golf Resort in Canada and Best Clubhouse Bar & Grill in Canada. See chapter 4, "Accommodations," for details of this beautiful property. Cross the Champlain Bridge over the Ottawa River to Hull and turn left on Hwy. 148 (boul. Alexander Taché/chemin d'Aylmer). The resort is a couple of minutes' drive on your left-hand side.

1170 chemin d'Aylmer, PQ. © **800/807-1088** or 819/777-1088.

Mont-Cascades   In a scenic country setting, this golf center has a mature championship course, clubhouse, and outdoor deck overlooking the Gatineau River and Gatineau Hills. To get to Mont-Cascades from Ottawa, take the Macdonald-Cartier Bridge to Hull, then take Highway 50 east. Take the first exit, which is boulevard Archambault. Turn right onto Highway 307. Turn left on chemin Mont-Cascades, and proceed 7km (4.3 miles) to Mont-Cascades. It's about a half-hour drive from Ottawa.

448 chemin Mont-Cascades, Cantley, PQ. © **819/459-2980.** www.golf.montcascades.com

Mont–Ste-Marie   This classic mountain course set in the rolling contours of the Gatineau Hills has a challenging layout. Driving range, power carts, locker room, golf boutique, and bar/restaurant. To reach Mont–Ste-Marie, take Highway 5 north through Hull and join Highway 105 north. Stay on 105 until you see the signs for Mont–Ste-Marie, a driving time of about 1 hour from Ottawa.

76 chemin de la Montagne, RR#1. Lac Ste-Marie, PQ. © **800/567-1256** or 819/467-3111. www. montstemarie.com.

Eagle Creek Golf Course   Eagle Creek course is a challenging 18-hole championship course designed by Ken Venturi with the aim of rewarding precision over power. The Eagle Creek Classic Tournament has been held for several years here as part of the Canadian Professional Golf Tour. The course has been a *Golf Digest* 4 Star Award winner from 1996 to 2001. Take Hwy. 417 (Queensway) west and exit at March Road/Kanata/Eagleson Road. Travel north on March Road for about 8km (5 miles), then turn right onto Dunrobin Rd. for 10km (6 miles). Turn right onto Vances Sideroad for around 3km (2 miles). Turn left onto Greenland Rd. About 1.5km (1 mile) along, turn left onto Ventor Boulevard. A few meters (yards) along here you'll find the club.

109 Royal Troon Lane, RR# 1 Dunrobin, ON. © **613/832-0728.**

Pine View Municipal Golf Course   Play a choice of two 18-hole courses here—one championship and one executive. Take Hwy. 417 (Queensway) east, and continue on Hwy. 174 when the highway splits in two (don't take 417 toward Montreal at exit 113). Exit Hwy. 174 at Blair Road. Turn left onto Blair Road for 400m (440 yd.) to the course.

1471 Blair Rd., Ottawa, ON. © **613/746-4301.**

ON THE RIVER

The Ottawa River, one of the most popular **white-water rafting and kayaking** rivers in Canada, has everything for the white-water enthusiast—dozens of islands, rapids, waterfalls, sandy beaches, and dramatic rock formations. It's even said that the water is warm (I can't confirm or deny that, but you're welcome to tackle the white water and find out for yourself). An hour or two northwest of Ottawa, a number of white-water tour operators have established businesses that allow novices and families to enjoy running the rapids just as much as experienced extreme-sports participants. Keep a lookout for one of the newest thrills, **riverboarding.** Equipped with a board, wetsuit, lifejacket, helmet, and fins, riverboarders ride the rapids lying prone on their board. They read the direction of the current and point the board where they want to go using their arms as paddles and their flippers as rudders.

Esprit Rafting Offering day trips and longer-stay outdoor adventure packages, Esprit Rafting operates on the Ottawa River about 90km (60 miles) from Ottawa; the company can arrange transportation between Ottawa and the rafting site. There's a wide range of adventure packages, including **white-water rafting, white-water canoeing, white-water kayaking, and riverboarding.** You can add horseback riding, mountain biking, or a bungee jump to your package. Esprit offers a great family white-water experience. In the morning, the family (children must be ages 7 or older) raft together with the assistance of an experienced guide. In the afternoon, children under age 12 take part in supervised shore activities while parents and children over age 12 take a more adventurous trip over the rapids. The day trip meets at a rendezvous point along the highway. Get directions when you call to make your reservation.

© 800/596-7238 or 819/683-3641. www.espritrafting.com.

Madawaska Kanu Center A summer camp runs at the Kanu Center. **Canoe and kayak instruction** is available at weekend clinics or as a 5-day course. The Madawaska River **Family Float Trip** is a 2-hour ride along a 5-km (3-mile) stretch of the Madawaska River near Algonquin Park. This is such a gentle ride that children ages 2 and over are accepted on the raft. The trips run Monday to Thursday in the summer, departing hourly from 10am to 2pm. Reservations are required.

Summer: P.O. Box 635, Barry's Bay, ON K0J 1B0. © 613/756-3620. Winter: 39 First Ave., Ottawa, ON K1S 2G1. © 613/594-5268. www.owl-mkc.ca.

Owl Rafting Owl Rafting operates on the Ottawa River near Forester's Falls, between Renfrew and Pembroke off Highway 17. Paddle your own course with a guide if you wish, and choose everything from chicken runs to a champion challenge. Two-person **inflatable kayaks** available. Owl Rafting also offers a half-day **family float trip** that takes you over 6km (3.7 miles) along the river, through white water and calm pools. They return you to base on a gentle cruising raft (with chairs and a barbecue lunch on board). Passengers must weigh a minimum of 22kg (50 lb.) and be at least 8 years old. Day care is available at the base for any child under age 12, at a cost of C$18 (US$12) per child. Trips run on weekdays, and lifejackets and helmets are provided. Wetsuits are available at extra cost. No paddling is required—just hold on and enjoy riding waves up to 1m (3 ft.) in height. Reservations are required.

Summer: P.O. Box 29, Forester's Falls, ON K0J 1V0. © 613/646-2263. Winter: 39 First Ave., Ottawa, ON K1S 2G1. © 613/238-7238. www.owl-mkc.ca.

River Run Rafting and Paddle Center   River Run, just a 90-minute drive northwest of Ottawa, is a 56-hectare (137-acre) riverfront resort on the Ottawa River. Choose from **white-water canoeing, white-water kayaking, or white-water rafting.** They offer a half-day **family rafting trip** on a gentle route over the rapids, and everyone on board gets involved—you get to paddle on this one. There's also a complete range of outdoor recreational activities at the resort, including horseback riding, camping, and splat ball. Packages with overnight accommodation can be arranged.

P.O. Box 179, Beachburg, ON K0J 1C0. ✆ **800/267-8504** or 613/646-2501. www.riverrunners.com.

Wilderness Tours   Wilderness Tours is a 266-hectare (650-acre) resort and adventure destination on the banks of the Ottawa River. Paddle a small, sporty **six-person raft** with a guide, or take a family raft trip geared toward families with children between the ages of 7 and 12. **Raft trips** are 4 to 6 hours long and include professional guides and a post-trip video and barbecue. They run a popular family program, which combines a gentle rafting day trip with a second day on the river in **sportyaks** or voyageur canoes. The package includes meals, scenic camping or cabin rental, use of the resort facilities, and a supervised children's program in the evenings.

P.O. Box 89, Beachburg, ON K0J 1C0. ✆ **800/267-9166** or 613/646-2291. www.wildernesstours.com.

OUT OF THE SKY

Great Canadian Bungee   Try to picture a majestic limestone quarry with 60-m (200-ft.) high sides, surrounding a spring-fed lagoon of deepest aqua blue. Now, imagine your loved ones jumping off a platform suspended above the water, attached by a bungee cord. You either love the idea or you hate it, but it's certainly an unusual spectacle. If you don't want to take part in the madness, come to enjoy the barbecue and picnic facilities, play and swim at the supervised beach area, rent a paddleboat or kayak, and be entertained by all those crazy dudes who are willing to pay up to C$100 (US$62) for the biggest adrenaline rush of all time. Note that there are no age restrictions, but jumpers must weigh at least 36kg (80 lb.). Recently another thrill ride was introduced at the site—the RIPRIDE. It's a 310-m (1,015-ft.) cable slide that accelerates as you travel along its length, reaching a top speed of 100kmph (62 mph). You can ride tandem on the slide if the combined weight is between 36 and 127kg (80 and 280 lb.). Life will never be the same again.

Morrison's Quarry, Wakefield, PQ. ✆ **877/828-8170** or 819/459-3714. www.bungee.ca.

UNDER THE GROUND

When you've explored air, land, and water, what do you do next? Go underground, of course.

Diefenbunker Cold War Museum   Visit an underground bunker built during the period of the Cold War and designed to shelter the Canadian government in the event of nuclear attack. This is a rare opportunity to glimpse a somber and alarming period of recent world history, when precautions were taken against the possible threat of nuclear war. The huge four-story bunker, buried deep under a farmer's field, is designed to house more than 500 people and enough supplies for a month in the event of nuclear war. The guided walking tour takes about 1½ hours. Many of the guides used to work in the Diefenbunker before it was decommissioned in 1994. During the tour you will see the blast tunnel and massive blast doors, the CBC radio studio, the Bank of Canada vault that was designed to hold Canada's gold reserves, the War Cabinet room, the decontamination unit, a detailed model of the bunker, a 1-megaton hydrogen "practice bomb," a reconstruction of a family fallout shelter, and lots more. To get to the Diefenbunker from Ottawa, follow Highway 417 (the Queensway) west, take the Carp–Stittsville exit, and bear right onto Carp Road. Travel about 8km (5 miles) into the village of Carp. Watch for signs on the left indicating the entrance to the Diefenbunker.

3911 Carp Rd., Carp, ON. (✆ 800/409-1965 or 613/839-0007. www.diefenbunker.ca. Admission C$12 (US$7) adults, C$10 (US$6) seniors and students, C$5 (US$3) children 6–17, free for children 5 and under. Guided tours begin in summer daily at 11am, noon, 1pm, 2pm, and 3pm; in fall, winter, and spring weekdays at 2pm and weekends at 1pm and 2pm. Reservations recommended.

Laflèche Caves Visit the white marble caverns at Laflèche Caves and explore the large network of domes, rooms, and tunnels that were carved into the rock by the pressure from water and ice during the last Ice Age. The general tour is suitable for all ages and takes about an hour. More adventurous souls can follow an experienced guide on a 3-hour tour of narrow spaces and galleries. The temperature inside the caves remains steady all year round between 3°C and 7°C (37°F–45°F). Wear sturdy walking shoes and warm clothing. Guides will provide you with hard hats and headlamps for both tours, as well as with the extra equipment needed for the caving adventure tour. Above ground, enjoy the skating rink, snowshoeing trails, and slides in winter and picnic areas and nature trails in summer. Reservations are required for cave tours. To reach Laflèche Caves, take Highway 50 north through Hull, exit on Highway 307 north, and travel to Val-des-Monts. It's about a half-hour drive from Ottawa.

Route 307, Val-des-Monts, PQ. (✆ 877/457-4033 or 819/457-4033. Admission C$12 (US$7) adults, C$8 (US$5) ages 13–18, C$6 (US$4) children 12 and under, C$30 (US$19) family (max. 2 adults and 2 children). Caving Adventure C$45 (US$28) per person. Open year-round.

Appendix:
Ottawa in Depth

Ottawa's transformation from wilderness to a camp for the builders of the Rideau Canal to Canada's capital spans a period of more than 200 years. The fascinating story of how this landscape of remarkable beauty, encompassing Chaudière Falls, Rideau Falls, and the Gatineau River became today's clean, green, high-tech national capital has been condensed in the next few pages.

History 101

The heart of Ottawa's history is the grand Ottawa River, Canada's second longest river at over 1,100km (700 miles). The river had been used as a major transportation route by Native peoples for thousands of years prior to the arrival of the first Europeans in the early 1600s.

Anxious to expand the fur trade, which was the basis of New France's economy, French governors encouraged exploration of the interior of the continent but did not give priority to establishing new settlements. Consequently, although many French explorers and fur traders paddled and portaged past the site of the future city of Ottawa, almost 200 years went by before the first settlers arrived.

The French explorer Samuel de Champlain, who had sent two Frenchmen on missions up the Ottawa River prior to his arrival in 1613, is often considered to be the first white man to visit the vicinity of present-day Ottawa and Hull. Champlain recorded detailed descriptions of Rideau Falls, Chaudière Falls, and the Native peoples in his diary.

Settlements finally began to be established in the Ottawa Valley toward the end of the 18th century, but it was Philemon Wright, a prosperous farmer from Massachusetts, who saw potential in the district. In 1800 he persuaded five homesteading families to join him, his wife, and six children to establish the first community in the area. Wright chose the north shore of the Ottawa River, and within 20 years Wrightsville became a thriving village of more than 700 residents. Wright's plan was to make the community self-sufficient, and with five mills, four stores, three schools, two hotels, two distilleries, a brewery, and agricultural endeavors, it seems he succeeded.

Wright was searching for additional income to boost the local economy, and timber was the obvious choice for an export commodity because of its quality and abundance. Wright established markets for the local lumber in Quebec and England, and the wood was transported down the Ottawa River.

At this time, 20 years after Wright's arrival, the south side of the Ottawa River was still covered in dense bush and swampland and sparsely populated by settlers. What sparked the establishment of a larger community on the south side of the Ottawa River was the need—following the War of 1812—for a more secure transportation route than the St. Lawrence River between Kingston and Montreal. It was the British, who by that time were governors of Upper and Lower Canada and therefore had the responsibility of defending the territory, who were pushing for a back door between Montreal and Lake Ontario as a security precaution in the event of an American invasion. They were unable to find any interested parties to share the cost of construction of a canal to link Lake Ontario with the Ottawa River. As a result, the canal project ended up as a costly operation for the British, but the advantage was that they had control over the building of the canal and its attendant settlement.

In 1826, Lieutenant-Colonel John By was assigned to oversee the construction of the Rideau Canal. By the end of that year, hundreds of people had arrived at the canal site in preparation for its construction. In the spring of the following year, the settlement was named Bytown.

The first buildings to be constructed were an engineering office and a commissariat, sited at the foot of the canal. At the head of the canal on the east side, civilian barracks were built in what would soon become known as "Lower Town." This area was an almost impenetrable swamp choked with cedars. As most of the land was uninhabitable, land purchasers were encouraged to buy or lease plots of land on the west side of the canal, then known as "Upper Town."

The canal works yard was located in Lower Town, and as it expanded, settlers found it necessary to drain the surrounding swampland in order to free up more land. Most of the new inhabitants of Lower Town were Irish and French laborers, thereby establishing a predominantly Roman Catholic community; some of the poorest Irish immigrants lived in shanties along the edge of the canal construction site.

Upper Town, which was not as densely populated, attracted more affluent and better-educated settlers, predominantly English and Scottish Protestants.

The 202-km (125-mile) Rideau Canal was completed in 1832. It was an enormous feat, all the more admirable for the fact that no fewer than 45 locks were constructed, manned by 24 lockstations; the locks allowed boats to ascend and descend the spine of the Precambrian Shield, an ancient rock formation that covers much of northern Canada and part of New York State. The highest point on the Rideau Waterway is Upper Rideau Lake. At one end of the lake, water flows down to Lake Ontario, dropping a distance of 50m (164 ft.) in total. At the other end, water flows in the opposite direction down to the Ottawa River, dropping a distance of 83m (273 ft.), ending in the 30-m (98 ft.) high Rideau Falls.

The canal never did fulfill its original purpose as a military transportation route, but for many years it operated as a commercial waterway before adopting its present recreational role for boaters and tourists.

Following the completion of the canal, Bytown evolved into a merchant-based community, supporting the growing timber trade by providing retail shops and services. Most of the supplies for the lumber camps up and down the Ottawa River were purchased in Bytown. Taverns, gaming houses, and brothels sprang up in response to demands from the rough, boisterous lumber workers. Street brawls were common, with racial and religious tensions running high, especially when fuelled by drink. As the timber trade continued to flourish, lawlessness and violence prevailed.

The native white pine, and to a lesser degree red pine and oak, were much in demand by the British for shipbuilding during the mid–19th century. As a result of interference by Napoleon, Great Britain's supply of timber from the Baltic countries was halted, and for a time the British began to purchase a large amount of timber from Canada. However, by 1842, Britain was able to obtain timber from the Baltic countries as it had in the past, and the timber trade in the Ottawa area began to decline.

The local lumber industry was launched into a new era of prosperity with the arrival of several American entrepreneurs in the early 1850s. These men established sawmills to supply sawn lumber to the United States.

Around the same time, a branch railway was built between Bytown and Prescott to serve as a link with the main line between Montreal and Toronto. Although the railway turned out to be a financial disaster, its presence was an important influence in the choice of a capital city.

As Bytown marched toward the future, it received a change in both name and status. On New Year's Day, 1855, Bytown became a city called Ottawa. It was time to move forward and put the community's sordid reputation of the past behind. The citizens were excited at the prospect of being considered a contender for the title of capital of the Province of Canada.

There was such bitter debate on the issue of a suitable location for the seat of government that Parliament finally asked Queen Victoria to select the city. Montreal, Quebec, Kingston, and Toronto were Ottawa's rivals and worthy contenders. Factors in Ottawa's favor were its geographical position on the border of Upper and Lower Canada and its origins as a mixed English- and French-speaking settlement, in addition to the presence of the Rideau Canal and the new railway link. Queen Victoria duly appointed Ottawa as the capital of the Province of Canada in 1857. In the years immediately following the announcement, Ottawa enjoyed a period of strong growth. Within six years, several hundred stone buildings were erected and the population grew by 50%, reaching 14,000 by 1863. Wellington Street and Bank Street were lined with shops, medical facilities were improved with two hospitals serving the city, and a police commission was established. There were dramatic increases in the commercial and professional classes as well as in the number of industrial workers.

The construction of the government buildings took more than five years to complete. At the end of 1865 about 350 civil servants from Quebec City transferred to the new buildings. By the time Ottawa had a mere 18 months' experience as capital of the Province of Canada, it took on the much larger role of capital of the new Dominion of Canada.

On July 1, 1867, there was a great celebration on Parliament Hill. The day was declared a public holiday. Viscount Monck was sworn in as Governor General of the Dominion of Canada at 10am, followed by a march-past of the troops. In the evening, revelers lit bonfires and watched a fireworks display. Since that first Dominion Day, Canadians have celebrated July 1st (now known as Canada Day) on Parliament Hill.

In the second half of the 19th century, Ottawa faced a number of conflicts: the lumber industry versus the government as economic influences; Catholics versus Protestants in terms of religious practices, culture, and education; and immigrants versus Canadian-born citizens, which often reflected differences in social class.

Despite the challenges of a growing city, growth in public and private enterprises surged ahead. A municipal water supply and electricity supply were established, and public transportation was improved with the installment of electric streetcars to replace horse-drawn trams. Many of Ottawa's recreational clubs were founded in the latter half of the 19th century. The Ottawa Field Naturalists Club, Rowing Club, Curling Club, Cricket Club, Tennis Club, Aquatic Club, and Golf Club all originated in the 1800s.

The urban landscape altered with the years. The Parliament Buildings dominated the skyline, while numerous mills crowded around Chaudière Falls. Stone
and brick commercial and residential properties abounded in Upper Town,
while Lower Town was marked by the twin spires of the Basilica and the more
modest wooden houses of the inhabitants of the Market district.

In the spring of 1900, a major fire swept through Hull and across the river to
the Chaudière area of Ottawa. Seven people died, 15,000 became homeless, and
more than 3,000 buildings were destroyed. The cities recovered, thanks mainly
to a relief fund and the resilience and strength of the citizens.

At the turn of the last century, Ottawa's prosperity could be attributed to
three major factors: the lumber industry, which was able to produce 500 million
board-feet of lumber annually by harnessing the power of Chaudière Falls;
growth of the civil service; and the trade generated by the railways. Downtown
Ottawa was a maze of tracks: four rail systems with nine different lines. In 1912,
the imposing Union Station with its domed ceiling and huge stone pillars
opened on the east bank of the Rideau Canal, bordered by Rideau Street. The
same year, one of Ottawa's most famous landmarks, the Château Laurier, which
sits directly opposite the Union Station building (now used as a convention
center), opened. Built of granite and sandstone in a Loire Valley Renaissance
style similar to that of the Château Frontenac Hotel in Quebec City, the building is topped with a copper roof, echoing the structure of the adjacent Parliament Buildings. Also in 1912, the Victoria Memorial Museum, now known
as the Canadian Museum of Nature, was completed. Three hundred Scottish
stone masons contributed their expertise to the intricately designed turreted
stonework.

In 1916, fire destroyed the Centre Block of the Parliament Buildings. Only
the Parliamentary Library was saved, due to the actions of a quick-thinking
employee who closed the steel fire-doors against the advancing flames. The
height of the drama occurred when the huge bell in the clock tower crashed to
the ground on the last stroke of midnight.

Rebuilding began a few months afterward, and the new Centre Block,
similar in appearance to the original, was completed six years later. The
central tower, named the Peace Tower, contains a memorial chamber dedicated to Canada's war dead, a 27.3-m (91-ft.) belfry with a carillon of 53 bells,
a four-faced clock, and an observation deck. Rising from the peak of the roof
of the Peace Tower is a 10.5-m (35-ft.) bronze flag mast proudly flying the
Canadian flag.

Ottawa, along with the rest of the world, suffered and survived two World
Wars, but by the end of World War II, Ottawa was a far cry from the beautiful
green capital of today. Rail lines choked the city. More than 100 trains, with
their associated smoke and soot, thundered into Ottawa every day, and there
were no fewer than 150 level crossings within city limits.

Much of the credit for the establishment of Ottawa's physical beauty goes to
Jacques Gréber, a French urban planner, and then prime minister William Lyon
Mackenzie King. Prior to World War II, in the late 1930s, King had invited
Gréber to Ottawa, initially as an advisor to plan the War Memorial and Con-
federation Square. World War II interrupted these plans, but following the war,
Gréber returned and prepared a report with recommendations for extensive
urban renewal. The report outlined several major proposed changes to the
urban landscape.

One of the most significant was the establishment of a wide swath of green-belt around the city. Gréber also recommended eliminating slum areas, creating parks and pathways, purchasing land in Quebec to further enhance Gatineau Park, and removing or relocating railway lines.

To implement Gréber's plan, the National Capital District was enlarged to 2,900km (1,800 miles), encompassing 72 municipalities in Ontario and Quebec, and the Federal District Commission (the official agency of capital planning) was restructured and renamed the National Capital Commission, and given a full-time chairman.

Removing the vast network of railway lines dramatically changed the face of Ottawa. In their place, sweeping scenic drives were created for vehicular traffic, and pathways for walkers and cyclists were built alongside the waterways, lined with grass verges, shrubbery, and flowerbeds.

To manage high volumes of through traffic, the multi-lane Queensway (Hwy. 417) was built on an old railway bed. Completed in 1965, the Queensway stretches for more than 50km (31 miles) from the city of Kanata in the west to the town of Orleans in the east.

In the mid-1900s, the number of diplomatic missions with embassies in Ottawa grew at an enormous pace. There are now more than 100 countries represented in Canada's capital, contributing vitality and diversity to the city's cultural and social life.

Throughout the 1970s, bilingualism became commonplace in the capital. The federal government adopted two official languages, and civil servants who could speak both English and French found themselves at a distinct advantage in the workplace. This move toward a bilingual population helped to break down the class barriers in the city. Added to this improved relationship between the two major cultures in Ottawa was the growth of immigrant populations, primarily German, Italian, Jewish, Lebanese, and Asian.

The presence of blue-collar workers dwindled in the years after the war, replaced by office workers to support the growing federal government and civil service. A second economic influence began to appear by the 1960s—one that was to become a major player in the region. The high-tech industry, with its emphasis on electronics and communications, thrived in Ottawa. The National Research Council, Communications Research Council, the two universities, and private companies such as Bell Northern Research were rich sources of research material and a highly skilled workforce. Demand for electronic equipment was increasing, and a ready customer, the federal government, was right on the doorstep. Other major markets, including Toronto, Montreal, the eastern seaboard of the United States, and Europe, were also within grasp.

The 1980s were characterized by the tech boom, when the more entrepre-neurial of the research scientists began to start up their own companies. Ottawa became known as Silicon Valley North and millions of dollars changed hands in the hot world of the tech sector in the 1990s. Despite a recent slump and mas-sive local layoffs in the industry, Ottawa's high-tech is here to stay. The injection of young, irreverent techies has brought new life to a city that was settling into a middle-income, middle-class snooze.

In all of this, the part played by the humble tourist must not be overlooked. Tourism is a major industry in Canada's capital city. Ottawa's natural beauty, its museums, attractions, and historic buildings, its many festivals and colorful ceremonies all draw millions of visitors each year, many of them Canadian.

As Ottawa shapes its future in the new millennium, it continues to wrestle with the challenge of its dual role as a city and a capital. The formation of the new city of Ottawa in 2001, an amalgamation of 12 local municipal governments, will perhaps make this challenge easier to manage. With the new city of Gatineau in 2002, also formed from several local municipalities, an opportunity exists for both cities to join with the National Capital Commission to plan for the growth of the entire region to the benefit of all.

Dateline

- **1610** Étienne Brûlé, by order of French explorer Samuel de Champlain, becomes the first white man to travel through the future site of Ottawa.
- **1613** Champlain records detailed descriptions of the Chaudière Falls and Rideau Falls while traveling up the Ottawa River.
- **1600s to 1900s** A large number of trading canoes travel up and down the Ottawa River, trading goods for furs.
- **1763** The first Treaty of Paris ends French rule in Canada, and land is granted to the British.
- **1800** A Massachusetts farmer, Philemon Wright, establishes the first non-Native settlement in the area on the north side of the Ottawa River. Wrightsville, now known as Hull, Quebec, grows and prospers along with the expanding lumber trade.
- **1812** The War of 1812 between the United States and England, which employed Canada as a battleground, sparks British military leaders to search for a more secure route between Montreal and Lake Ontario, to protect against a possible future invasion by the Americans.
- **1822** The first steamboat to travel up the Ottawa River, *Union of the Ottawa*, makes its inaugural journey.
- **1826** Lieutenant-Colonel John By arrives on the south shore of the Ottawa River to oversee the construction of the Rideau Canal, a 202-km (125-mile) waterway between Lake Ontario and the Ottawa River, designed to provide a safe transportation route between Kingston and Montreal.
- **1827** A settlement, population 1,000, is established on the south side of the Ottawa River and named Bytown.
- **1841** Work begins on Notre-Dame Cathedral Basilica on Sussex Drive.
- **1848**   Population 6,000.
- **1855** Bytown becomes a city called Ottawa.
- **1857** Queen Victoria chooses Ottawa as the capital of the British Provinces of Upper and Lower Canada, ahead of Montreal, Toronto, Kingston, and Quebec City.
- **1860** Queen Victoria's son Edward, Prince of Wales, visits Ottawa and becomes the first member of the Royal Family to visit North America.
- **1866** The Parliament Buildings, modeled on the British Houses of Parliament, are completed.
- **1866** The University of Ottawa is founded.
- **1867** With Confederation, Ottawa becomes the capital of the new Dominion of Canada. Population now 18,000.
- **1870** The capital's first streetcar service, Ottawa City Passenger Railway, begins operation.
- **1873** The grounds of Parliament Hill are laid out by Calvert Vaux, a landscape architect who also designed New York's Central Park.
- **1874** The city's municipal water supply is established.
- **1877** A new city hall is constructed of limestone on Elgin Street.
- **1879** Cartier Square Drill Hall, the oldest armory in Canada still in use, is built.
- **1880** A group of 26 prominent Canadian artists decides to found a National Gallery. The gallery has many temporary homes in the years to come.
- **1888** Lansdowne Park fairgrounds are built on what was then the outskirts of town.

- **1891** The region's first strike takes place, as 2,400 millworkers walk out in protest at wage cuts.
- **1899** The Ottawa Improvement Commission (ancestor of today's National Capital Commission aka NCC) is created to oversee city planning.
- **1901** The Alexandra Railway Bridge opens; its construction was at the forefront of engineering in its day.
- **1908** The Royal Canadian Mint is established as a branch of the British Royal Mint.
- **1911** Population 87,000.
- **1914** World War I begins.
- **1916** A devastating fire sweeps the Parliament Buildings—only the Parliamentary Library is saved. The Parliament Buildings must be almost completely rebuilt.
- **1916** The National Research Council is founded in Ottawa.
- **1927** A carillon of 53 bells is rung for the first time in the Peace Tower.
- **1930s** The Great Depression; thousands are out of work.
- **1938** The federal government purchases the first lands of what is now Gatineau Park following pressure from local citizens to protect the wilderness.
- **1939** World War II begins.
- **1941** Population 155,000.
- **1945** Queen Juliana of the Netherlands presents a gift of thousands of tulip bulbs to the city in appreciation of Canada's granting a safe haven to the Dutch Royal Family during World War II.
- **1965** Canada gains its own flag, and it is raised for the first time on the top of the Peace Tower on February 15.
- **1967** Then prime minister Lester B. Pearson lights the Centennial Flame on Parliament Hill to commemorate 100 years of Confederation.

- **1969** The National Arts Centre, with its distinctive series of repeating triangles and hexagons, opens.
- **1971** Population 302,000.
- **1970s** The NCC constructs the first section of recreational pathway, marking the beginning of the "greening" of the city.
- **1980s** The growth of Ottawa's tech industry continues to strengthen and Silicon Valley North takes hold.
- **1988** A permanent location for the National Gallery of Canada opens at 380 Sussex Drive. Canadian architect Moshe Safdie creates a marvelous glass, steel, and concrete structure.
- **1989** The outstanding Canadian Museum of Civilization opens in Hull.
- **1992** Ottawa's National Hockey League team, the Ottawa Senators, is reborn.
- **1990s** Ottawa's high-tech industry explodes, bringing new jobs to the district and indirectly causing traffic congestion and a housing shortage.
- **1999** Population 324,000 in the city, but surrounding communities continue to experience rapid population growth
- **2000** Hull's Jacques-Cartier Park is designated "Mile 0" of the new Trans Canada Trail, a multi-use trail that will eventually stretch from coast to coast.
- **2001** Canada and the World Pavilion opens, an exhibit to celebrate Canadian success stories around the world.
- **2001** A new city of Ottawa is born, as 12 local municipal governments are amalgamated to create one new municipality of Ottawa. Population of the new city is 800,000 and projected to pass the 1-million mark by 2003.

Index

See also Accommodations and Restaurant indexes, below.